CLYMER®
MANUALS

HONDA
ATC • TRX • FOURTRAX 70-125 • 1970-1987

WHAT'S IN YOUR TOOLBOX?

More information available at haynes.com
Phone: 805-498-6703

Haynes UK
Sparkford Nr Yeovil
Somerset BA22 7JJ England

Haynes North America, Inc
859 Lawrence Drive
Newbury Park
California 91320 USA

ISBN-10: 0-89287-214-4
ISBN-13: 978-0-89287-214-5

Cover: Photographed by Michael Brown Photographic Productions, Los Angeles, California.

© Haynes North America, Inc. 1987
With permission from J.H. Haynes & Co. Ltd.

Clymer is a registered trademark of Haynes North America, Inc.

All rights reserved. No part of this book may be reproduced or transmitted in any form or by any means, electronic or mechanical, including photocopying, recording or by any information storage or retrieval system, without permission in writing from the copyright holder.

While every attempt is made to ensure that the information in this manual is correct, no liability can be accepted by the authors or publishers for loss, damage or injury caused by any errors in, or omissions from, the information given.

Common spark plug conditions

NORMAL
Symptoms: Brown to grayish-tan color and slight electrode wear. Correct heat range for engine and operating conditions.
Recommendation: When new spark plugs are installed, replace with plugs of the same heat range.

WORN
Symptoms: Rounded electrodes with a small amount of deposits on the firing end. Normal color. Causes hard starting in damp or cold weather and poor fuel economy.
Recommendation: Plugs have been left in the engine too long. Replace with new plugs of the same heat range. Follow the recommended maintenance schedule.

TOO HOT
Symptoms: Blistered, white insulator, eroded electrode and absence of deposits. Results in shortened plug life.
Recommendation: Check for the correct plug heat range, over-advanced ignition timing, lean fuel mixture, intake manifold vacuum leaks, sticking valves and insufficient engine cooling.

CARBON DEPOSITS
Symptoms: Dry sooty deposits indicate a rich mixture or weak ignition. Causes misfiring, hard starting and hesitation.
Recommendation: Make sure the plug has the correct heat range. Check for a clogged air filter or problem in the fuel system or engine management system. Also check for ignition system problems.

PREIGNITION
Symptoms: Melted electrodes. Insulators are white, but may be dirty due to misfiring or flying debris in the combustion chamber. Can lead to engine damage.
Recommendation: Check for the correct plug heat range, over-advanced ignition timing, lean fuel mixture, insufficient engine cooling and lack of lubrication.

ASH DEPOSITS
Symptoms: Light brown deposits encrusted on the side or center electrodes or both. Derived from oil and/or fuel additives. Excessive amounts may mask the spark, causing misfiring and hesitation during acceleration.
Recommendation: If excessive deposits accumulate over a short time or low mileage, install new valve guide seals to prevent seepage of oil into the combustion chambers. Also try changing gasoline brands.

HIGH SPEED GLAZING
Symptoms: Insulator has yellowish, glazed appearance. Indicates that combustion chamber temperatures have risen suddenly during hard acceleration. Normal deposits melt to form a conductive coating. Causes misfiring at high speeds.
Recommendation: Install new plugs. Consider using a colder plug if driving habits warrant.

OIL DEPOSITS
Symptoms: Oily coating caused by poor oil control. Oil is leaking past worn valve guides or piston rings into the combustion chamber. Causes hard starting, misfiring and hesitation.
Recommendation: Correct the mechanical condition with necessary repairs and install new plugs.

DETONATION
Symptoms: Insulators may be cracked or chipped. Improper gap setting techniques can also result in a fractured insulator tip. Can lead to piston damage.
Recommendation: Make sure the fuel anti-knock values meet engine requirements. Use care when setting the gaps on new plugs. Avoid lugging the engine.

GAP BRIDGING
Symptoms: Combustion deposits lodge between the electrodes. Heavy deposits accumulate and bridge the electrode gap. The plug ceases to fire, resulting in a dead cylinder.
Recommendation: Locate the faulty plug and remove the deposits from between the electrodes.

MECHANICAL DAMAGE
Symptoms: May be caused by a foreign object in the combustion chamber or the piston striking an incorrect reach (too long) plug. Causes a dead cylinder and could result in piston damage.
Recommendation: Repair the mechanical damage. Remove the foreign object from the engine and/or install the correct reach plug.

CONTENTS

QUICK REFERENCE DATA

ATV INFORMATION

MODEL:_____ YEAR:_____

VIN NUMBER:_____

ENGINE SERIAL NUMBER:_____

CARBURETOR SERIAL NUMBER OR I.D. MARK:_____

TUNE-UP SPECIFICATIONS

Valve clearance (intake and exhaust)	
All 70 cc and 90 cc engines	0.05 mm (0.002 in.)
All 110 cc and 125 cc engines	0.07mm (0.003 in.)
Compression pressure (at sea level)	
ATC70, ATC90	10-12 kg/cm^2 (142-170 psi)
Fourtrax 70	10.5-13.5 kg/cm^2 (149-191 psi)
ATC110, ATC125M, TRX125 and Fourtrax 125	11.0-14.0 kg/cm^2 (156.5-199 psi)
Spark plug type	
ATC70, Fourtrx 70	NGK CR7HS, ND U22FSR-L
ATC90, Fourtrax 70	NGK D-8HS, ND X24FS
ATC110	
1979-1981	NGK D-8HS
1982-1985	NGK DR8HS
ATC125M, TRX125 and Fourtrax 125	NGK DR8ES-L, ND X24ESR-U or Champion RA6YC
Spark plug gap	0.6-0.7 mm (0.024-0.028 in.)
Contact breaker point gap	0.3-0.4 mm (0.012-0.016 in.)
Ignition timing @ idle	Timing mark "F"
Idle speed	
ATC70	1,500 ± 100 rpm
ATC90	1,300 ± 100 rpm
ATC110, ATC125M, Fourtrax 70, TRX125 and Fourtrax 125	1,700 ± 100 rpm

ENGINE OIL CAPACITY

Model	Liters	U.S. qt.	Imp. qt.
ATC70	0.8	0.9	0.65
Fourtrax 70	0.7	0.74	0.62
ATC80, 1979-1980 ATC110	0.9	1.0	0.79
1981-1985 ATC110	1.1	1.12	0.9
ATC125M, TRX125 and Fourtrax 125	1.0	1.06	0.88

FRAME SUSPENSION TORQUE SPECIFICAIONS

Item	N·m	ft.-lb.
Front wheel (or lug) nuts		
ATC70	60-80	43-57
Fourtrax 70	24-30	17-22
ATC90	NA*	NA
ATC110, ATC125M	50-70	36-51
TRX125 and Fourtrax 125	50-60	36-43
Front hub nut		
Fourtrax 70	55-65	40-47
TRX125 and Fourtrax 125	60-80	36-43
Handlebar upper holder bolts		
ATC70	6-9	4-6
Fourtrax 70	24-30	17-22
ATC90	NA	NA
ATC110, ATC125M	18-30	13-22
TRX125 and Fourtrax 125	24-30	17-22
Handlebar holder nuts		
All models	40-48	29-34
Steering stem nut (3 wheel models)	50-70	36-51
Front fork bridge bolt		
ATC70	40-48	29-34
ATC90	NA	NA
ATC110, ATC125M	50-70	36-51
Rear axle drum nut		
ATC70 and Fourtrax 70	DNA	DNA
ATC90	40-45	29-32
ATC110	40-60	29-34
ATC125M, TRX125 and Fourtrax 125		
Inner	35-45	25-33
Outer	120-140	87-101
Rear bearing holder		
ATC70 and Fourtrax 70	20-24	14-17
(right-hand side)		
ATC90	20-24	14-17
ATC110	DNA	DNA
ATC125M, TRX125 and and Fourtrax 125	50-70	36-51
Drive sprocket to axle		
ATC70 and Fourtrax 70	DNA	DNA
ATC90	40-48	29-35
ATC110	44-52	32-38
ATC125M, TRX125 and and Fourtrax 125	21-27	15-20
Wheel rim bolts and nuts		
(3 wheel models only)	19-25	14-18
4 WHEEL MODELS ONLY		
Steering shaft		
Holder nuts 70 cc	24-30	17-22
Shaft nut 70 cc	50-60	36-51
Shaft bearing locknut	40-60	29-43
in frame 125 cc		
Tie rod		
End nuts	35-43	25-31
Locknuts		
70 cc	35-43	25-31
125 cc	25-31	18-22
Kingpin		
Nut 70 cc	30-40	22-29
Bolt and nut 125 cc	50-60	36-43

NA—Honda does not provide specifications for all models.　　DNA—Does not apply to this model.

NOTE: If you own a 1985 or later model, first check the Supplement at the back of the book for any new service information.

1

CHAPTER ONE

GENERAL INFORMATION

This detailed, comprehensive manual covers the Honda ATC 70-125 cc singles manufactured from 1970-on. All of the models and years covered are listed in **Table 1** at the end of this chapter.

The expert text gives complete information on maintenance, tune-up, repair and overhaul. Hundreds of photos and drawings guide you through every step. The book includes all you need to keep your Honda ATC running right and performing well.

A shop manual is a reference. You want to be able to find information fast. As in all Clymer books, this one is designed with you in mind. All chapters are thumb tabbed. Important items are extensively indexed at the rear of the book. All procedures, tables, photos, etc., in this manual assume that the reader may be working on the ATC or using this manual for the first time. All the most frequently used specifications and capacities are summarized on the *Quick Reference Data* pages at the front of the book.

Keep the book handy in your tool box or tow vehicle. It will help you to better understand how the vehicle runs, lower repair and maintenance costs and generally improve your satisfaction with the ATC.

Table 1 contains engine and frame serial numbers and year of manufacture. This may help if you have purchased a "well-used" 3-wheeler and are not sure of its origin. **Table 1** and **Table 2** are located at the end of this chapter.

MANUAL ORGANIZATION

All dimensions and capacities are expressed in English units familiar to U.S. mechanics as well as in metric units.

This chapter provides general information and discusses equipment and tools useful both for preventive maintenance and troubleshooting.

Chapter Two provides methods and suggestions for quick and accurate diagnosis and repair of problems. Troubleshooting procedures discuss typical symptoms and logical methods to pinpoint the trouble.

Chapter Three explains all periodic lubrication and routine maintenance necessary to keep the Honda running well. Chapter Three also includes recommended tune-up procedures, eliminating the need to constantly consult chapters on the various assemblies.

Subsequent chapters describe specific systems such as the engine, clutch, transmission, fuel system, exhaust system, wheels, tires and brakes. Each chapter provides disassembly, repair and assembly procedures in simple step-by-step form. If a repair is impractical for a home mechanic, it is so indicated. It is usually faster and less expensive to take such repairs to a dealer or competent repair shop. Specifications concerning a particular system are included at the end of the appropriate chapter.

Some of the procedures in this manual specify special tools. In most cases, the tool is illustrated either in actual use or alone. Well-equipped mechanics may find they can substitute similar tools already on hand or can fabricate their own.

The terms NOTE, CAUTION and WARNING have a specific meaning in this manual. A NOTE provides additional information to make a step or procedure easier or clearer. Disregarding a NOTE could cause inconvenience, but would not cause equipment damage or personal injury.

A CAUTION emphasizes areas where equipment damage could result. Disregarding a CAUTION could cause permanent mechanical damage; however, personal injury is unlikely.

A WARNING emphasizes areas where personal injury or even death could result from negligence. Mechanical damage may also occur. WARNINGS *are to be taken seriously.* In some cases, serious injury or death has resulted from disregarding similar warnings.

Throughout this manual keep in mind 2 conventions. "Front" refers to the front of the ATC. The front of any component, such as the engine, is the end which faces toward the front of the ATC. The "left-" and "right-hand" side refer to the position of the parts as viewed by a rider sitting on the seat facing forward. For example, the throttle lever is on the right-hand side and the shift lever is on the left-hand side. These rules are simple, but even experienced mechanics occasionally become disoriented.

SERVICE HINTS

Most of the service procedures covered are straightforward and can be performed by anyone reasonably handy with tools. It is suggested, however, that you consider your own capabilities carefully before attempting any operation involving major disassembly of the engine.

Some operations, for example, require the use of a press. It would be wiser to have these performed by a shop equipped for such work, rather than to try to do the job yourself with makeshift equipment. Other procedures require precise measurements. Unless you have the skills and equipment required, it would be better to have a qualified repair shop make the measurements for you.

There are many items available that can be used on your hands before and after working on your ATC. A little preparation prior to getting "all greased up" will help when cleaning up later.

Before starting out, work Vaseline, soap or a product such as Pro-Tek (**Figure 1**) onto your forearms, into your hands and under your fingernails and cuticles. This will make cleanup a lot easier.

For cleanup, use a waterless hand soap such as Sta-Lube and then finish up with powdered Boraxo and a fingernail brush.

Repairs go much faster and easier if the ATC is clean before you begin work. There are special cleaners, such as Gunk or Bel-Ray Degreaser, for washing the engine and related parts. Just spray or brush on the cleaning solution, let it stand, then rinse it away with a garden hose. Clean all oily or greasy parts with cleaning solvent as you remove them.

A number of solvents can be used to remove old dirt, oil and grease. Kerosene is readily available and comparatively inexpensive. Another inexpensive solvent similar to kerosene is ordinary

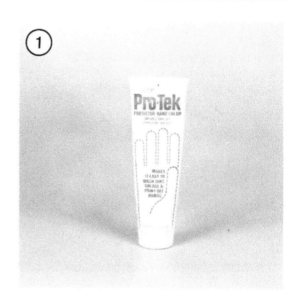

diesel fuel. Both of these solvents have a very high temperature flash point (they have to be very hot in order to ignite and catch fire) and can be used safely in any adequately ventilated area away from open flames (this includes pilot lights on home water heaters and clothes driers that are sometimes located in the garage).

> *WARNING*
> ***Never use gasoline*** *as a solvent. Gasoline is extremely volatile and contains tremendously destructive potential energy. The slightest spark from metal parts accidently hitting or a tool slipping could cause a fatal explosion. Work in well ventilated area and keep a fire extinguisher, rated for gasoline fires, handy in any case.*

Special tools are required for some repair procedures. These may be purchased at a dealer, rented from a tool rental dealer or fabricated by a mechanic or machinist (often at a considerable savings).

Much of the labor charged for repairs made by dealers is for the removal and disassembly of other parts to reach the defective unit. You can often save money by removing the defective part yourself and then taking it to a dealer for repair.

Once you have decided to tackle the job yourself, read the entire section in this manual which pertains to it, making sure you have identified the proper section. Study the illustrations and text until you have a good idea of what is involved in completing the job satisfactorily. If special tools are required, make arrangements to get them before you start. It is frustrating and time-consuming to get partly into a job and then be unable to complete it.

Simple wiring checks can be easily made at home, but a knowledge of electronics is almost a necessity for performing tests with complicated electronic testing gear.

During disassembly of parts keep a few general cautions in mind. Force is rarely needed to get things apart. If parts are a tight fit, such as a bearing in a case, there is usually a tool designed to separate them. Never use a screwdriver to pry apart parts with machined surfaces such as crankcase halves. You will mar the surfaces and end up with leaks.

Make diagrams (or take a Polaroid picture) wherever similar-appearing parts are found. For instance, crankcase bolts are often not the same length. You may think you can remember where everything came from, but mistakes are costly. There is also the possibility you may be sidetracked and not return to work for days or even weeks, in which interval carefully laid out parts may have become disturbed.

Tag all similar internal parts for location and mark all mating parts for position. Record number and thickness of any shims as they are removed. Small parts such as bolts can be identified by placing them in plastic sandwich bags. Seal and label them with masking tape.

Wiring should be tagged with masking tape and marked as each wire is removed. Again, do not rely on memory alone.

Protect finished surfaces from physical damage or corrosion. Keep gasoline off painted surfaces.

Frozen or very tight bolts and screws can often be loosened by soaking with penetrating oil, such as WD-40 or Liquid Wrench, then sharply striking the bolt head a few times with a hammer and punch (or screwdriver for screws). Avoid heat unless absolutely necessary, since it may melt, warp or remove the temper from many parts.

No parts, except those assembled with a press fit, require unusual force during assembly. If a part is hard to remove or install, find out why before proceeding.

Cover all openings after removing parts to keep dirt, small tools, etc., from falling in.

When assembling 2 parts, start all fasteners, then tighten evenly.

Wiring connections and brake components should be kept clean and free of grease and oil.

When assembling parts, be sure all shims and washers are installed exactly as they came out.

Whenever a rotating part butts against a stationary part, look for a shim or washer. Use new gaskets if there is any doubt about the condition of the old ones. A thin coat of oil on gaskets may help them seal effectively.

Heavy grease can be used to hold small parts in place if they tend to fall out during assembly. However, keep grease and oil away from electrical and brake components.

High spots may be sanded off a piston with sandpaper, but fine emery cloth and oil will do a much more professional job.

Carbon can be removed from the head, the piston crown and the exhaust port with a dull screwdriver. *Do not* scratch the surfaces. Wipe off the surface with a clean cloth when finished.

The carburetor is best cleaned by disassembling it and soaking the parts in a commercial carburetor cleaner. Never soak gaskets and rubber parts in these cleaners. Never use wire to clean out jets and air passages; they are easily damaged. Use compressed air to blow out the carburetor only if the float has been removed first.

A baby bottle makes a good measuring device for adding oil to the engine, transmission or forks. Get one that is graduated in fluid ounces and cubic centimeters. After it has been used for this purpose, do not let a small child drink out of it as there will always be an oil residue in it.

Take your time and do the job right. Do not forget that a newly rebuilt engine must be broken in the same as a new one. Keep the rpm within the limits given in your owner's manual when you get back in the dirt or sand.

TORQUE SPECIFICATIONS

Torque specifications throughout this manual are given in Newton meters (N•m) and foot pounds (ft.-lb.). Newton meters have been adopted in place of meter kilograms (mkg) in accordance with the International Modernized Metric System. Tool manufacturers offer torque wrenches calibrated in Newton meters and Sears has a Craftsman line calibrated in both values.

Existing torque wrenches calibrated in meter kilograms can be used by performing a simple conversion. All you have to do is move the decimal point one place to the right; for example, 4.7 mkg = 47 N•m. This conversion is sufficient for use in this manual even though the exact mathematical conversion is 3.5 mkg = 34.3 N•m.

SAFETY FIRST

Professional mechanics can work for years and never sustain a serious injury. If you observe a few rules of common sense and safety, you can enjoy many hours servicing your own machine. If you ignore these rules you can hurt yourself or damage the ATC.

1. Never use gasoline as a cleaning solvent.
2. Never smoke or use a torch in the vicinity of flammable liquids such as cleaning solvent in open containers.
3. If welding or brazing is required on the ATC, remove the fuel tank to a safe distance, at least 50 ft. (15 m) away.
4. Use the proper sized wrenches to avoid damage to nuts and injury to yourself.
5. When loosening a tight or stuck nut, watch out for what might happen if the wrench should slip. Be careful; protect yourself accordingly.
6. Keep your work area clean and uncluttered.
7. Wear safety goggles during all operations involving drilling, grinding or the use of a cold chisel.
8. Never use worn tools.
9. Keep a fire extinguisher handy and be sure it is rated for gasoline and electrical fires.

SPECIAL TIPS

Because of the extreme demands placed on an ATC, several points should be kept in mind when performing service and repair. The following items are general suggestions that may improve the overall life of the machine and help avoid costly failures.

1. Use a locking compound such as Loctite 242 on all bolts and nuts, even if they are secured with lockwashers. This type of Loctite does not harden completely and allows easy removal of the bolt or nut. A screw or bolt lost from an engine cover or bearing retainer could easily cause serious and expensive damage before its loss is noticed. When applying Loctite, use a small amount. If too much is used, it can work its way down the threads and enter bearings or seals.
2. Use a hammer-driven impact tool to remove tight fasteners. These tools help prevent the rounding off of bolt heads.
3. When straightening out the "fold over" type lockwasher, use a wide-blade chisel such as an old and dull wood chisel. Such a tool provides a better purchase on the folded tab, making straightening out easier.

4. When installing the "fold over" type lockwasher, always use a new washer if possible. If a new washer is not available, always fold over a part of the washer that has not been previously folded.

Reusing the same fold may cause the washer to break, resulting in the loss of its locking ability and a loose piece of metal adrift in the engine.

When folding the washer over, start the fold with a screwdriver and finish it with a pair of pliers. If a punch is used to make the fold, the fold may be too sharp, thereby increasing the chances of the washer breaking under stress.

These washers are relatively inexpensive and it is suggested that you keep several of each size in your tool box for field repairs.

5. When replacing missing or broken fasteners (bolts, nuts and screws), especially on the engine or frame components, always use Honda replacement parts. They are specially hardened for each application. The wrong 75-cent bolt could easily cause many dollars worth of serious damage, not to mention rider injury.
6. When installing gaskets in the engine, always use Honda replacement gaskets *without* sealer, unless otherwise designated. These gaskets are designed to swell when they come in contact with oil. Gasket sealer will prevent the gaskets from swelling as intended, which can result in oil leaks. These Honda gaskets are also cut from material of the precise thickness needed. Installation of a too thick or too thin gasket in a critical area could cause engine damage.

PARTS REPLACEMENT

Honda makes frequent changes during a model year—some minor, some relatively major. When you order parts from the dealer or other parts distributor, always order by engine and frame number. Write the numbers down and carry them with you. Compare new parts to old before purchasing them. If they are not alike, have the parts manager explain the difference to you.

EXPENDABLE SUPPLIES

Certain expendable supplies are also required. These include grease, oil, gasket cement, wiping rags and cleaning solvent. Ask your dealer for the special locking compounds, silicone lubricants and lube products which make ATC maintenance simpler and easier. Cleaning solvent, kerosene and diesel fuel are available at many service stations.

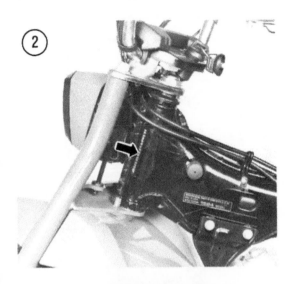

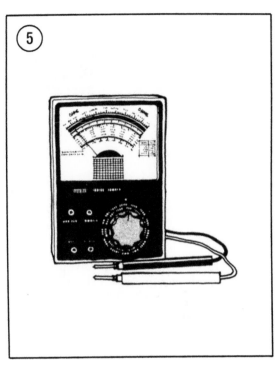

SERIAL NUMBERS

You must know the model serial number for registration purposes and when ordering replacement parts.

The frame serial number is stamped on the side of the steering head (**Figure 2**). The engine serial number is located on the lower left-hand side of the crankcase (**Figure 3**). The carburetor identification number is located on the left-hand side of the carburetor body mounting flange adjacent to the intake tube (**Figure 4**).

TUNE-UP AND TROUBLESHOOTING TOOLS

Multimeter or VOM

This instrument (**Figure 5**) is invaluable for electrical system troubleshooting and service. A few of its functions may be duplicated by homemade test equipment, but for the serious mechanic it is a must. Its uses are described in the applicable sections of the book.

Strobe Timing Light

This instrument is necessary for tuning. By flashing a light at the precise instant the spark plug fires, the position of the timing mark can be seen. Marks on the alternator flywheel line up with the stationary mark on the crankcase while the engine is running.

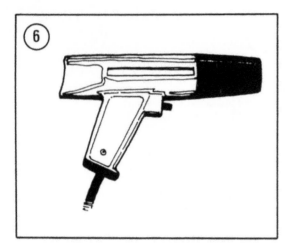

Suitable lights range from inexpensive neon bulb types to powerful xenon strobe lights (**Figure 6**). Neon timing lights are difficult to see and must be used in dimly lit areas. Xenon strobe timing lights can be used outside in bright sunlight. Both types work on the ATC; use according to the manufacturer's instructions.

Portable Tachometer

A portable tachometer (**Figure 7**) is necessary for tuning. Ignition timing and carburetor adjustments must be performed at the specified idle speed. The best instrument for this purpose is one with a low range of 0-1,000 or 0-2,000 rpm range and a high range of 0-4,000 rpm. Extended range (0-6,000 or 0-8,000 rpm) instruments lack accuracy at lower speeds. The instrument should be capable of detecting changes of 25 rpm on the low range.

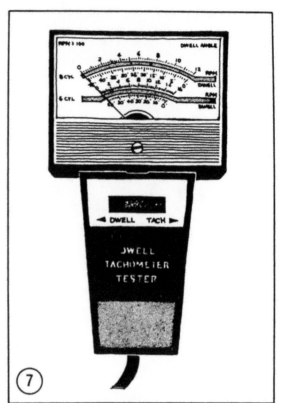

Compression Gauge

A compression gauge measures the engine compression. The one shown in **Figure 8** is the type used for the Honda ATCs covered in this book.

Ignition Gauge

This tool has both flat and round wire measuring gauges (**Figure 9**) and is used to measure contact breaker point gap or ignition pulse generator air gap and to set the spark plug gap. A good one is available at most auto or motorcycle supply stores. Get one calibrated in millimeters.

"OFF THE ROAD" RULES

Areas set aside for off-road riding by the Federal Government or by state or local agencies are continuing to disappear. The loss of many of these areas is usually due to the few who really don't care

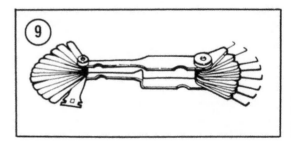

and therefore ruin the sport of off-road fun for those who do. Following these basic rules will enable you and others to always have an area open for this type of recreational use.

1. When riding, always observe the basic practice of good sportsmanship and recognize that other people will judge all off-road vehicle owners by your actions.
2. Don't litter the trails or camping areas. Leave the area cleaner than it was before you came.
3. Don't pollute lakes, streams or the ocean.
4. Be careful not to damage living trees, shrubs or other natural terrain.
5. Respect other people's rights and property.
6. Help anyone in distress.
7. Make yourself and your vehicle available for assistance in any search and rescue parties.
8. Don't harass other people using the same area as you are. Respect the rights of others enjoying the recreation area.
9. Be sure to obey all Federal, state, provincial and other local rules regulating the operation of the ATC.
10. Inform public officials when using public lands.
11. Don't harass wildlife. Stay out of areas posted for the protection and feeding of wildlife.
12. Always run with the spark arrester in place and keep your exhaust noise to a minimum.

SAFETY

General Tips

1. Read your owner's manual and know your machine.
2. Check the throttle and brake controls before starting the engine.
3. Know how to make an emergency stop.
4. Know all state, Federal and local laws concerning the ATC. Respect private property.

NOTE
*The Honda ATC is designed and manufactured for **off-road use only**. It does not conform to Federal Motor Vehicle Safety Standards and it is illegal to operate it on public streets, roads or highways.*

5. Never add fuel while anyone is smoking in the area or when the engine is running.
6. Never wear loose scarves, belts or boot laces that could catch on moving parts or tree limbs.
7. Always wear eye protection and a helmet.
8. Never allow anyone to operate the ATC without proper instruction. This is for their protection and to keep your machine from damage or destruction.

CAUTION
***Do not** "pop wheelies" and run for any distance with the ATC. The oil capacity is relatively small and the oil will drain out of the oil pump area, causing a loss of oil pressure and costly engine damage.*

9. Use the "buddy system" for long trips, just in case you have a problem or run out of gas.
10. Never attempt to repair your machine with the engine running except when necessary for certain tune-up procedures.
11. Check all of the machine's components and hardware frequently, especially the wheels and the steering.
12. Push the ATC onto a trailer bed—never ride it on. Secure it firmly to the trailer and be sure that the trailer lights operate properly.
13. Always wear comfortable clothing and warm clothing in cool or cold weather. Even mild temperatures can be very uncomfortable and dangerous when combined with a strong wind or high-speed travel. See **Table 2** for wind chill factors. Always dress according to what the wind chill factor is, not the ambient temperature.

Operating Tips

1. Never operate the machine in crowded areas or steer toward persons.
2. Avoid dangerous terrain.
3. Cross highways (where permitted) at a 90 degree angle after looking in both directions. Post traffic guards if crossing in groups.
4. Do not ride the vehicle on or near railroad tracks. The ATC engine and exhaust noise can drown out the sound of an approaching train.
5. On models so equipped, keep the headlight free of dirt and never ride at night without the headlight on.
6. Do not ride the ATC without the seat/fender assembly in place.
7. Always steer with both hands.
8. Be aware of the terrain and avoid operating the ATC at excessive speed.
9. Do not panic if the throttle sticks. Turn the engine stop switch to the OFF position.
10. Do not speed through wooded areas. Hidden obstructions, hanging tree limbs, unseen ditches, wild animals and hikers can cause injury and damage to the ATC.
11. Do not tailgate. Rear end collisions can cause injury and machine damage.
12. Do not mix alcoholic beverages with riding.
13. Keep both feet on the foot pegs. Do not permit your feet to hang out to stabilize the machine when

making turns or in near spill situations; broken limbs could result.

14. Check your fuel supply regularly. Do not travel farther than your fuel supply will permit you to return.

15. Do not run without the spark arrester in place.

16. On models so equipped, check to make sure that the parking brake is *completely released* while riding. If left on, the rear brake shoes will be damaged.

Table 1 MODEL, YEAR AND FRAME NUMBER

Model and year	Engine serial no.	Frame serial no.
ATC70		
1973	1000001-on	1000001-on
1974*	1100001-on	1100001-on
1978	ATC70E-2000001-2010823	ATC70-2000036-2010823
1980	TB03E-2000001-2011736	TB03-2000001-2011706
1981	TBO3E-2600001-2611751	TBO3O-BC600001-BC611215
1982	TB03E-2700003-2718283	TB03-CC700001-CC717796
1983	TBO3E-2800001-2827785	TBO3O-DC800006-DC827275
1984	TBO3E-2900001-on	TBO3O-EC900001-on
ATC90		
1970	US90E-100122-on	US90-100122-on
1972 (K1)	US90E-1100001-on	US90-200001-on
1974 (K2)	ATC90E-1300001-on	ATC90-1300001-on
1975 (K3)	ATC90E-1400001-on	ATC90-1400001-on
1976	ATC90E-1500001-on	ATC90-1500001-on
1977	ATC90E-1600001-on	ATC90-1600001-on
1978	ATC90E-1700001-on	ATC90-1700001-on
ATC110		
1979	ATC110E-2000007-2064904	ATC110-2000005-2069494
1980	TB02E-2000001-2075408	TB02-2000001-2075225
1981	TBO2E-2200001-2226679	TBO2O-BC200001-BC225984
1982	TB02E-2300003-2352963	TB02-CC300001-CC352101
1983	TBO2E-2500005-2553946	TBO2O-DC400008-DC453423
1984	TBO2E-2600001-on	TBO2O-EC000001-on
ATC125M		
1984	TE01E-2000014-on	TEO1O-EC000001-on

* ATC70 not manufactured 1975-1977.

Table 2 WIND CHILL FACTORS

Estimated Wind Speed in MPH	Actual Thermometer Reading (° F)											
	50	40	30	20	10	0	—10	—20	—30	—40	—50	—60
	Equivalent Temperature (° F)											
Calm	50	40	30	20	10	0	—10	—20	—30	—40	—50	—60
5	48	37	27	16	6	—5	—15	—26	—36	—47	—57	—68
10	40	28	16	4	—9	—21	—33	—46	—58	—70	—83	—95
15	36	22	9	—5	—18	—36	—45	—58	—72	—85	—99	—112
20	32	18	4	—10	—25	—39	—53	—67	—82	—96	—110	—124
25	30	16	0	—15	—29	—44	—59	—74	—88	—104	—118	—133
30	28	13	—2	—18	—33	—48	—63	—79	—94	—109	—125	—140
35	27	11	—4	—20	—35	—49	—67	—82	—98	—113	—129	—145
40	26	10	—6	—21	—37	—53	—69	—85	—100	—116	—132	—148

* Little Danger (for properly clothed person) | Increasing Danger | Great Danger

• Danger from freezing of exposed flesh •

*Wind speeds greater than 40 mph have little additional effect.

CHAPTER TWO

TROUBLESHOOTING

Diagnosing mechanical problems is relatively simple if you use orderly procedures and keep a few basic principles in mind. The troubleshooting procedures in this chapter analyze typical symptoms and show logical methods of isolating causes. These are not the only methods. There may be several ways to solve a problem, but only a systematic, methodical approach can guarantee success.

Never assume anything. Do not overlook the obvious. If you are riding along and the engine suddenly quits, check the easiest, most accessible problem spot first. Is there gasoline in the tank? Is the fuel shutoff valve in the ON position? Has the spark plug wire fallen off? Check the ignition switch to make sure it is in the RUN position. If nothing turns up in a quick check, look a little further.

Learning to recognize and describe symptoms will make repairs easier for you or a mechanic at the shop. Describe problems accurately and fully. Saying that "it won't run" isn't the same as saying "it quit climbing a hill and won't start" or that "it sat in my garage for 3 months and then wouldn't start." Gather as many symptoms together as possible to aid in diagnosis. Note whether the engine lost power gradually or all at once, what color smoke, if any, came from the exhaust and so on. Remember that the more complicated a machine is, the easier it is to troubleshoot because symptoms point to specific problems. After the symptoms are defined, areas which could cause the problems are tested and analyzed. Guessing at the cause of a problem may provide the solution, but it can also easily lead to frustration, wasted time and a series of expensive, unnecessary parts replacements.

You do not need fancy equipment or complicated test gear to determine whether repairs can be attempted at home. A few simple checks could save a large repair bill and time lost while the ATC sits in a dealer's service department. On the other hand, be realistic and don't attempt repairs beyond your abilities. Service departments tend to charge heavily for putting together a disassembled engine that may have been abused. Some dealers won't even take on such a job—so use common sense and don't get in over your head.

OPERATING REQUIREMENTS

To run properly, an engine needs these three basics: correct fuel-air mixture, compression and a spark at the correct time. If one or more are missing, the engine won't run. The electrical system is the weakest link of the three basics. More problems result from electrical breakdowns than from any other source. Keep that in mind before you begin tampering with carburetor adjustments.

Figure 1 shows typical spark plug conditions and the engine problems they indicate.

If the ATC has been sitting for any length of time and refuses to start, check and clean the spark plug and then look to the gasoline delivery system. This includes the fuel tank cap, fuel shutoff valve, lines and the carburetor. Rust may have formed in the gas tank, restricting fuel flow. Gasoline deposits may have formed and gummed up the carburetor jets and air passages. Gasoline tends to lose its potency after standing for long periods and condensation may contaminate it with water. Drain old gas and try starting with fresh gasoline.

① SPARK PLUG CONDITION

NORMAL
- Identified by light tan or gray deposits on the firing tip.
- Can be cleaned.

GAP BRIDGED
- Identified by deposit buildup closing gap between electrodes.
- Caused by oil or carbon fouling. If deposits are not excessive, the plug can be cleaned.

OIL FOULED
- Identified by wet black deposits on the insulator shell bore and electrodes.
- Caused by excessive oil entering combustion chamber through worn rings and pistons, excessive clearance between valve guides and stems, or worn or loose bearings. Can be cleaned. If engine is not repaired, use a hotter plug.

CARBON FOULED
- Identified by black, dry fluffy carbon deposits on insulator tips, exposed shell surfaces and electrodes.
- Caused by too cold a plug, weak ignition, dirty air cleaner, too rich a fuel mixture, or excessive idling. Can be cleaned.

LEAD FOULED
- Identified by dark gray, black, yellow, or tan deposits or a fused glazed coating on the insulator tip.
- Caused by highly leaded gasoline. Can be cleaned.

WORN
- Identified by severely eroded or worn electrodes.
- Caused by normal wear. Should be replaced.

FUSED SPOT DEPOSIT
- Identified by melted or spotty deposits resembling bubbles or blisters.
- Caused by sudden acceleration. Can be cleaned.

OVERHEATING
- Identified by a white or light gray insulator with small black or gray brown spots and with bluish-burnt appearance of electrodes.
- Caused by engine overheating, wrong type of fuel, loose spark plugs, too hot a plug, or incorrect ignition timing. Replace the plug.

PREIGNITION
- Identified by melted electrodes and possibly blistered insulator. Metallic deposits on insulator indicate engine damage.
- Caused by wrong type of fuel, incorrect ignition timing or advance, too hot a plug, burned valves, or engine overheating. Replace the plug.

EMERGENCY TROUBLESHOOTING

When the ATC is difficult or impossible to start or won't start at all, it does not help to keep pulling on the recoil starter rope. Check for obvious problems even before getting your tools by following the steps listed below. Don't omit any. You may be embarrassed to find your engine stop switch in the OFF position but that is better than wearing out your arm trying to start the engine. If it still will not start, refer to the appropriate troubleshooting procedure in this chapter.

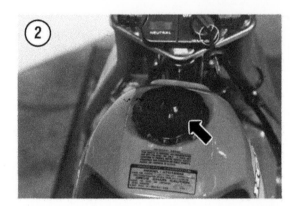

1. Is there fuel in the tank? Remove the filler cap (**Figure 2**) and rock the ATC; listen for sloshing fuel. Also make sure that the lever is in the ON position. The cap must be in this position to open the internal vent in the cap and allow the fuel to flow.

> *WARNING*
> *Do not use an open flame to check in the tank. A serious explosion is certain to result.*

2. Is the fuel shutoff valve (**Figure 3**) in the ON position?
3. Make sure the engine stop switch (**Figure 4**) is not stuck in the OFF position.
4. Is the spark plug wire (**Figure 5**) on tight? Push the wire on and slightly rotate it to clean the electrical connection between the plug and the connector.
5. Is the choke in the right position? The lever or knob should be moved *up* for a cold engine and *down* for a warm engine.

ENGINE STARTING

An engine that refuses to start or is difficult to start is very frustrating. More often than not, the problem is very minor and can be found with a simple and logical troubleshooting approach.

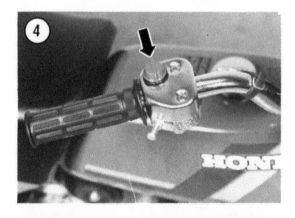

The following items show a beginning point from which to isolate engine starting problems.

Engine Fails to Start

Perform the following spark test to determine if the ignition system is operating properly.
1. Remove the spark plug from the cylinder.
2. Connect the spark plug wire and connector to the spark plug and touch the spark plug's base to a good ground such as the engine cylinder head (**Figure 6**). Position the spark plug so you can see the electrode.
3. Crank the engine over with the recoil starter. A fat blue spark should be evident across the spark plug electrodes.

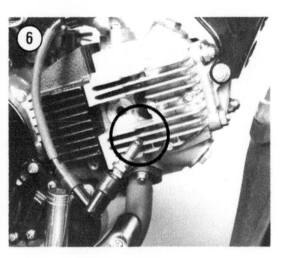

WARNING
On models with a CDI ignition system,
if it is necessary to hold the high voltage
lead, do so with an insulated pair of
pliers. The high voltage generated by
the CDI could produce serious or fatal
shocks.

4. If the spark is good, check for one or more of the following possible malfunctions:
  a. Obstructed fuel line.
  b. Leaking head gasket.
  c. Low compression.
5. If spark is not good, check for one or more of the following:
  a. Weak ignition coil.
  b. Faulty contact breaker points (models so equipped).
  c. Weak CDI pulse generator (models so equipped).
  d. Broken or shorted high tension lead to the spark plug.
  e. Loose electrical connections.
  f. Loose or broken ignition coil ground wire.

Engine Is Difficult to Start

Check for one or more of the following possible malfunctions:
  a. Fouled spark plug.
  b. Improperly adjusted choke.
  c. Contaminated fuel system.
  d. Improperly adjusted carburetor.
  e. Weak ignition coil.
  f. Faulty contact breaker points (models so equipped).
  g. Weak CDI pulse generator (models so equipped).
  h. Incorrect type ignition coil.
  i. Poor compression.

Engine Will Not Crank

Check for one or more of the following possible malfunctions:
  a. Broken recoil starter.
  b. Seized piston.
  c. Seized crankshaft bearings.
  d. Broken connecting rod.
  e. Locked up transmission or clutch.

ENGINE PERFORMANCE

The following check lists assume that the engine runs, but is not operating at peak performance. This will serve as a starting point from which to isolate a performance malfunction.

The possible causes for each malfunction are listed in a logical sequence and in order of probability.

Engine Will Not Idle

  a. Carburetor incorrectly adjusted.
  b. Fouled or improperly gapped spark plug.
  c. Leaking head gasket.
  d. Ignition timing incorrect.
  e. Incorrect contact breaker point gap (models so equipped).
  f. Weak or faulty pulse generator (models so equipped).
  g. Valve clearance incorrect.
  h. Obstructed fuel line or fuel shutoff valve.

Engine Misses at High Speed

  a. Fouled or improperly gapped spark plug.
  b. Improper ignition timing.
  c. Improper valve clearance.
  d. Improper carburetor main jet selection.
  e. Clogged jets in the carburetor.
  f. Weak ignition coil.
  g. Incorrect contact breaker point gap (models so equipped).
  h. Weak or faulty pulse generator (models so equipped).
  i. Obstructed fuel line or fuel shutoff valve.

Engine Overheating

  a. Obstructed cooling fins on cylinder head and cylinder.
  b. Improper ignition timing.
  c. Improper spark plug heat range.

Smoky Exhaust and Engine Runs Roughly

  a. Carburetor adjustment incorrect (mixture too rich).
  b. Choke not operating correctly.

c. Water or other contaminants in the fuel.
d. Clogged fuel line.
e. Clogged air filter element.

Engine Loses Power

a. Carburetor incorrectly adjusted.
b. Engine overheating.
c. Improper ignition timing.
d. Incorrectly gapped spark plug.
e. Weak ignition coil.
f. Faulty contact breaker points (models so equipped).
g. Weak CDI pulse generator (models so equipped).
h. Obstructed muffler.
i. Dragging brake(s).

Engine Lacks Acceleration

a. Carburetor mixture too lean.
b. Clogged fuel line.
c. Improper ignition timing.
d. Improper valve clearance.
e. Dragging brake(s).

ENGINE NOISES

1. *Knocking or pinging during acceleration—* Caused by using a lower octane fuel than recommended or by poor fuel. Pinging can also be caused by using a spark plug of the wrong heat range. Refer to *Spark Plug Selection* in Chapter Three.

2. *Slapping or rattling noises at low speed or during acceleration—* May be caused by piston slap (excessive piston to cylinder wall clearance).

3. *Knocking or rapping while decelerating—* Usually caused by excessive rod bearing clearance.

4. *Persistent knocking and vibration—* Usually caused by excessive main bearing clearance.

5. *Rapid on-off squeal—* Compression leak around cylinder head gasket or spark plug.

EXCESSIVE VIBRATION

This can be difficult to find without disassembling the engine. Usually this is caused by loose engine mounting hardware.

FRONT SUSPENSION AND STEERING

Poor handling may be caused by improper front tire pressure or uneven rear tire pressure, a damaged or bent frame or front steering components, a worn front fork assembly, worn wheel bearings or dragging brakes.

BRAKE PROBLEMS

A sticking drum brake may be caused by worn or weak return springs, dry pivot and cam bushings or improper adjustment. Grabbing brakes may be caused by greasy linings which must be replaced. Brake grab may also be due to an out-of-round drum. Glazed linings will cause loss of stopping power.

NOTE: If you own a 1985 or later model, first check the Supplement at the back of the book for any new service information.

CHAPTER THREE

3

LUBRICATION, MAINTENANCE AND TUNE-UP

If this is your first experience with an ATC or motorcycle, you should become acquainted with products that are available in auto or motorcycle parts and supply stores. Look into the tune-up tools and parts and check out the different lubricants such as motor oil, locking compounds and greases. Also check engine degreasers, such as Gunk or Bel-Ray Degreaser, for cleaning your engine prior to working on it.

The more you get involved in your ATC the more you will want to work on it. Start out by doing simple tune-up, lubrication and maintenance. Tackle more involved jobs as you gain experience.

The Honda ATC is a relatively simple machine but to gain the utmost in safety, performance and useful life from it, it is necessary to make periodic inspections and adjustments. It frequently happens that minor problems are found during such inspections that are simple and inexpensive to correct at the time, but which could lead to major problems if not corrected.

This chapter explains lubrication, maintenance and tune-up procedures. **Table 1** is a suggested factory maintenance schedule. **Tables 1-5** are located at the end of this chapter.

DAILY CHECKS

The following checks should be performed prior to the first ride of the day.
1. Inspect all fuel lines and fittings for wetness.
2. Make sure the fuel tank is full of fresh gasoline.
3. Make sure the engine oil level is correct.
4. Check the operation of the clutch and adjust if necessary.
5. Check the throttle and the brake lever(s). Make sure they operate properly with no binding.
6. Make sure the engine stop switch works properly.
7. Inspect the front and rear suspension; make sure it has a good solid feel with no looseness.
8. Check the drive chain for wear and correct tension.
9. Check tire pressure or circumference measurement. Refer to **Table 2**.
10. Check the exhaust system for damage.
11. Check the tightness of all fasteners, especially engine mounting hardware.

SERVICE INTERVALS

The services and intervals shown in **Table 1** are recommended by the factory. Strict adherence to these recommendations will ensure long service from your Honda ATC. However, if the vehicle is run in an area of high humidity the lubrication and services must be done more frequently to prevent possible rust damage. This is especially true if you have run the ATC through water (especially salt water).

For convenience when maintaining your vehicle, most of the services shown in **Table 1** are described in this chapter. However, some procedures which require more than minor disassembly or adjustment are covered elsewhere in the appropriate chapter.

TIRES AND WHEELS

Tire Pressure

Tire pressure should be checked and adjusted to maintain the smoothness of the tire, good traction and handling and to get the maximum life out of the tire. A simple, accurate gauge (**Figure 1**) can be purchased for a few dollars and should be carried in your tool box in the tow vehicle. The appropriate tire pressures and circumference measurements are shown in **Table 2**.

> *WARNING*
> *Always inflate both rear tires to the same pressure. If the ATC is run with unequal air pressures it will cause poor handling.*

> *CAUTION*
> *Do not over-inflate the stock tires as they will be permanently distorted and damaged. If overinflated, they will bulge out similar to inflating an inner tube that is not within the constraints of a tire. If this happens the tire **will not** return to its original contour.*

Tire Inspection

The tires take a lot of punishment due to the variety of terrain they are subject to. Inspect them periodically for excessive wear, cuts, abrasions, etc. If you find a nail or other object in the tire, mark its location with a light crayon prior to removing it. This will help locate the hole for repair. Refer to Chapter Eight for tire changing and repair information.

Rim Inspection

Frequently inspect the wheel rims, especially the outer side. If the wheel has hit a tree or large rock, rim damage may be sufficient to cause an air leak or knock it out of alignment. Improper wheel alignment can cause severe vibration and result in an unsafe riding condition.

Make sure that the cotter pins are securely in place on all 3 wheels. If they are lost and the castellated nut works loose, it's good-bye wheel.

BATTERY
(MODELS SO EQUIPPED)

Removal/Installation and Electrolyte Level Check

The battery is the heart of the electrical system. It should be checked and serviced as indicated in **Table 1**. The majority of electrical system troubles can be attributed to neglect of this vital component.

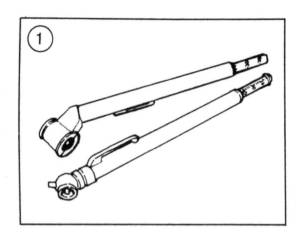

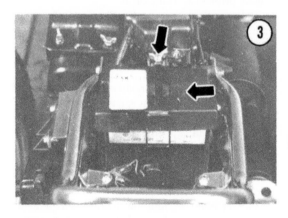

The electrolyte level may be checked with the battery installed in the frame and without removing any parts. Look directly over the taillight and observe the electrolyte level at the rear of the battery. The electrolyte level should be maintained between the 2 marks on the battery case (**Figure 2**).

If the electrolyte level is low, it's a good idea to remove the battery from the ATC so it can be thoroughly serviced and checked.

1. Remove the seat/rear fender assembly.
2. Unscrew the wing nut and remove the battery holder and cover (**Figure 3**).
3. Remove the vent tube (**Figure 4**) from the battery.
4. Disconnect the battery negative (-) and positive (+) leads from the battery (**Figure 5**).
5. Pull the battery up and out of its tray. Wipe off any of the highly corrosive residue that may have dripped from the battery during removal.

> *CAUTION*
> *Be careful not to spill battery electrolyte on painted surfaces. The liquid is highly corrosive and will damage the finish. If it is spilled, wash it off immediately with soapy water and thoroughly rinse with clean water.*

6. Remove the caps from the battery cells and add distilled water to correct the fluid level. Never add electrolyte (acid) to correct the level. Do not use ordinary tap water as it will shorten the service life of the battery.
7. After the fluid level has been corrected, gently shake the battery to mix the existing electrolyte with the new water and allow the battery to stand a few minutes.
8. Check the specific gravity of the electrolyte in each cell with a hydrometer (**Figure 6**) as described under *Testing* in this chapter.
9. After the battery has been refilled, recharged or replaced, install it by reversing these removal steps.

> *CAUTION*
> *If the breather tube was moved during battery removal be sure to route it through the clips on the drive chain case so that residue from it will not drain onto any part of the ATC's frame. The tube must be free of bends or twists as any restriction may pressurize the battery and damage it.*

Testing

Hydrometer testing is the best way to check battery condition. Use a hydrometer with numbered graduations from 1.100 to 1.300 rather than one with color-coded bands. To use the hydrometer, squeeze the rubber ball, insert the tip into the cell and release the pressure on the ball. Draw enough electrolyte to float the weighted float inside the hydrometer. Note the number in line with the surface of the electrolyte; this is the specific gravity for this cell. Squeeze the rubber ball again and return the electrolyte to the cell from which it came.

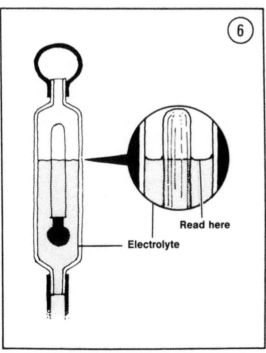

Read here
Electrolyte

The specific gravity of the electrolyte in each battery cell is an excellent indication of that cell's condition. A fully charged cell will read 1.260-1.280, while a cell in acceptable condition reads from 1.230-1.250 and anything below 1.160 is discharged.

Specific gravity varies with temperature. For each 10° the electrolyte temperature exceeds 80° F (27° C), add 0.004 to readings indicated on the hydrometer. Subtract 0.004 for each 10° below 80° F (27° C).

If the cells test in the poor range, the battery requires recharging. The hydrometer is useful for checking the progress of the charging operation. **Table 3** shows approximate state of charge.

Charging

WARNING
During the charging process, highly explosive hydrogen gas is released from the battery. The battery should be charged only in a well-ventilated area and away from any open flames (including pilot lights on home gas appliances). Do not allow any smoking in the area. Never check the charge of the battery by arcing across the terminals; the resulting spark can ignite the hydrogen gas.

CAUTION
Always remove the battery from the vehicle before connecting the battery charger. Never recharge a battery in the ATC's frame due to the corrosive mist that is emitted during the charging process. If this mist settles on the frame it will damage it.

1. Connect the positive (+) charger lead to the positive (+) battery terminal (or lead) and the negative (-) charger lead to the negative (-) battery terminal (or lead).
2. Remove all vent caps from the battery, set the charger at 12 volts and switch the charger on. If the output of the charger is variable, it is best to select a low setting—1 1/2 to 2 amps.

CAUTION
The electrolyte level must be maintained at the upper level during the charging cycle; check and refill as necessary.

3. After the battery has been charged for about 8 hours, turn the charger off, disconnect the leads and check the specific gravity. It should be within the limits specified in **Table 3**. If it is, and remains stable for 1 hour, the battery is considered charged.

4. Clean the battery terminals, surrounding case and tray and reinstall them in the ATC, reversing the removal steps. Coat the battery terminals with Vaseline or silicone spray to retard corrosion and decomposition of the terminals.

CAUTION
Route the breather tube through the clips on the drive chain case so that it does not drain onto any part of the ATC's frame. The tube must be free of bends or twists as any restriction may pressurize the battery and damage it.

New Battery Installation

When replacing the old battery with a new one, be sure to charge it completely (specific gravity 1.260-1.280) before installing it in the ATC. Failure to do so, or using the battery with a low electrolyte level, will permanently damage the new battery.

PERIODIC LUBRICATION

Oil

Oil is graded according to its viscosity, which is an indication of how thick it is. The Society of Automotive Engineers (SAE) system distinguishes oil viscosity by numbers. Thick oils have higher viscosity numbers than thin oils. For example, an SAE 5 oil is a thin oil while an SAE 90 oil is relatively thick.

Grease

A good quality grease (preferably waterproof) should be used. Water does not wash grease off parts as easily as it washes off oil. In addition, grease maintains its lubricating qualities better than oil on long and strenuous rides. In a pinch, though, the wrong lubricant is better than none at all. Correct the situation as soon as possible.

Engine Oil Level Check

Engine oil level is checked with the dipstick/oil filler cap, located on the rear right-hand side of the engine behind the clutch mechanism cover (**Figure 7**).
1. Start the engine and let it warm up approximately 2-3 minutes. Shut off the engine and let the oil settle.
2. Place the ATC on a level surface.
3. Unscrew the dipstick/oil filler cap and wipe it clean. Reinsert it onto the threads in the hole; do not screw it in. Remove it and check the oil level. The ATC must be level for a correct reading.

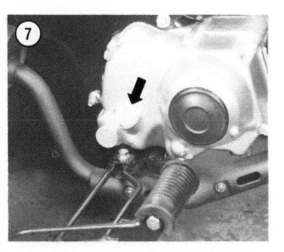

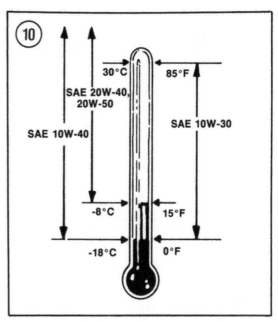

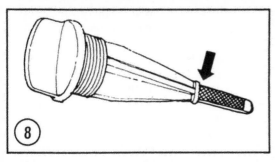

filter screen and rotor are listed in **Table 1**. These intervals assume that the ATC is operated in moderate climates. If it is operated under dusty conditions, the oil will get dirty more quickly and should be changed more frequently than recommended.

Use only a high quality detergent motor oil with an API classification of SE or SF. The classification is stamped or printed on top of the can (**Figure 9**). Try to use the same brand of oil at each oil change. Refer to **Figure 10** for correct oil viscosity to use under anticipated ambient temperatures (not engine oil temperature).

CAUTION
Do not add any friction reducing additives to the oil as they will cause clutch slippage. Also, do not use an engine oil with graphite added. The use of graphite oil will void any applicable Honda warranty. It is not established at this time if graphite will build up on the clutch friction plates and cause clutch problems. Until further testing is done by the oil and motorcycle industry, do not use this type of oil.

4. The level should be between the 2 lines, not above the upper one (**Figure 8**). If necessary, add the recommended type oil to correct the level. Install the dipstick/oil filler cap and tighten it securely.

Engine Oil Change

Regular oil changes will contribute more to engine longevity than any other maintenance operation performed. The factory-recommended oil change interval and the interval for cleaning the oil

To change the engine oil and filter you will need the following:

a. Drain pan.

b. Funnel.

c. Can opener or pour spout.

d. 17 mm wrench (supplied in the owner's tool kit).

e. Oil (see **Table 4** for capacity).

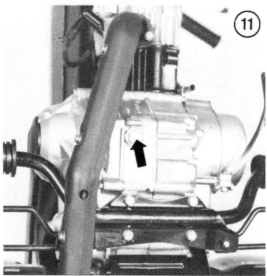

NOTE
Never dispose of motor oil in the trash or pour it on the ground, or down a storm drain. Many service stations accept used motor oil. Many waste haulers provide curbside used motor oil collection. Do not combine other fluids with motor oil to be recycled. To find a recycling location contact the American Petroleum Institute (API) at www.recycleoil.org.

1. Place the ATC on level ground and set the parking brake or block the wheels so the vehicle will not roll in either direction.
2. Start the engine and let it reach operating temperature.
3. Shut the engine off and place a drain pan under the engine drain plug.

NOTE
In the following step, use the 17 mm wrench provided in the owner's tool kit.

4. Remove the 17 mm drain plug (**Figure 11**). Remove the dipstick/oil filler cap; this will speed up the flow of oil.
5. Let it drain for at least 15-20 minutes. During this time, turn the engine over a couple of times with the recoil starter to drain any remaining oil.

CAUTION
Do not let the engine start and run without oil in the crankcase. Make sure the ignition switch is in the OFF position.

6. Inspect the sealing washer on the drain plug; replace if necessary.
7. Install and tighten the drain plug to 20-25 N•m (14-18 ft.-lb.).

8. Clean the oil filter screen and the oil filter rotor prior to refilling the crankcase with fresh oil. Both procedures are described in this chapter.
9. Insert a funnel into the oil fill hole and fill the engine with the correct viscosity and quantity of oil. Refer to **Table 4** for engine oil capacity for each model.
10. Screw in the dipstick/oil filler cap securely.
11. Start the engine, let it run at moderate speed and check for leaks.
12. Turn the engine off and check for correct oil level; adjust as necessary.

Centrifugal Oil Filter Rotor
and Oil Filter Screen Cleaning

The centrifugal oil filter rotor and oil filter screen should be cleaned every time the engine oil is changed.
1. Drain the engine oil as described in this chapter.
2. Move an oil drain pan under the right-hand crankcase cover (residual oil will drain out when this cover is removed). Remove the bolts securing the right-hand crankcase cover and remove the cover and the gasket. Don't lose the locating dowels.
3. Remove the clutch ball retainer (**Figure 12**), the oil guide and spring (**Figure 13**), the clutch release lever (**Figure 14**) and the cam plate assembly (**Figure 15**).
4. Remove the screws securing the clutch outer housing cover (**Figure 16**) and remove the cover.
5. Thoroughly clean the clutch outer housing cover in solvent and dry with compressed air.

CAUTION
Do not allow any dirt or sludge to enter the opening in the end of the cranckshaft (Figure 17). This is the crankshaft oil passageway.

3

6. Use a lint-free shop cloth moistened in solvent and clean the inside of the rotor (**Figure 18**). If necessary, scrape out any oil sludge with a broad-tipped dull screwdriver.

7. Install the clutch outer housing cover and install the screws. Tighten the screws securely.

8. Install the cam plate assembly, the clutch release lever, the oil guide and spring and the clutch ball retainer.

9. Pull the oil filter screen (**Figure 19**) out of the right-hand crankcase. Clean it with solvent and a medium soft toothbrush and carefully dry with compressed air.

NOTE
Figure 19 is shown with the engine removed and partially disassembled for clarity.

10. Inspect the screen; replace it if there are any breaks or holes in it. Install the screen.

11. Install the dowel pins and the gasket.

12. Install the right-hand crankcase cover. Push it all the way into place. Install the screws and tighten securely in a crisscross pattern.

CAUTION
Do not install any of the crankcase cover screws until the crankcase cover is snug up against the crankcase surface. Do not try to force the cover into place with screw pressure. If the cover will not fit up against the crankcase, remove the crankcase cover and repeat Step 12.

13. Refill the engine with the recommended type and quantity of oil; refer to *Engine Oil Change* in this chapter.

Drive Chain Lubrication
(With O-rings)

The 1981-on ATC110 and the ATC125M models are equipped with an O-ring type drive chain. Special care must be taken when cleaning

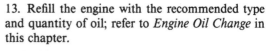

and lubricating this type of chain. The chain should be removed and cleaned prior to lubricating it. Refer to *Drive Chain Cleaning and Lubrication* in Chapter Eight.

Drive Chain Lubrication (Without O-rings)

Lubricate the drive chain every 30 days of operation or more frequently if required. A properly maintained chain will provide maximum service life and reliability.

1. Remove the seat/rear fender assembly.

2A. On ATC70 models, remove the inspection cap (**Figure 20**) on the side of the drive chain case.

2B. On ATC90 and 1979-1980 ATC110 models, remove the rubber inspection cap at the rear of the drive chain case.

> *NOTE*
> *One way to make sure that you lubricate the entire run of the chain is to mark one of the links with a light colored paint.*

3. Shift the transmission into NEUTRAL and push the ATC in either direction until the light colored link is visible through the inspection hole.

4. Starting at this point, lubricate the chain with a good grade of chain lubricant, carefully following the manufacturer's instructions. If a chain lubricant isn't available, use 10W-30 motor oil. Continue to push the ATC forward while lubricating the drive chain through the inspection hole (**Figure 21**). To make sure the entire chain is lubricated, start with the light-colored link and end up with the light-colored link.

Control Cables

The control cables should be lubricated every 30 days of operation. They should be also inspected at this time for fraying and the cable sheath should be checked for chafing. The cables are relatively inexpensive and should be replaced when found to be faulty.

The control cables can be lubricated either with oil or with any of the popular cable lubricants and a cable lubricator. The first method requires more time and the complete lubrication of the entire cable is less certain.

Examine the exposed end of the inner cable. If it is dirty or the cable feels gritty when moved up and down in its housing, first spray it with a lubricant/solvent such as LPS-25 or WD-40. Let this solvent drain out, then proceed with the following steps.

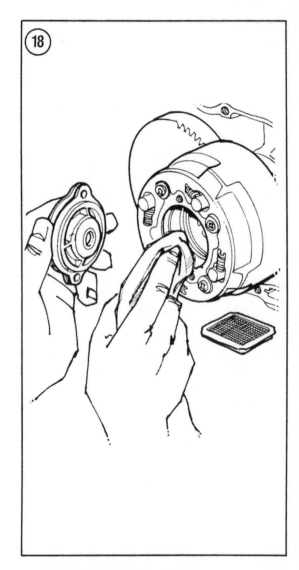

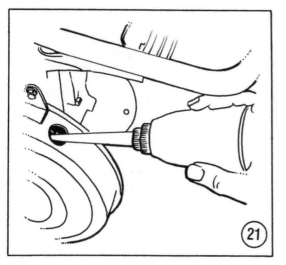

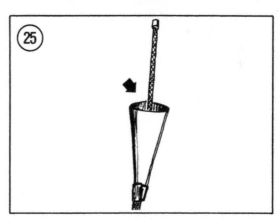

Oil method

1. Disconnect the cable from the throttle lever (**Figure 22**), the rear brake lever (**Figure 23**) and, on models so equipped, the front brake lever (**Figure 24**).

2. Make a cone of stiff paper and tape it to the end of the cable sheath (**Figure 25**).

3. Hold the cable upright and pour a small amount of thin oil (SAE 10W-30) into the cone. Work the cable in and out of the sheath for several minutes to help the oil work its way down to the end of the cable.

NOTE
To avoid a mess, place a shop cloth at the end of the cable to catch the oil as it runs out.

4. Remove the cone, reconnect the cable and adjust the cable as described in this chapter.

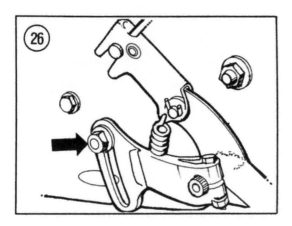

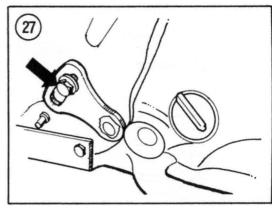

Lubricator method

1. Disconnect the cable from the throttle lever (**Figure 22**), the rear brake lever (**Figure 23**) and, on models so equipped, the front brake lever (**Figure 24**).
2. Attach a lubricator following the manufacturer's instructions.
3. Insert the nozzle of the lubricant can in the lubricator, press the button on the can and hold it down until the lubricant begins to flow out of the other end of the cable.

NOTE
Place a shop cloth at the end of the cable(s) to catch all excess lubricant that will flow out.

4. Remove the lubricator, reconnect the cable and adjust the cable as described in this chapter.

Miscellaneous Lubrication Points

Lubricate the front brake lever (models so equipped), rear brake lever and rear brake pedal pivot point.

PERIODIC MAINTENANCE

Drive Chain Adjustment

The drive chain should be checked and adjusted every 30 days of operation.

NOTE
Drive chain removal, inspection, cleaning and installation is covered in Chapter Eight.

1973-1974 ATC70; ATC90; 1979-1980 ATC110

1. Set the ATC on level ground.
2. On ATC90 and 1979-1980 ATC110 models, remove the seat/rear fender assembly.
3A. On 1973-1974 ATC70 models, loosen the drive chain tensioner lock bolt (**Figure 26**). Using your

hand, pull or push the tensioner plate and shaft upward until it will no longer move; tighten the lock bolt.
3B. On ATC90 and 1979-1980 ATC110 models, loosen the drive chain tensioner locknut (**Figure 27**). Using your hand, pull or push the tensioner plate and shaft upward until it will no longer move; tighten the locknut.
4. Remove the drive chain inspection hole cover (**Figure 20**) on the left-hand side of the drive chain case.
5. Through the inspection hole (**Figure 28**), push up on the drive chain and then let it fall back down. The correct amount of free play is 10-20 mm (3/8-3/4 in.); refer to **Figure 29**.
6. If additional adjustment is necessary, repeat Step 3.

CAUTION
On a well run-in ATC, if the drive chain becomes slack shortly after being properly adjusted, chances are the drive chain tensioner arm and shaft need replacing. The splines on the shaft and the matching teeth on the chain tensioner arm tend to flatten out after long hard use and can no longer grab

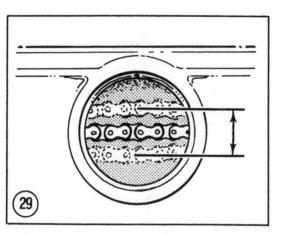

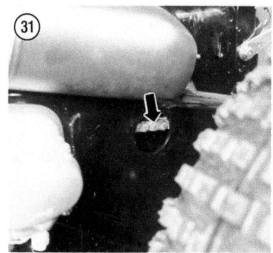

3

onto each other sufficiently to maintain proper tension. If this condition exists refer to Chapter Eight and replace the tensioner shaft as described in the rear axle removal and disassembly procedure.

7. Move the ATC forward to move the drive chain to another position. Recheck the adjustment; chains rarely wear or stretch evenly and, as a result, the free play will not remain constant over the entire chain. If the drive chain cannot be adjusted within these limits, it is excessively worn and stretched and should be replaced as described in Chapter Eight.

8. Install the inspection hole cover.

1978-on ATC70

1. Set the ATC on level ground and shift the transmission into NEUTRAL.

2. Remove the drive chain inspection hole cover (**Figure 20**) on the left-hand side of the drive chain case.

3. Through the inspection hole, push up on the drive chain and then let it fall back down. The correct amount of free play is 10-20 mm (3/8-3/4 in.); refer to **Figure 29**.

4. To adjust the tension, loosen the drive chain adjuster locknuts (A, **Figure 30**) and move the adjuster (B, **Figure 30**) until the correct amount of free play is achieved.

5. Tighten the locknuts to 25-33 N•m (18-23 ft.-lb.).

6. Move the ATC forward to move the drive chain to another position. Recheck the adjustment; chains rarely wear or stretch evenly and, as a result, the free play will not remain constant over the entire chain. If the drive chain cannot be adjusted within these limits, it is excessively worn and stretched and should be replaced as described in Chapter Eight.

7. Install the inspection hole cover.

1981-1983 ATC110

1. Set the ATC on level ground and set the parking brake.

2. Shift the transmission into NEUTRAL.

3. Remove the seat/rear fender assembly.

4. Remove the drive chain inspection hole cover (**Figure 31**) on the left-hand side of the drive chain case.

5. Through the inspection hole, push up on the drive chain and then let it fall back down. The correct amount of free play is 10-20 mm (3/8-3/4 in.); refer to **Figure 29**.

6. To adjust the tension, loosen the drive chain adjuster locknut (A, **Figure 32**) and move the tensioner plate (B, **Figure 32**) until the correct amount of free play is achieved.

NOTE
Move the tensioner plate up to decrease tension or move it down to increase tension.

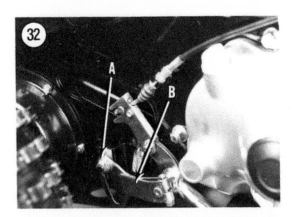

7. Tighten the locknut to 35-45 N•m (25-33 ft.-lb.).
8. Move the ATC forward to move the drive chain to another position. Recheck the adjustment; chains rarely wear or stretch evenly and, as a result, the free play will not remain constant over the entire chain. If the drive chain cannot be adjusted within these limits, it is excessively worn and stretched and should be replaced as described in Chapter Eight.
9. Install the inspection hole cover.

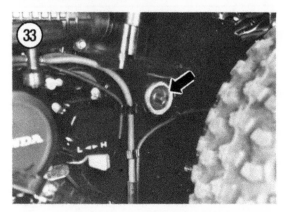

1984 ATC110; 1984 ATC125M

1. Set the ATC on level ground and set the parking brake.
2. Shift the transmission into NEUTRAL.
3. Remove the seat/rear fender assembly.
4. Remove the drive chain inspection hole cover (**Figure 33**) on the left-hand side of the drive chain case.
5. Through the inspection hole, push up on the drive chain and then let it fall back down. The correct amount of free play is 10-20 mm (3/8-3/4 in.); refer to **Figure 29**.
6. To adjust the tension, loosen the rear axle bearing holding bolts (A, **Figure 34**) (2 on each side) and turn the drive chain adjustment nut (B, **Figure 34**) in or out as required. Turn the nut *clockwise* will decrease free play and *counterclockwise* will increase free play.

7. Tighten the bearing holding bolts to 50-70 N•m (36-51 ft.-lb.).
8. Move the ATC forward to move the drive chain to another position. Recheck the adjustment; chains rarely wear or stretch evenly and, as a result, the free play will not remain constant over the entire chain. If the drive chain cannot be adjusted within these limits, it is excessively worn and stretched and should be replaced as described in Chapter Eight.
9. Install the inspection hole cover.
10. After the drive chain has been adjusted, the rear brake pedal free play must be adjusted as described in this chapter.

Brake Lining Inspection

Every 30 days of operation, inspect the front (models so equipped) and rear brake lining wear indicator. Apply the rear brake fully. If the wear indicator on the brake arm aligns with the reference mark on the brake panel, the brake shoes must be replaced. Refer to **Figure 35** for the front or **Figure 36** for the rear brake. Refer to Chapter Nine for service procedures.

Front Brake Lever Adjustment
(Models So Equipped)

The front brake lever should be inspected every 30 days of operation and adjusted if necessary to maintain the proper amount of free play. The brake lever should travel about 15-20 mm (5/8-3/4 in.) before the brake shoes come in contact with the brake drum, but must not be adjusted so closely that the brake shoes contact the brake drum with the lever relaxed.

If adjustment is necessary, turn the adjustment nut (**Figure 37**) in or out to achieve the correct amount of free play.

NOTE
Make sure the cut-out relief in the adjustment nut is properly seated on the brake arm pivot pin.

Rear Brake Adjustment

The rear brake lever should be inspected every 30 days of operation and adjusted if necessary to maintain the proper amount of free play. The brake lever should travel the specified amount of travel before the brake shoes come in contact with the brake drum, but must not be adjusted so closely that the brake shoes contact the brake drum with the lever relaxed.

ATC70

On the ATC70 the rear brake is operated only with the lever located on the left-hand side of the handlebar. There is no brake pedal.

The brake lever should travel about 15-20 mm (5/8-3/4 in.) before the brake shoes come in contact with the brake drum. If adjustment is necessary, turn the adjustment nut (**Figure 38**) on the end of the brake cable, in or out to achieve the correct amount of free play.

NOTE
Make sure the cut-out relief in the adjustment nut is properly seated on the brake arm pivot pin.

NOTE
If the correct amount of free play cannot be achieved, the brake cable has stretched and must be replaced; see Chapter Nine.

ATC90, ATC110 and ATC125M

The ATC90, ATC110 and ATC125M are equipped with both a left-hand brake lever and a foot-operated brake pedal. The brake pedal should travel about 15-20 mm (5/8-3/4 in.) before the brake shoes come in contact with the brake drum. If adjustment is necessary, perform the following steps in this order.

1. Set the ATC on level ground and set the parking brake.
2. Remove the seat/rear fender assembly.
3. Release the parking brake.
4. Depress the brake pedal until the brake shoes come in contact with the brake drum. The correct amount of free play is 15-20 mm (5/8-3/4 in.) as shown in **Figure 39**.
5. If adjustment is necessary, turn the adjustment nut (**Figure 40**) on the end of the brake rod in or out to achieve the correct amount of free play.

NOTE
Make sure the cut-out relief in the adjustment nut is properly seated on the brake arm pivot pin.

The brake lever must be adjusted after the brake pedal is adjusted.

6A. On ATC90 models, the brake lever should travel about 20-30 mm (3/4-1 1/4 in.) before the brake shoes come in contact with the brake drum.

6B. On ATC110 and ATC125M models, the brake lever should travel about 15-20 mm (5/8-3/4 in.) before the brake shoes come in contact with the brake drum.

7. If adjustment is necessary, perform the following:
   a. At the brake cable, loosen the locknut (A, **Figure 41**).
   b. Turn the adjustment nut (B, **Figure 41**) on the brake cable in or out to achieve the correct amount of free play.

8. After adjusting both the pedal and lever free play, apply the parking brake and make sure it holds the ATC securely in place. If necessary, repeat this procedure until the parking brake operates properly.

NOTE
If the parking brake does not operate properly or the correct amount of free play cannot be achieved, the brake

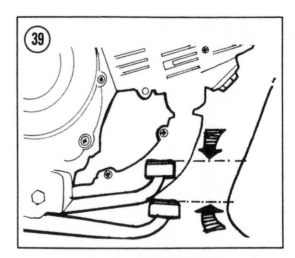

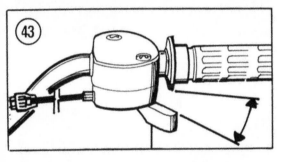

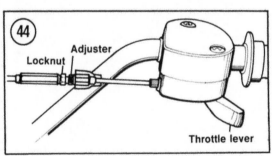

Adjuster
Locknut
Throttle lever

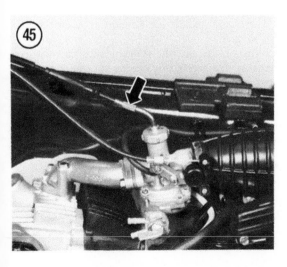

cable has stretched and must be replaced; refer to Chapter Nine.

Clutch Mechanism Adjustment

This is the only clutch adjustment provided for the automatic (centrifugal) clutch. This adjustment takes up slack due to clutch component wear. The adjustment of the clutch must be made with the engine off.

1. Remove the rubber protective cap from the right-hand crankcase cover.
2. Loosen the locknut (A, **Figure 42**) on the clutch adjusting screw.
3. Slowly turn the clutch adjuster screw (B, **Figure 42**) *clockwise* 1 full turn.
4. Slowly turn the clutch adjuster screw *counterclockwise* until *slight* resistance is felt, then stop.
5. Turn the adjuster screw *clockwise* 1/8 turn.

NOTE
Make sure the adjuster screw does not move when tightening the locknut.

6. Hold the adjuster screw in this position and tighten the locknut securely.
7. Test ride the ATC to make sure the clutch is operating correctly; readjust if necessary.
8. If the clutch cannot be properly adjusted using this method, some of the internal components in the clutch are worn and need replacing; refer to Chapter Five.

Throttle Lever Adjustment

The throttle lever should have 5-10 mm (3/16-3/8 in.) free play measured at the tip of the lever (**Figure 43**).

1. On 1982-on ATC110 models, if adjustment is necessary, perform the following:
   a. At the upper end of the throttle cable, loosen the locknut and turn the adjuster (**Figure 44**) in either direction to achieve the correct amount of free play.
   b. Tighten the locknut.
2. On all other models, if adjustment is necessary, perform the following:
   a. Remove the seat/rear fender assembly.
   b. Remove the fuel tank as described in Chapter Six.
   c. At the carburetor, slide up the rubber boot where the throttle cable enters the top of the carburetor.
   d. Turn the adjuster (**Figure 45**) to obtain the correct amount of free play. Looking down onto the carburetor top, turning the adjuster *clockwise* will increase free play while *counterclockwise* will decrease free play.

e. Slide the rubber boot back down onto the carburetor top.

f. Check the throttle cable from grip to carburetor. Make sure it is not kinked or chafed. Check for smooth operation of the throttle from the open to closed position while moving the handlebar from one limit to the other.

g. If the throttle cable requires replacing, refer to Chapter Six.

h. Reinstall the fuel tank and seat/rear fender assembly.

Air Filter Element Cleaning

The air filter element should be removed and cleaned every 30 operating days and replaced whenever it is damaged or starts to deteriorate.

The air filter removes dust and abrasive particles before the air enters the carburetor and engine. Without the air filter, very fine particles could enter into the engine and cause rapid wear of the piston rings, cylinder and bearings. They also might clog small passages in the carburetor. Never run the ATC without the element installed.

Proper air filter servicing can ensure long service from your engine.

ATC70

1. Remove the acorn nut (A, **Figure 46**) securing the filter cover and remove the cover (B, **Figure 46**).

2. Withdraw the filter element assembly from the air filter case (**Figure 47**).

3. Remove the inner pipe from the element holder and remove the element.

4. Clean and inspect the element as described in this chapter.

5. Wipe out the interior of the air filter case with a shop rag dampened in cleaning solvent. Remove any foreign matter that may have passed through a broken element.

6. Assemble and install the element by reversing these steps. Make sure the filter cover is correctly seated onto the filter housing on the carburetor.

ATC90; 1979-1982 ATC110

1. Place the ATC on level ground and set the parking brake.

2. Remove the seat/rear fender assembly.

3. Remove the screws securing the air filter case (A, **Figure 48**) to the frame.

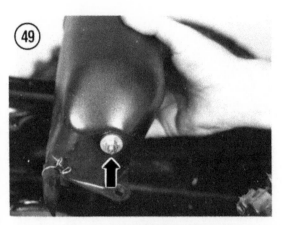

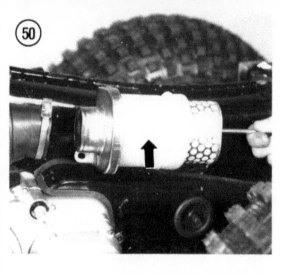

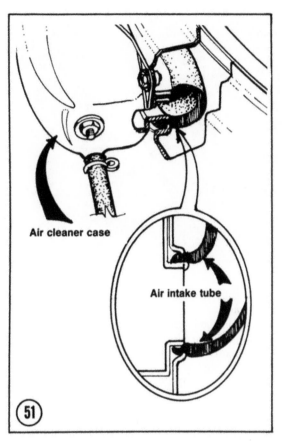

Air cleaner case

Air intake tube

4A. On 1981-1982 ATC110 models, loosen the screw (B, **Figure 48**) on the clamping bands securing the air filter case to the carburetor.

4B. On all other models, remove the nut at the rear of the filter case.

5. Remove the air filter assembly and case from the frame.

6A. On 1981-1982 ATC110 models, remove the nut (**Figure 49**) at the rear of the filter case and withdraw the element assembly.

6B. On all other models, remove the nut at the rear of the filter bolt and withdraw the element assembly.

7A. On 1982 ATC110 models, carefully slide the foam element off of the paper element assembly (**Figure 50**).

7B. On all other models, carefully slide the foam element off the element assembly.

8. Clean and inspect the element(s) as described in this chapter.

9. Wipe out the interior of the air filter case with a shop rag dampened in cleaning solvent. Remove any foreign matter that may have passed through a broken element.

10. Assemble and install the element by reversing these steps, noting the following.

11A. On 1982 ATC110 models, make sure the air intake tube fits correctly into the opening in the air filter case assembly (**Figure 51**).

11B. On all other models, make sure the filter cover is correctly seated onto the filter housing on the carburetor.

1983-on ATC110; ATC125M

1. Place the ATC on level ground and set the parking brake.

2. Remove the seat/rear fender assembly.

3. Remove the wing nuts (**Figure 52**) securing the air filter case cover and remove the cover.

4. Loosen the screw (A, **Figure 53**) on the clamping band securing the air filter assembly to the carburetor.

5. Remove the wing nut (B, **Figure 53**) securing the air filter assembly to the air box.

6. Remove the air filter assembly from the air box.

7. Carefully slide the foam element off the element assembly.

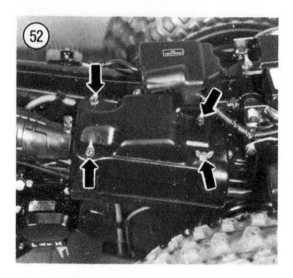

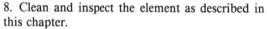

8. Clean and inspect the element as described in this chapter.

9. Wipe out the interior of the air box with a shop rag dampened in cleaning solvent. Remove any foreign matter that may have passed through a broken element.

10. Assemble and install the element by reversing these steps.

Foam Air Filter Element
Cleaning and Inspection

1A. On 1982 ATC110 models, gently wash the element in liquid detergent and water. Rinse thoroughly in clean water. Repeat if necessary until the element is clean. Let the element dry for about one hour.

1B. On all other models, clean the element gently in cleaning solvent until all dirt is removed. Thoroughly dry in a clean shop cloth until all solvent residue is removed. Let it dry for about one hour.

NOTE
Inspect the element; if it is torn or broken in any area it should be replaced. Do not run with a damaged element as it may allow dirt to enter the engine.

2. On all models except the 1982 ATC110, pour a small amount of SAE 80 or SAE 90 gear oil or special foam air filter oil onto the element and work it into the porous foam material. Do not oversaturate the element as too much oil will restrict air flow. The element will be discolored by the oil and should have an even color indicating that the oil is distributed evenly. Let it dry for

another hour prior to installation. If installed too soon, the chemical carrier in the special foam air filter oil will be drawn into the engine and may cause damage.

Paper Air Filter Element
Cleaning and Inspection

1. Gently tap the paper filter assembly to loosen the dust and dirt.

2. Apply compressed air to the *inside* of the element to remove all loosened dirt and dust from the element.

3. Tap the element again and repeat Step 2 until all loose dust and dirt is removed.

NOTE
If the paper element is extremely dirty, wash it in a solution of liquid detergent and water. Rinse thoroughly in clean water and allow to dry thoroughly. If it does not come clean, replace the foam and paper elements as a set.

4. Inspect the element; if it is torn or broken in any area it should be replaced. Do not run with a damaged element as it may allow dirt to enter the engine.

Fuel Filter Cleaning

The integral fuel filter in the carburetor or in the fuel shutoff valve removes particles in the fuel which might otherwise enter the carburetor. This could cause the float needle to stay in the open position or clog one of the jets.

3

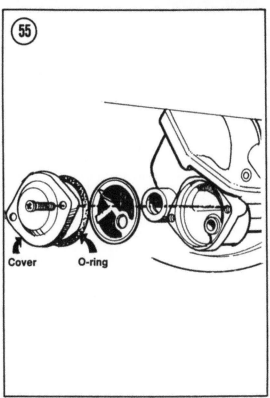

Cover   O-ring

1973-1974 ATC70; ATC90

1. Turn the fuel shutoff valve to the S or OFF position.
2. Place the loose end of the drain tube into a clean, sealable metal container. If the fuel is kept clean, it can be reused.
3. Loosen the drain screw knob or the drain screw (**Figure 54**) and drain all gasoline from the carburetor.

4. Remove the screws securing the cover and remove the cover, O-ring and filter screen (**Figure 55**) from the carburetor float chamber.
5. After removing the filter screen, insert a corner of a clean shop rag into the opening in the carburetor to stop the dribbling of fuel onto the engine and frame.
6. Clean the filter screen with a medium soft toothbrush and blow out with compressed air. Replace the filter screen if it is defective.
7. Install by reversing these removal steps, noting the following.
8. Do not forget to install the O-ring between the cover and the carburetor float bowl.
9. Turn the fuel shutoff valve to the ON position and check for fuel leakage after installation is completed.

1978-on ATC70; ATC110; ATC125M

NOTE
Some of the photos in this procedure show the carburetor removed for clarity. It is not necessary to remove the carburetor for this procedure.

1. Turn the fuel shutoff valve to the OFF position.
2. Place the loose end of the drain tube into a clean, sealable metal container. If the fuel is kept clean, it can be reused.
3. Loosen the drain screw and drain all gasoline from the carburetor.
4A. On ATC70 and 1979-1983 ATC110 models, perform the following:
  a. Remove the screws (**Figure 56**) securing the fuel shutoff valve to the carburetor and remove the valve.

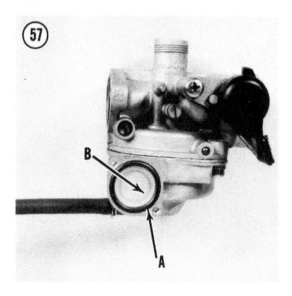

b. Remove the O-ring (A, **Figure 57**) and the filter screen (B, **Figure 57**).

4B. On 1984 ATC110 and ATC125M models perform the following:

a. Unscrew the fuel cup (**Figure 58**) from the base of the carburetor float bowl.

b. Remove the fuel cup, filter screen and O-ring seals from the carburetor (**Figure 59**).

5. After removing the valve, insert a corner of a clean shop rag into the opening in the carburetor to stop the dribbling of fuel onto the engine and frame.

6. Clean the filter screen with a medium soft toothbrush and blow out with compressed air. Replace the filter screen if it is defective.

7. Inspect all parts for wear, damage or deterioration.

8. Install by reversing these removal steps, noting the following.

9. On ATC70 and 1979-1983 ATC110 models, install the filter screen with the cupped face in toward the carburetor body (**Figure 60**).

10. Do not forget to install the O-ring between the valve or cup and the carburetor float bowl.

11. Turn the fuel shutoff valve to the ON position and check for fuel leakage after installation is completed.

Fuel Line Inspection

Inspect the fuel line from the fuel tank to the carburetor. If it is cracked or starting to deteriorate it must be replaced. Make sure the small hose clamps are in place and holding securely.

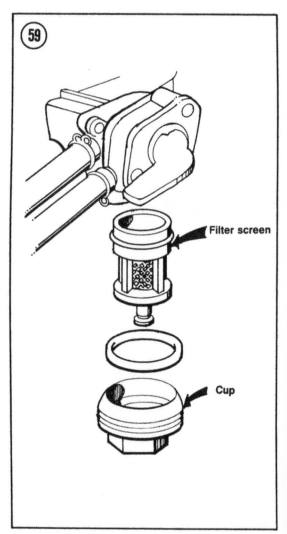

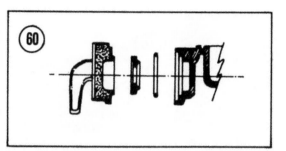

3

3. Clean off accumulated carbon from the spark arrester with a scraper and wash off with solvent. Thoroughly dry with compressed air.

4. With the spark arrester removed, start the engine and rev it up a few times to blow out accumulated carbon from the tail section of the muffler. Continue until carbon stops coming out.

5. Turn the engine off and let the exhaust system cool down.

6. Install the spark arrester and install the bolt.

Wheel Bearings

There is no factory-recommended interval for cleaning and repacking the wheel bearings. They should be serviced whenever they are removed from the wheel hub or whenever there is the likelihood of water contamination (especially salt water). Service procedures are covered in Chapter Eight.

Steering Head Adjustment Check

The steering head is fitted with loose ball bearings. It should be checked every year of operation or after a serious spill.

Place the ATC up on wood block(s) so the front wheel is off the ground.

Hold onto the front fork tubes and gently rock the fork assembly back and forth. If you can feel looseness, refer to Chapter Eight.

Nuts, Bolts and Other Fasteners

Constant vibration can loosen many of the fasteners on the ATC. Check the tightness of all fasteners, especially the following:

a. Engine mounting hardware.
b. Engine crankcase covers.
c. Handlebar and front forks.
d. Gearshift lever.
e. Brake pedal and lever.
f. Exhaust system.

WARNING
A damaged or deteriorated fuel line presents a very dangerous fire hazard to both the rider and the vehicle if fuel should spill onto a hot engine or exhaust pipe.

Spark Arrester Cleaning

The spark arrester should be cleaned every 30 operating days.

WARNING
To avoid burning your hands, do not perform this cleaning operation with the exhaust system hot. Work in a well ventilated area (outside your garage) that is free of any fire hazards. Be sure to protect your eyes with safety glasses or goggles.

1. Place the ATC on level ground and set the parking brake.

2. Remove the bolt (A, **Figure 61**) securing the spark arrester and slide the unit out of the tailpipe (B, **Figure 61**).

ENGINE TUNE-UP

A tune-up is general adjustment and maintenance to ensure peak engine performance. A complete tune-up should be performed every 30 operating days with normal riding. More frequent tune-ups may be required if the ATC is ridden hard or raced.

Table 5 summarizes tune-up specifications.

The spark plug should be routinely replaced at every other tune-up or if the electrodes show signs of erosion. Have new parts on hand before you begin.

Because different systems in an engine interact, the procedures should be done in the following order:

a. Clean or replace the air filter element.
b. Adjust valve clearance.
c. Adjust camshaft chain tension.
d. Run a compression test.
e. Check or replace the spark plug.
f. Check and adjust the ignition timing.
g. Adjust the carburetor idle speed.

To perform a tune-up on your Honda, you will need the following tools and equipment:

a. 18 mm spark plug wrench.
b. Socket wrench and assorted sockets.
c. Flat feeler gauge.
d. 9 mm box wrench for adjusting valve clearance.
e. Spark plug wire feeler gauge and gapper tool.
f. Compression gauge.
g. Ignition timing light.
h. Portable tachometer.

VALVE CLEARANCE ADJUSTMENT

Valve clearance adjustment must be made with the engine cool, at room temperature (below 95° F/35° C). The correct valve clearance for both the intake and exhaust valves are as follows:

a. ATC70 and ATC90: 0.05 mm (0.002 in.).
b. ATC110 and ATC125M: 0.07 mm (0.005 in.).

The exhaust valve is located on the bottom of the engine and the intake valve is at the top of the engine.

1. Place the ATC on level ground and set the parking brake.
2. Remove the seat/rear fender assembly.
3. Remove the bolt securing the gearshift lever and remove the gearshift lever.
4. Remove the recoil starter assembly as described in Chapter Seven.
5. Remove both valve adjustment covers (**Figure 62**).
6. Remove the spark plug—this will make it easier to rotate the engine by hand.
7. On models so equipped, remove the timing inspection cover on the left-hand crankcase cover.
8. Using the nut (or bolt) on the alternator rotor, rotate the crankshaft *counterclockwise* until the piston is at top dead center (TDC) on the compression stroke.

NOTE
A piston at TDC on its compression stroke will have free play in both of the rocker arms, indicating that both the intake and exhaust valves are closed.

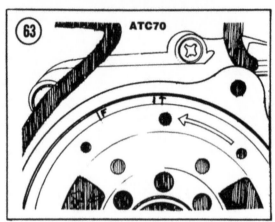

9. Make sure the "T" mark on the alternator rotor aligns with the fixed pointer either on the crankcase or alternator stator assembly. Refer to **Figure 63** for ATC70 models or **Figure 64** for ATC90, ATC110 and ATC125M models.
10. If both rocker arms are not loose with the engine timing mark on the "T," rotate the engine an additional 360° until both valves have free play.
11. Check the clearance of both the intake and exhaust valves by inserting a flat feeler gauge between the rocker arm pad and the camshaft lobe (**Figure 65**). If the clearance is correct, there will be a slight resistance on the feeler gauge when it is inserted and withdrawn.
12. To correct the clearance, use a 9 mm wrench and back off the locknut. Screw the adjuster in or out so there is a slight resistance felt on the feeler gauge. Hold the adjuster to prevent it from turning further and tighten the locknut securely. Then recheck the clearance to make sure the adjuster did

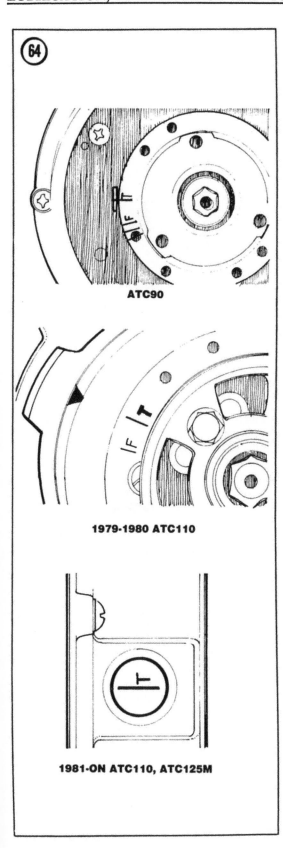

ATC90

1979-1980 ATC110

1981-ON ATC110, ATC125M

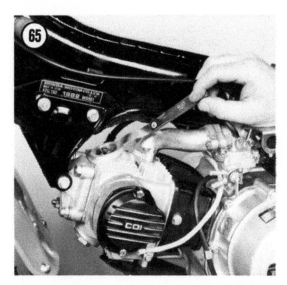

3

not slip when the locknut was tightened. Readjust if necessary.

13. Rotate the engine 360° and repeat Step No. 11 to make sure the adjustment is correct. If the clearance is still not correct, repeat Step 12 until it is correct.

14. Inspect the rubber gasket on each valve adjusting cover. Replace if they are starting to deteriorate or harden; replace as a set even if only one is bad. Install both covers and tighten securely.

15. Install the spark plug and attach the spark plug lead.

16. On models so equipped, install the timing inspection cover on the left-hand crankcase cover.

17. Install the valve adjuster covers, the recoil starter assembly, the gearshift lever and the seat/rear fender assembly.

CAMSHAFT CHAIN TENSIONER ADJUSTMENT

In time, the camshaft chain and guide will wear and develop slack. This will cause engine noise and, if neglected too long, will cause engine damage. The chain tension should be adjusted every 30 days of operation or if it becomes noisy.

1. Place the ATC on level ground and set the parking brake.

2. Start the engine and let it reach normal operating temperature. Shut off the engine.

3. Restart the engine and let it idle.

4. Loosen the cam chain tensioner locknut (A, **Figure 66**).

5. Slowly loosen the cam chain tensioner adjust bolt (B, **Figure 66**) *counterclockwise* 1/2 to 1 1/2

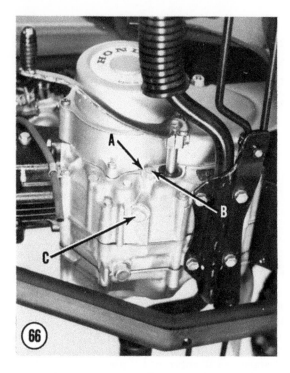

66

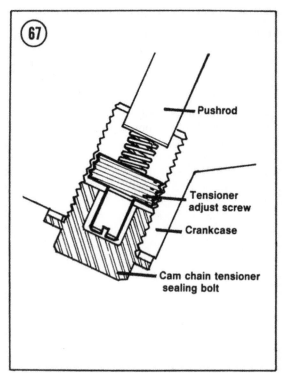

67

Pushrod

Tensioner
adjust screw

Crankcase

Cam chain tensioner
sealing bolt

turns. The tensioner will automatically adjust. Retighten the adjust bolt and locknut.

6. If the cam chain is still noisy, remove the 14 mm cam chain tensioner sealing bolt (C, **Figure 66**). Use a screwdriver and gradually turn in the tensioner adjust screw (**Figure 67**) until the cam chain is no longer noisy. Install the sealing bolt.

NOTE
If the cam chain is still noisy after Step 6, there is a problem with the cam chain tensioner assembly. Remove the tensioner assembly and inspect it as described in Chapter Four.

COMPRESSION TEST

A compression test should be run every 30 operating days. Record the results and compare them with the readings at the next test interval. A running record will show trends in deterioration so that corrective action can be taken before complete failure occurs.

The results, when properly interpreted, can indicate general cylinder, piston ring and valve condition.

1. Place the ATC on level ground and set the parking brake or block the wheels so the vehicle will not roll in either direction.

2. Start the engine and let it reach normal operating temperature. Shut the engine off.

3. Fully open the throttle lever. Raise the choke lever or push the knob all the way down to the completely open position.

4. Disconnect the spark plug wire and remove the spark plug.

5. Connect a compression gauge to the cylinder following the manufacturer's instructions (**Figure 68**).

6. Operate the recoil starter several times and check the readings.

CAUTION
On models with a CDI ignition, do not turn the engine over more than absolutely necessary. When the spark plug lead is disconnected the electronic ignition will produce the highest voltage possible and the ignition coil may overheat and be damaged.

7. Remove the compression gauge and record the reading. The readings should be as follows:

   a. ATC70 and ATC90: 10-12 kg/cm² (142-170 psi).

   b. ATC110 and ATC125M: 11-14 kg/cm² (156-198 psi).

If the reading is higher than normal, there may be a buildup of carbon deposits in the combustion chamber or on the piston crown.

If a low reading is obtained it can be caused by one or more of the following faulty items:

    a. A leaking cylinder head gasket.

    b. Incorrect valve clearance.

    c. Valve leakage (burned valve face).

    d. Worn or broken piston rings.

If the head gasket is okay, perform a wet test to determine which other component is faulty. Pour about one teaspoon of engine oil through the spark plug hole onto the top of the piston. Turn the engine over once to clear the oil, then take another compression reading. If the compression increases significantly, the valves are good but the piston rings are defective. If compression does not increase, the valves require servicing. A valve could be hanging open but not burned or a piece of carbon could be on a valve seat.

Install the spark plug and connect the spark plug lead.

SPARK PLUG

Selection

Spark plugs are available in various heat ranges, hotter or colder than the plugs originally installed at the factory.

Select a plug of the heat range designed for the loads and conditions under which the ATC will be run. Use of incorrect heat ranges can cause a seized piston, scored cylinder wall or a damaged piston crown.

In general, use a hot plug for low speeds and low temperatures. Use a cold plug for high speeds, high engine loads and high temperatures. The plug should operate hot enough to burn off unwanted deposits, but not so hot that it is damaged or causes preignition. A spark plug of the correct heat range will show a light tan color on the portion of the insulator within the cylinder after the plug has been in service.

The reach (length) of a plug is also important. A longer than normal plug could interfere with the piston, causing permanent and severe damage; refer to **Figure 69**. Refer to **Table 5** for recommended spark plug types.

Removal and Cleaning

1. Grasp the spark plug lead as near the plug as possible and pull it off the plug. If it is stuck to the plug, twist it slightly to break it loose.

2. Blow away any dirt that has accumulated in the spark plug well.

> *CAUTION*
> *The dirt could fall into the cylinder when the plug is removed, causing serious engine damage.*

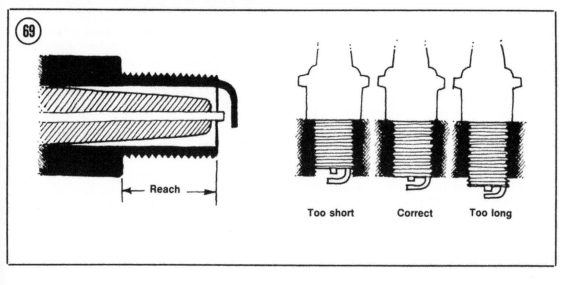

Too short   Correct   Too long

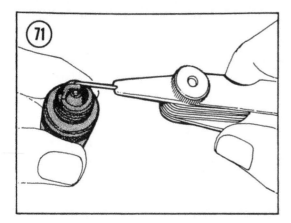

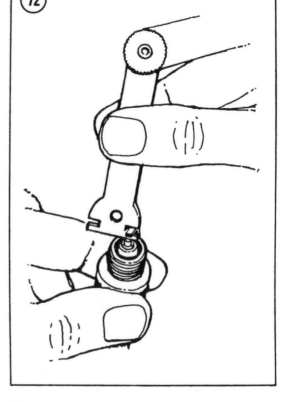

3. Remove the spark plug with an 18 mm spark plug wrench.

NOTE
If the plug is difficult to remove, apply penetrating oil such as WD-40 or Liquid Wrench around the base of the plug and let it soak in about 10-20 minutes.

4. Inspect the plug carefully. Look for a broken center porcelain, excessively eroded electrodes and excessive carbon or oil fouling. If any of these problems are present, replace the plug. If deposits are light, the plug may be cleaned in solvent with a wire brush or cleaned in a special spark plug sandblast cleaner. Regap the plug as explained in this chapter.

Gapping and Installation

A spark plug should be carefully gapped to ensure a reliable, consistant spark. You must use a special spark plug gapping tool and a wire feeler gauge.
1. Remove the new spark plug from its box. *Do not* screw on the small piece that is loose in the box (**Figure 70**); it is not used.

2. Insert a wire feeler gauge between the center and side electrode of each plug (**Figure 71**). The correct gap is 0.6-0.7 mm (0.024-0.028 in.). If the gap is correct, you will feel a slight drag as you pull the wire through. If there is no drag or the gauge won't pass through, bend the side electrode with a gapping tool (**Figure 72**) to set the proper gap.
3. Put a small drop of oil or aluminum anti-seize compound on the threads of the spark plug.
4. Screw the spark plug in by hand until it seats. Very little effort is required. If force is necessary, you have the plug cross-threaded; unscrew it and try again.
5. Use a spark plug wrench and tighten the plug an additional 1/4 to 1/2 turn after the gasket has made contact with the head. If you are installing an old, regapped plug and reusing the old gasket, only tighten an additional 1/4 turn.

NOTE
Do not overtighten. This will only squash the gasket and destroy its sealing ability.

6. Install the spark plug lead; make sure it is on tight.

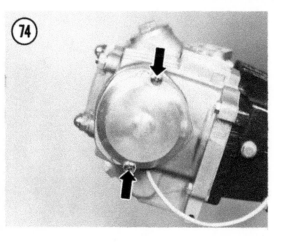

Reading Spark Plugs

Much information about engine and spark plug performance can be determined by careful examination of the spark plug. This information is more valid after performing the following steps.

1. Ride the ATC a short distance at full throttle in any gear.

2. Turn the ignition switch to OFF before closing the throttle and simultaneously shift to NEUTRAL; coast and brake to a stop.

3. Remove the spark plug and examine it. Compare it to the illustrations in Chapter Two:

   a. If the insulator is white or burned, the plug is too hot and should be replaced with a colder one.

   b. A too-cold plug will have sooty or oily deposits ranging in color from dark brown to black. Replace with a hotter plug and check for too-rich carburetion or evidence of oil blow-by at the piston rings.

   c. If the plug has a light tan or gray colored deposit and no abnormal gap wear or electrode erosion is evident, the plug and the engine are running properly.

   d. If the plug exhibits a black insulator tip, a damp and oily film over the firing end and a carbon layer over the entire nose, it is oil fouled. An oil-fouled plug can be cleaned, but it is better to replace it.

CONTACT BREAKER POINT IGNITION (ATC70, ATC90, 1979-1980 ATC110)

The following procedures describe breaker point adjustment and ignition timing. Breaker point replacement is described in Chapter Seven.

Gap Adjustment

The contact breaker point assembly is located on the left-hand end of the crankshaft next to the alternator on ATC70 models. On ATC90 and ATC110 models, the contact breaker point assembly is attached to the left-hand end of the camshaft in the cylinder head.

Contact breaker point adjustment is basically the same on all models. Where differences occur they are identified.

1. Place the ATC on level ground and set the parking brake or block the wheels so the vehicle will not roll in either direction.

2. Shift the transmission into NEUTRAL.

3. Remove the spark plug – this will make it easier to rotate the engine.

4A. On ATC70 models, perform the following:

   a. Remove the recoil starter and left-hand crankcase (alternator) cover as an assembly.

   b. Remove the bolts securing the recoil starter ring (**Figure 73**) and remove the ring from the alternator rotor.

4B. On ATC90 and ATC110 models, remove the screws (**Figure 74**) securing the ignition cover and remove the cover and the gasket. Remove the timing inspection cover on the left-hand crankcase cover.

5. Rotate the crankshaft with the nut on the alternator rotor counterclockwise until the point gap is at the maximum opening.

6. Insert a flat feeler gauge and measure the gap. The gap should be 0.3-0.4 mm (0.012-0.016 in.).

7. If the gap is not within these limits, loosen the contact breaker point attachment screw(s). Refer to A, **Figure 75** for ATC70 models or A, **Figure 76** for ATC90 and ATC110 models. Insert a screwdriver into the pry point (B, **Figure 75** or B, **Figure 76**) and move the point assembly until the gap is correct. Tighten the screw(s) securely.

NOTE
Make sure the point assembly does not move while tightening the screw(s).

NOTE
Figure 75 is shown with the contact breaker point assembly and backing plate removed for clarity. Do not remove the assembly for this procedure.

8. After tightening the screw(s), repeat Step 6 to make sure the gap is correct. Readjust if necessary.
9. Leave all components that were removed off for the next procedure.
10. Adjust the ignition timing as described in this chapter.

NOTE
Ignition timing must be adjusted after the contact breaker point gap has been changed.

Static Timing Adjustment (ATC70)

Static ignition timing is acceptable but if you have a stroboscopic timing light, dynamic timing (as described in this chapter) is more accurate.

This procedure requires a test light. It can be a homemade unit (**Figure 77**) that consists of 2 C or D size flashlight batteries and a light bulb mounted on a piece of wood, some light gauge electrical wire and alligator clips. These items can be purchased from any hardware store.

The following procedure is based on the test light shown in **Figure 77**. If another type is used, follow the manufacturer's instructions.
1. Adjust the contact breaker point gap as described in this chapter.
2. Disconnect the electrical connector from the alternator.

NOTE
Before attaching the test light unit, check the condition of the batteries by touching the test leads together. The light should go on. If not, replace the batteries and/or the light bulb and check all electrical connections on the tester. The test light must be operating correctly.

3. Connect one lead of the test light unit to a good ground, such as one of the cooling fins on the cylinder, and connect the other lead to the black wire in the electrical connector disconnected in Step 2. The test light should be on. If a commercial tester is used, follow the manufacturer's instructions.

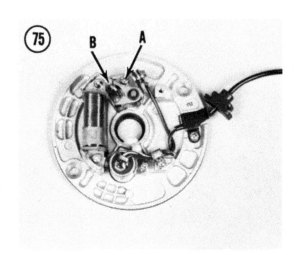

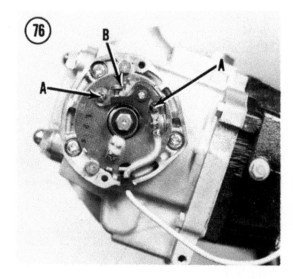

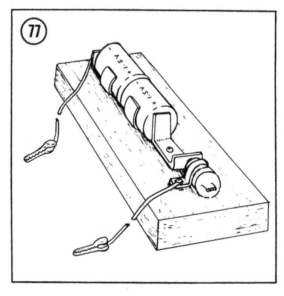

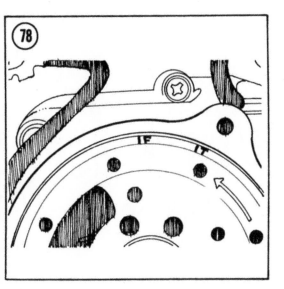

4. Rotate the crankshaft with the nut on the alternator rotor *counterclockwise* until the "F" mark on the alternator rotor aligns with the fixed pointer (**Figure 78**). At this exact moment the contact breaker points should just begin to open. If they open at this moment, the test light will dim indicating that the ignition timing is correct. If the timing is incorrect, proceed to Step 5.

5. To adjust the timing, loosen the contact breaker point attachment screw (A, **Figure 75**). Insert a screwdriver into the pry point (B, **Figure 75**) and slightly move the point assembly until the breaker points just begin to open. The light will dim when the points open; tighten the screw securely. Make sure the point assembly does not move while tightening the screw.

> *NOTE*
> *Increasing the point gap will **advance** the timing. Decreasing the point gap will **retard** the timing.*

6. Repeat Step 4.

7. After the timing is correct, recheck the maximum point gap. Rotate the crankshaft with the nut on the alternator rotor *counterclockwise* until the point gap is at its maximum. Insert a flat feeler gauge and measure the gap. The gap should be 0.3-0.4 mm (0.012-0.016 in.). If the maximum gap cannot be maintained when the ignition timing is correct, the contact breaker point assembly is worn and must be replaced. Refer to Chapter Seven.

8. Install the recoil starter ring.

9. Install the recoil starter and left-hand crankcase (alternator) cover as an assembly.

10. Install the spark plug and spark plug lead.

Static Timing Adjustment
(ATC90 and ATC110)

Static ignition timing is acceptable but if you have a stroboscopic timing light, dynamic timing (as described in this chapter) is more accurate.

This procedure requires a test light. It can be a homemade unit (**Figure 77**) that consists of 2 C or D size flashlight batteries and a light bulb mounted on a piece of wood, some light gauge electrical wire and alligator clips. These items can be purchased from any hardware store.

The following procedure is based on the test light shown in **Figure 77**. If another type is used, follow the manufacturer's instructions.

1. Adjust the contact breaker point gap as described in this chapter.

> *NOTE*
> *Before attaching the test light, check the condition of the batteries by touching the test leads together. The light should go on. If not, replace the batteries and/or the light bulb and check all electrical connections on the tester. The test light unit must be operating correctly.*

2. Connect one lead of the test light to a good ground, such as one of the cooling fins on the cylinder, and connect the other lead to the contact breaker point terminal. The test light should be on. If a commercial tester is used, follow the manufacturer's instructions.

3. Rotate the crankshaft with the bolt on the alterator rotor *counterclockwise* until the "F" mark on the alterator rotor aligns with the fixed pointer (**Figure 79**). At this exact moment the contact breaker points should just begin to open. If they open at this moment, the test light will dim indicating that the ignition timing is correct. If the timing is incorrect, proceed to Step 4.

4. To adjust the timing, loosen the contact breaker point base plate attachment screws (A, **Figure 76**). Insert a screwdriver into the pry point (B, **Figure 76**) on the outer perimeter of the base plate and slightly move the base plate assembly until the breaker points just begin to open. The light will dim when the points open; tighten the screws securely. Make sure the base plate assembly does not move while tightening the screws.

> *NOTE*
> *Rotating the base plate clockwise will **advance** the timing. Rotating the base plate counterclockwise will **retard** the timing.*

5. Repeat Step 3.

6. After the timing is correct, recheck the minimum point gap. Rotate the crankshaft with the bolt on the alternator *counterclockwise* until the point gap is at its maximum. Insert a flat feeler gauge and measure the gap. The gap should be 0.3-0.4 mm (0.012-0.016 in.). If the maximum gap cannot be maintained when the ignition timing is correct, the contact breaker point assembly is worn and must be replaced. Refer to Chapter Seven.

7. Install the ignition cover gasket and cover. Install the timing inspection cover on the left-hand crankcase cover.

8. Install the spark plug and spark plug lead.

Dynamic Timing Adjustment
(All Models)

1. Perform *Gap Adjustment* as described in this chapter.

2. Start the engine and let it reach normal operating temperature. Turn the engine off.

3. Connect a portable tachometer and timing light following the manufacturer's instructions.

4. Restart the engine and let it idle at the following rpm:

    a. ATC70: 1,500 ±100 rpm.

    b. ATC 90 and ATC110: 1,300 ±100 rpm.

5. Adjust the idle speed, if necessary, as described in this chapter.

6. Shine the timing light at the alternator rotor and pull the trigger. The timing is correct if the "F" mark aligns with the fixed index mark. Refer to **Figure 78** or **Figure 79**.

7. If timing is incorrect, stop the engine and continue with this procedure.

8A. On ATC70 models, to adjust the timing, loosen the contact breaker point attachment screw (A, **Figure 75**). Insert a screwdriver into the pry point (B, **Figure 75**) and slightly move the point assembly:

    a. Increasing the point gap will advance timing.

    b. Decreasing the point gap will retard timing.

Tighten the screw securely. Make sure the point assembly does not move while tightening the screw.

8B. On ATC90 and ATC110 models, to adjust the timing, loosen the contact breaker point base plate attachment screws (A, **Figure 76**). Insert a screwdriver into the pry point (B, **Figure 76**) on the outer perimeter of the base plate and slightly move the base plate assembly:

    a. Rotating the base plate clockwise will advance timing.

    b. Rotating the base plate counterclockwise will retard timing.

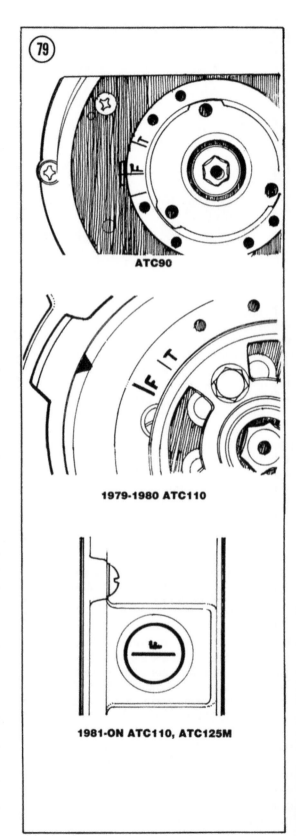

ATC90

1979-1980 ATC110

1981-ON ATC110, ATC125M

80

81

82

Tighten the screws securely. Make sure the base plate assembly does not move while tightening the screws.

9. Repeat Steps 4-6 and readjust if necessary until timing is correct.

10. Disconnect the timing light and portable tachometer.

11. Install all items removed.

SOLID STATE IGNITION
(1981-ON ATC110; ATC125M)

The 1981-on ATC110 and 1984 ATC125M models are equipped with a capacitor discharge ignition (CDI) system. This system uses no breaker points, but timing does have to be checked to make sure that the base plate has not moved. Faulty ignition system components can also affect timing. This system's timing can only be checked dynamically—there is no static method. Dynamic timing requires a stroboscopic timing light as described in Chapter One. If timing cannot be adjusted correctly using this method, either the CDI unit or the alternator may be faulty and must be replaced; refer to Chapter Seven.

Before starting on this procedure, check all electrical connections related to the ignition system. Make sure all connections are tight and free from corrosion and that all ground connections are clean and tight.

1. Place the ATC on level ground and set the parking brake.

2. Start the engine and let it reach normal operating temperature. Turn the engine off.

3. Remove the timing mark hole cap (A, **Figure 80**).

4. Connect a portable tachometer and timing light following the manufacturer's instructions.

5. Restart the engine and let it idle at 1,500 ±100 rpm. Adjust the idle speed if necessary as described in this chapter.

6. Shine the timing light at the timing window and pull the trigger (**Figure 81**). The timing is correct if the "F" mark aligns with the fixed index mark (**Figure 79**).

7. If timing is incorrect, perform the following:

    a. Remove the screws securing the ignition cover (B, **Figure 80**) and remove the cover.

    b. Loosen the base plate screws (A, **Figure 82**) and rotate the base plate in either direction. Tighten the screws.

    c. Restart the engine and recheck the timing.

    d. Repeat this step until the timing marks align.

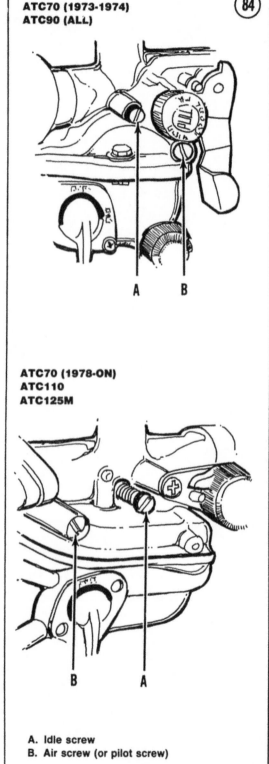

ATC70 (1973-1974)
ATC90 (ALL)

A   B

ATC70 (1978-ON)
ATC110
ATC125M

B   A

A. Idle screw
B. Air screw (or pilot screw)

NOTE
*If correct timing cannot be achieved,
inspect and test all ignition components
as described in Chapter Seven.*

8. After timing is correct, check the air gap
between the rotor and the pulse generator with a
non-magnetic flat feeler gauge (**Figure 83**). The
correct air gap is 0.3-0.4 mm (0.001-0.002 in.). If
the air gap is incorrect, adjust as follows:

  a. Loosen the pulse generator mounting screws
    (B, **Figure 82**).

  b. Move the pulse generator assembly until the
    air gap is correct.

  c. Tighten the screws securely.

  d. Repeat Step 6 (and Step 7 if necessary) to
    make sure the timing is still correct. Readjust
    if necessary.

9. Shut off the engine and disconnect the timing
light and the portable tachometer.

10. Install the timing mark hole cap.

CARBURETOR

Idle Mixture Adjustment

The idle mixture (pilot screw) is preset at the
factory and *is not to be reset*. Do not adjust the
pilot screw unless the carburetor has been
overhauled. If so, refer to *Pilot Screw Adjustment*
in Chapter Six.

Idle Speed Adjustment

Before making this adjustment, the air cleaner
must be clean and the engine must have adequate
compression; see *Compression Test* in this chapter.
Otherwise, this procedure cannot be done properly.

1. Place the ATC on level ground and set the parking brake or block the wheels so the vehicle will not roll in either direction.
2. Connect a portable tachometer following the manufacturer's instructions.
3. Start the engine and let it reach normal operating temperature.
4. Set the idle speed by turning the idle speed stop screw (A, **Figure 84**). For correct idle speed refer to **Table 5**.
5. Open and close the throttle a couple of times; check for variation in idle speed. Readjust if necessary.

> *WARNING*
> *With the engine idling, move the handlebar from side to side. If idle speed increases during this movement, the throttle cable needs adjusting or may be incorrectly routed through the frame. Correct this problem immediately. Do not ride the ATC in this unsafe condition.*

6. Turn the engine off and disconnect the portable tachometer.

STORAGE

Several months of inactivity can cause serious problems and a general deterioration of the ATC's condition. This is especially true in areas of weather extremes. During the winter months it is advisable to specially prepare the ATC for lay-up.

Selecting a Storage Area

Most owners store their vehicles in their home garages. If you do not have a home garage, facilities suitable for long-term storage are readily available for rent or lease in most areas. In selecting a building, consider the following points.
1. The storage area must be dry, free from dampness and excessive humidity. Heating is not necessary, but the building should be well-insulated to minimize extreme temperature variations.
2. Buildings with large window areas should be avoided or such windows should be masked if direct sunlight can fall on the ATC. This is also a good security measure.
3. Buildings in industrial areas, where factories are liable to emit corrosive fumes, are not desirable nor are facilities near bodies of salt water.
4. The area should be selected to minimize the possibility of loss from fire, theft or vandalism. The area should be fully insured, perhaps with a package covering fire, theft, vandalism, weather and liability. The advice of your insurance agent

should be sought in these matters. The building should be fireproof and items such as the security of doors and windows, alarm facility and proximity of police should be considered.

Preparing ATC for Storage

Careful preparation will minimize deterioration and make it easier to restore the ATC to service later. Use the following procedure.
1. Wash everything completely. Make certain to remove all dirt from all the hard to reach parts like the cooling fins on the head and cylinder. Completely dry all parts of the vehicle to remove all moisture. Wax all painted and polished surfaces, including any chromed areas.
2. Run the engine for about 20-30 minutes to warm up the oil in the engine. Drain the oil, regardless of the time since the last oil change. Fill the engine with the normal quantity and type of oil.
3. Drain all gasoline from the fuel tank, the interconnecting hose and the carburetor. Leave the fuel shutoff valve in the RES position. As an alternative, a fuel preservative may be added to the fuel. This preservative is available from many motorcycle shops and marine equipment suppliers.
4. Lubricate the drive chain and control cables; refer to specific procedures in this chapter.
5. Remove the spark plug and pour about one teaspoon of SAE 10W-30 motor oil into the cylinder. Turn the engine over a few revolutions by hand to distribute the oil and then install the spark plug.
6. On models so equipped, remove the battery from the frame. If there is evidence of acid spillage in the battery box, neutralize it with a baking soda solution, wash clean and repaint the damaged area. Store the battery in a warm area and recharge it every 2 weeks.
7. One additional safeguard for winter or prolonged storage is the Engine Protection Dispenser that screws into the spark plug hole. It dispenses a vapor into the cylinder, crankcase, carburetor and muffler which works against rust and acid damage. It is rated to be good for up to 2 years and is available from the Brookstone Company, 127 Voss Farm Road, Peterborough, NH 03458. The catalog number is P-3304.
8. Tape or tie a plastic bag over the end of the muffler to prevent the entry of moisture.
9. Check the tire pressure, inflate to the correct pressure and move the ATC to the storage area. Place it securely on a wood blocks with all 3 wheels off the ground.

10. Cover the ATC with a tarp, blanket or heavy plastic drop cloth. Place this cover mainly as a dust cover—do not wrap it tightly especially if it is plastic, as it may trap moisture. Leave room for air to circulate around the vehicle.

Inspection During Storage

Try to inspect the ATC weekly while in storage. Any deterioration should be corrected as soon as possible. For example, if corrosion of bright metal parts is observed, cover them with a light coat of grease or silicone spray after a thorough polishing.

Turn the engine over a couple of times—don't start it; use the recoil starter with the ignition switch in the OFF position.

Restoring the ATC to Service

An ATC that has been properly prepared and stored in a suitable area requires only light maintenance to restore it to service. It is advisable, however, to perform a tune-up.

1. Before removing the ATC from the storage area, reinflate the tires to the correct pressures. Air loss during storage may have nearly flattened the tires and moving the ATC can cause damage to tires and rims.

> *WARNING*
> *During the next step, place a metal container under the carburetor to catch all fuel or it will create a real fire danger if allowed to drain onto the ATC and the floor. Dispose of the fuel properly.*

2. When the ATC is brought to the work area, drain the fuel tank if fuel preservative was used. Turn the fuel shutoff valve to the OFF position and refill the fuel tank with fresh gasoline.

3. Turn the fuel shutoff valve to the RES position and check for leaks in the fuel system.

> *WARNING*
> *For the next step, place a metal container under the drain outlet on the float bowl to catch the expelled fuel—this presents a real fire danger if allowed to drain on the floor. Dispose of fuel properly.*

4. Open the drain screw and allow several cups of fuel to pass through the fuel system. Turn the fuel shutoff valve to the OFF position and close the drain screw.

5. Remove the spark plug and squirt a small amount of fuel into the cylinder to help remove the oil coating.

6. Remove the engine protection dispenser (if installed) and install a fresh spark plug. Start up the engine.

7. Perform the standard tune-up as described in this chapter.

8. Check the operation of the ignition switch and (on models so equipped) the head and taillight switch. Oxidation of the switch contacts during storage may make them inoperative.

9. On models so equipped, fully charge the battery and install it.

10. Clean and test ride the ATC.

Table 1 MAINTENANCE SCHEDULE*

Every 30 days of operation

- Change engine oil
- Clean oil filter screen and filter rotor
- Clean and oil air filter element
  (perform sooner if used in wet or dusty terrain)
- Inspect spark plug, regap if necessary
- Inspect valve clearance, adjust if necessary
- Adjust cam chain tensioner
- Check and adjust the carburetor
- Check and adjust ignition timing
- Inspect fuel lines for chafed, cracked
  or swollen ends, replace if necessary
- Clean fuel strainer, replace if necessary
- Check throttle operation, adjust if necessary
- Clean spark arrester
- Lubricate drive chain
- Adjust drive chain tension
- Check and adjust clutch free play
- Check and adjust brake(s)
- Check brake lining wear indicator(s)
- Check and adjust rear brake pedal height and free play
- Lubricate rear brake pedal and shift lever
- Check tire and wheel condition
- Inspect front steering for looseness
- Check wheel bearings for smooth operation
- Check engine mounting bolts for tightness

* This Honda Factory maintenance schedule should be considered as a guide to general maintenance and lubrication intervals. Harder than normal use (racing) and exposure to mud, water, sand, high humidity, etc. will naturally dictate more frequent attention to most maintenance items.

Table 2 TIRE INFLATION PRESSURE AND CIRCUMFERENCE MEASUREMENTS

Model	Tire size (Front and rear)	Tire pressure kg/cm²	psi	Circumference mm	in.
ATC70	16×8-7	0.2	2.8	1,520	60
ATC90					
1970-1974	NA	NA	NA	NA	NA
1975-1978	22×11-8 ATV	0.15	2.2	1,742	68.6
ATC110	22×11-8 ATV	0.15	2.2	1,742	68.6
ATC125	22×11-8 ATV	0.15	2.2	1,742	68.6

NA—Honda does not provide service information for all models.

Table 3 BATTERY STATE OF CHARGE

Specific Gravity	State of Charge
1.110-1.130	Discharged
1.140-1.160	Almost discharged
1.170-1.190	One-quarter charged
1.200-1.220	One-half charged
1.230-1.250	Three-quarters charged
1.260-1.280	Fully charged

Table 4 ENGINE OIL CAPACITY

Model	Liters	U.S. qt.	Imp. qt.
ATC70	0.8	0.9	0.65
ATC90; 1979-1980 ATC110	0.9	1.0	0.79
1981-on ATC110	1.1	1.12	0.9
ATC125M	1.0	1.06	0.88

Table 5 TUNE-UP SPECIFICATIONS

Valve clearance	
Intake and exhaust	
ATC70, ATC90	0.05 mm (0.002 in.)
ATC110, ATC125M	0.07 mm (0.005 in.)
Compression pressure	
(at sea level)	
ATC70, ATC90	10-12 kg/cm² (142-170 psi)
ATC110, ATC125M	11-14 kg/cm² (156-198 psi)
Spark plug type	
ATC70	NGK C7HS, ND U22FS
ATC90	NGK D-8HS, ND X24FS
ATC110	
1979-1981	NGK D-8HS
1982-on	NGK DR8HS
ATC125M	NGK DR8ES-L, ND X24ESR-U, Champion RA6YC
Spark plug gap	0.6-0.7 mm (0.024-0.028 in.)
Contact breaker point gap	0.3-0.4 mm (0.012-0.016 in.)
Ignition timing @ idle	Timing mark "F"
Idle speed	
ATC70	1,500 ±100 rpm
ATC90	1,300 ±100 rpm
ATC110, ATC125M	1,700 ±100 rpm

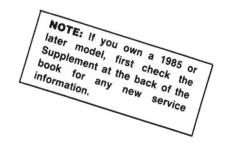

NOTE: If you own a 1985 or later model, first check the Supplement at the back of the book for any new service information.

CHAPTER FOUR

ENGINE

4

All models covered in this book are equipped with an air-cooled, 4-stroke, single cylinder engine with a single overhead camshaft. The crankshaft is supported by 2 main ball bearings. The camshaft is chain-driven from the sprocket on the left-hand side of the crankshaft and operates rocker arms that are individually adjustable.

Engine lubrication is by wet sump with the oil pump located on the right-hand side of the engine next to the clutch. The oil pump delivers oil under pressure throughout the engine and is driven by the cam chain guide sprocket shaft.

The main difference between the ATC70 engine and the larger displacement ATC90, ATC110 and ATC125M engine is in the upper end (cylinder head, cylinder, cam and cam chain). The lower end (crankshaft assembly and crankcase) are almost identical in all models. To avoid confusion, some procedures are separated according to engine displacement.

This chapter contains information for removal, inspection, service and reassembly of the engine. In order to simplify this material the following components are covered in separate chapters:

a. Alternator and ignition advance mechanism—Chapter Seven.

b. Clutch and transmission—Chapter Five.

Table 1 provides complete specifications for the engine and **Table 2** lists all of the engine torque specifications. **Tables 1-3** are located at the end of this chapter.

Before beginning work, re-read Chapter One of this book. You will do a better job with this information fresh in your mind.

Throughout the text there is frequent mention of the right-hand and left-hand side of the engine. This refers to the engine as it sits in the ATC's frame, not as it sits on your workbench. The right- and left-hand refers to a rider sitting on the seat facing forward.

ENGINE PRINCIPLES

Figure 1 explains how the engine works. This will be helpful when troubleshooting or repairing the engine.

ENGINE COOLING

Cooling is provided by air passing over the cooling fins on the engine cylinder head and cylinder. It is very important to keep these fins free from buildup of dirt, oil, grease and other foreign matter. Brush out the fins with a whisk broom or small stiff paint brush.

CAUTION
Remember, these fins are thin in order to dissipate heat and may be damaged if struck too hard.

ENGINE LUBRICATION

The oil flow path through a typical engine is shown in **Figure 2**. The oil pressure is supplied by the oil pump that is driven by the cam chain guide sprocket shaft.

SERVICING ENGINE IN FRAME

The following components can be serviced while the engine is mounted in the frame (the ATC's frame is a great holding fixture for breaking loose stubborn bolts and nuts):

a. Camshaft.

b. Cylinder head.

c. Cylinder.

d. Carburetor.

e. Recoil starter.

f. Alternator.

g. Clutch assembly.

h. External shift mechanism.

i. Starter (ATC125M).

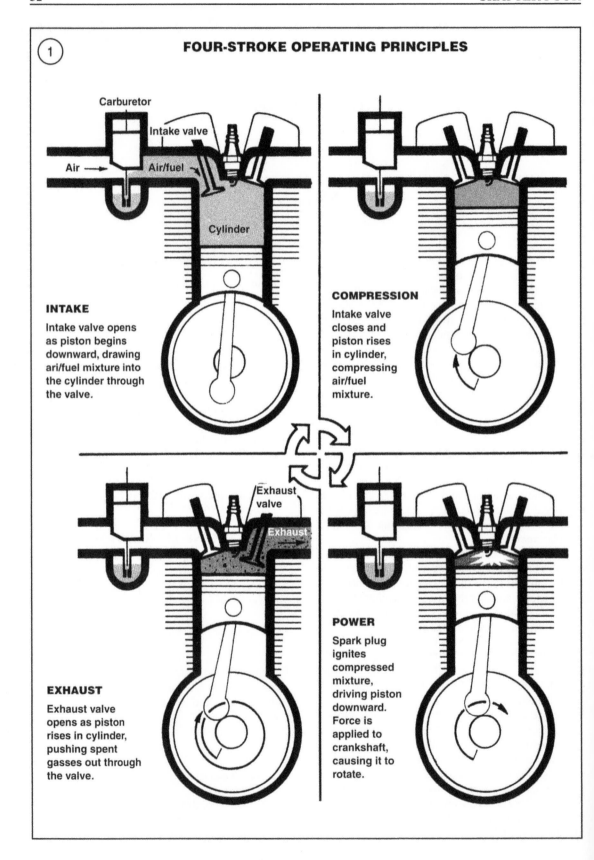

① FOUR-STROKE OPERATING PRINCIPLES

INTAKE
Intake valve opens as piston begins downward, drawing ari/fuel mixture into the cylinder through the valve.

COMPRESSION
Intake valve closes and piston rises in cylinder, compressing air/fuel mixture.

EXHAUST
Exhaust valve opens as piston rises in cylinder, pushing spent gasses out through the valve.

POWER
Spark plug ignites compressed mixture, driving piston downward. Force is applied to crankshaft, causing it to rotate.

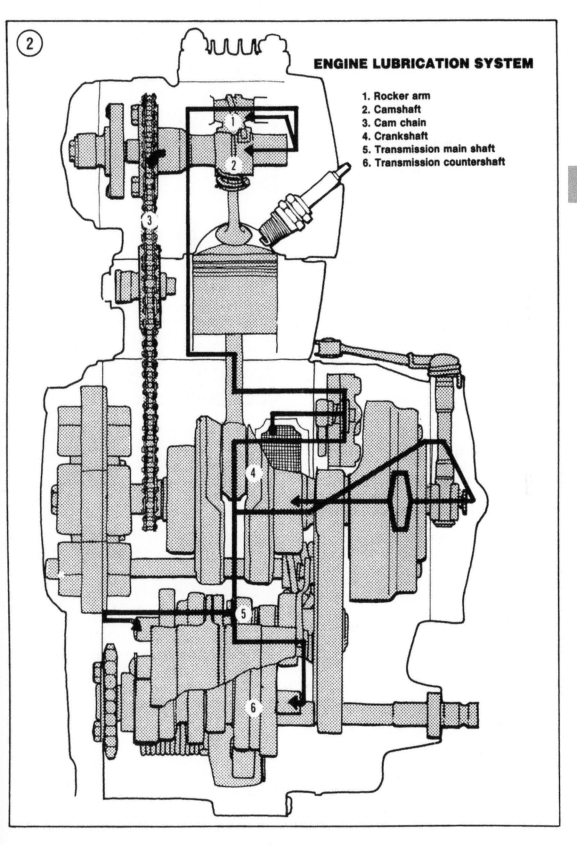

ENGINE LUBRICATION SYSTEM

1. Rocker arm
2. Camshaft
3. Cam chain
4. Crankshaft
5. Transmission main shaft
6. Transmission countershaft

ENGINE

Removal/Installation

1. Drain the engine oil as described under *Engine Oil Change* in Chapter Three.
2. Remove the seat/rear fender assembly.
3. Remove the fuel tank as described in Chapter Six.
4. Remove the exhaust system as described in Chapter Six.
5. Remove the carburetor as described in Chapter Six.
6. Disconnect the spark plug lead and tie it up out of the way.
7. On ATC70 models, remove the bolts securing the under plate and chain cover (**Figure 3**) and remove the assembly.
8. Remove the bolts (**Figure 4**) securing the footpeg assembly and remove the assembly.

> *NOTE*
> *If you are just removing the engine and are not planning to disassemble it, do not perform Step 8. The engine is small enough so that external components can be left on during removal.*

9. If the engine is going to be disassembled, remove the following parts:
   a. On 1981-on ATC70 models, shift the transmission into NEUTRAL and remove the E-clip on the neutral indicator (A, **Figure 5**).
   b. On 1981-on ATC70 models, remove the recoil starter and left-hand crankcase cover as an assembly (B, **Figure 5**).
   c. On all other models, remove the recoil starter assembly as described in Chapter Seven.
   d. Remove the alternator as described in Chapter Seven.
   e. Remove the clutch assembly as described in Chapter Five.
   f. Remove the external shift mechanism as described in Chapter Five.
   g. Remove the camshaft, cylinder head, cylinder, piston and oil pump assembly as described in this chapter.
10. On 90-125 cc models, remove the bolts securing the skid plate and remove the skid plate.
11. Remove the brake pedal assembly as described in Chapter Nine.
12. On models so equipped, remove the screws (**Figure 6**) securing the chain guide and remove the guide.

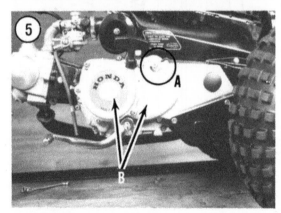

13A. On 1981-on ATC70 models, loosen the bolts (**Figure 7**) on the drive chain tensioner and move the tensioner so there is little tension on the drive chain.

13B. On all other models, loosen the drive chain tensioner bolt or nut (**Figure 8**) and move the tensioner plate so there is little tension on the drive chain.

14. On 90-125 cc models, remove the subtransmission as described in Chapter Five.

15A. On all models except 1981-on ATC110, perform the following:
  a. Remove the left-hand crankcase cover.
  b. Remove the bolts securing the chain case and slide it along the rear axle toward the left-hand wheel.
  c. Remove the drive chain master link and remove the drive chain from both sprockets.

15B. On 1981-1983 ATC110 models, remove the rear axle assembly as described in Chapter Eight. These models are equipped with a drive chain without a master link.

16. Disconnect the electrical connector from the alternator to the wiring harness (**Figure 9**).

17. Take a final look all over the engine to make sure everything has been disconnected.

18. Place a suitable size jack, with a piece of wood to protect the crankcase, under the engine. Apply a *small amount* of jack pressure up on the engine.

CAUTION
The following steps require the aid of a helper to safely remove the engine assembly from the frame.

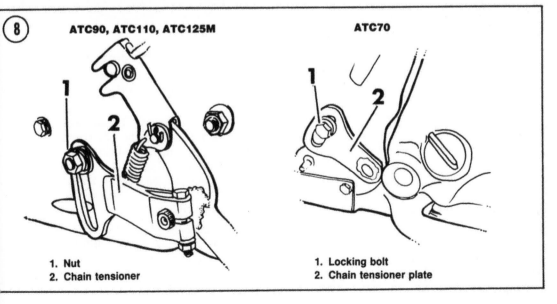

ATC90, ATC110, ATC125M

ATC70

1. Nut
2. Chain tensioner

1. Locking bolt
2. Chain tensioner plate

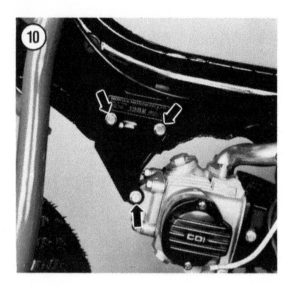

19. On all models except ATC70, remove the bolts (**Figure 10**) securing the engine hanger and remove the engine hanger.

20. Remove the nuts and washers from the upper and lower engine mounting through bolts (**Figure 11**). Withdraw the bolts from the left-hand side.

21. Pull the engine slightly forward and lower the engine from the frame. Take it to a workbench for further disassembly.

22. Install by reversing these removal steps, noting the following.

23. Tighten the mounting bolts to the torque specifications in **Table 2**.

24. Fill the engine with the recommended type and quantity of oil; refer to Chapter Three.

25. Adjust the clutch, drive chain and rear brake pedal as described in Chapter Three.

26. Start the engine and check for leaks.

CYLINDER HEAD AND CAMSHAFT

Removal (70 cc)

This procedure is shown with the engine removed from the frame. It is not necessary to remove the engine to perform this procedure. Refer to **Figure 12** for this procedure.

CAUTION
To prevent any warpage and damage, remove the cylinder head and cam only when the engine is at room temperature.

1. Place the ATC on level ground and set the parking brake or block the wheels so the vehicle will not roll in either direction.

2. Remove the seat/rear fender assembly.

3. Shift the transmission into NEUTRAL.

4. Remove the fuel tank as described in Chapter Six.

5. On the right-hand side of the engine, loosen the bolt (**Figure 13**) securing the side cover. Tap the bolt with a plastic mallet to help break loose the left-hand side cover. Remove the bolt and remove both side covers and the gasket (**Figure 14**).

6. Remove the screw (**Figure 15**) securing the cylinder head to the cylinder.

7. Remove the bolts (**Figure 16**) securing the cam sprocket. Insert a screwdriver or drift into the hole in the cam and cam sprocket to keep the sprocket and chain from sliding into the cam chain cavity on the side of the cylinder.

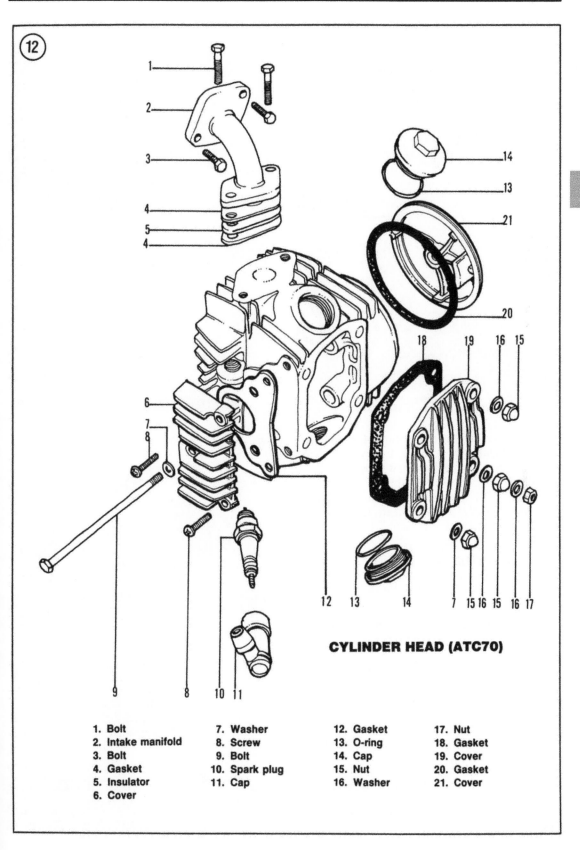

CYLINDER HEAD (ATC70)

1. Bolt	7. Washer	12. Gasket	17. Nut
2. Intake manifold	8. Screw	13. O-ring	18. Gasket
3. Bolt	9. Bolt	14. Cap	19. Cover
4. Gasket	10. Spark plug	15. Nut	20. Gasket
5. Insulator	11. Cap	16. Washer	21. Cover
6. Cover			

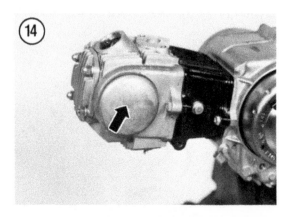

8. In a crisscross pattern, remove the nuts and washers (**Figure 17**) securing the cylinder head cover and remove the cover and the gasket.

9. Loosen the head by tapping around the perimeter with a rubber or plastic mallet. If necessary, *gently* pry the head loose with a broad-tipped screwdriver.

> *CAUTION*
> *Remember, the cooling fins are fragile and may be damaged if tapped or pried on too hard. Never use a metal hammer.*

10. Remove the screwdriver (A, **Figure 18**) or drift from the cam sprocket and remove the cam sprocket.

11. Pull the cylinder head and gasket (B, **Figure 18**) straight off the crankcase studs.

12. After the cylinder head is removed, reinstall the cam sprocket onto the cam chain to hold the chain in position (**Figure 19**).

13. Remove the cylinder head gasket and discard it. Don't lose any locating dowels.

14. Place a clean shop cloth into the cam chain opening in the cylinder to prevent the entry of foreign matter.

15. Remove the cam from the cylinder head (**Figure 20**).

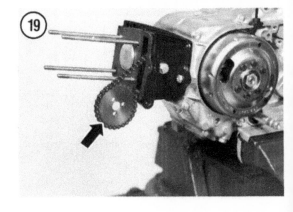

Removal (90-125 cc)

Refer to **Figure 21** (ATC90 and 1979-1980 ATC110) or **Figure 22** (1981-on ATC110 and all ATC125M) for this procedure.

Damage to the valves and cylinder head can be caused by over-revving the engine on 1981-1984 ATC110 and 1984 ATC125M models. To eliminate this problem, Honda has developed a new CDI unit with a built-in rpm limiter. Some early ATC110 models that have experienced this problem will also benefit from the installation of a new valve set that consists of new valves, valve keepers and valve spring collars.

If your ATC is still covered by the factory warranty, take it to a Honda dealer and have this engine modification performed under the conditions of your warranty. If your ATC is out of the warranty period, this modification should still be performed to eliminate the possibility of engine damage.

All ATCs that have the new parts installed are identified by an "X" mark stamped directly under the engine serial number on the crankcase.

The models that are affected by this problem are as follows:

  a. 1981-1983 ATC110: All models (CDI unit and valve set).

  b. 1984 ATC110: Engine serial No. 2600001-2607160 inclusive (CDI unit and valve set).

  c. 1984 ATC110: Engine serial No. 2607161-on (CDI unit only).

  d. 1984 ATC125M: All models (CDI unit only).

CAUTION
To prevent any warpage and damage, remove the cylinder head and cam only when the engine is at room temperature.

1. Place the ATC on level ground and set the parking brake.
2. Remove the seat/rear fender assembly.
3. Remove the fuel tank as described in Chapter Six.

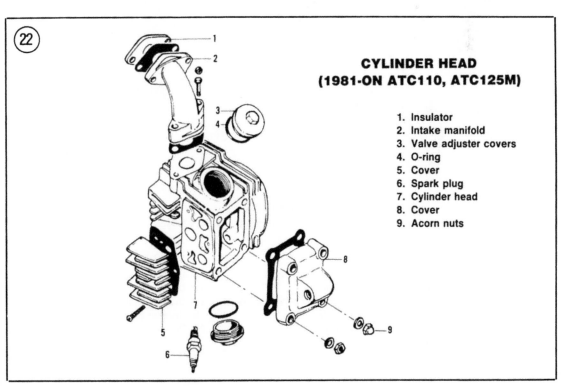

CYLINDER HEAD (1981-ON ATC110, ATC125M)

1. Insulator
2. Intake manifold
3. Valve adjuster covers
4. O-ring
5. Cover
6. Spark plug
7. Cylinder head
8. Cover
9. Acorn nuts

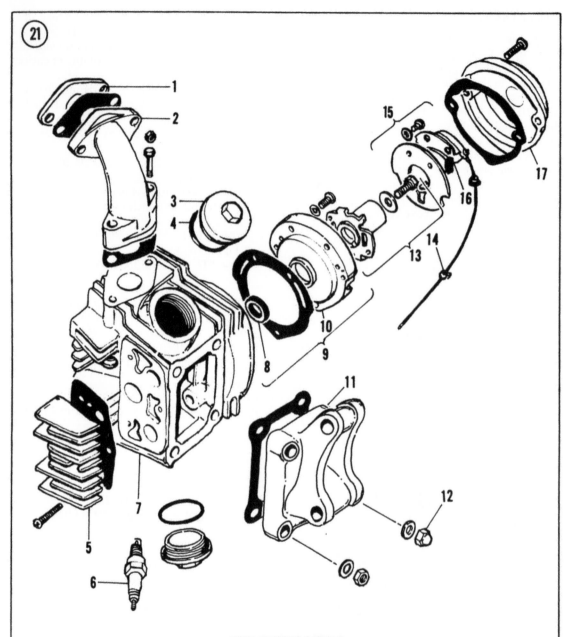

**CYLINDER HEAD
(ALL ATC90, 1979-1980 ATC110)**

1. Insulator
2. Intake manifold
3. Tappet cover
4. O-ring
5. Cover
6. Spark plug
7. Cylinder head
8. Spacer
9. Point base assembly
10. Point base
11. Cover
12. Acorn nut
13. Ignition advance assembly
14. Clip
15. Breaker point assembly
16. Breaker points
17. Breaker point assembly cover

4

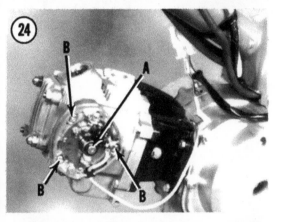

4. Remove the carburetor and intake tube as described in Chapter Six.

5. Remove the screws (**Figure 23**) securing the ignition cover and remove the cover and the gasket.

6. Disconnect the electrical connector to the contact breaker point assembly (A, **Figure 24**) or CDI pulse generator assembly.

7A. On breaker point ignition models, remove the screws securing the contact breaker point assembly and base plate (B, **Figure 24**). Remove the assembly.

7B. On CDI ignition models, remove the screws (A, **Figure 25**) securing the CDI pulse generator assembly. Remove the screw and clamp (B, **Figure 25**) securing the electrical wires to the cylinder head and remove the assembly.

8A. On breaker point ignition models, remove the bolt (A, **Figure 26**) securing the ignition advance mechanism and remove the mechanism.

8B. On CDI ignition models, remove the bolt (**Figure 27**) securing the pulse rotor and ignition advance mechanism and remove the mechanism.

9. Remove the dowel pin on the camshaft (A, **Figure 28**).

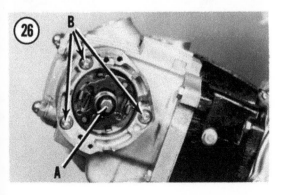

10A. On breaker point ignition models, remove the bolts (B, **Figure 26**) securing the contact breaker point base and remove the base.

10B. On models with a CDI ignition, remove the screws (B, **Figure 28**) securing the pulse generator base and remove the base.

11. Rotate the crankshaft with the recoil starter until the camshaft sprocket "O" timing mark aligns with the index mark on the cylinder head (A, **Figure 29**).

12. Loosen the cam chain tensioner locknut and adjust bolt.

13. Remove both cam sprocket bolts (B, **Figure 29**). Hold the cam chain sprocket with one finger and withdraw the camshaft (**Figure 30**).

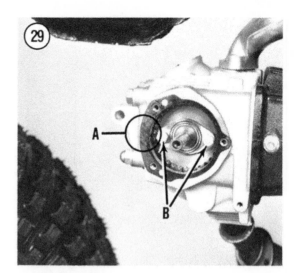

NOTE
Prior to removing the nuts and washers, note the location of the copper washer(s) and cap nut(s). The location varies with different models and years. They must be installed on the same crankcase stud from which they were removed. If installed incorrectly, an oil leak will result.

14. Using a crisscross pattern, remove the nuts and washers (**Figure 31**) securing the cylinder head cover.

15. Remove the cylinder head cover and gasket.

16. On ATC125M models, remove the screws (C, **Figure 25**) securing the cylinder head to the cylinder.

17. Loosen the head by tapping around the perimeter with a rubber or plastic mallet. If necessary, *gently* pry the head loose with a broad-tipped screwdriver.

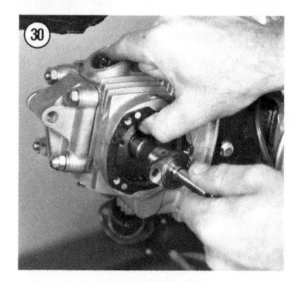

CAUTION
Remember the cooling fins are fragile and may be damaged if tapped or pried on too hard. Never use a metal hammer.

18. Remove the cam sprocket and pull the cylinder head and gasket straight off the crankcase studs.

19. After the cylinder head is removed, reinstall the cam sprocket onto the cam chain to hold the chain in position.

20. Remove the cylinder head gasket and discard it. Don't lose any locating dowels.

21. Place a clean shop cloth into the cam chain opening in the cylinder to prevent the entry of foreign matter.

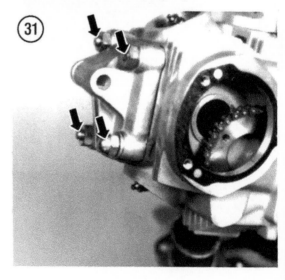

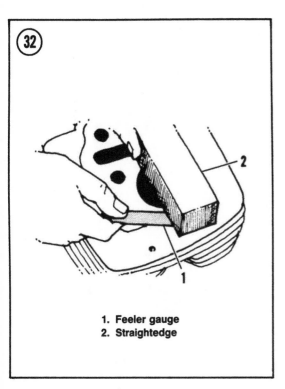

1. Feeler gauge
2. Straightedge

Disassembly/Inspection/Assembly (All Models)

It is recommended that one rocker arm assembly be disassembled, inspected and then assembled to avoid the interchanging of parts. This is especially true on a well run-in (high mileage) engine as the parts have developed wear patterns.

The cylinder head shown in this procedure is from an ATC70. There are slight differences

between this cylinder head and the type used on 90-125 cc engines. Where differences occur they are identified.

Because the cylinder head and cover are machined as a set during manufacture, they must be replaced as a set if either is damaged or defective.

NOTE
Honda does not provide service limit specifications for all components on all models. The specifications given in **Table 1** *are the only ones given by the manufacturer.*

1. Remove all traces of gasket material from the cylinder head mating surfaces.
2. *Without removing the valves,* remove all carbon deposits from the combustion chamber and valve ports with a wire brush. A blunt screwdriver or chisel may be used if care is taken not to damage the head, valves and spark plug threads.
3. After the carbon is removed from the combustion chamber and the valve intake and exhaust ports, clean the entire head in cleaning solvent. Blow dry with compressed air.
4. Clean away all carbon from the piston crown. Do not remove the carbon ridge at the top of the cylinder bore.
5. Check for cracks in the combustion chamber and exhaust ports. A cracked head must be replaced.
6. After the head has been thoroughly cleaned, place a straightedge across the cylinder head/cylinder gasket surface (**Figure 32**) at several points. Measure the warp by inserting a flat feeler gauge between the straightedge and the cylinder head at each location. There should be no warpage; if a small amount is present, the head can be resurfaced by a dealer or qualified machine shop.
7. Inspect the valves, valve springs and valve guides as described in this chapter.

NOTE
Both intake and exhaust rocker arms and rocker arm shafts are identical (same Honda part numbers) when new but after prolonged mileage do wear differently. If you remove both rocker arm assemblies at the same time, mark them in sets with "I" (intake—top) or "E" (exhaust—bottom) so they will be reinstalled in the correct location in the cylinder head.

8. Remove the screws securing the rocker arm shaft set plate (**Figure 33**) and remove the set plate and gasket.

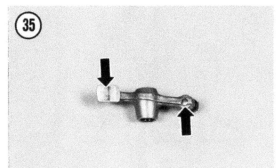

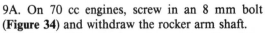

NOTE
One of the engine mounting bolts can
be used for the next step.

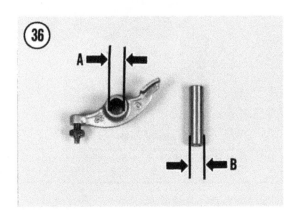

9A. On 70 cc engines, screw in an 8 mm bolt
(**Figure 34**) and withdraw the rocker arm shaft.

9B. On 90-125 cc engines, tap on the side of the
cylinder head next to the rocker arm shafts with a
plastic mallet and the rocker arm shafts will work
their way out of the cylinder head. Remove the
rocker arm shaft.

10. Remove the rocker arm.

11. Wash all parts in cleaning solvent and
thoroughly dry.

12. Inspect the rocker arm pad (**Figure 35**) where it
rides on the cam lobe and where the adjuster rides
on the valve stem. If the pad is scratched or
unevenly worn, inspect the cam lobe for scoring,
chipping or flat spots. Replace the rocker arm if
defective.

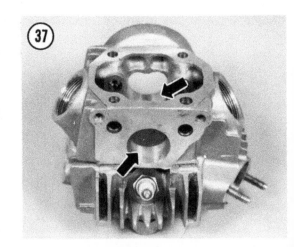

13. Measure the inside diameter of the rocker arm
bore (A, **Figure 36**) with an inside micrometer and
check against the dimensions in **Table 1**. Replace if
worn to the service limit or greater.

14. Inspect the rocker arm shaft for signs of wear
or scoring. Measure the outside diameter (B,
Figure 36) with a micrometer and check against the
dimensions in **Table 1**. Replace if worn to the
service limit or less.

15. Inspect the cam bearing surfaces (**Figure 37**)
for excessive wear. If worn excessively, the cylinder
head must be replaced.

16. Coat the rocker arm shaft and rocker arm bore
with assembly oil.

17A. On 70 cc engines, install the rocker arm shaft
with the threaded hole facing out. Partially insert
the rocker arm shaft into the cylinder head and
position the rocker arm into the cylinder head
(**Figure 38**).

17B. On 90-125 cc engines, the rocker arm shaft
can be inserted in either direction. Partially insert
the rocker arm shaft into the cylinder head and
position the rocker arm into the cylinder head.

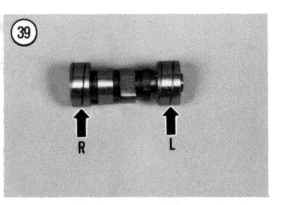

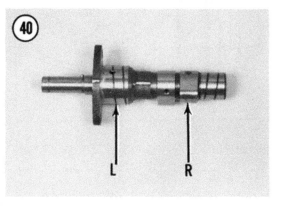

18. Repeat Steps 8-17 for the other rocker arm assembly.

19. Install the rocker arm shaft set plate and tighten the screws securely.

20. Check the cam bearing journals for wear and scoring. Measure both the left-hand (L) and right-hand (R) bearing journals with a micrometer. Refer to **Figure 39** for 70 cc engines or **Figure 40** for 90-125 cc engines. Compare to the dimensions given in **Table 1**. If worn to the service limit or greater, the cam must be replaced.

21. Check the cam lobes for wear. The lobes should show no signs of scoring and the edges should be square. Slight damage may be removed with a silicone carbide oilstone. Use No. 100-120 grit stone initially, then polish with a No. 280-320 grit stone.

22. Even though the cam lobe surface appears to be satisfactory with no visible signs of wear, the cam lobes must be measured with a micrometer. Compare to the dimensions given in **Table 1**.

23. Inspect the cam sprocket for wear; replace if necessary.

Installation
(70 cc Engines)

1. Lubricate the cam lobes and the bearing journals with molybdenum disulfide grease. Also coat the cam bearing surfaces in the cylinder head. Install the cam into the cylinder head (**Figure 41**) with the threaded holes for the cam sprocket facing out.

CAUTION
When rotating the crankshaft, keep the cam chain taut and engaged with the timing sprocket on the crankshaft.

2. Remove the recoil starter as described in Chapter Seven.

3. The engine must be at top dead center (TDC) during the following steps for correct valve timing. Hold the cam drive chain taut while rotating the crankshaft to avoid damage to the chain and/or the crankcase.

4. Rotate the crankshaft with the nut on the alternator rotor *counterclockwise* until the "T" timing mark is aligned with the fixed pointer on the crankcase (**Figure 42**).

5. Loosen the cam chain tensioner locknut and loosen the adjusting screw. Remove the cam chain tensioner sealing bolt (**Figure 43**) and loosen the tensioner adjust screw until it is almost unscrewed from the crankcase. This is to gain the maximum amount of cam chain slack.

6. Install a new head gasket and locating dowels.

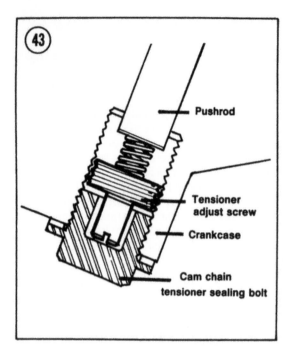

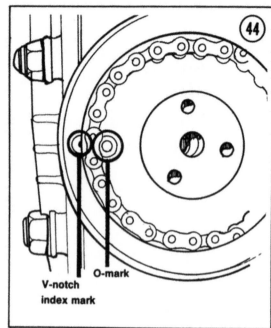

7. If removed, install the cam sprocket (with the "O" mark facing out) onto the cam chain in the following manner. Hold the cam sprocket and cam chain straight out in line with the crankcase studs. Place the sprocket with the alignment mark "O" on the center top end of the cam chain. Let the cam sprocket and cam chain swing down and rest on the cylinder.

8. Install the cylinder head onto the crankcase studs. With your fingers, carefully insert the cam sprocket and cam chain into the cam chain cavity on the side of the cylinder head while pushing the cylinder head down into position.

9. Insert a screwdriver or drift into the hole in the cam sprocket and cam to hold the assembly in place.

10. Check the alignment of the cam sprocket. Make sure that the "O" mark is aligned with the V-notch index mark on the cylinder head (**Figure 44**). If alignment is not correct, reposition the cam chain on the sprocket so alignment is correct.

CAUTION
Very expensive damage could result from improper cam and chain alignment. Recheck your work several times to be sure alignment is correct.

11. When alignment is correct, install the cam sprocket bolts (**Figure 16**) and tighten to the torque specifications listed in **Table 2**.

12. Make one final check to make sure alignment is correct. The "T" timing mark must be aligned

with the stationary pointer (**Figure 42**) and the "O" mark on the sprocket must align with the V-notch in the cylinder head (**Figure 44**).

13. Install the cylinder head cover with the arrow (A, **Figure 17**) facing down toward the exhaust port. Install the copper washer on the lower left-hand crankcase stud (B, **Figure 17**). Install sealing washers on all other crankcase studs.

14. Install the regular nut on the lower left-hand crankcase stud (B, **Figure 17**) and cap nuts on all other crankcase studs.

15. Using a crisscross pattern, tighten the nuts to the torque specifications listed in **Table 2**.

16. Install the screw securing the cylinder head to the cylinder and tighten securely.

17. Align the locating tab on the side cover with the notch in the cylinder head and install the side cover with a new gasket. Install the long bolt from the right-hand side, screw it into the side cover and tighten securely.

18. Install the recoil starter, fuel tank and seat/rear fender assembly.

19. Adjust the valves and the cam chain tension as described in Chapter Three.

Installation
(90-125 cc Engines)

1. Lubricate all cam lobes and bearing journals with molybdenum disulfide grease. Also coat the cam bearing surfaces in the cylinder head.

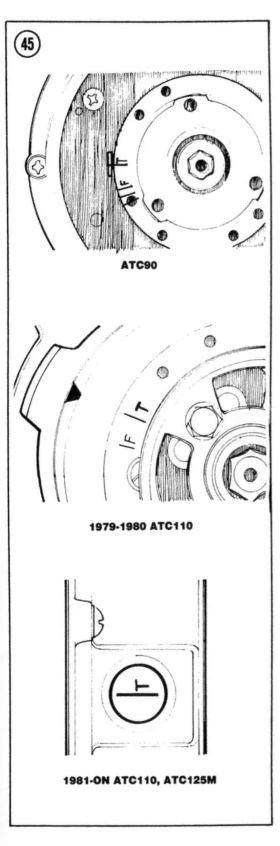

ATC90

1979-1980 ATC110

1981-ON ATC110, ATC125M

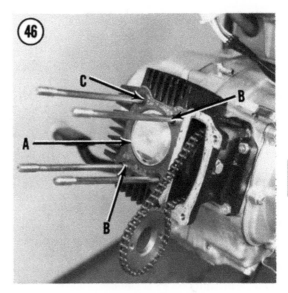

4

CAUTION
When rotating the crankshaft, keep the cam chain taut and engaged with the timing sprocket on the crankshaft.

2. The engine must be at top dead center (TDC) during the following steps for correct valve timing. Hold the cam drive chain out and taut while rotating the crankshaft to avoid damage to the chain and/or the crankcase.

3. Remove the recoil starter as described in Chapter Seven.

4. Rotate the crankshaft with the nut or bolt on the alternator rotor. Turn it *counterclockwise* until the "T" timing mark is aligned with the fixed pointer either on the crankcase or alternator stator assembly (**Figure 45**).

5. Loosen the cam chain tensioner locknut and loosen the adjusting screw. Remove the cam chain tensioner sealing bolt (**Figure 43**) and loosen the tensioner adjust screw until it is almost unscrewed from the crankcase. This is to gain the maximum amount of cam chain slack.

6. Install a new head gasket (A, **Figure 46**), locating dowels (B, **Figure 46**) and O-ring seal (C, **Figure 46**).

7. If removed, install the cam sprocket (with the "O" mark facing out) onto the cam chain in the following manner. Hold the cam chain straight out in line with the crankcase studs. Place the sprocket "O" mark on the center top end of the cam chain. Let the cam sprocket and cam chain swing down and rest on the cylinder.

8. Install the cylinder head onto the crankcase studs. With your fingers, carefully insert the cam

sprocket and cam chain into the cam chain cavity on the side of the cylinder head while pushing the cylinder head down into position.

9. Insert a screwdriver or drift into the hole in the cam sprocket to hold the sprocket in place.

10. Loosen all valve adjusters fully. This is to allow maximum room for the cam during installation.

11. Position the cam with the lobes facing toward the crankcase and the dowel pin hole facing forward toward the top of the cylinder head.

12. Hold onto the cam sprocket, remove the screwdriver and install the cam through the cam sprocket and into position in the cylinder head.

13. Check the alignment of the cam sprocket. Make sure that the "O" mark is aligned with the V-notch index mark on the cylinder head (**Figure 44**). If alignment is not correct, reposition the cam chain on the sprocket so alignment is correct.

> *CAUTION*
> *Very expensive damage could result from improper cam and chain alignment. Recheck your work several times to be sure alignment is correct.*

14. When alignment is correct, install the cam sprocket bolts (B, **Figure 29**) and tighten to the torque specifications listed in **Table 2**.

15. Make one final check to make sure alignment is correct. The "T" timing mark must be aligned with the stationary pointer (**Figure 45**) and the "O" mark on the sprocket must align with the V-notch in the cylinder head (**Figure 44**).

16. Install the cylinder head cover. The cover can be installed in one direction only as the crankcase studs are offset.

> *NOTE*
> *In the next 2 steps, install the copper washer(s) and cap nut(s) in the same location from which they were removed. Refer to Step 14, **Removal**.*

17. Install the copper washer(s) and sealing washers on the crankcase studs in the correct location.

18. Install the cap nuts and regular nuts on the crankcase studs in the correct location.

19. Using a crisscross pattern, tighten the nuts to the torque specification listed in **Table 2**.

20. On ATC125M models, install the screws securing the cylinder head to the cylinder and tighten securely.

> *CAUTION*
> *Be careful when installing the base in the next step. The shoulder on the cam is very sharp and tends to turn the oil*

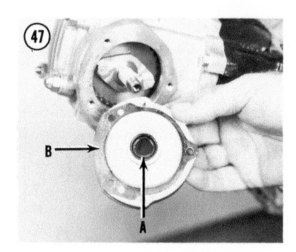

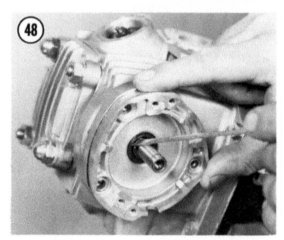

*seal (A, **Figure 47**) inside out. This oil seal has an internal circle spring that may pop out if the oil seal is turned inside out. Be sure to reinstall the spring in the seal if it comes out. As you slowly push the base into place, **carefully** work the seal over the shoulder of the cam with a narrow bladed screwdriver (**Figure 48**).*

21. Make sure the base gasket (B, **Figure 47**) is in place and install the contact breaker point base or CDI pulse generator base. Tighten the screws securely.

22. Install the dowel pin into the camshaft.

23. Install the ignition advance mechanism. Install the bolt and tighten it securely.

24. Connect the electrical connector to the contact breaker point assembly or CDI pulse generator assembly.

25. Install the ignition cover and gasket and tighten the screws securely.

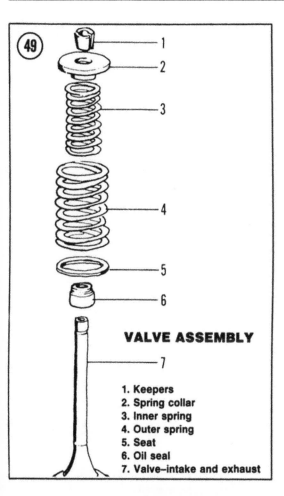

VALVE ASSEMBLY

1. Keepers
2. Spring collar
3. Inner spring
4. Outer spring
5. Seat
6. Oil seal
7. Valve—intake and exhaust

26. Install the recoil starter, fuel tank and seat/rear fender assembly.
27. Adjust the valves and cam chain tension as described in Chapter Three.

VALVES AND VALVE COMPONENTS

Removal

Refer to **Figure 49** for this procedure.

CAUTION
When replacing valve parts on 1981 to mid-year 1984 ATC110 models, refer to **Cylinder Head and Camshaft Removal (90-125 cc)** *regarding a special set of valve components that may have been installed on these models. Do* **not** *mix old valve parts with parts from a new valve kit that may have been installed by a Honda dealer. There are 2 punch marks on the top surface of the valve spring retainers in the* **new** *kit. All ATCs that have the new valve kit are identified by an "X" mark stamped directly under the engine serial number on the crankcase.*

1. Remove the cylinder head as described in this chapter.
2. Compress the valve springs with a valve compressor tool (**Figure 50**). Remove the valve keepers and release the compression. Remove the valve compressor tool.

CAUTION
To avoid loss of spring tension, do not compress the springs any more than necessary to remove the keepers.

3. Remove the valve spring retainer and valve springs (**Figure 51**). Do not intermix the springs as the intake valve springs are different than those on the exhaust valve.

NOTE
The inner and outer valve seats and valve stem seal will stay in the cylinder head. On some models there is only an inner valve seat on the exhaust valve.

4. Prior to removing the valve, remove any burrs from the valve stem (**Figure 52**). Otherwise the valve guide will be damaged.
5. Mark all parts as they are disassembled so that they will be installed in their original location.

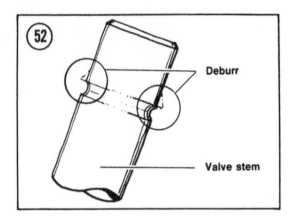

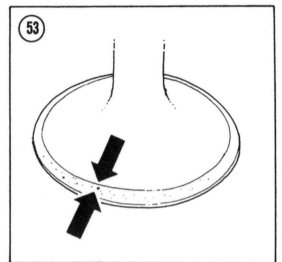

Inspection

1. Clean valves with a wire brush and solvent.
2. Inspect the contact surface of each valve for burning or pitting (**Figure 53**). Unevenness of the contact surface is an indication that the valve is not serviceable. The valve contact surface *cannot be ground*; the valve must be replaced if defective.
3. Measure the valve stem for wear (**Figure 54**). Compare with specifications given in **Table 1**.
4. Remove all carbon and varnish from the valve guide with a stiff spiral wire brush.
5. Insert each valve in its guide. Hold the valve with the head just slightly off the valve seat and rock it sideways. If it rocks more than slightly, the guide is probably worn and should be replaced. As a final check, take the cylinder head to a dealer and have the valve guides measured.
6. Measure each valve spring free length with a vernier caliper (**Figure 55**). All should be within the length specified in **Table 1** with no signs of bends or distortion. Replace defective springs in pairs (inner and outer).
7. Check the valve spring retainer and valve keepers. If they are in good condition they may be reused; replace as necesary.
8. Inspect the valve seats. If worn or burned, they must be reconditioned. This should be performed by a dealer or qualified machine shop.

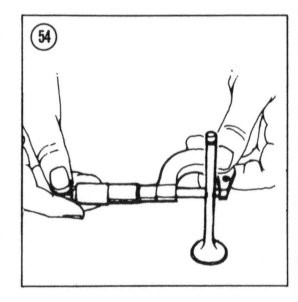

Installation

1. Coat the valve stems with molybdenum disulfide grease. To avoid damage to the valve stem seal, turn the valve slowly while inserting the valve into the cylinder head.
2A. On 1982-on ATC110 and all ATC125M models, install the valve springs with their closer wound coils facing the cylinder head.
2B. On all other models, the valve springs are not progressively wound so they can be installed with either end facing the cylinder head.

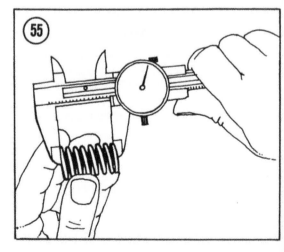

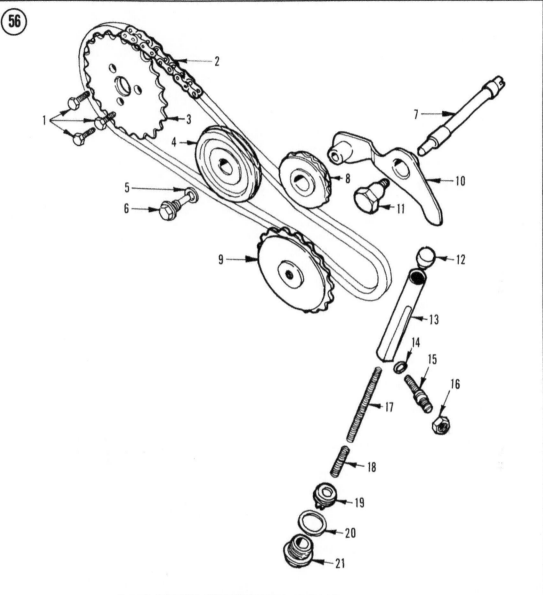

CAM CHAIN TENSIONER (ATC70)

1. Bolt
2. Drive chain
3. Sprocket
4. Roller (cam chain guide)
5. Washer
6. Guide roller pin
7. Spindle
8. Roller (cam chain guide)
9. Sprocket
10. Tensioner arm
11. Pivot
12. Pushrod head
13. Pushrod
14. Washer
15. Tensioner adjuster bolt
16. Locknut
17. Tensioner spring "A"
18. Tensioner spring "B"
19. Tensioner adjuster bolt
20. Sealing washer
21. Sealing bolt

3. Install the valve spring retainer.

4. Compress the valve springs with a compressor tool (**Figure 50**) and install the valve keepers.

> *CAUTION*
> *To avoid loss of spring tension, do not compress the springs any more than necessary to install the keepers.*

5. After all springs have been installed, gently tap the end of the valve stems with a soft aluminum or brass drift and hammer. This will ensure that the keepers are properly seated.

Valve Guide Replacement

When valve guides are worn so that there is excessive stem-to-guide clearance or valve tipping, the guides must be replaced. Replace both, even if only one is worn. This job should ony be done by a dealer as special tools are required. If the valve guides are replaced, replace both valves also.

Valve Seat Reconditioning

This job is best left to a dealer or qualified machine shop. They have special equipment and knowledge for this exacting job. You can still save considerable money by removing the cylinder head and taking the head to the shop for repairs.

Valve Lapping or Grinding

Valve lapping or grinding the valves is not recommended as the valve face may be coated with a special material. Lapping or grinding the valve will remove this surface and will lead to almost instant valve failure. *Do not* lap or grind the valves.

CAMSHAFT CHAIN AND TENSIONER

Removal/Installation
(70 cc Engines)

This procedure is shown with the engine removed from the frame for clarity. All components can be removed with the engine in the frame.

Refer to **Figure 56** for this procedure.

1. Remove the cylinder head and cylinder as described in this chapter.

2. Remove the alternator rotor and stator assembly as described in Chapter Seven.

3. Loosen the cam chain tensioner locknut and unscrew the adjust bolt (**Figure 57**).

4. Unscrew the sealing bolt (**Figure 58**) and, on models so equipped, unscrew the tensioner adjust screw (**Figure 59**).

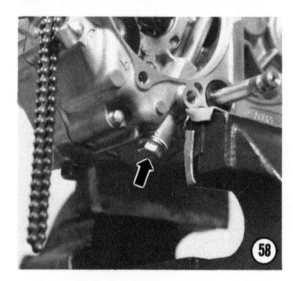

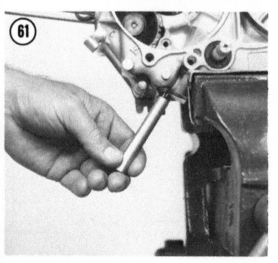

5. Remove the springs (**Figure 60**) and the pushrod (**Figure 61**).

6. Remove the bolt (A, **Figure 62**) securing the tensioner arm and remove the tensioner arm and the roller.

7. Remove the cam chain (B, **Figure 62**).

8. Inspect all components as described in this chapter.

9. Install by reversing these removal steps, noting the following.

10. Apply fresh engine oil to all components prior to installation.

11. Adjust the cam chain tensioner as described in Chapter Three.

Removal/Installation
(90-125 cc Engines)

Refer to **Figure 63** for this procedure.

1. Remove the cylinder head and cylinder as described in this chapter.

2. Remove the alternator rotor and stator assembly as described in Chapter Seven.

3. Loosen the cam chain tensioner locknut and unscrew the adjust bolt (A, **Figure 64**).

4. Unscrew the sealing bolt (B, **Figure 64**) and, on models so equipped, unscrew the tensioner adjust screw (**Figure 65**).

5. Remove the springs (**Figure 66**) and the pushrod (**Figure 67**).

6. Remove the chain guide sprocket (**Figure 68**).

7. Remove the cam chain (A, **Figure 69**).

8. Remove the screw securing the set plates (B, **Figure 69**) and remove the tensioner assembly (C, **Figure 69**).

9. Inspect all components as described in this chapter.

10. Install by reversing these removal steps, noting the following.

11. Apply fresh engine oil to all components prior to installation.

12. Slightly rotate the chain guide sprocket assembly so the notch in the shaft will mesh with the raised tab on the oil pump rotor shaft (located within the crankcase on the opposite side of the engine).

13. Adjust the cam chain tensioner as described in Chapter Three.

Inspection (All Models)

1. Clean all parts in solvent and thoroughly dry with compressed air.

2A. On 70 cc engines, inspect the cam sprocket, chain guide sprocket, roller and cam chain (**Figure 70**).

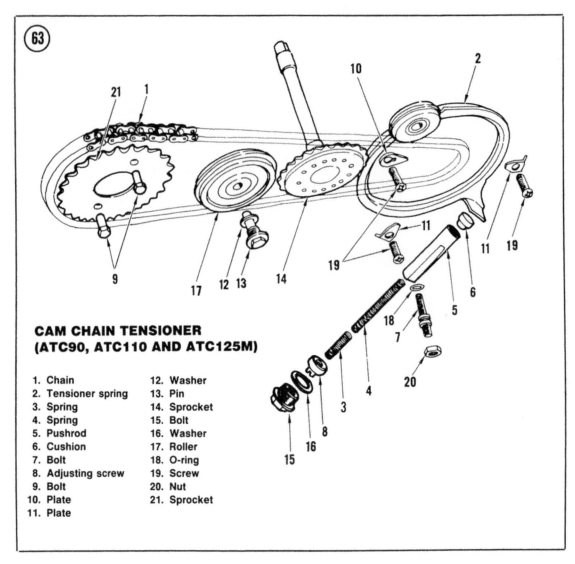

CAM CHAIN TENSIONER
(ATC90, ATC110 AND ATC125M)

1. Chain
2. Tensioner spring
3. Spring
4. Spring
5. Pushrod
6. Cushion
7. Bolt
8. Adjusting screw
9. Bolt
10. Plate
11. Plate
12. Washer
13. Pin
14. Sprocket
15. Bolt
16. Washer
17. Roller
18. O-ring
19. Screw
20. Nut
21. Sprocket

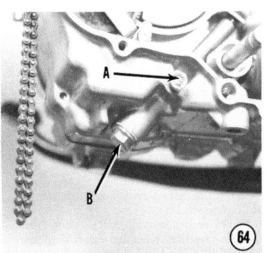

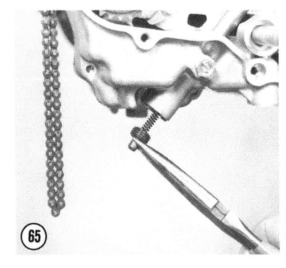

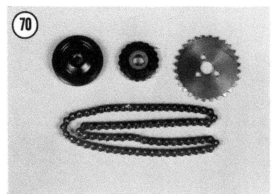

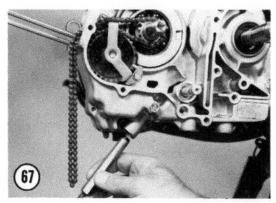

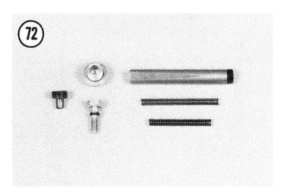

2B. On 90-125 cc engines, inspect the roller, tensioner assembly and the chain guide sprocket (**Figure 71**).

3. If any of the components are worn or any rubber-coated parts are starting to disintegrate, they must be replaced. If the cam chain is replaced it is a good idea to replace the sprocket at the same time and vice versa.

4. Inspect the tensioner pushrod and its related components for wear or damage (**Figure 72**). If the springs appear to be weak or if they are broken, they must be replaced. Replace both springs even if only one needs replacing. Make sure the cushion

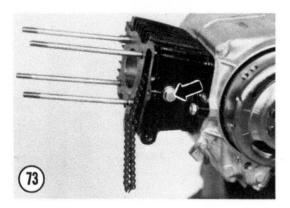

on the end of the pushrod is not worn or cracked; replace if necessary.

CYLINDER

Removal

1. Remove the cylinder head as described in this chapter.
2. Remove the bolt (**Figure 73**) securing the cam chain roller and remove the roller (**Figure 74**).
3A. On ATC70 engines, remove the bolt (**Figure 75**) securing the cylinder to the crankcase.
3B. On ATC125M engines, remove the bolts (**Figure 76**) securing the cylinder to the crankcase.
4. Loosen the cylinder by tapping around the perimeter with a rubber or plastic mallet. If necessary, *gently* pry the cylinder loose with a broad-tipped screwdriver.
5. Pull the cylinder straight out and off of the crankcase studs. Work the cam chain wire through the opening in the cylinder.

> *NOTE*
> *Note the location of the locating dowels and O-ring seals prior to removing them. The location varies with different models and years. They must be installed on the same crankcase stud from which they were removed. If installed incorrectly, an oil leak will result.*

6. Remove the cylinder base gasket and discard it. Remove the dowel pins from the crankcase studs.
7. Install a piston holding fixture under the piston (**Figure 77**) to protect the piston skirt from damage. This fixture may be purchased or may be a homemade unit of wood. See **Figure 78** for dimensions.

Inspection

The following procedure requires the use of highly specialized and expensive measuring

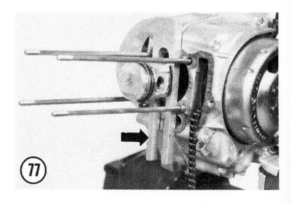

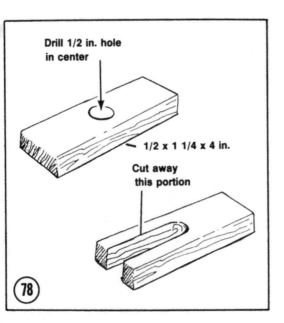

Drill 1/2 in. hole
in center

1/2 x 1 1/4 x 4 in.

Cut away
this portion

(78)

(80)

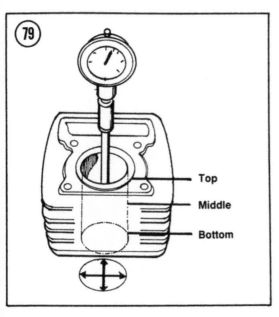

(79)

Top

Middle

Bottom

instruments. If such equipment is not readily available, have the measurements performed by a dealer or qualified machine shop.

1. Soak with solvent any old cylinder head gasket material on the cylinder. Use a broad-tipped *dull* chisel and gently scrape off all gasket residue. Do not gouge the sealing surface as oil and air leaks will result.

2. Measure the cylinder bore with a cylinder gauge or inside micrometer at the points shown in **Figure 79**. Measure in 2 axes—in line with the piston pin and at 90°degrees to the pin. If the taper or

out-of-round is 0.10 mm (0.004 in.) or greater, the cylinder must be rebored to the next oversize and a new piston installed.

NOTE
The new piston should be obtained before the cylinder is rebored so that the piston can be measured; slight manufacturing tolerances must be taken into account to determine the actual size and working clearance.

3. Check the cylinder wall for scratches; if evident, the cylinder should be rebored.

NOTE
*The maximum wear limit on the cylinder is listed in **Table 1**. If the cylinder is worn to this limit, it must be replaced. Never rebore a cylinder if the finished rebore diameter will be this dimension or greater.*

Installation

1. Check that the top surface of the crankcase and the bottom surface of the cylinder are clean prior to installing a new base gasket.
2. Install a new cylinder base gasket.

NOTE
*In the next step, install the dowel pins and O-ring seals in the same location from which they were removed. Refer to Step 6, **Removal**.*

3. Install the dowel pins (A, **Figure 80**) and O-ring seals (B, **Figure 80**) onto the correct crankcase studs.
4. Install a piston holding fixture under the piston (**Figure 77**). This can be a purchased unit or a homemade unit (**Figure 78**).

5. Make sure the end gaps of the piston rings are *not* lined up with each other—they must be staggered. Lightly oil the piston rings and the inside of the cylinder bores with assembly oil.
6. Install the cylinder and slide it down onto the crankcase studs.
8. Carefully feed the cam chain and wire up through the opening in the cylinder and tie it to the engine.
9. Start the cylinder down over the piston (**Figure 81**). Compress each piston ring with your fingers as it enters the cylinder.
10. Slide the cylinder down until it bottoms on the piston holding fixture (**Figure 82**).
11. Remove the piston holding fixture and slide the cylinder down into place on the crankcase.
12A. On 70 cc engines, install the bolt (**Figure 75**) securing the cylinder to the crankcase and tighten it securely.
12B. On 125 cc engines, install the bolts (**Figure 76**) securing the cylinder to the crankcase and tighten securely.
13. Install the cam chain roller **Figure 74** in between the cam chain runs and install the bolt (**Figure 73**). Tighten the bolt securely.
14. Install the cylinder head as described in this chapter.
15. Adjust the valves and the cam chain tensioner as described in Chapter Three.
16. Follow the *Break-in Procedure* in this chapter if the cylinder was rebored, honed or a new piston or piston rings were installed.

PISTON, PISTON PIN AND PISTON RINGS

The piston is made of an aluminum alloy. The piston pin is made of steel and is a precision fit. The piston pin is held in place by a clip at each end.

Piston Removal

1. Remove the cylinder head and cylinder as described in this chapter.

WARNING
The edges of all piston rings are very sharp. Be careful when handling them to avoid cutting fingers.

2. Remove the top ring with a ring expander tool or by spreading the ends with your thumbs just enough to slide the ring up over the piston (**Figure 83**). Repeat for the remaining rings.

3. Before removing the piston, hold the rod tightly and rock the piston as shown in **Figure 84**. Any rocking motion (do not confuse with the normal sliding motion) indicates wear on the piston pin, piston pin bore or connecting rod small-end bore (more likely a combination of these).

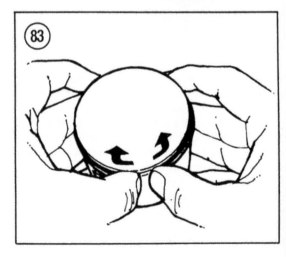

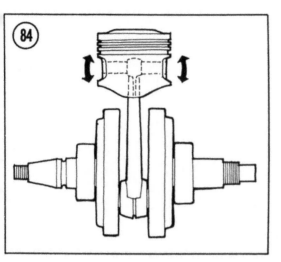

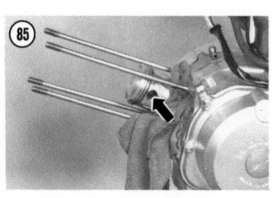

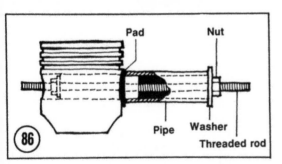

Pad   Nut

Pipe   Washer

Threaded rod

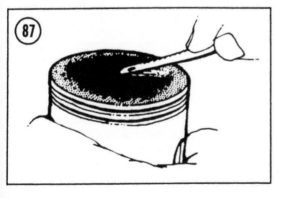

NOTE
Wrap a clean shop cloth under the piston so that the piston pin clip will not fall into the crankcase.

4. Remove the clips from each side of the piston pin bore (**Figure 85**) with a small screwdriver or scribe. Hold your thumb over one edge of the clip when removing it to prevent the clip from springing out.

5. Use a proper size wooden dowel or socket extension and push out the piston pin.

CAUTION
Be careful when removing the pin to avoid damaging the connecting rod. If it is necessary to gently tap the pin to remove it, be sure that the piston is properly supported so that lateral shock is not transmitted to the lower connecting rod bearing.

6. If the piston pin is difficult to remove, heat the piston and pin with a butane torch. The pin will probably push right out. Heat the piston to only about 140° F (60° C), i.e., until it is too warm to touch, but not excessively hot. If the pin is still difficult to push out, use a homemade tool as shown in **Figure 86**.

7. Lift the piston off the connecting rod.

8. If the piston is going to be left off for some time, place a piece of foam insulation tube over the end of the rod to protect it.

Inspection

1. Carefully clean the carbon from the piston crown with a chemical remover or with a soft scraper (**Figure 87**). Do not remove or damage the carbon ridge around the circumference of the piston above the top ring. If the piston, rings and cylinder are found to be dimensionally correct and can be reused, removal of the carbon ring from the top of the piston or the carbon ridge from the top of the cylinder will promote excessive oil consumption.

CAUTION
Do not wire brush the piston skirts.

2. Examine each ring groove for burrs, dented edges and wide wear. Pay particular attention to the top compression ring groove as it usually wears more than the others.

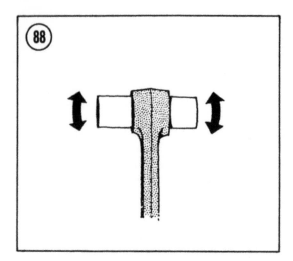

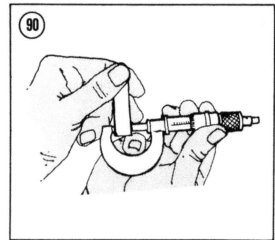

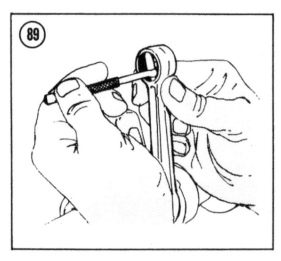

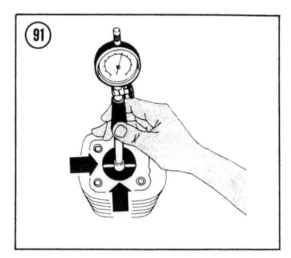

3. If damage or wear indicates piston replacement, select a new piston as described under *Piston Clearance* in this chapter.

4. Oil the piston pin and install it in the connecting rod. Slowly rotate the piston pin and check for radial and axial play (**Figure 88**). If any play exists, the piston pin should be replaced, providing the rod bore is in good condition. Measure the inside diameter of the piston pin bore with a snap gauge (**Figure 89**) and measure the outside diameter of the piston pin with a micrometer (**Figure 90**). Compare with dimensions given in **Table 1**. Replace the piston and piston pin as a set if either or both are worn.

5. Check the piston skirt for galling and abrasion which may have been caused by piston seizure. If light galling is present, smooth the affected area with No. 400 emery paper and oil or a fine oilstone. However, if galling is severe or if the piston is deeply scored, replace it.

Piston Clearance

1. Make sure the piston and cylinder walls are clean and dry.

2. Measure the inside diameter of the cylinder bore at a point 13 mm (1/2 in.) from the upper edge with a bore gauge (**Figure 91**).

3. Measure the outside diameter of the piston across the skirt (**Figure 92**) at right angles to the piston pin. Measure at a distance 10 mm (0.40 in.) up from the bottom of the piston skirt.

4. Piston clearance is the difference between the maximum piston diameter and the minimum cylinder diameter. Subtract the dimension of the piston from the cylinder dimension. Honda does not provide service specifications for piston-to-cylinder clearance service limit, but if the clearance exceeds 0.10 mm (0.004 in.) the cylinder should be rebored to the next oversize and a new piston installed.

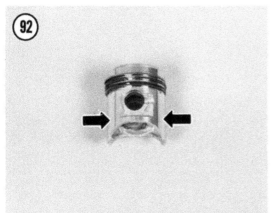

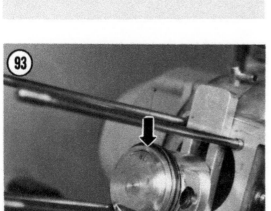

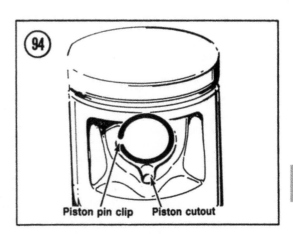

Piston pin clip   Piston cutout

CAUTION
If it is necessary to tap the piston pin into the connecting rod, do so gently with a block of wood or a soft-faced hammer. Make sure you support the piston to prevent the lateral shock from being transmitted to the connecting rod bearing.

NOTE
In the next step, install the clips with the gap away from the cutout in the piston (Figure 94).

5. Install new piston pin clips in both ends of the pin boss. Make sure they are seated in the grooves in the piston.
6. Check the installation by rocking the piston back and forth around the pin axis and from side to side along the axis. It should rotate freely back and forth but not from side to side.
7. Install the piston rings as described in this chapter.
8. Install the cylinder and cylinder head as described in this chapter.

Piston Ring Removal/Inspection/Installation

WARNING
The edges of all piston rings are very sharp. Be careful when handling them to avoid cutting fingers.

1. Remove the top ring by spreading the ends with your thumbs just enough to slide the ring up over the piston (**Figure 83**). Repeat for the remaining rings.
2. Carefully remove all carbon buildup from the ring grooves with a broken piston ring. Inspect the grooves carefully for burrs, nicks or broken and cracked lands. Recondition or replace the piston if necessary.

5. To establish a final overbore dimension with a new piston, add the piston skirt measurement to the specified clearance. This will determine the dimension for the cylinder overbore size. Remember, do not exceed the cylinder maximum service limit inside diameter indicated in **Table 1**.
6. Refer to **Table 3** for oversize piston dimensions and cylinder bore dimensions for the 1981-on ATC110 and the ATC125M. Honda provides service information for these models only.

Piston Installation

1. Apply molybdenum disulfide grease to the inside surface of the connecting rod.
2. Oil the piston pin with assembly oil and install it in the piston until its end extends slightly beyond the inside of the boss.
3. Place the piston over the connecting rod with the "IN" (**Figure 93**) on the piston crown directed upward toward the intake port.
4. Line up the piston pin with the hole in the connecting rod. Push the piston pin through the connecting rod and into the other side of the piston until it is even with the piston pin clip grooves.

3. Roll each ring around its piston groove as shown in **Figure 95** to check for binding. Minor binding may be cleaned up with a fine-cut file.

4. Measure the side clearance of each ring in its groove with a flat feeler gauge (**Figure 96**) and compare to dimensions given in **Table 1**. If the clearance is greater than specified, the rings must be replaced. If the clearance is still excessive with the new rings, the piston must also be replaced.

5. Measure each ring for wear. Place each ring, one at a time, into the cylinder and push it in about 20 mm (3/4 in.) with the crown of the piston to ensure that the ring is square in the cylinder bore. Measure the gap with a flat feeler gauge (**Figure 97**) and compare to dimensions in **Table 1**. If the gap is greater than specified, the rings should be replaced. When installing new rings, measure their end gap in the same manner as for old ones. If the gap is less than specified, carefully file the ends (**Figure 98**) with a fine-cut file until the gap is correct.

6. Install the piston rings in the order shown in **Figure 99**.

NOTE
Install all rings with their markings facing up.

7. Install the piston rings—first the bottom one, then the middle one, then the top—by carefully spreading the ends of the ring with your thumbs and slipping the ring over the top of the piston. Remember that the marks on the piston rings are toward the top of the piston.

8. Make sure the rings are seated completely in their grooves all the way around the piston and that the ends are distributed around the piston as shown in **Figure 100**. The important thing is that the ring gaps are not aligned with each other when installed.

9. If new rings were installed, measure the side clearance of each ring in its groove with a flat feeler gauge (**Figure 96**) and compare to dimensions given in **Table 1**.

10. Follow the *Break-in Procedure* in this chapter if a new piston or piston rings have been installed or the cylinder was rebored or honed.

OIL PUMP

The oil pump is located on the right-hand side of the engine forward of the clutch assembly. The oil pump can be removed with the engine in the frame.

Removal/Installation

1. Drain the engine oil as described in Chapter Three.

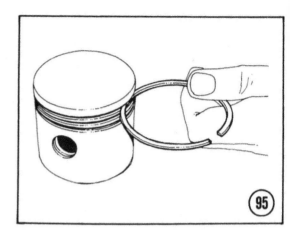

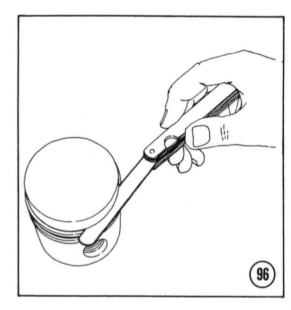

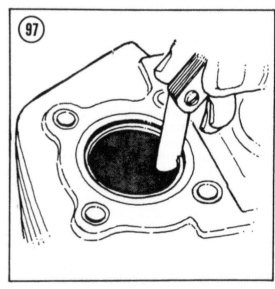

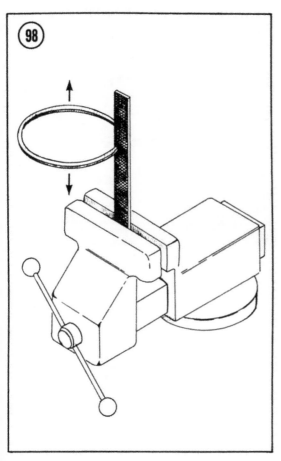

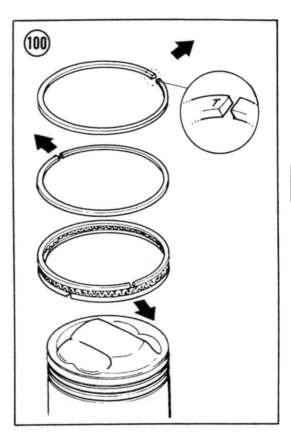

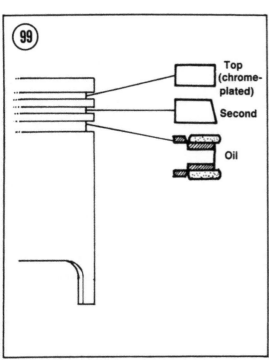

2. Remove the clutch assembly as described in Chapter Five.

3A. On 70 cc engines, remove the Phillips head screws (**Figure 101**) securing the oil pump and remove the oil pump assembly.

3B. On 90-125 cc engines, remove the bolt (A, **Figure 102**) and Phillips head screws (B, **Figure 102**) securing the oil pump and remove the oil pump assembly.

4. Install by reversing these removal steps, noting the following.

5. Make sure the gasket is located on the backside of the oil pump body prior to installation.

6. Align the tab on the oil pump rotor shaft with the notch in the cam chain guide sprocket shaft (**Figure 103**) and push the oil pump assembly into place. Tighten the fasteners securely.

7. Refill the crankcase with the recommended type and quantity of engine oil; refer to Chapter Three.

Disassembly/Inspection/Assembly

Refer to **Figure 104** this procedure.

1. Remove the rotor shaft.

2. Remove the Phillips screws (**Figure 105**) securing the pump cover to the body and remove the cover.

3. Remove the inner and outer rotors. Inspect both parts for scratches and abrasions. Replace both parts if evidence of this is found.

4. If damaged, remove the gasket.

5. Clean all parts in solvent and thoroughly dry. Coat all parts with fresh engine oil prior to assembly.

6. Inspect the pump body for cracks (**Figure 106**).

7. Install the inner and outer rotor into the pump body.

8. Measure the clearance between the inner rotor tip and the outer rotor as shown in **Figure 107**. If the clearance is 0.2 mm (0.008 in.) or greater, replace the worn part.

9. Measure the clearance between the outer rotor and the oil pump body with a flat feeler gauge (**Figure 108**). If the clearance is 0.20 mm (0.008 in.) or greater, replace the worn part.

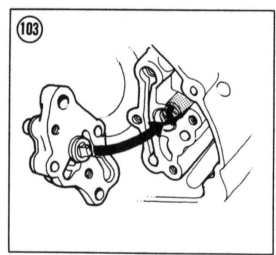

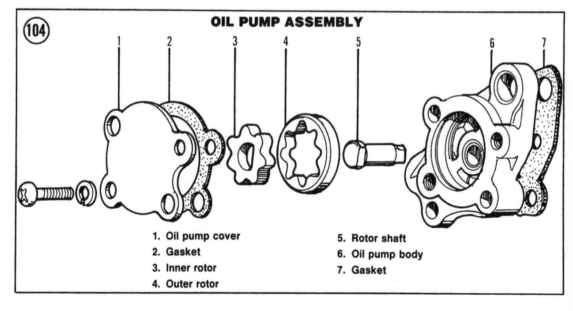

OIL PUMP ASSEMBLY

1. Oil pump cover
2. Gasket
3. Inner rotor
4. Outer rotor
5. Rotor shaft
6. Oil pump body
7. Gasket

10. Install the rotor shaft. Align the flat of the shaft with the flat of the inner rotor (**Figure 109**).

11. Install a new gasket (**Figure 110**).

12. Install the cover and screws and tighten the screws securely.

LEFT-HAND CRANKCASE COVER (ATC90 AND ATC110)

This cover is not used on the ATC70 because that model is not equipped with a subtransmission. For ATC125M models, refer to *Electric Starter Gears and Left-Hand Crankcase Cover Spacer Removal/Installation* in this chapter.

Removal/Installation

1. Drain the engine oil as described in Chapter Three.

2. Remove the subtransmission as described in Chapter Five.

3. Remove the recoil starter and the alternator as described in Chapter Seven.

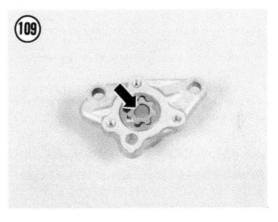

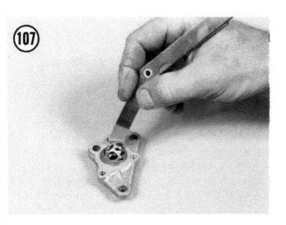

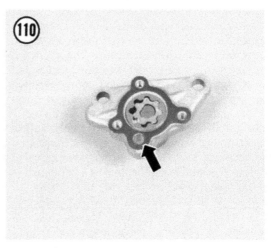

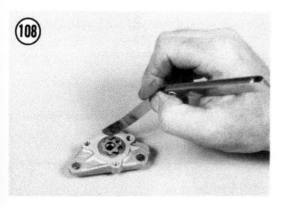

4. Remove the E-clip on the neutral indicator and remove the neutral indicator.

5. Remove the bolts (**Figure 111**) securing the left-hand crankcase cover and remove the cover and the gasket. Don't lose the locating dowels.

6. Remove the drive chain sprocket (**Figure 112**) and, on models so equipped, the bushing(s).

7. Install by reversing these removal steps, noting the following.

8. Install a new gasket and reinstall the locating dowels.

9. Position the neutral indicator shaft so the flats are horizontal.

10. The neutral indicator must be pointed toward the arrow (**Figure 113**) on the cover or the cover will not fit on properly.

CRANKCASE AND CRANKSHAFT

Disassembly of the crankcase (splitting the cases) and removal of the crankshaft assembly require that the engine be removed from the frame.

The crankcase is made in 2 halves of precision diecast aluminum alloy and is of the "thin-walled" type. To avoid damage, do not hammer or pry on any of the interior or exterior projected walls. These areas are easily damaged. The cases are assembled with a gasket between the 2 halves and dowel pins align the halves when they are bolted together.

The crankshaft assembly is made up of 2 full-circle flywheels pressed together on a hollow crankpin. The connecting rod big end bearing on the crankpin is a needle bearing assembly. The crankshaft assembly is supported in 2 ball bearings in the crankcase. Service to the crankshaft assembly is limited to removal and replacement.

The procedure which follows is presented as a complete, step-by-step, major lower end rebuild

that should be followed if an engine is to be completely reconditioned. However, if you're replacing a part that you know is defective, the disassembly should be carried out only until the failed part is accessible; there is no need to disassemble the engine beyond that point so long as you know the remaining components are in good condition and that they were not affected by the failed part.

Crankcase Disassembly

1. Remove all exterior engine assemblies as described in this chapter and other related chapters:
   a. Cylinder head.
   b. Cylinder and piston.
   c. Cam chain and cam chain tensioner assembly.
   d. Clutch assembly.
   e. Recoil starter.

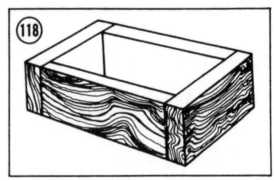

4. Remove the engine as described in this chapter.

5A. On 70 cc engines, remove the bolts from the left-hand crankcase side that secure the crankcase halves together (**Figure 116**). To prevent warpage, loosen them in a crisscross pattern.

5B. On 90-125cc engines, remove the bolts from the right-hand crankcase side that secure the crankcase halves together (**Figure 117**). To prevent warpage, loosen them in a crisscross pattern.

> *NOTE*
> *Set the engine on wood blocks or fabricate a holding fixture of 2×4 inch wood as shown in **Figure 118**.*

> *CAUTION*
> *Perform the next step directly over and close to the workbench as the crankcase halves may separate easily. **Do not** hammer on the crankcase halves or they will be damaged.*

f. Alternator.

g. Subtransmission (models so equipped).

h. Primary driven gear.

i. External shift mechanism.

j. Oil pump.

k. Starter motor, starter gears and left-hand crankcase spacer (models so equipped).

2. On 70 cc engines, remove the rubber plug (**Figure 114**) and remove the shift drum setting bolt and washer (**Figure 115**).

3. On 90-125 cc engines, remove the neutral indicator shaft.

6. Hold onto the right-hand crankcase and studs and tap on the right-hand end of the crankshaft and transmission shafts with a plastic or rubber mallet until the crankshaft and crankcase separate.

7. If the crankcase and crankshaft will not separate using this method, check to make sure that all screws are removed. If you still have a problem, take the crankcase assembly to a dealer and have it separated.

NOTE
Never pry between case halves. Doing so may result in oil leaks, requiring replacement of the case halves.

8. Don't lose the locating dowels if they came out of the case. They do not have to be removed from the case if they are secure.

9. Lift up and carefully remove the transmission, shift drum and shift fork shaft assemblies.

10. Carefully remove the crankshaft assembly from the crankcase half.

11. Inspect the crankcase halves and crankshaft as described in this chapter.

Crankcase Assembly

1. Apply assembly oil to the inner race of all bearings in both crankcase halves.

NOTE
Set the crankcase half assembly on wood blocks or the wood holding fixture shown in the disassembly procedure.

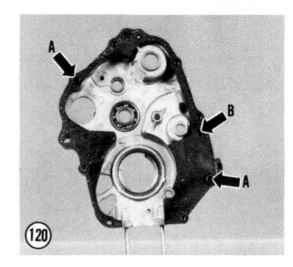

2. Install the transmission assemblies, shift shafts and shift drum in the left-hand crankcase half and lightly oil all shaft ends. Refer to Chapter Five for the correct procedure.

3. Install the crankshaft with the tapered end and cam chain sprocket on the left-hand side (**Figure 119**). The crankshaft can be installed backward, so make sure you have installed it correctly.

NOTE
Make sure the mating surfaces are clean and free of all old gasket material. Make sure you get a leak-free seal.

4. Install the locating dowels (A, **Figure 120**) if they were removed.

5. Install a new crankcase gasket (B, **Figure 120**).

6. Set the upper crankcase half over the one on the blocks. Push it down squarely into place until it reaches the crankshaft bearing. There is usually about 1/2 inch left to go (**Figure 121**).

7. Lightly tap the case halves together with a plastic or rubber mallet until they seat.

CAUTION
Crankcase halves should fit together without force. If the crankcase halves do not fit together completely, do not attempt to pull them together with the crankcase screws. Separate the crankcase halves and investigate the cause of the interference. If the transmission shafts were disassembled, recheck to make sure that a gear is not

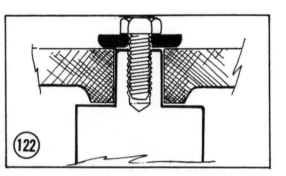

installed backwards. Do not risk damage by trying to force the cases together.

8A. On 70 cc engines, install the bolts on the right-hand side that secure the crankcase halves together (**Figure 116**). Tighten only finger-tight.
8B. On 90-125 cc engines, install the bolts on the right-hand side that secure the crankcase halves together (**Figure 117**). Tighten only finger-tight.
9. Securely tighten the screws in 2 stages in a crisscross pattern until they are firmly hand-tight.

NOTE
*Install the shift drum setting bolt washer with the rounded side against the crankcase (**Figure 122**).*

10. On 70 cc engines, install the shift drum setting bolt and washer and tighten to 8-12 N•m (6-9 ft.-lb.). Install the rubber plug.
11. On 90-125 cc engines, install the neutral indicator shaft.
12. After the crankcase halves are completely assembled, rotate the crankshaft and transmission shafts to make sure there is no binding. If any is present, disassemble the crankcase and correct the problem.

NOTE
After a new crankcase gasket is installed, it must be trimmed. Carefully trim off all excess crankcase gasket material where the cylinder base gasket comes in contact with the crankcase. If it is not trimmed the cylinder base gasket will not seal properly.

13. Install all exterior engine assemblies as described in this chapter and other related chapters:
   a. Cylinder head.
   b. Cylinder and piston.
   c. Cam chain and cam chain tensioner assembly.
   d. Clutch assembly.
   e. Recoil starter.
   f. Alternator.
   g. Subtransmission (models so equipped).
   h. Primary driven gear.
   i. External shift mechanism.
   j. Starter motor, starter gears and left-hand crankcase spacer (models so equipped).

Crankcase and Crankshaft Inspection

1. Clean both crankcase halves inside and out with cleaning solvent. Thoroughly dry with compressed air and wipe off with a clean shop cloth. Be sure to remove all traces of old gasket material from all mating surfaces.
2. Check the transmission bearings (**Figure 123**) for roughness, pitting, galling and play by rotating them slowly by hand. If any roughness or play can be felt in the bearing it must be replaced.
3. Carefully inspect the cases for cracks and fractures, especially in the lower areas (A, **Figure 124**); they are vulnerable to rock damage. Also check the areas around the stiffening ribs, around bearing bosses and threaded holes. If damage is found, have them repaired by a shop specializing

in the repair of precision aluminum castings or replace them.

4. Make sure the crankcase studs (B, **Figure 124**) are tight in each case half. Retighten if necessary.

5. Check the crankshaft main bearings (**Figure 125**) for roughness, pitting, galling and play by rotating them slowly by hand. If any roughness or play can be felt in the bearing it must be replaced. This must be entrusted to a dealer as special tools are required. The cam chain sprocket and oil pump drive gear must also be removed and realigned properly upon installation.

6. Inspect the cam chain sprocket (**Figure 126**) for wear or missing teeth. If the sprocket is damaged, replacement should be entrusted to a dealer.

7. Measure the inside diameter of the connecting rod small end (**Figure 127**) with a snap gauge and an inside micrometer. Compare to dimensions given in **Table 1**. If worn to the service limit the crankshaft assembly must be replaced.

8. Check the condition of the connecting rod big end bearing by grasping the rod in one hand and lifting up on it. With the heel of your other hand, rap sharply on the top of the rod. A sharp metallic sound, such as a click, is an indication that the bearing or crankpin or both are worn and the crankshaft assembly should be replaced.

9. Check the connecting rod-to-crankshaft side clearance with a flat feeler gauge (**Figure 128**). Compare to dimensions given in **Table 1**. If the clearance is greater than specified the crankshaft assembly must be replaced.

10. Other inspections of the crankshaft assembly involve accurate measuring equipment and should be entrusted to a dealer or competent machine shop. The crankshaft assembly operates under severe stress and dimensional tolerances are critical. These dimensions are given in **Table 1**. If any are off by the slightest amount it may cause a considerable amount of damage or destruction of the engine. The crankshaft assembly must be replaced as a unit as it cannot be serviced without the aid of a 10-12 ton (9,000-11,000 kilogram) capacity press, holding fixtures and crankshaft jig.

11. Inspect the oil seals. They should be replaced every other time the crankcase is disassembled. Refer to *Bearing and Oil Seal Replacement* in this chapter.

Bearing and Oil Seal Replacement

1. Pry out the oil seals (**Figure 129**) with a small screwdriver, taking care not to damage the crankcase bore. If the seals are old and difficult to remove, heat the cases as described in Step 2 and

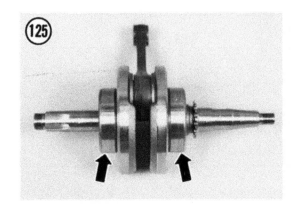

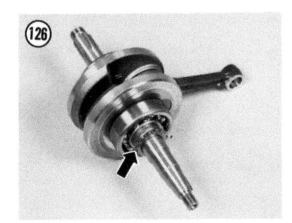

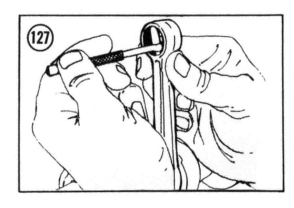

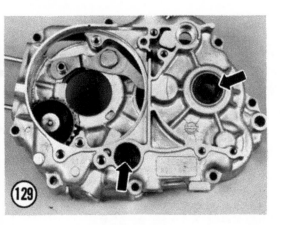

use an awl to punch a small hole in the steel backing of the seal. Install a small sheet metal screw part way into the seal and pull the seal out with a pair of pliers.

CAUTION
Do not install the screw too deep or it may contact and damage the bearing behind it.

2. The bearings are installed with a slight interference fit. The crankcase must be heated in an oven to a temperature of about 212° F (100° C). An easy way to check the proper temperature is to drop tiny drops of water on the case; if they sizzle and evaporate immediately, the temperature is correct. Heat only one case at a time.

CAUTION
Do not heat the cases with a torch (propane or acetylene); never bring a flame into contact with the bearing or case. The direct heat will destroy the case hardening of the bearing and will likely cause warpage of the case.

3. Remove the case from the oven and hold onto the 2 crankcase studs with a kitchen pot holder, heavy gloves or heavy shop cloths—*it is hot.*
4. Remove the oil seals if not already removed (see Step 1).
5. Hold the crankcase with the bearing side down and tap it squarely on a piece of soft wood. Continue to tap until the bearing(s) fall out. Repeat for the other half.

CAUTION
Be sure to tap the crankcase squarely on the piece of wood. Avoid damaging the sealing surface of the crankcase.

6. If the bearings are difficult to remove, they can be gently tapped out with a socket or piece of pipe the same size as the bearing outer race.

NOTE
If the bearings or seals are difficult to remove or install, don't take a chance on expensive damage. Have the work performed by a dealer or competent machine shop.

7. While heating up the crankcase halves, place the new bearings in a freezer if possible. Chilling them will slightly reduce their overall diameter while the hot crankcase is slightly larger due to heat expansion. This will make bearing installation much easier.
8. While the crankcase is still hot, press each new bearing(s) into place in the crankcase by hand until it seats completely. Do not hammer it in. If the bearing will not seat, remove it and cool it again. Reheat the crankcase and install the bearing again.
9. Oil seals are best installed with a special tool available at a dealer or motorcycle supply store. However, a proper size socket or piece of pipe can be substituted. Make sure that the bearings and seals are not cocked in the crankcase hole and that they are seated properly.

ELECTRIC STARTER GEARS AND LEFT-HAND CRANKCASE COVER SPACER (ATC125M)

Removal/Installation

Refer to **Figure 130** for this procedure.
1. Remove the alternator stator and rotor as described in Chapter Seven.
2. Remove the left-hand rear wheel and the drive chain cover as described in Chapter Eight.
3. Remove the subtransmission as described in Chapter Five.
4. Remove the thrust washer (A, **Figure 131**) and the starter idler gear (B, **Figure 131**).
5. Remove the thrust washer (**Figure 132**) from the reduction gear shaft.
6. Remove the screw securing the driven gear set plate (**Figure 133**) and remove the set plate.
7. Disconnect the neutral indicator switch electrical connector and withdraw the rubber grommet from the left-hand crankcase spacer (**Figure 34**).
8. Remove the bolts (**Figure 135**) securing the crankcase cover spacer and remove the spacer from the crankcase. Don't lose the locating dowels.
9. Remove the starter driven gear (**Figure 136**), the needle bearing (**Figure 137**) and the spacer (A, **Figure 138**).
10. Remove the neutral indicator shaft, dowel pin and gasket (B, **Figure 138**).

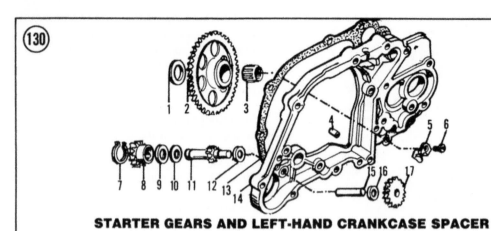

STARTER GEARS AND LEFT-HAND CRANKCASE SPACER

1. Spacer	7. Circlip	13. Gasket
2. Driven gear	8. Reduction gear	14. Left-hand crankcase spacer
3. Needle bearing	9. Thrust washer	15. Shaft
4. Dowel pin	10. Thrust washer	16. Thrust washer
5. Driven gear set plate	11. Reduction gear and shaft	17. Starter idle gear
6. Screw	12. Thrust washer	

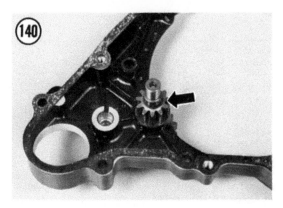

11. Remove the circlip (**Figure 139**) securing the starter reduction gear to the crankcase cover spacer.

12. Remove the starter reduction gear and thrust washer from the inside surface of the crankcase cover spacer.

13. From the outside surface of the crankcase spacer, withdraw the reduction gear/shaft (**Figure 140**) and thrust washer.

14. Install by reversing these removal steps.

Disassembly/Inspection/Assembly

1. Use an impact driver and a T-30 Torx driver bit to remove the screws (**Figure 141**) securing the

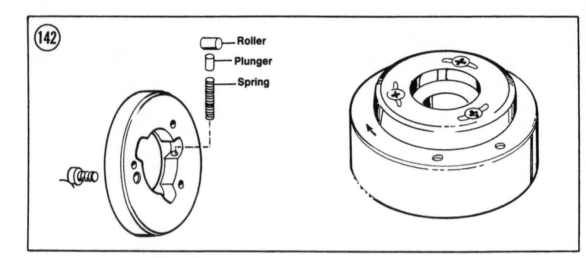

Roller
Plunger
Spring

starter clutch cover to the starter clutch
housing/alternator rotor assembly. Remove the
cover.

2. Remove the rollers, the plungers and the
springs.

3. Inspect the rollers for uneven or excessive wear.
Replace as a set if any require replacing.

4. Inspect the driven gear, idler gear and reduction
gears. Check for chipped or missing teeth; replace if
necessary.

5. Inspect the driven gear needle bearing for wear
or damage. Rotate the bearing by hand and check
for roughness, noise or play. If the bearing is
suspect it should be replaced.

6. Install the springs, the plungers and the rollers
into the starter clutch housing (**Figure 142**).

7. Inspect the starter idler gear and shaft (**Figure
143**) for wear and damage. Replace if necessary.

8. Inspect the needle bearing (**Figure 144**) for wear
or damage; replace if necessary.

9. Install the starter cover and the screws. Use an
impact driver and tighten the screws (**Figure 141**).

10. Use a punch and stake each screw head into the
groove next to each screw head.

RECOIL STARTER (70-110 CC)

Removal/Installation

1. Place the ATC on level ground and set the
parking brake or block both wheels so the vehicle
will not roll in either direction.

2. Shift the transmission into NEUTRAL and
remove the gearshift lever.

3. Remove the bolts (**Figure 145**) securing the
recoil starter assembly and remove the assembly.

4. Install by reversing these removal steps. Make
sure to install a new gasket on the assembly prior to
installation.

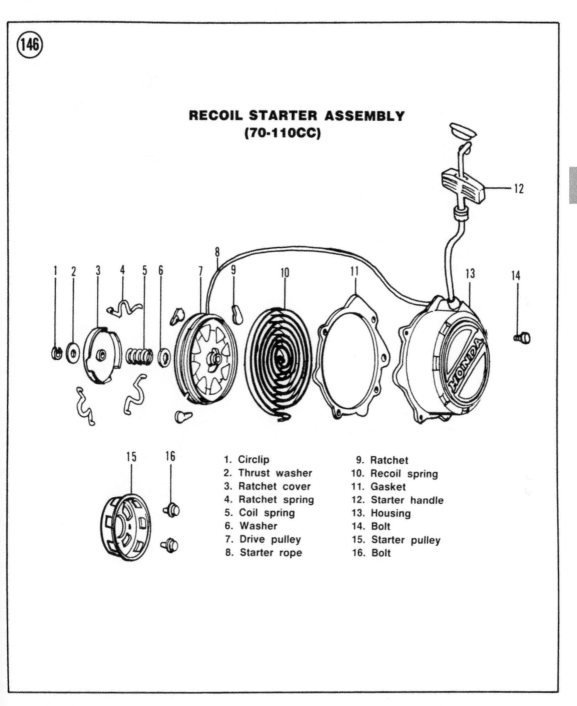

(146)

**RECOIL STARTER ASSEMBLY
(70-110CC)**

1. Circlip
2. Thrust washer
3. Ratchet cover
4. Ratchet spring
5. Coil spring
6. Washer
7. Drive pulley
8. Starter rope
9. Ratchet
10. Recoil spring
11. Gasket
12. Starter handle
13. Housing
14. Bolt
15. Starter pulley
16. Bolt

**Disassembly and
Starter Rope Removal**

NOTE
*Consider replacing the Honda starter
rope with an aftermarket vinyl coated
flexible wire cable. These cables are
available from many dealers and mail
order houses.*

Refer to **Figure 146** for this procedure.

WARNING
*The return spring is under pressure and
may jump out during the disassembly
procedure. It is a very strong spring and
may cut fingers or cause eye damage.
Wear safety glasses and gloves when
disassembling and assembling.*

1. Remove and discard the gasket.

2. If the starter rope is still attached to the starter handle (the rope hasn't broken), tie a knot (A, **Figure 147**) in the rope and remove the starter handle.

3. Remove the circlip and thrust washer (B, **Figure 147**) and ratchet cover (C, **Figure 147**).

4A. On ATC70 models, remove the set spring, ratchets and the washer.

4B. On ATC90 and ATC110 models, remove the ratchet springs (A, **Figure 148**), ratchets (B, **Figure 148**), coil spring and washer (C, **Figure 148**).

5. Untie the knot and release the starter rope slowly into the housing.

WARNING
*The recoil spring may jump out at this time—**protect yourself accordingly**.*

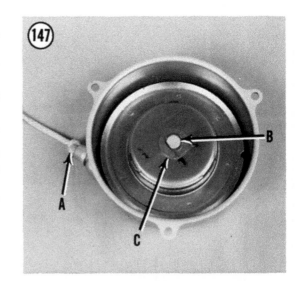

6. Remove the drive pulley (D, **Figure 148**).

7. Untie and remove the starter rope from the drive pulley.

NOTE
It is a good idea to replace the starter rope every time the recoil starter is disassembled.

8. Clean all parts in solvent and thoroughly dry.

9. Inspect all parts for wear or damage and replace as necessary.

Assembly and
Starter Rope Installation

1. Install a new starter rope in the drive pulley (A, **Figure 149**) and tie a special knot at the end (**Figure 150**). Apply heat to the knot (a match is sufficient) and *slightly* melt the nylon rope. This will hold the knot securely.

2. Apply multipurpose grease to the housing shaft (A, **Figure 151**). Install the recoil spring into the housing. Hook the end of the spring onto the hook (B, **Figure 151**) in the housing.

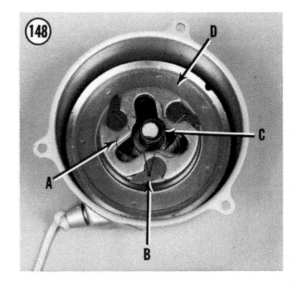

3. Coil the rope onto the ratchet in a *clockwise* direction (B, **Figure 149**).

4. Position the end of the rope in the drive pulley so the starter grip end is located within the notch (C, **Figure 149**) in the drive pulley.

5. Install the drive pulley into the housing while rotating it in a *clockwise* direction. Make sure the rope is positioned up through the notch in the drive pulley. The pin on the bottom of the drive pulley must engage with the end of the recoil spring. If they engage, proceed to Step 8. If the 2 will not engage, remove the drive pulley and use the procedure in Step 6 and Step 7.

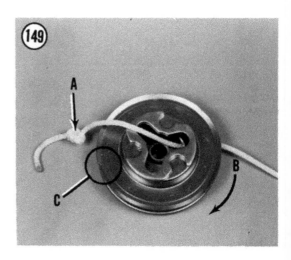

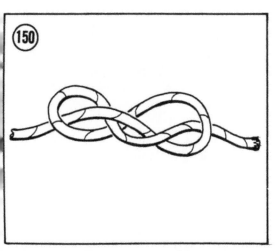

(150)

(153)

4

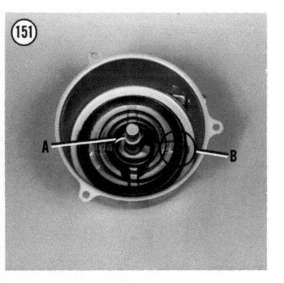

(151)

A———————————B

(154)

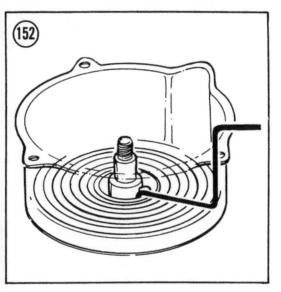

(152)

6. Make a *soft* wire hook (do not use stiff wire) and hook it onto the inner end of the recoil spring as shown in **Figure 152**. The other end of the hook must lay flat on top of the spring coils to allow the drive pulley to drop into position. The wire must be long enough so it can be pulled on.

7. Reinstall the drive pulley into the housing while rotating it in a *clockwise* direction. Make sure the rope is positioned up through the notch in the drive pulley. When the drive pulley comes into contact with the recoil spring, pull sideways on the hook to bring the inner end of the recoil spring away from the shaft in the housing. Continue to rotate the drive pulley and push it the rest of the way down until it seats and engages with the spring hook. Pull the soft wire hook out from between the drive pulley and the spring.

8. After engagement with the spring, rotate the drive pulley 2 turns *clockwise* to preload the recoil spring.

9. Hold onto the drive pulley and feed the rope out through the hole in the housing. Secure the rope with Vise Grips or tie a knot in it (**Figure 153**).

10. Apply a light coat of multipurpose grease to the washer and install the washer (**Figure 154**) and coil spring (A, **Figure 155**).

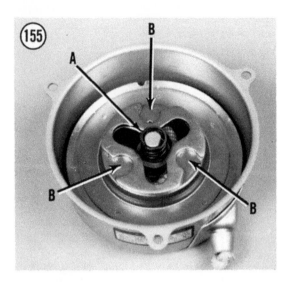

11. Apply a light coat of grease to the areas where the ratchets ride (B, **Figure 155**).
12. Install the ratchets as shown in **Figure 156**.
13A. On ATC70 models, install the washer and the set spring.
13B. On ATC90 and ATC110 models, install the ratchet springs (**Figure 157**).
14. Install the ratchet cover (**Figure 158**).
15. Install thrust washer and circlip (**Figure 159**).

NOTE
Make sure the circlip is seated correctly in the groove in the shaft.

16. Install the rope through the starter handle and tie the end using the same special knot as shown in **Figure 150**. Apply heat to the knot (a match is sufficient) and *slightly* melt the nylon rope. This will hold the knot securely.
17. After assembly is complete, check the operation of the recoil starter by pulling on the starter handle. Make sure the drive pulley rotates freely and returns completely. Also make sure the ratchets move out and in correctly. If either does not operate correctly, disassemble and correct the problem.
18. Inspect the square holes in the starter pulley. If they are damaged in the area where the ratchets make contact it should be replaced.

RECOIL STARTER (125 CC)

Removal/Installation

1. Place the ATC on level ground and set the parking brake.
2. Shift the transmission into NEUTRAL and remove the gearshift lever.

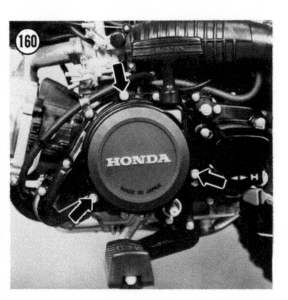

3. Remove the bolts (**Figure 160**) securing the recoil starter assembly and remove the assembly.
4. Install by reversing these removal steps. Make sure to install a new gasket on the assembly prior to installation.

**Disassembly and
Starter Rope Removal**

NOTE
Consider replacing the Honda starter rope with an aftermarket vinyl coated flexible wire cable. These cables are available from many dealers and mail order houses.

Refer to **Figure 161** for this procedure.

WARNING
The return spring is under pressure and may jump out during the disassembly procedure. It is a very strong spring and

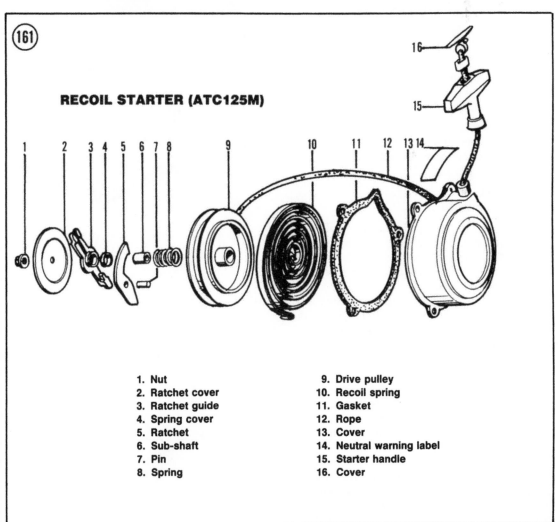

RECOIL STARTER (ATC125M)

1. Nut
2. Ratchet cover
3. Ratchet guide
4. Spring cover
5. Ratchet
6. Sub-shaft
7. Pin
8. Spring
9. Drive pulley
10. Recoil spring
11. Gasket
12. Rope
13. Cover
14. Neutral warning label
15. Starter handle
16. Cover

may cut fingers or cause eye damage. Wear safety glasses and gloves when disassembling and assembling.

1. Remove the cover from the starter handle and untie the knot in the starter rope.
2. Hold the starter rope with Vise Grips (A, **Figure 162**) and remove the starter handle from the rope.
3. Remove and discard the gasket.
4. Remove the nut (B, **Figure 162**) and ratchet cover (C, **Figure 162**).
5. Remove the ratchet guide (**Figure 163**).
6. Remove the ratchet (A, **Figure 164**) and the friction spring and cup (B, **Figure 164**).
7. Remove the Vise Grips and release the starter rope slowly into the housing.

WARNING
The recoil spring may jump out at this time—protect yourself accordingly.

8. Remove the drive pulley (C, **Figure 164**).
9. Untie and remove the starter rope from the drive pulley.

NOTE
It is a good idea to replace the starter rope every time the recoil starter is disassembled.

10. Clean all parts in solvent and thoroughly dry.
11. Inspect all moving parts (**Figure 165**) for wear or damage and replace as necessary.

**Assembly and
Starter Rope Installation**

1. Install a new starter rope in the drive pulley (A, **Figure 166**) and tie a special knot at the end (**Figure 150**). Apply heat to the knot (a match is sufficient) and *slightly* melt the nylon rope. This will hold the knot securely.
2. Apply multipurpose grease to the housing shaft (A, **Figure 167**). Install the recoil spring into the housing. Hook the end of the spring onto the hook (B, **Figure 167**) in the housing.
3. Coil the rope onto the ratchet in a *clockwise* direction (B, **Figure 166**).
4. Position the end of the rope in the drive pulley so the starter grip end is located within the notch (C, **Figure 166**) in the drive pulley.
5. Install the drive pulley into the housing while rotating it in a *clockwise* direction. Make sure the rope is positioned up through the notch in the drive pulley. The tab (A, **Figure 168**) on the bottom of the drive pulley must engage with the hook (B, **Figure 168**) in the end of the recoil spring. If they engage, proceed to Step 8. If the 2 will not

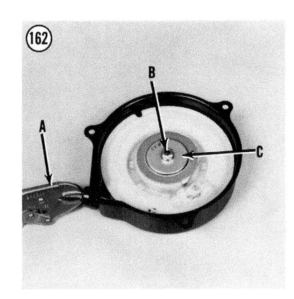

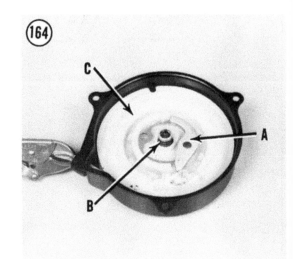

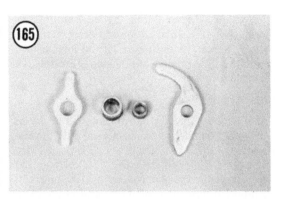

engage, remove the drive pulley and use the procedure in Step 6 and Step 7.

6. Make a *soft* wire hook (do not use stiff wire) and hook it onto the inner end of the recoil spring as shown in **Figure 152**. The other end of the hook must lay flat on top of the spring coils to allow the drive pulley to drop into position. The wire must be long enough so it can be pulled on.

7. Reinstall the drive pulley into the housing while rotating it in a *clockwise* direction. Make sure the rope is positioned up through the notch in the drive pulley. When the drive pulley comes into contact with the recoil spring, pull sideways on the hook to bring the inner end of the recoil spring away from the shaft in the housing. Continue to rotate the drive pulley and push it the rest of the way down until it seats and engages with the spring hook. Pull the soft wire hook out from between the drive pulley and the spring.

8. After engagement with the spring, rotate the drive pulley 2 turns *clockwise* to preload the recoil spring.

9. Hold onto the drive pulley and feed the rope out through the hole in the housing. Secure the rope with Vise Grips (A, **Figure 162**).

10. Apply a light coat of multipurpose grease to the ratchet and install the ratchet (A, **Figure 164**).

11. Install the friction spring and spring cover (B, **Figure 164**).

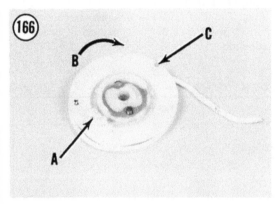

12. Install the ratchet guide onto the spring cover.

13. Install the ratchet cover and secure with the nut (B, **Figure 162**).

14. Install the rope through the starter handle and tie the end using the same special knot as shown in **Figure 150**. Apply heat to the knot (a match is sufficient) and *slightly* melt the nylon rope. This will hold the knot securely. Install the cover in the starter handle.

15. After assembly is complete, check the operation of the recoil starter by pulling on the starter handle. Make sure the drive pulley rotates freely and returns completely. Also make sure the ratchet moves out and in correctly. If either does not operate correctly, disassemble and correct the problem.

16. Inspect the slots in the starter driven pulley. If they are damaged it should be replaced.

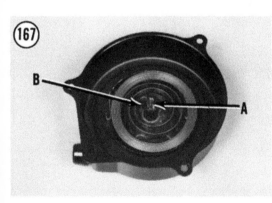

BREAK-IN PROCEDURE

If the rings were replaced, a new piston installed, the cylinder rebored or honed or major lower end work performed, the engine should be broken in just as though it were new. The performance and service life of the engine depends greatly on a careful and sensible break-in.

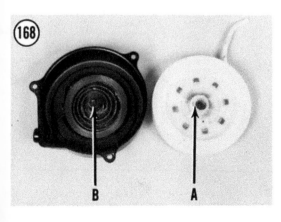

For the first 5-10 hours of operation, no more than one-third throttle should be used and speed should be varied as much as possible within the one-third throttle limit. Prolonged steady running at one speed, no matter how moderate, is to be avoided as well as hard acceleration.

Following the first 5-10 hours of operation more throttle should not be used until the ATC has run for 100 hours and then it should be limited to short bursts of speed until 150 hours have been logged.

The mono-grade oils recommended for break-in and normal use provide a better bedding pattern for rings and cylinder than do multi-grade oils. As a result, piston ring and cylinder bore life are greatly increased. During this period, oil consumption will be higher than normal. It is therefore important to frequently check and correct oil level. At no time, during the break-in or later, should the oil level be allowed to drop below the bottom line on the dipstick; if the oil level is low, the oil will become overheated resulting in insufficient lubrication and increased wear.

10 Hour Service

It is essential that the oil be changed and the oil filter rotor and filter screen be cleaned after the first 10 hours of operation. In addition, it is a good idea to change the oil and clean the oil filter rotor and filter screen at the completion of 100 hours of operation to ensure that all of the particles produced during break-in are removed from the lubrication system. The small added expense may be considered a smart investment that will pay off in increased engine life.

Table 1 ENGINE SPECIFICATIONS

Item	Specification	Wear limit
General		
Type	4-stroke, air-cooled, SOHC	
Number of cylinders	1	
Bore and stroke		
70 cc	47.0×41.4 mm (1.85×1.63 in.)	
90 cc	50.0×45.6 mm (1.97×1.79 in.)	
110 cc	52.0×49.5 mm (2.05×1.95 in.)	
125 cc	55.0×52.2 mm (2.16×2.05 in.)	
Displacement		
70 cc	72 cc (4.4 cu. in.)	
90 cc	89.5 cc (5.46 cu. in.)	
110 cc	105.1 cc (6.39 cu. in.)	
125 cc	124 cc (7.6 cu. in.)	
Compression ratio		
70 cc	7.5 to 1	
90 cc	7.5 to 1	
110 cc	8.2 to 1	
125 cc	8.8 to 1	
Compression pressure (at sea level)		
ATC70, ATC90	10-12 kg/cm^2 (142-170 psi)	
ATC110, ATC125M	11-14 kg/cm^2 (156-198 psi)	
Lubrication	Wet sump	
Cylinder		
Bore		
70 cc	47.005-47.015 mm (1.8506-1.8510 in.)	47.05 mm (1.852 in.)
90 cc	50.000-50.010 mm (1.9685-1.9689 in.)	50.10 mm (1.972 in.)
110 cc	52.020-52.030 mm (2.0480-2.0483 in.)	52.06 mm (2.049 in.)
125 cc	55.000-55.010 mm (2.1654-2.1657 in.)	55.01 mm (2.169 in.)
Out of round	–	0.05 mm (0.002 in.)

(continued)

Table 1 ENGINE SPECIFICATIONS (continued)

Item	Specification	Wear limit
Piston		
Diameter		
70 cc	46.98-47.00 mm (1.850-1.8504 in.)	46.90 mm (1.847 in.)
90 cc	49.975-49.99 mm (1.9673-1.9681 in.)	49.80 mm (1.9606 in.)
110 cc	51.970-51.990 mm (2.0461-2.0468 in.)	51.80 mm (2.039 in.)
125 cc	54.955-54.985 mm (2.2029-2.1648 in.)	54.90 mm (2.161 in.)
Piston pin bore		
70 cc	13.002-13.008 mm (0.5119-0.5121 in.)	13.10 mm (0.516 in.)
90 cc	14.002-14.008 mm (0.5513-0.5515 in.)	14.04 mm (0.555 in.)
110-125 cc	15.002-15.008 mm (0.5906-0.5909 in.)	15.04 mm (0.592 in.)
Piston pin outer diameter		
70 cc	12.994-13.000 mm (0.5116-0.5118 in.)	12.98 mm (0.511 in.)
90 cc	13.994-14.000 mm (0.5509-0.5512 in.)	13.96 mm (0.549 in.)
110-125 cc	14.994-15.000 mm (0.5903-0.5906 in.)	14.96 mm (0.589 in.)
Piston to pin clearance		
70 cc	0.002-0.014 mm (0.0001-0.0006 in.)	0.075 mm (0.003 in.)
90 cc	NA	NA
110-125 cc	0.002-0.014 mm (0.0001-0.0006 in.)	0.02 mm (0.001 in.)
Piston rings		
Number of rings		
Compression	2	
Oil control	1	
Ring end gap		
Top and second		
70-90 cc	0.15-0.35 mm (0.006-0.014 in.)	0.5 mm (0.02 in.)
110-125 cc	0.10-0.25 mm (0.004-0.010 in.)	0.5 mm (0.02 in.)
Oil (side rail)		
70 cc	0.3-0.9 mm (0.02-0.036 in.)	–
90 cc	0.15-0.40 mm (0.006-0.016 in.)	0.50 mm (0.020 in.)
110-125 cc	0.3-0.9 mm (0.01-0.04 in.)	–
Ring side clearance		
Top and second ring		
70-90 cc	0.010-0.045 mm (0.0004-0.0018 in.)	0.12 mm (0.005 in.)
Top ring		
110-125 cc	0.015-0.050 mm (0.0006-0.0020 in.)	0.12 mm (0.005 in.)

(continued)

4

Table 1 ENGINE SPECIFICATIONS (continued)

Item	Specification	Wear limit
Second ring		
110-125 cc	0.010-0.045 mm (0.0004-0.0018 in.)	0.12 mm (0.005 in.)
Oil ring		
70 cc	0.010-0.045 mm (0.0004-0.0018 in.)	0.12 mm (0.0047 in.)
90-125 cc	NA	NA
Connecting rod small end inner diameter		
70 cc	13.013-13.043 mm (0.5123-0.5135 in.)	13.1 mm (0.52 in.)
90 cc	14.012-14.028 mm (0.5517-0.5523 in.)	14.05 mm (0.553 in.)
110-125 cc	15.016-15.034 mm (0.5912-0.5919 in.)	15.05 mm (0.593 in.)
Crankshaft		
Runout	–	0.10 mm (0.004 in.)
Connecting rod big end side clearance	0.10-0.35 mm (0.004-0.014 in.)	0.60 mm (0.02 in.)
Camshaft		
Cam lobe height (intake and exhaust)		
70 cc	26.07 mm (1.026 in.)	25.69 mm (1.011 in.)
90-110 cc	24.90-24.98 mm (0.9803-0.9835 in.)	24.6 mm (0.9685 in.)
125 cc	24.118-24.278 mm (0.9495-0.9558 in.)	23.8 mm (0.94 in.)
Cam journal OD		
Right-hand end		
70 cc	NA	NA
90-110 cc	17.927-17.938 mm (0.7058-0.7062 in.)	17.90 mm (0.705 in.)
125 cc	17.934-17.945 mm (0.7060-0.7065 in.)	17.90 mm (0.705 in.)
Left-hand end		
70 cc	NA	NA
90-110 cc	25.917-25.930 mm (1.0204-1.0209 in.)	25.90 mm (1.019 in.)
125 cc	25.932-25.945 mm (1.0210-1.0215 in.)	25.90 mm (1.019 in.)
Valves		
Valve stem outer diameter		
Intake		
70-90 cc	5.455-5.465 mm (0.2148-0.2152 in.)	5.40 mm (0.213 in.)
110-125 cc	5.450-5.465 mm (0.2146-0.2152 in.)	5.43 mm (0.2139 in.)
Exhaust		
70-125 cc	5.430-5.445 mm (0.2138-0.2144 in.)	5.40 mm (0.213 in.)
90 cc	5.435-5.445 mm (0.2140-0.2144 in.)	5.41 mm (0.2132 in.)

(continued)

Table 1 ENGINE SPECIFICATIONS (continued)

Item	Specification	Wear limit
Valve guide inner diameter		
Intake	5.475-5.485 mm (0.2156-0.2159 in.)	5.50 mm (0.217 in.)
Exhaust	5.475-5.485 mm (0.2156-0.2159 in.)	5.50 mm (0.217 in.)
Stem to guide clearance		
Intake	0.010-0.030 mm (0.0004-0.0012 in.)	0.08 mm (0.0032 in.)
Exhaust	0.030-0.050 mm (0.0012-0.0020 in.)	0.10 mm (0.004 in.)
Valve seat width	1.0 mm (0.047 in.)	1.6 mm (0.064 in.)
Valve face width		
70 cc	NA	NA
90-125 cc	1.2-1.5 mm (0.048-0.060 in.)	1.8 mm (0.072 in.)
Valve springs free length		
Inner spring		
70 cc	25.1 mm (0.99 in.)	23.8 mm (0.94 in.)
90-110 cc	26.5 mm (1.043 in.)	25.5 mm (1.004 in.)
125 cc	31.1 mm (1.22 in.)	29.9 mm (1.18 in.)
Outer spring		
70 cc	28.1 mm (1.11 in.)	26.8 mm (1.06 in.)
90-110 cc	31.8 mm (1.252 in.)	30.6 mm (1.205 in.)
125 cc	35.0 mm (1.38 in.)	33.7 mm (1.32 in.)
Rocker arm assembly		
Rocker arm bore ID	10.000-10.015 mm (0.3937-0.3943 in.)	10.10 mm (0.398 in.)
Rocker arm shaft OD		
70 cc	9.978-9.989 mm (0.3928-0.3933 in.)	9.91 mm (0.390 in.)
90-125 cc	9.972-9.987 mm (0.3926-0.3932 in.)	9.92 mm (0.3906 in.)
Cylinder head warpage	–	0.004 in. (0.10 mm)
Oil pump (all models)		
Inner to outer rotor tip clearance	–	0.20 mm (0.008 in.)
Outer rotor to body clearance	–	0.20 mm (0.008 in.)
End clearance	–	0.12 mm (0.005 in.)

NA—Honda does not provide specifications for all items and all models.

Table 2 ENGINE TORQUE SPECIFICATIONS

Item	N•m	ft-lb.
Cylinder head cover nuts		
70 cc	9-12	7-9
90 cc	20-25	14-18
110-125 cc	18-21	13-15
Cam sprocket bolt		
70 cc	5-9	4-7
90-125 cc	9-12	7-9
Cam chain roller bolt	9-14	6-10
Ignition advance unit		
(models so equipped)	9-12	7-9
Pulse rotor bolt		
(models so equipped)	8-12	6-9
Alternator rotor (bolt or nut)		
70 cc	33-38	24-27
90 cc	20-30	14-22
110 cc	65-75	47-51
125 cc	40-45	29-33

**Table 3 OVERSIZE PISTON AND CYLINDER
BORE DIMENSION (1981-ON ATC110, ATC125M)***

Oversize piston	Cylinder dimension
ATC110	
0.25 mm (0.01 in.)	52.27-52.28 mm (2.0579-2.0583 in.)
0.50 mm (0.02 in.)	52.52-52.53 mm (2.0677-2.0681 in.)
ATC125M	
0.25 mm (0.01 in.)	55.25-55.26 mm (2.1752-2.1756 in.)
0.50 mm (0.02 in.)	55.50-55.51 mm (2.1850-2.1854 in.)

* Honda provides service information for these models only.

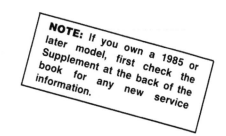
NOTE: If you own a 1985 or later model, first check the Supplement at the back of the book for any new service information.

CHAPTER FIVE

5

CLUTCH AND TRANSMISSION

This chapter includes service procedures for the centrifugal clutch, the transmission and the subtransmission (used on some models).

Tables 1-4 are at the end of the chapter.

CENTRIFUGAL CLUTCH

The clutch design varies among the different models. Each clutch type is covered in a separate procedure. Within each of the clutch assembly types there are variations, so pay particular attention to the location and positioning of the friction discs, the clutch plates and to any spacers, washers and springs. Make sure they are assembled in the correct location. Always refer to the exploded view drawing relating to the specific model and year on which you are working.

Operation

The centrifugal clutch is a wet multi-plate type which operates immersed in the engine oil. It is mounted on the right-hand end of the transmission main shaft. The drive plate is splined to the transmission main shaft and the outer clutch housing can rotate freely on the main shaft. The outer clutch housing is geared to the crankshaft by the primary driven gear. The clutch is released by gearshift pedal movement and engagement is achieved by centrifugal effect as engine speed increases.

The clutch release mechanism is mounted within the right-hand crankcase cover.

Removal/Disassembly (70 cc)

The centrifugal clutch shown in **Figure 1** is used on the 1973-1974 ATC70.

The centrifugal clutch shown in **Figure 2** is found on the 1978-on ATC70.

1. Drain the engine oil as described in Chapter Three.
2. Remove the bolts securing the right-hand crankcase cover. Hold the rear brake lever down and remove the cover and the gasket. Don't lose the locating dowels.
3. Remove the ball retainer (**Figure 3**) and the spring.
4. Remove the oil guide and the spring (**Figure 4**).
5. Remove the clutch release lever (**Figure 5**).
6. Remove the cam plate assembly (**Figure 6**).

> *NOTE*
> *The following steps are shown with the engine removed. The clutch outer housing can be removed with this assembly installed in the frame.*

7. Remove the bearing (**Figure 7**) from the clutch outer cover.
8. Remove the screws (**Figure 8**) securing clutch outer cover and remove the cover.
9. Straighten out the locking tab on the lockwasher.
10. Place a copper washer (or copper penny) into mesh with the primary driven gear and the primary drive gear. This will keep the clutch housing from

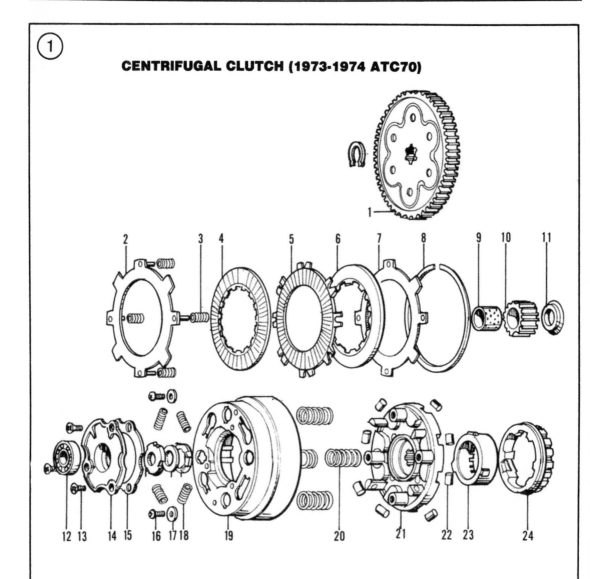

CENTRIFUGAL CLUTCH (1973-1974 ATC70)

1. Primary driven gear
2. Clutch plate A
3. Spring
4. Friction disc A
5. Friction disc B
6. Friction disc A
7. Clutch plate B
8. Circlip
9. Center guide bushing
10. Primary drive gear
11. Collar
12. Bearing
13. Screw
14. Clutch cover
15. Gasket
16. Screw
17. Washer
18. Damper spring
19. Clutch outer housing
20. Clutch spring
21. Drive plate
22. Roller
23. Drive gear outer
24. Clutch center

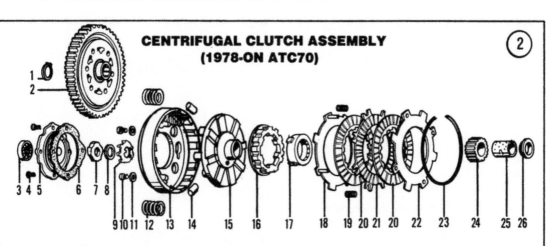

**CENTRIFUGAL CLUTCH ASSEMBLY
(1978-ON ATC70)**

1. Circlip	10. Screw	18. Clutch plate A
2. Primary drive gear	11. Washer	19. Clutch plate coil spring
3. Bearing	12. Clutch spring	20. Friction disc A
4. Screw	13. Clutch outer housing	21. Friction disc B
5. Clutch cover	14. Roller	22. Clutch plate B
6. Gasket	15. Drive plate	23. Circlip
7. Locknut (14 mm)	16. Clutch center	24. Primary drive gear
8. Washer	17. Drive gear outer	25. Center guide bushing
9. Lockwasher		26. Collar

turning during the next step. If the engine is partially disassembled, install a socket drive extension or piece of smooth metal rod into the piston pin hole in the connecting rod to keep the crankshaft and clutch from turning.

NOTE
Clutch outer housing locknut removal requires a special tool available from a Honda dealer (14 mm Locknut Wrench part No. 07716-0010100) or the double pin spanner that is available from most motorcycle supply stores.

11. Remove the locknut, conical lockwasher and lockwasher securing the clutch outer housing.
12. Remove the clutch outer housing and the copper washer from the engine. The primary drive gear may stay in place on the crankshaft. There is no need to remove it.

NOTE
*If the primary drive gear does come off, don't lose the center guide bushing and collar (**Figure 9**) on the crankshaft. It is not necessary to remove them.*

13. From the backside of the clutch outer housing, press down on the clutch plate "B" (A, **Figure 10**).
14. With a screwdriver, work the set spring (B, **Figure 10**) out of the grooves in the clutch outer housing and remove the set spring.
15. Remove the clutch plates and friction plates from the clutch outer housing.

NOTE
Don't lose the small coil springs mounted onto the pins on clutch plate "A".

16. Remove the clutch center and the drive gear outer.
17. Remove the rollers from the drive plate.
18. Remove the damper springs (**Figure 11**) from the front of the clutch outer housing where they are indexed into the fingers of the drive plate.
19. Loosen the Philips screws (**Figure 12**) in a crisscross pattern and remove the screws and washers securing the drive plate to the clutch outer housing. Remove the drive plate and the drive plate springs.
20. Inspect the clutch components as described in this chapter.

Assembly/Installation (70 cc)

NOTE
If either or both friction discs and clutch plates have been replaced with new ones, apply new engine oil to all surfaces to

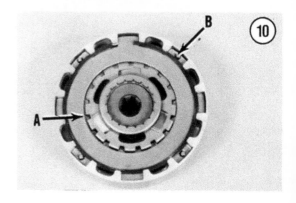

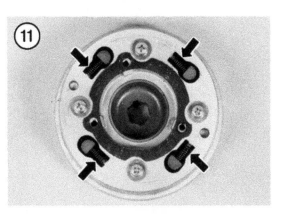

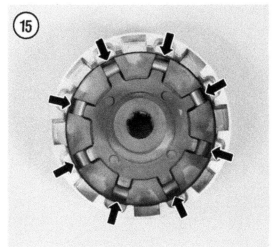

5

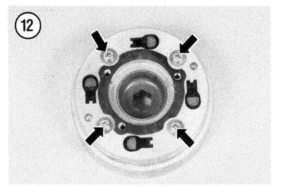

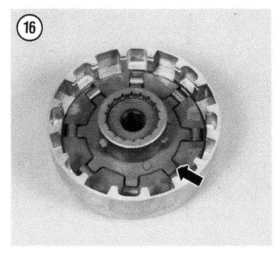

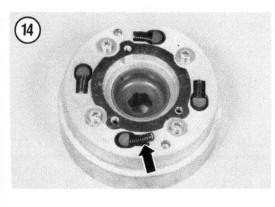

avoid having the clutch lock up when used for the first time.

1. Assemble the clutch outer housing on your workbench.

2. Install the drive plate springs (**Figure 13**) onto the drive plate.

3. Set the clutch outer housing onto the drive plate springs and the drive plate.

4. Install the Phillips head screws and washers. Securely tighten the screws in a crisscross pattern.

5. Install the damper springs into the front of the clutch housing and into the recesses in the fingers of the drive plate (**Figure 14**).

6. Turn the clutch outer housing over and install the drive plate.

7. Install all rollers into the recesses in the drive plate (**Figure 15**).

8. Install the drive gear outer (**Figure 16**) and the clutch center (**Figure 17**).

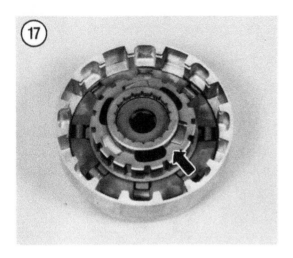

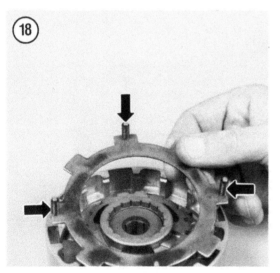

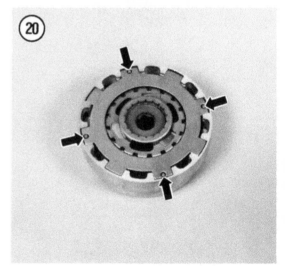

NOTE
Make sure the 2 parts mesh properly.

9. Install the small coil springs onto the pins on clutch plate "A" (**Figure 18**).

10A. On 1973-1974 models, install clutch plate "A" (**Figure 19**), friction disc "A," friction disc "B," clutch disc "A" and clutch plate "B." Make sure the small holes in the tabs on clutch plate "B" are indexed into the pins of clutch plate "A" (**Figure 20**).

NOTE
Friction disc "B" has notches cut into all tabs to clear the small springs installed on clutch plate "A."

10B. On 1978-on models, install clutch plate "A" (**Figure 19**), the clutch friction disc "A," friction disc "B," another friction disc "A" and clutch plate "B." Make sure the small holes in the tabs are indexed into the pins of clutch plate "A" (**Figure 20**).

11. Push down on clutch plate "B" and install the set spring into the backside of the clutch outer housing. Work the set spring into the grooves in the clutch outer housing and make sure it is properly seated.

12. Make sure the center guide bushing and collar (**Figure 9**) are installed onto the crankshaft.

13. If removed, install the primary drive gear (**Figure 21**) onto the crankshaft.

14. If removed, install the drive gear and circlip (**Figure 22**).

15. Install the clutch assembly onto the crankshaft.

16. Install the lockwasher (**Figure 23**) and the additional conical lockwasher with the "OUTSIDE" mark (**Figure 24**) facing out toward the outside of the clutch assembly.

17. Place a copper washer (or copper penny) into mesh with the primary drive gear and the primary driven gear. If the engine is partially disassembled, install a socket drive extension or smooth metal rod into the piston pin hole in the connecting rod to keep the crankshaft and clutch from turning.

18. Install the locknut (**Figure 25**) and tighten to 35-45 N•m (28-33 ft.-lb.).

19. Bend one locking tab down into one of the grooves in the locknut (**Figure 26**). If the locking tab will not fit into a groove, tighten the locknut (*do not loosen*) until a locking tab will fit.

20. Install the clutch outer cover and new gasket. Tighten the screws securely.

21. Install the bearing (**Figure 7**) into the clutch outer cover.

22. Install the cam plate assembly (**Figure 6**).

23. Install the clutch release lever (**Figure 5**).

24. Install the spring and oil guide (**Figure 4**).

25. Apply a light coat of grease to the spring to hold the spring in place. Install the spring and the ball retainer (**Figure 3**).

26. Install the dowel pins (**Figure 27**) and a new crankcase cover gasket.

27. Hold the rear brake pedal down and install the right-hand crankcase cover. Install the screws and tighten in a crisscross pattern until they are secure.

CAUTION
Do not install any of the crankcase cover screws until the crankcase cover is snug up against the crankcase surface. Do not try to force the cover into place with screw pressure. If the cover will not fit up against the crankcase, remove the crankcase cover and repeat Step 27.

28. Refill the engine with the recommended type and quantity of oil; refer to Chapter Three.

29. Adjust the clutch as described in Chapter Three.

Removal/Disassembly (90-125 cc)

The centrifugal clutch shown in **Figure 28** is used on the following models:

   a. All ATC90.

   b. All ATC110.

   c. ATC125M.

1. Drain the engine oil as described in Chapter Three.

2. Remove the bolts securing the right-hand crankcase cover.

3. Remove the ball retainer (**Figure 29**) and the spring.

4. Remove the oil guide and the spring.

5. Remove the clutch release lever (**Figure 30**).

6. Remove the cam plate assembly (**Figure 31**).

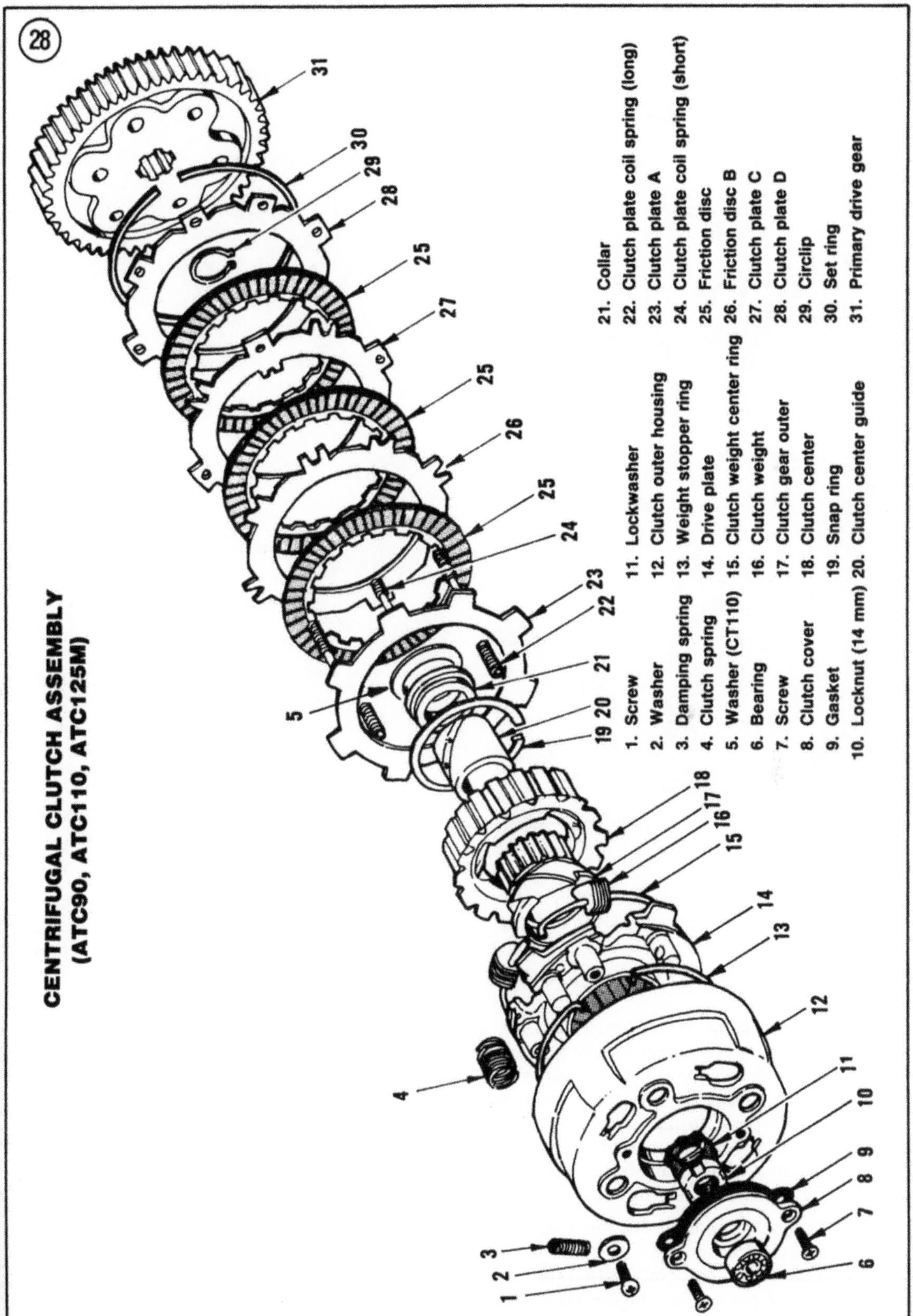

CENTRIFUGAL CLUTCH ASSEMBLY
(ATC90, ATC110, ATC125M)

1. Screw
2. Washer
3. Damping spring
4. Clutch spring
5. Washer (CT110)
6. Bearing
7. Screw
8. Clutch cover
9. Gasket
10. Locknut (14 mm)
11. Lockwasher
12. Clutch outer housing
13. Weight stopper ring
14. Drive plate
15. Clutch weight center ring
16. Clutch weight
17. Clutch gear outer
18. Clutch center
19. Snap ring
20. Clutch center guide
21. Collar
22. Clutch plate coil spring (long)
23. Clutch plate A
24. Clutch plate coil spring (short)
25. Friction disc
26. Friction disc B
27. Clutch plate C
28. Clutch plate D
29. Circlip
30. Set ring
31. Primary drive gear

5

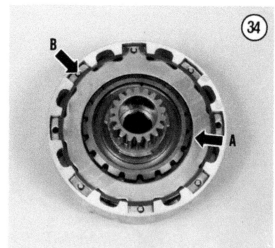

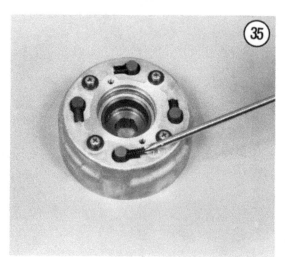

7. Remove the screws securing the clutch outer cover (**Figure 32**) and remove the cover and the bearing.

8. Straighten out the locking tab on the lockwasher.

9. Place a copper washer (or copper penny) into mesh with the primary driven gear and the primary drive gear. This will keep the clutch housing from turning during the next step. If the engine is partially disassembled, install a socket drive extension or piece of smooth metal rod into the piston pin hole in the connecting rod to keep the crankshaft and clutch from turning.

10. The clutch outer housing locknut removal requires a special tool available from a Honda dealer (Locknut Wrench part No. 07916-3710000) or a 16 mm double pin spanner (**Figure 33**) that is available from most motorcycle supply stores.

11. Remove the locknut and lockwasher securing the clutch outer housing in place. Remove the clutch outer housing and the copper washer from the engine.

12. From the backside of the clutch outer housing, press down on clutch plate "D" (A, **Figure 34**).

13. With a screwdriver, work the set ring (B, **Figure 34**) out of the grooves in the clutch outer housing and remove the set ring.

14. Remove the clutch plates and friction plates from the clutch outer housing.

NOTE
Don't lose the small coil springs mounted onto the pins on clutch plate "A."

15. Remove the clutch center assembly.

16. Remove the damper springs (**Figure 35**) from the front of the clutch outer housing.

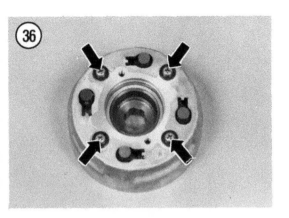

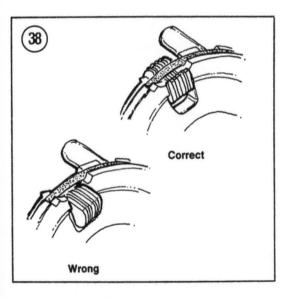

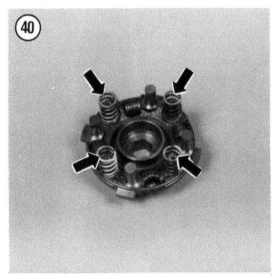

Assembly/Installation (90-125 cc)

NOTE
If either or both friction discs and clutch plates have been replaced with new ones, apply new engine oil to all surfaces to avoid having the clutch lock up when used for the first time.

1. Assemble the clutch outer housing on your workbench.
2. If the clutch weight assembly (A, **Figure 37**) was removed from the drive plate (B, **Figure 37**), the clutch weight assembly must be reinstalled with the weights placed as shown in **Figure 38** and **Figure 39**.
3. Install the drive plate springs (**Figure 40**) onto the drive plate.
4. Set the clutch outer housing onto the drive plate springs and the drive plate.

17. Loosen the Phillips screws (**Figure 36**) in a crisscross pattern then remove the screws and washers securing the drive plate assembly to the clutch other housing. Remove the drive plate assembly and the drive plate springs.
18. Inspect the clutch components as described in this chapter.

5. Install the Phillips head screws and washers (**Figure 36**). Securely tighten the screws in a crisscross pattern.

6. Install the damper springs into the front of the clutch outer housing and into the recesses in the fingers of the drive plate (**Figure 35**).

7. Install the short length small coil springs (A, **Figure 41**) on the middle pins of clutch plate "A." Install the long length small coil springs (B, **Figure 41**) onto the other pins of clutch plate "A."

8. Turn the clutch outer housing over and install the clutch plate "A" (**Figure 42**).

9. Install the clutch center assembly (**Figure 43**).

10. Install clutch plates and friction discs as follows:

   a. Install a friction disc (**Figure 44**) then clutch plate "B" (**Figure 45**).

   b. Install a friction disc and clutch plate "C." Align clutch plate "C" so the tabs with the small holes are installed onto clutch plate "A" pins where the *short* coil springs are installed (**Figure 46**).

   c. Install a friction disc and then clutch plate "D" (**Figure 47**). Make sure the small holes in the tabs of clutch plate "D" are indexed into the pins of clutch plate "A."

11. Push down on clutch plate "D" and install the set spring into the backside of the clutch outer housing. Work the set spring into the grooves in the clutch outer housing and make sure it is properly seated.

CAUTION
Install the set spring ends into one of the recesses with sharp corners as shown in

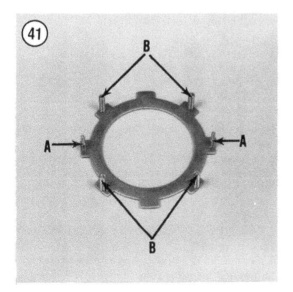

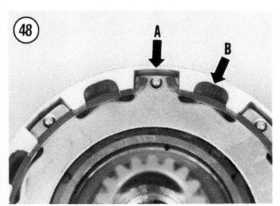

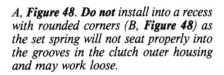

*A, **Figure 48**. **Do not** install into a recess with rounded corners (B, **Figure 48**) as the set spring will not seat properly into the grooves in the clutch outer housing and may work loose.*

12. Make sure the center guide bushing is installed in the primary drive gear.

13. If removed, install the collar and conical washer with the "OUTSIDE" mark facing out toward the clutch assembly onto the crankshaft.

14. Install the lockwasher (**Figure 49**).

15. Place a copper washer (or copper penny) into mesh with the primary drive gear and the primary driven gear. If the engine is partially disassembled, install a socket drive extenson (A, **Figure 50**) or smooth metal rod into the piston pin hole in the connecting rod to keep the crankshaft and clutch from turning.

16. Install the locknut (B, **Figure 50**) and tighten to 35-45 N•m (28-33 ft.-lb.). Use the same tool setup used in Step 10, *Removal.*

17. Bend one locking tab down into one of the grooves in the locknut (**Figure 51**). If the locking tab will not fit into a groove, tighten the locknut (*do not loosen*) until a locking tab will fit.

18. Install the clutch outer cover, bearing and new gasket. Tighten the screws securely (**Figure 32**).

19. Install the cam plate assembly (**Figure 31**).
20. Install the clutch release lever (**Figure 30**).
21. Install the spring and oil guide.
22. Apply a light coat of grease to the spring to hold the spring in place. Install the spring and the ball retainer (**Figure 29**).
23. Install the dowel pins and a new crankcase cover gasket.
24. Install the right-hand crankcase cover. Install the screws and tighten in a crisscross pattern until they are secure.

> *CAUTION*
> *Do not install any of the crankcase cover screws until the crankcase cover is snug up against the crankcase surface. Do not try to force the cover into place with screw pressure. If the cover will not fit up against the crankcase, remove the crankcase cover and repeat Step 24.*

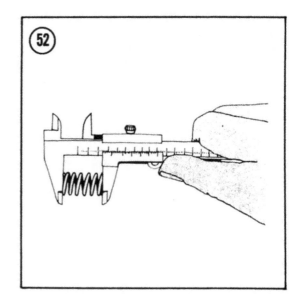

25. Refill the engine with the recommended type and quantity of oil; refer to Chapter Three.
26. Adjust the clutch as described in Chapter Three.

CLUTCH INSPECTION (ALL MODELS)

Refer to **Table 1** for clutch specifications.
1. Clean all parts in a petroleum based solvent such as kerosene and thoroughly dry with compressed air.
2. Measure the free length of each clutch spring as shown in **Figure 52**. If any of the springs are worn to the service limit shown in **Table 1** they should be replaced. Replace all springs as a set.
3. Measure the thickness of each friction disc at several places around the disc as shown in **Figure 53**.
4. Replace any friction disc that is worn to the service limit shown in **Table 1**. For optimum performance, replace all friction discs as a set even if only a few need replacement.
5. Check the clutch plates for warpage on a surface plate such as a piece of plate glass (**Figure 54**). Replace any clutch plates that are warped to the service limit shown in **Table 1**. For optimum performance, replace all plates as a set even if only a few need replacement.
6. On 70 cc models, inspect the ramps in the drive plate (A, **Figure 55**) and the grooves in the clutch outer housing (B, **Figure 55**). If either show signs of wear or galling they should be replaced.
7. On 70 cc models, inspect the splines of the drive gear outer (A, **Figure 56**) and the clutch center (B, **Figure 56**). If either show signs of wear or damage they should be replaced.

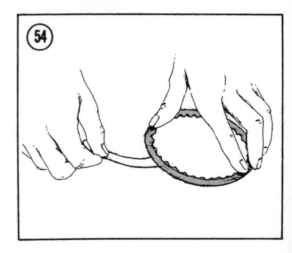

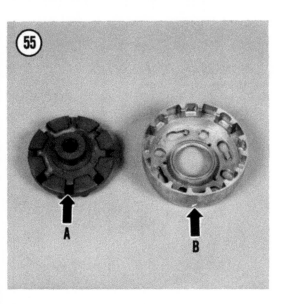

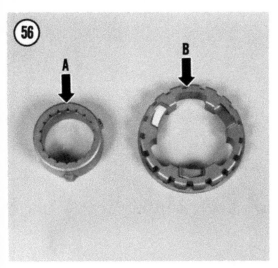

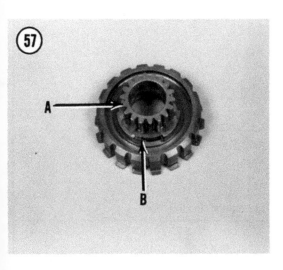

8. On 90-125 cc clutch models, inspect the splines of the clutch outer housing (A, **Figure 57**). If it show signs of wear or damage they should be replaced. This is a 2-part assembly; if disassembly is necessary, remove the circlip (B, **Figure 57**) and separate the 2 parts.

9. On 90-125 cc models, inspect the centrifugal weights on the drive plate (**Figure 39**). They must move freely or be replaced.

CLUTCH RELEASE MECHANISM

The clutch release mechanism is located within the right-hand crankcase cover (**Figure 58**).

1. Drain the engine oil as described in Chapter Three.

2. Remove the bolts securing the right-hand crankcase cover and remove the cover and the gasket. Don't lose the locating dowels.

3. From the exterior of the crankcase cover, remove the locknut and washer from the adjuster screw.

4. Within the right-hand crankcase cover, remove the adjuster screw and the O-ring seal.

5. Install by reversing these removal steps, noting the following.

6. Refill the engine with the recommended type and quantity of engine oil; refer to Chapter Three.

7. Adjust the clutch as described in Chapter Three.

EXTERNAL SHIFT MECHANISM

The external shift mechanism is located on the right-hand side of the engine, under the crankcase cover and next to the clutch assembly. The mechanism can be removed with the engine in the frame. To remove the shift drum and shift forks it is necessary to remove the engine and split the crankcase. This procedure is covered under *Shift Drum and Shift Forks* in this chapter.

The gearshift lever is subject to a lot of abuse. If the ATC has hit a large rock or other obstruction, the gearshift lever may have been hit and the shift shaft bent. It is very hard to straighten the shaft without subjecting the crankcase to abnormal stress where the shaft enters the case. If the shaft is bent enough to prevent it from being withdrawn from the crankcase, there is little recourse but to cut the shaft off with a hacksaw very close to the crankcase. It is much cheaper in the long run to replace the shaft than risk damaging a very expensive crankcase.

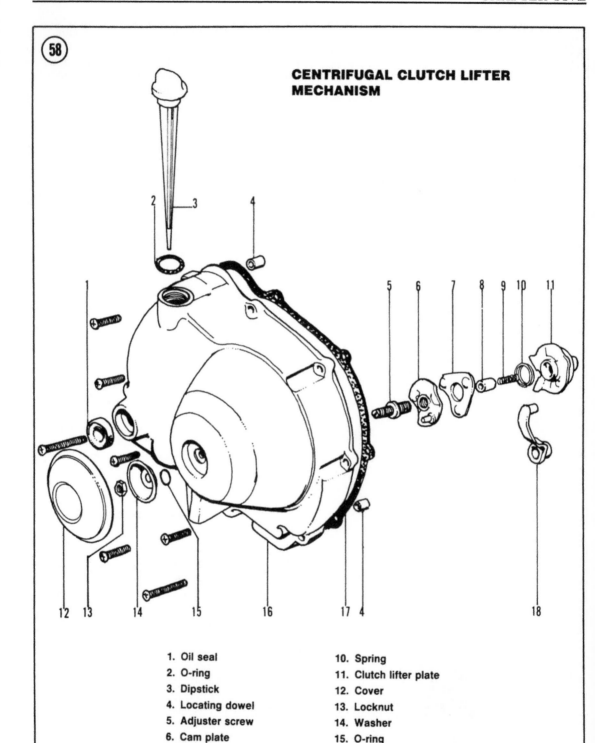

58

CENTRIFUGAL CLUTCH LIFTER MECHANISM

1. Oil seal
2. O-ring
3. Dipstick
4. Locating dowel
5. Adjuster screw
6. Cam plate
7. Ball retainer
8. Oil guide
9. Spring
10. Spring
11. Clutch lifter plate
12. Cover
13. Locknut
14. Washer
15. O-ring
16. Cover
17. Gasket
18. Clutch release lever

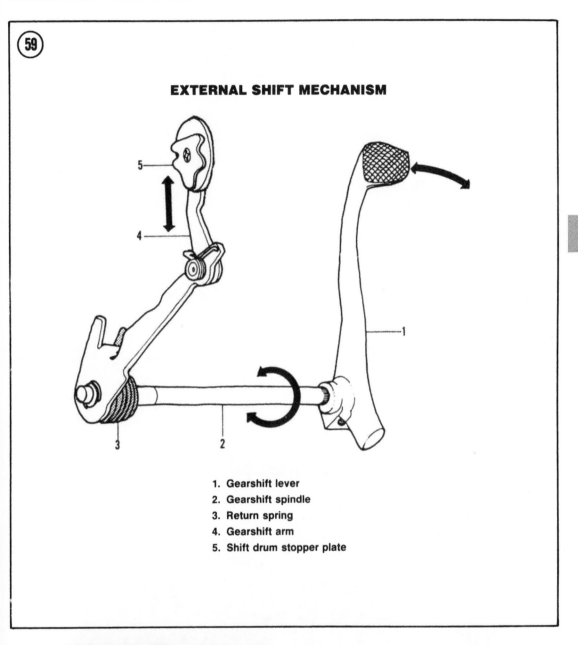

EXTERNAL SHIFT MECHANISM

5

1. Gearshift lever
2. Gearshift spindle
3. Return spring
4. Gearshift arm
5. Shift drum stopper plate

Removal

Refer to **Figure 59** for this procedure.

1. Place the ATC on level ground and set the parking brake or block the wheels so the vehicle will not roll in either direction.

2. Drain the engine oil as described in Chapter Three.

3. Remove the clutch assembly as described in this chapter.

4. Remove the circlip (**Figure 60**) securing the primary driven gear. Slide the primary driven gear off of the transmission main shaft.

5. Remove the bolt securing the gear shift lever (**Figure 61**) on the left-hand side and remove the gearshift lever.

6. Loosen the bolt securing the stopper arm. Unhook the return spring from the arm (**Figure 62**) and let the arm pivot down out of the way.

NOTE
See the introduction to this procedure if the assembly is difficult to remove.

7. Disengage the gearshift lever portion of the lever from the shift drum (**Figure 63**) and withdraw the gearshift spindle assembly.

8. Remove the screw (**Figure 64**) securing the stopper plate to the shift drum and remove the stopper plate. Don't lose the loose pins on the shift drum.

Inspection

1. Inspect the return springs on the gearshift spindle assembly (**Figure 65**). If broken or weak they must be replaced.

2. Inspect the gearshift lever assembly shaft (**Figure 66**) for bending, wear or other damage; replace if necessary.

3. Inspect the ramps on the stopper plate. They must be smooth and free of burrs or cracks. Replace if necessary.

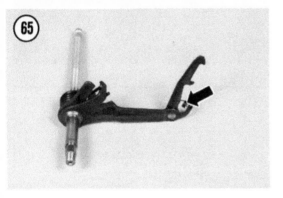

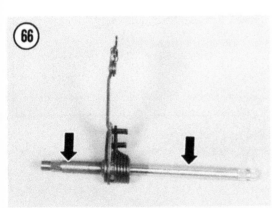

Installation

1. Make sure all the pins are installed in the shift drum.

2. Install the gearshift spindle assembly. Make sure the return spring is correctly positioned onto the stopper pin in the crankcase.

3. Engage the gearshift lever portion of the lever into the shift drum pins.

4. Align the recess in the back of the stopper plate with the long pin in the shift drum. Install the stopper plate and tighten the bolt securely.

5. Correctly position the return spring onto the stopper arm. Move the stopper arm into position and tighten the stopper arm bolt securely.

6. Install the primary driven gear onto the transmission main shaft. From the other side of the engine, push on the main shaft and install the circlip. The main shaft must be pushed on slightly so that the circlip will seat correctly into the groove in the main shaft.

7. Install the clutch assembly as described in this chapter.

8. Refill the engine with the correct type and quantity of oil; refer to Chapter Three.

9. Adjust the clutch as described in Chapter Three.

DRIVE SPROCKET

Removal/Installation (70 cc)

1. Place the ATC on level ground.

2. Remove the seat/rear fender assembly.

3. Remove the bolts securing the under plate and the chain cover (**Figure 67**).

4. Shift the transmission into NEUTRAL and remove the E-clip and the neutral indicator (A, **Figure 68**).

5. Remove the recoil starter assembly and left-hand crankcase cover as an assembly (B, **Figure 68**).

6. Loosen the bolts on the drive chain tensioner (**Figure 69**).

7. Shift the transmission into any gear. Push the ATC forward until the master link is visible next to the drive sprocket.

8. Have an assistant hold the rear brake on while you loosen the bolts (A, **Figure 70**) securing the drive sprocket and drive sprocket holding plate.

9. Remove the drive chain master link (B, **Figure 70**).

10. Rotate the holding plate in either direction to disengage it from the splines on the transmission countershaft; slide off the holding plate and drive sprocket.

11. Install by reversing these removal steps, noting the following.

12. Install a new drive chain master link so that the closed end of the clip is facing the direction of chain travel (**Figure 71**).

13. Adjust the drive chain as described in Chapter Three.

Removal/Installation
(All 90 and 125 cc; 1979-1980 and 1984 110 cc)

1. Remove the subtransmission as described in this chapter.

2. Remove the left-hand crankcase cover as described in Chapter Four.

3. Loosen the drive chain adjusting nut.

4. Loosen the rear axle bearing holder and move the rear axle forward to allow slack in the drive chain.

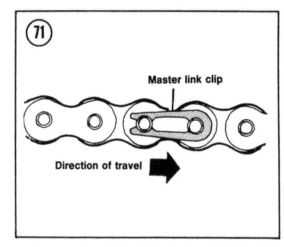

Master link clip

Direction of travel

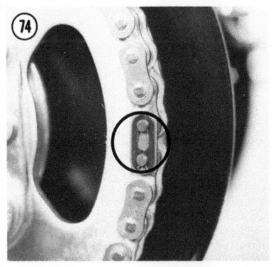

5. Remove the left-hand rear wheel and hub as described in Chapter Eight.

6. On ATC125M models, remove the carburetor, crankcase vent and battery vent tubes (A, **Figure 72**) from the drive chain cover.

7. Remove the bolts securing the axle seal cover (B, **Figure 72**) and slide off the cover.

8. Remove the bolts securing the drive chain cover and remove the cover.

NOTE
*On ATC125M models, there is one additional bolt (**Figure 73**) at the rear of the cover.*

9. Remove the drive chain master link (**Figure 74**).

10. On models equipped with O-rings, don't lose the 2 O-ring seals (**Figure 75**) on the link pins.

11. Slide off the sprocket (**Figure 76**) and, on ATC110 and ATC125M models, the bushings.

12. Install by reversing these removal steps, noting the following.

13. On models equipped with O-rings, be sure to install the 2 O-ring seals (**Figure 75**) on the link pins.

14. Install a new drive chain master link so that the closed end of the clip is facing the direction of chain travel (**Figure 71**).

15. Adjust the drive chain and rear brake as described in Chapter Three.

Removal/Installation
(1981-1983 ATC110)

The factory equipped drive chain is a continous loop with no master link. To remove the drive sprocket (as well as the drive chain or rear axle) it

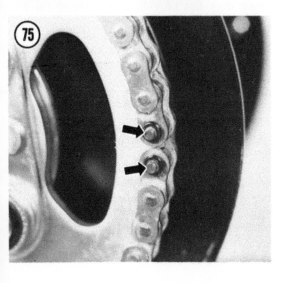

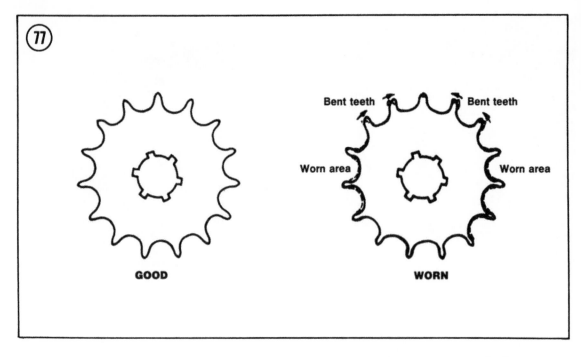

is necessary to partially disassemble the rear axle. Consider replacing the factory drive chain with an aftermarket type chain equipped with a master link.

1. Remove the recoil starter and alternator as described in Chapter Seven.
2. Remove the subtransmission as described in this chapter.
3. Remove the left-hand crankcase cover as described in Chapter Four.
4. Remove the rear axle, drive chain, drive sprocket and bushings as an assembly as described in Chapter Eight.
5. Install by reversing these removal steps, noting the following.
6. Adjust the drive chain as described in Chapter Three.

Inspection

1. Inspect the teeth on the drive sprocket. If the teeth are visibly worn (**Figure 77**), replace the sprocket with a new one.
2. If the sprocket requires replacement, the drive chain is probably worn also and should be replaced.
3. On ATC110 and ATC125M models, measure the inside and outside diameter of the drive sprocket bushings. Replace if worn to the following service limit dimensions:
    a. Inside diameter: 19.94 mm (0.785 in.).
    b. Outside diameter: 21.90 mm (0.862 in.).

TRANSMISSION AND INTERNAL SHIFT MECHANISM

To gain access to the transmission and internal shift mechanism it is necessary to remove the engine and split the crankcase. Once the crankcase has been split, removal of the transmission and shift drum and forks is a simple task of pulling the assemblies up and out of the crankcase. Installation is more complicated and is covered more completely than the removal sequence.

Refer to **Table 2** for specifications for the internal shift mechanism and **Table 3** for specifications for the transmission components. Honda does not provide specifications for all models.

Different transmissions are used among the various models. They are covered in separate procedures; be sure to use the correct procedure for your specific model.

PRELIMINARY TRANSMISSION INSPECTION (ALL MODELS)

After the transmission shaft assemblies have been removed from the crankcase halves, clean and inspect the assemblies prior to disassembling them. Place the assembled shaft into a large can or plastic bucket and thoroughly clean with a petroleum based solvent such as kerosene and a stiff brush. Dry with compressed air or let it sit on rags to drip dry. Repeat for the other shaft assembly.

1. After they have been cleaned, visually inspect the components of the assemblies for excessive wear. Any burrs, pitting or roughness on the teeth of a gear will cause wear on the mating gear. Minor roughness can be cleaned up with an oilstone but there's little point in attempting to remove deep scars.

NOTE
Defective gears should be replaced. It's a good idea to replace the mating gear on the other shaft even though it may not show as much wear or damage.

2. Carefully check the engagement dogs. If any are chipped, worn, rounded or missing, the affected gear must be replaced.
3. Rotate the transmission bearings in the crankcases by hand. Refer to **Figure 78**. Check for roughness, noise and radial play. Any bearing that is suspect should be replaced. Refer to *Bearing and Oil Seal Replacement* in Chapter Four.
4. If the transmission shafts are satisfactory and are not going to be disassembled, apply assembly oil or engine oil to all components and reinstall them in the crankcase as described in this chapter.

NOTE
If disassembling a used, well run-in transmission for the first time by yourself, pay particular attention to any additional shims that may have been added by a previous owner. These may have been added to take up the tolerance of worn components and must be reinstalled in the same position since the shims have developed a wear

pattern. *If new parts are going to be installed these shims may be eliminated. This is something you will have to determine upon reassembly.*

3-SPEED TRANSMISSION AND INTERNAL SHIFT MECHANISM (70 CC)

The 3-speed transmission shown in **Figure 79** is used on the 1973-1981 ATC70.

Removal/Installation

1. Remove the engine and split the crankcase as described in Chapter Four.
2. Pull the shift fork shaft assembly, main shaft assembly and the countershaft assembly up and out of the crankcase as an assembly.
3. Disassemble and inspect the shift forks and transmission assemblies as described in this chapter.
4. Coat all bearings and sliding surfaces of both transmission assemblies and the shift drum with assembly oil.
5. Install the 2 transmission assemblies and the shift drum assembly by meshing them together in their proper relationship to each other. Install them in the left-hand crankcase. Hold the thrust washer on the main shaft in place with your fingers (**Figure 80**). Make sure it is still positioned correctly after the assemblies are completely installed. After both assemblies are installed, tap on the end of both shafts and the shift drum assembly (**Figure 81**) with a plastic or rubber mallet to make sure they are completely seated.

NOTE
If the thrust washer on the end of the main shaft does not seat correctly it will hold the transmission shaft up a little and prevent the crankcase halves from seating completely.

6. Spin the transmission shafts and shift through the gears using the shift drum. Make sure you can shift into all gears. This is the time to find that something may be installed incorrectly—not after the crankcase is completely assembled.

NOTE
This procedure is best done with the aid of a helper as the assemblies are loose and won't spin very easily. Have the helper spin the transmission shaft while you turn the shift drum through all the gears.

7. Make sure that the thrust washer (**Figure 82**) is installed on the countershaft.
8. Assemble the crankcase as described in Chapter Four.

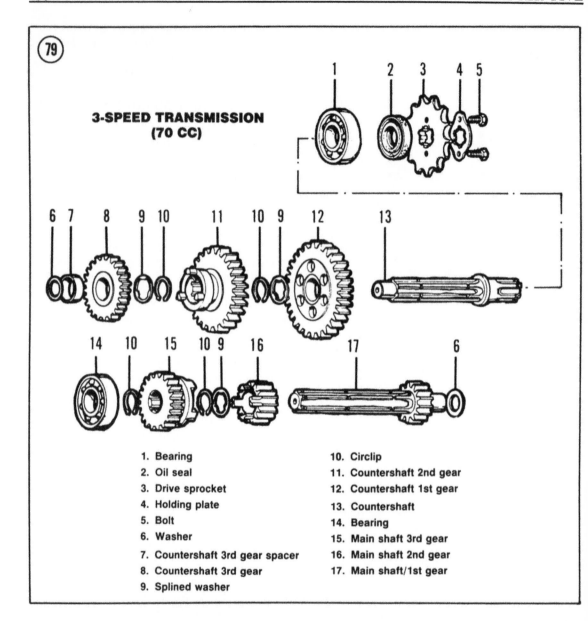

3-SPEED TRANSMISSION (70 CC)

1. Bearing
2. Oil seal
3. Drive sprocket
4. Holding plate
5. Bolt
6. Washer
7. Countershaft 3rd gear spacer
8. Countershaft 3rd gear
9. Splined washer
10. Circlip
11. Countershaft 2nd gear
12. Countershaft 1st gear
13. Countershaft
14. Bearing
15. Main shaft 3rd gear
16. Main shaft 2nd gear
17. Main shaft/1st gear

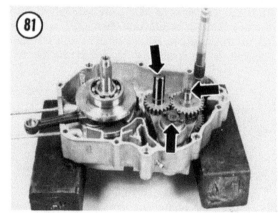

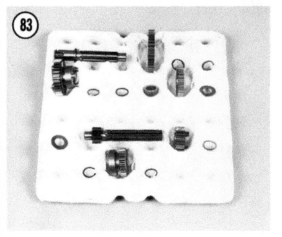

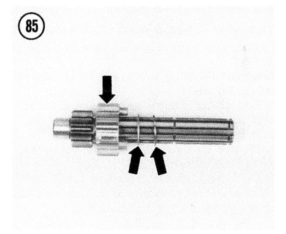

Main Shaft Disassembly/Inspection/Assembly

Refer to **Figure 79** for this procedure.

> *NOTE*
> *A helpful "tool" that should be used for transmission disassembly is a large egg flat (the type that restaurants get their eggs in). As you remove a part from the shaft set it in one of the depressions in the same position from which it was removed (**Figure 83**). This is an easy way to remember the correct relationship of all parts.*

1. Clean the shaft as described under *Preliminary Transmission Inspection (All Models)* in this chapter.
2. Remove the circlip and slide off the 3rd gear.
3. Remove the circlip and splined washer.
4. Slide off the 2nd gear.
5. From the other end of the shaft, remove the thrust washer.

6. Check each gear for excessive wear, burrs, pitting or chipped or missing teeth. Make sure the lugs (**Figure 84**) on the gears are in good condition.

> *NOTE*
> *Defective gears should be replaced. It is a good idea to replace the mating gear on the countershaft even though it may not show as much wear or damage.*

> *NOTE*
> *The 1st gear is part of the shaft. If the gear is defective, the shaft must be replaced.*

7. Make sure that all gears slide smoothly on the main shaft splines.

> *NOTE*
> *It is a good idea to replace all circlips every other time the transmission is disassembled to ensure proper gear alignment.*

8. Slide on the 2nd gear and install the splined washer and circlip (**Figure 85**).

9. Slide on the 3rd gear and install the circlip (**Figure 86**).

10. Onto the other end of the main shaft, slide on the thrust washer (**Figure 87**).

11. Before installation, double-check the placement of all gears (**Figure 88**). Make sure all circlips are seated in the main shaft grooves.

Countershaft Disassembly/Inspection/Assembly

Refer to **Figure 79** for this procedure.

NOTE
*Use the same large egg flat (used on the main shaft disassembly) during the countershaft disassembly (**Figure 83**). This is an easy way to remember the correct relationship of all parts.*

1. Clean the shaft as described under *Preliminary Transmission Inspection (All Models)* in this chapter.

2. Remove the thrust washer, the 3rd gear spacer and the 3rd gear.

3. Slide off the splined washer and remove the circlip.

4. Slide off the 2nd gear.

5. Remove the circlip and splined washer and slide off the 1st gear.

6. Check each gear for excessive wear, burrs, pitting or chipped or missing teeth. Make sure the lugs on the gears are in good condition.

NOTE
Defective gears should be replaced. It is a good idea to replace the mating gear on the main shaft even though it may not show as much wear or damage.

7. Make sure that all gears slide smoothly on the countershaft splines.

NOTE
It is a good idea to replace all circlips every other time the transmission is disassembled to ensure proper gear alignment.

8. Slide on the 1st gear, circlip and splined washer (**Figure 89**).

9. Slide on the 2nd gear, circlip and thrust washer (**Figure 90**).

10. Slide on the 3rd gear (**Figure 91**).

11. Slide on the collar and the thrust washer (**Figure 92**).

12. Before installation, double-check the placement of all gears (**Figure 93**). Make sure the circlips are seated correctly in the countershaft groove.

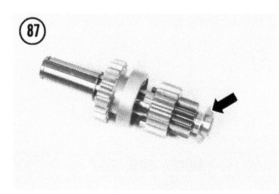

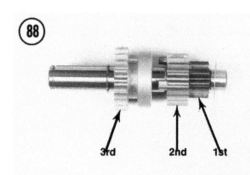

3rd   2nd   1st

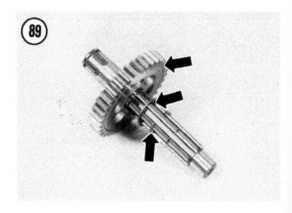

(90)

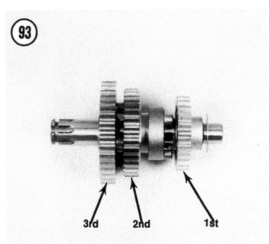

(93)

3rd   2nd   1st

(91)

(94)

(92)

NOTE
*After both transmission shafts have been assembled, mesh the 2 assemblies together in the correct position (**Figure 94**). Check that all gears meet correctly. This is your last check prior to installing the assemblies into the crankcase; make sure they are correctly assembled.*

4-SPEED TRANSMISSION AND INTERNAL SHIFT MECHANISM (70 CC)

The 4-speed transmission shown in **Figure 95** is used on the 1982-on ATC70.

Removal/Installation

1. Remove the engine and split the crankcase as described in Chapter Four.

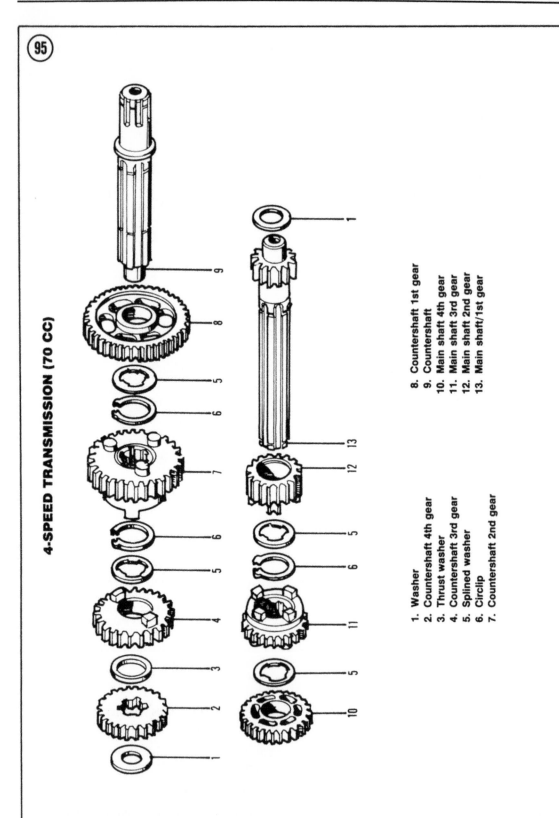

4-SPEED TRANSMISSION (70 CC)

1. Washer
2. Countershaft 4th gear
3. Thrust washer
4. Countershaft 3rd gear
5. Splined washer
6. Circlip
7. Countershaft 2nd gear
8. Countershaft 1st gear
9. Countershaft
10. Main shaft 4th gear
11. Main shaft 3rd gear
12. Main shaft 2nd gear
13. Main shaft/1st gear

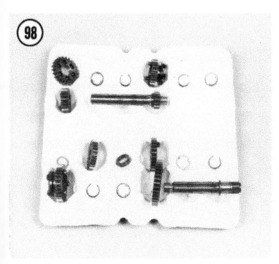

2. Pull the shift fork shaft assembly, main shaft assembly and the countershaft assembly up and out of the crankcase as an assembly.

3. Disassemble and inspect the shift forks and transmission assemblies as described in this chapter.

4. Coat all bearings and sliding surfaces of both transmission assemblies and the shift drum with assembly oil.

5. Install the 2 transmission assemblies and the shift drum assembly by meshing them together in their proper relationship to each other. Install them in the left-hand crankcase. Hold the thrust washer on the main shaft in place with your fingers (**Figure 96**). Make sure it is still positioned correctly after the assemblies are completely installed. After both assemblies are installed, tap on the end of both shafts and the shift drum assembly (**Figure 97**) with a plastic or rubber mallet to make sure they are completely seated.

NOTE
If the thrust washer on the end of the main shaft does not seat correctly it will hold the transmission shaft up a little and prevent the crankcase halves from seating completely.

6. Spin the transmission shafts and shift through the gears using the shift drum. Make sure you can shift into all gears. This is the time to find that something may be installed incorrectly—not after the crankcase is completely assembled.

NOTE
This procedure is best done with the aid of a helper as the assemblies are loose and won't spin very easily. Have the helper spin the transmission shaft while you turn the shift drum through all the gears.

7. Make sure that the thrust washer is installed on the countershaft.

8. Assemble the crankcase as described in Chapter Four.

Main Shaft Disassembly/Inspection/Assembly

Refer to **Figure 95** for this procedure.

NOTE
*A helpful "tool" that should be used for transmission disassembly is a large egg flat (the type that restaurants get their eggs in). As you remove a part from the shaft set it in one of the depressions in the same position from which it was removed (**Figure 98**). This is an easy way to remember the correct relationship of all parts.*

1. Clean the shaft as described under *Preliminary Transmission Inspection (All Models)* in this chapter.

2. Slide off the 4th gear.

3. Slide off the splined washer.

4. Slide off the 3rd gear.

5. Remove the circlip and slide off the splined washer.

6. Slide off the 2nd gear.

7. From the other end of the shaft, remove the thrust washer.

8. Check each gear for excessive wear, burrs, pitting or chipped or missing teeth. Make sure the lugs on the gears are in good condition.

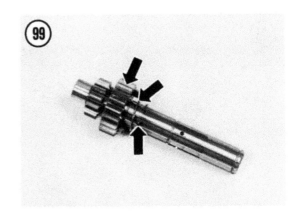

> *NOTE*
> *Defective gears should be replaced. It is a good idea to replace the mating gear on the countershaft even though it may not show as much wear or damage.*

> *NOTE*
> *The 1st gear is part of the shaft. If the gear is defective the shaft must be replaced.*

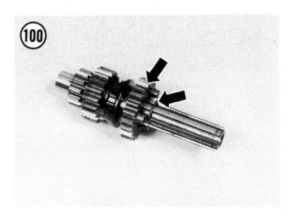

9. Make sure that all gears slide smoothly on the main shaft splines.

> *NOTE*
> *It is a good idea to replace all circlips every other time the transmission is disassembled to ensure proper gear alignment.*

10. Slide on the 2nd gear and install the splined washer and circlip (**Figure 99**).

11. Slide on the 3rd gear and the splined washer (**Figure 100**).

12. Slide on the 4th gear (**Figure 101**).

13. Slide the thrust washer onto the other end of the main shaft.

14. Before installation, double-check the placement of all gears (**Figure 102**). Make sure all circlips are seated correctly in the main shaft grooves.

Countershaft Disassembly/Inspection/Assembly

Refer to **Figure 95** for this procedure.

> *NOTE*
> *Use the same large egg flat (used on the main shaft disassembly) during the countershaft disassembly (**Figure 98**). This is an easy way to remember the correct relationship of all parts.*

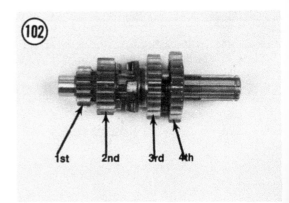

1. Clean the shaft as described under *Preliminary Transmission Inspection (All Models)* in this chapter.

5

2. Remove the thrust washer and slide off the 4th gear.

3. Slide off the thrust washer and the 3rd gear.

4. Slide off the splined washer and remove the circlip.

5. Slide off the 2nd gear.

6. Remove the circlip and splined washer and slide off the 1st gear.

7. Check each gear for excessive wear, burrs, pitting or chipped or missing teeth. Make sure the lugs on the gears are in good condition.

> *NOTE*
> *Defective gears should be replaced. It is a good idea to replace the mating gear on the main shaft even though it may not show as much wear or damage.*

8. Make sure that all gears slide smoothly on the countershaft splines.

> *NOTE*
> *It is a good idea to replace all circlips every other time the transmission is disassembled to ensure proper gear alignment.*

9. Slide on the 1st gear, splined washer and circlip (**Figure 103**).

10. Slide on the 2nd gear, circlip and thrust washer (**Figure 104**).

11. Slide on the 3rd gear and the thrust washer (**Figure 105**).

12. Slide on the 4th gear and the thrust washer (**Figure 106**).

13. Before installation, double-check the placement of all gears (**Figure 107**). Make sure the circlips are seated correctly in the countershaft groove.

NOTE
After both transmission shafts have been assembled, mesh the 2 assemblies together in the correct position (Figure 108). Check that all gears meet correctly. This is your last check prior to installing the assemblies into the crankcase; make sure they are correctly assembled.

4-SPEED TRANSMISSION AND INTERNAL SHIFT MECHANISM (90-125 CC)

The 4-speed transmission shown in **Figure 109** is used on the following models:

a. All ATC90.
b. All ATC110.
c. ATC125M.

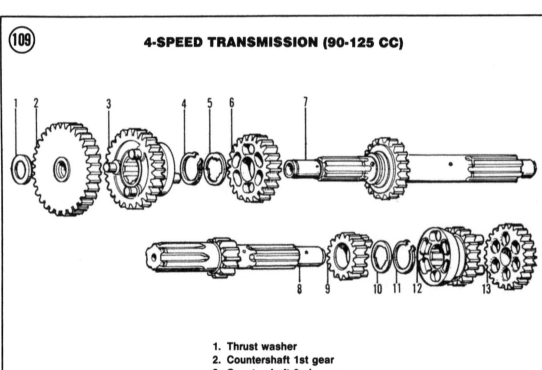

4-SPEED TRANSMISSION (90-125 CC)

1. Thrust washer
2. Countershaft 1st gear
3. Countershaft 2nd gear
4. Circlip
5. Splined washer
6. Countershaft 3rd gear
7. Countershaft/4th gear
8. Main shaft/1st gear
9. Main shaft 2nd gear
10. Splined washer
11. Circlip
12. Main shaft 3rd gear
13. Main shaft 4th gear

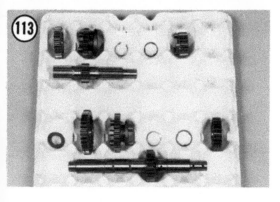

Removal/Installation

1. Remove the engine and split the crankcase as described in Chapter Four.

2. Pull the shift fork shaft assembly, main shaft assembly and the countershaft assembly up and out of the crankcase as an assembly.

3. Disassemble and inspect the shift forks and transmission assemblies as described in this chapter.

4. Coat all bearings and sliding surfaces of both transmission assemblies and the shift drum with assembly oil.

5. Install the 2 transmission assemblies and the shift drum assembly by meshing them together in their proper relationship to each other. Install them in the left-hand crankcase (**Figure 110**). After both assemblies are installed, tap on the end of both shafts and the shift drum assembly (**Figure 111**) with a plastic or rubber mallet to make sure they are completely seated.

> *NOTE*
> *Figure 110 and Figure 111 are shown with the crankshaft assembly removed. It is not necessary to remove the assembly for this procedure.*

6. Spin the transmission shafts and shift through the gears using the shift drum. Make sure you can shift into all gears. This is the time to find that something may be installed incorrectly—not after the crankcase is completely assembled.

> *NOTE*
> *This procedure is best done with the aid of a helper as the assemblies are loose and won't spin very easily. Have the helper spin the transmission shaft while you turn the shift drum through all the gears.*

7. Make sure that the thrust washer (**Figure 112**) is installed on the countershaft.

8. Assemble the crankcase as described in Chapter Four.

Main Shaft Disassembly/Inspection/Assembly

Refer to **Figure 109** for this procedure.

> *NOTE*
> *A helpful "tool" that should be used for transmission disassembly is a large egg flat (the type that restaurants get their eggs in). As you remove a part from the shaft set it in one of the depressions in the same position from which it was removed (**Figure 113**). This is an easy way to remember the correct relationship of all parts.*

1. Clean the shaft as described under *Preliminary Transmission Inspection (All Models)* in this chapter.
2. Slide off the 4th gear and the 3rd gear.
3. Remove the circlip and slide off the splined washer and the 2nd gear.
4. Check each gear for excessive wear, burrs, pitting or chipped or missing teeth. Make sure the lugs (**Figure 114**) on the gears are in good condition.

NOTE
Defective gears should be replaced. It is a good idea to replace the mating gear on the countershaft even though it may not show as much wear or damage.

NOTE
The 1st gear is part of the shaft. If the gear is defective the shaft must be replaced.

5. Make sure that all gears slide smoothly on the main shaft splines.

NOTE
It is a good idea to replace the circlip every other time the transmission is disassembled to ensure proper gear alignment.

6. Slide on the 2nd gear and install the splined washer and circlip (**Figure 115**).
7. Slide on the 3rd gear (**Figure 116**).
8. Slide on the 4th gear (**Figure 117**).
9. Before installation, double-check the placement of all gears (**Figure 118**). Make sure the circlip is seated correctly in the main shaft grooves.

Countershaft Disassembly/Inspection/Assembly

Refer to **Figure 109** for this procedure.

NOTE
*Use the same large egg flat (used on the main shaft disassembly) during the countershaft disassembly (**Figure 113**). This is an easy way to remember the correct relationship of all parts.*

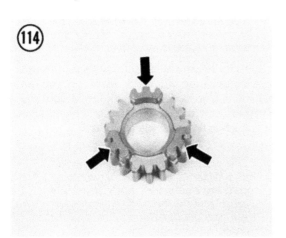

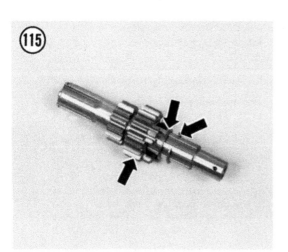

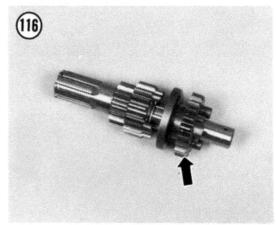

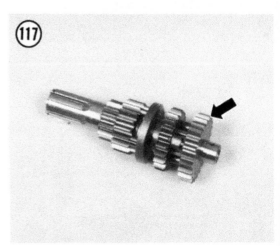

1. Clean the shaft as described under *Preliminary Transmission Inspection (All Models)* in this chapter.
2. Remove the thrust washer and slide off the 1st gear.
3. Slide off the 2nd gear.
4. Remove the circlip and slide off the splined washer and the 3rd gear.
5. Check each gear for excessive wear, burrs, pitting or chipped or missing teeth. Make sure the lugs on the gears are in good condition.

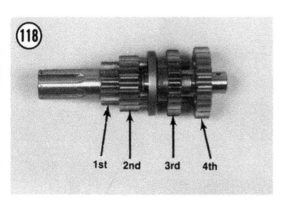

NOTE
Defective gears should be replaced. It is a good idea to replace the mating gear on the main shaft even though it may not show as much wear or damage.

NOTE
The 4th gear is part of the shaft. If the gear is defective the shaft must be replaced.

6. Make sure that all gears slide smoothly on the countershaft splines.

NOTE
It is a good idea to replace the circlip every other time the transmission is disassembled to ensure proper gear alignment.

7. Slide on the 3rd gear and install the circlip and splined washer (**Figure 119**).
8. Slide on the 2nd gear (**Figure 120**).
9. Slide on the 1st gear and the thrust washer (**Figure 121**).
10. Before installation, double-check the placement of all gears (**Figure 122**). Make sure the circlip is seated correctly in the countershaft groove.

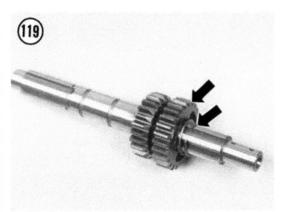

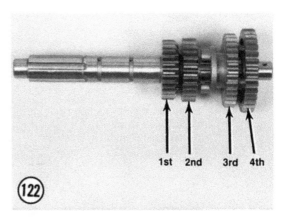

NOTE
After both transmission shafts have been assembled, mesh the 2 assemblies together in the correct position (Figure 123). Check that all gears meet correctly. This is your last check prior to installing the assemblies into the crankcase; make sure they are correctly assembled.

INTERNAL SHIFT MECHANISM (ALL MODELS)

Refer to **Figure 124** for 70 cc models or **Figure 125** for 90-125 cc models for this procedure.

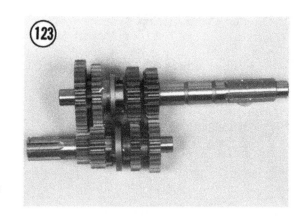

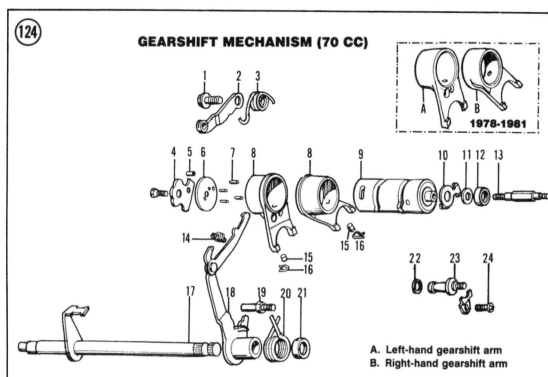

GEARSHIFT MECHANISM (70 CC)

1978-1981

A. Left-hand gearshift arm
B. Right-hand gearshift arm

1. Bolt
2. Stopper pawl
3. Spring
4. Shift drum stopper plate
5. Pin
6. Plate (1982-on)
7. Pin
8. Gearshift fork
9. Gearshift drum
10. Neutral indicator contact plate
11. Washer
12. Oil seal
13. Gear position indicator shaft
14. Spring
15. Guide pin
16. Clip
17. Gearshift shaft
18. Gearshift arm
19. Stud
20. Return spring
21. Collar
22. O-ring seal
23. Neutral indicator
24. Screw

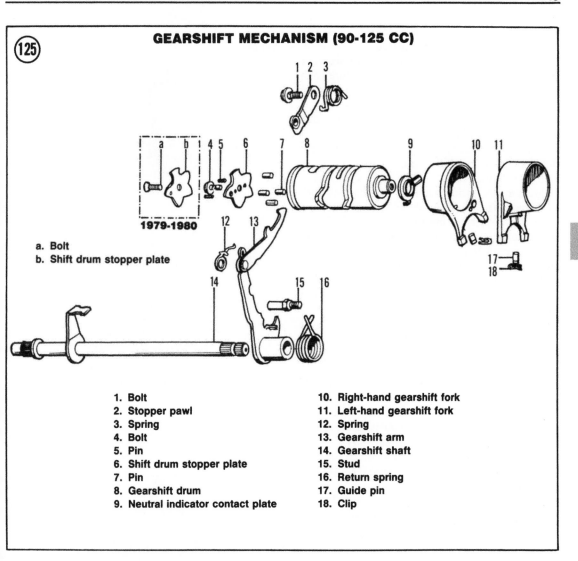

GEARSHIFT MECHANISM (90-125 CC)

125

a. Bolt
b. Shift drum stopper plate

1979-1980

1. Bolt
2. Stopper pawl
3. Spring
4. Bolt
5. Pin
6. Shift drum stopper plate
7. Pin
8. Gearshift drum
9. Neutral indicator contact plate
10. Right-hand gearshift fork
11. Left-hand gearshift fork
12. Spring
13. Gearshift arm
14. Gearshift shaft
15. Stud
16. Return spring
17. Guide pin
18. Clip

5

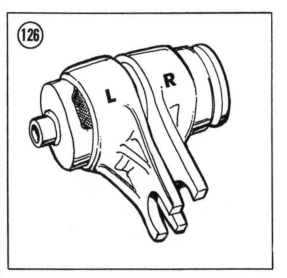

126

Disassembly/Inspection/Assembly

NOTE
*Prior to disassembly, mark the shift forks with an "R" (right-hand side) and "L" (left-hand side—toward the shift drum stopper plate). Refer to **Figure 126**. The right- and left-hand side refer to the shift fork as it is installed in the engine, not as it sits on your workbench. The shift forks are not identical (even though they look alike) and they must be reinstalled onto the shift drum in the correct position.*

1. Clean the assembly in solvent and thoroughly dry with compressed air.
2. Check for any arc-shaped wear or burned marks on the shift forks (**Figure 127**). This indicates that the shift fork has come in contact with the gear.

The shift fork fingers have become excessively worn and the fork must be replaced.

3. Inspect each shift fork for signs of wear or cracking. Check for bending and make sure each fork slides smoothly on the shift drum (**Figure 128**). Replace any worn or damaged forks.

4. Remove the clip (**Figure 129**) securing the guide pin in the shift fork.

5. Remove the guide pin (**Figure 130**) and slide the shift fork off of the shift drum.

6. Repeat Steps 4 and 5 for the other shift fork.

7. Measure the inside diameter of each shift fork (A, **Figure 131**) with an inside micrometer. Replace if worn to the service limit shown in **Table 2**.

8. Measure the width of the gearshift fork fingers with a micrometer (**Figure 132**). Replace any that are worn to the service limit shown in **Table 2**.

9. Measure the outside diameter of the shift drum (B, **Figure 131**) with a micrometer. Replace if worn to the service limit shown in **Table 3**.

10. Check the grooves in the shift drum (**Figure 133**) for wear or roughness. If any of the groove profiles have excessive wear or damage, replace the shift drum.

11. On models so equipped, inspect the neutral switch rotor on the end of the shift drum. If damaged, remove it and install a new one. Make sure the locating tang on the rotor is installed into the hole in the shift drum (C, **Figure 131**).

12. Apply a light coat of assembly oil to the shift drum and the inside bores of the shift forks prior to installation.

13. Be sure to install the shift forks correctly onto the shift drum; refer to marks made during disassembly.

SUBTRANSMISSION

The ATC90, ATC110 and ATC125M have a dual-range subtransmission that is equipped with 2 reduction gears. On the ATC90, the unit is called "Posi-Torque." The unit is driven by the countershaft of the main transmission. It offers 2 different riding ranges or ratios—a low and a high range. Shifting is accomplished by moving a small lever on the subtransmission cover.

The dual-range subtransmission used on all models is basically the same. Where differences occur they are noted. The dual-range subtransmission is shown in the following illustrations:

a. ATC90—**Figure 134**.
b. ATC110—**Figure 135**.
c. ATC125M—**Figure 136**.

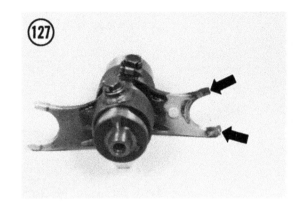
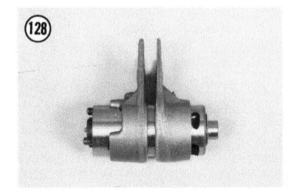
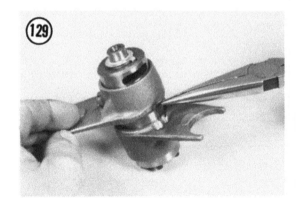
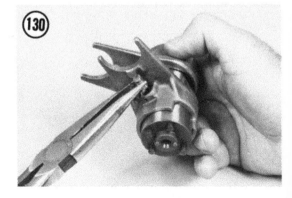

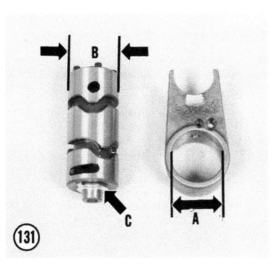

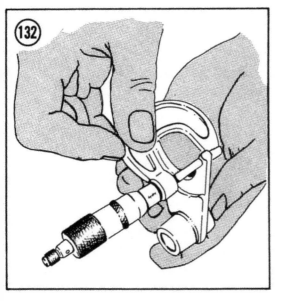

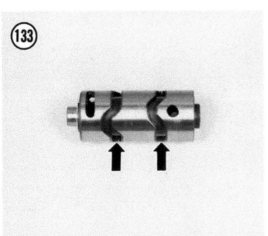

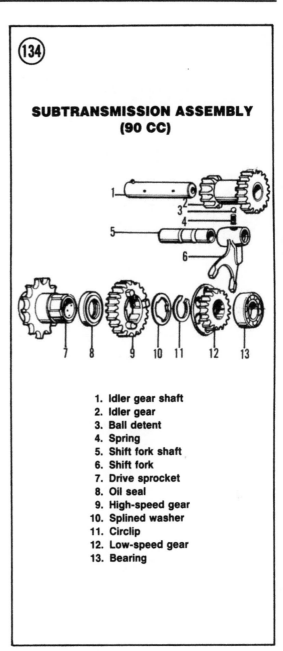

SUBTRANSMISSION ASSEMBLY (90 CC)

1. Idler gear shaft
2. Idler gear
3. Ball detent
4. Spring
5. Shift fork shaft
6. Shift fork
7. Drive sprocket
8. Oil seal
9. High-speed gear
10. Splined washer
11. Circlip
12. Low-speed gear
13. Bearing

Removal/Disassembly

NOTE
This procedure is shown with the recoil starter assembly and the drive chain cover removed. It is not necessary to remove either for this procedure.

1. Place the ATC on level ground and set the parking brake.
2. Remove the seat/rear fender assembly.
3. Drain the engine oil as described in Chapter Three.

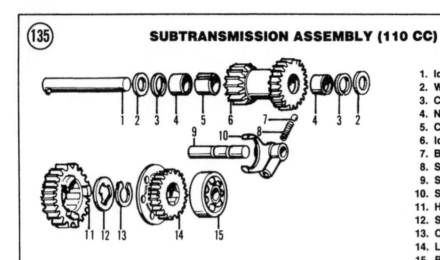

SUBTRANSMISSION ASSEMBLY (110 CC)

1. Idler gear shaft
2. Washer
3. Circlip
4. Needle bearing
5. Collar
6. Idler gear
7. Ball detent
8. Spring
9. Shift fork shaft
10. Shift fork
11. High-speed gear
12. Splined washer
13. Circlip
14. Low-speed gear
15. Bearing

SUBTRANSMISSION ASSEMBLY (125 CC)

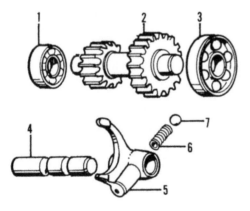

1. Bearing
2. Idler gear
3. Bearing
4. Shift fork shaft
5. Shift fork
6. Spring
7. Ball detent
8. Splined washer
9. High-speed gear
10. Bushing
11. Splined washer
12. Circlip
13. Low-speed gear
14. Bearing

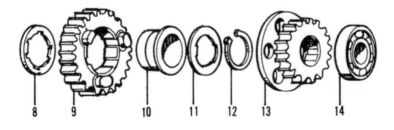

4. Remove the screws (**Figure 137**) securing the subtransmission cover and remove the cover.

5A. On 90 cc models, move the shift lever to LOW and remove the idler gear assembly (**Figure 138**).

5B. On 110 cc models, slide off the idler drive gear washer, idler gear, idler gear shaft and washer (**Figure 139**).

> *NOTE*
> *On 110 cc models, don't lose the dowel pin on the inside end of the idler gear shaft.*

5C. On 125 cc models, slide off the idler drive gear assembly (**Figure 140**).

6. Withdraw the shift fork, the shift fork shaft and the low speed gear as an assembly (**Figure 141**).

7. Remove the circlip (**Figure 142**) securing the high speed gear.

8A. On 90 cc models, slide off the high speed gear splined washer and the high speed gear.

8B. On 110-125 cc models, slide off the high speed gear splined washer, the drive sprocket bushing and the high speed gear.

9. On 125 cc models, slide off the splined thrust washer (**Figure 143**) from the transmission countershaft.

10. If necessary, remove the drive sprocket bushing (**Figure 144**).

Inspection

1. Check each gear for excessive wear, burrs, pitting or chipped or missing teeth.

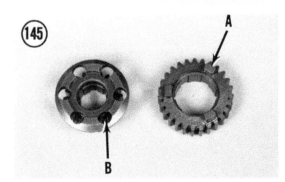

> *NOTE*
> *Defective gears should be replaced. It is a good idea to replace the mating gear even though it may not show as much wear or damage.*

2. Make sure the low gear moves smoothly on the main transmission's countershaft.

3. Check the engagement lugs on the gear (A, **Figure 145**). If worn or damaged the gear should be replaced.

4. Check the engagement lug receptacles in the low gear (B, **Figure 145**). If worn or damaged the gear must be replaced.

5. On 90-110 cc models, make sure the idler gear turns smoothly on the idler gear shaft. It must rotate smoothly with no signs of wear or damage.

6. On 110 cc models, measure the inside diameter (**Figure 146**) and the outside diameter (**Figure 147**) of the drive sprocket bushing with a micrometer or a vernier caliper. Replace if worn to the service limits listed in **Table 4**.

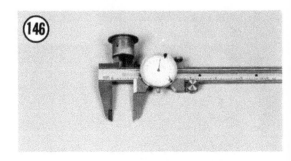

> *NOTE*
> *90 cc models are also equipped with a drive sprocket bushing but Honda does not provide specifications.*

7. On 110 cc models, perform the following:
   a. Check the needle bearings within each end of the idler gear.

b. Rotate each bearing with your finger. They should rotate smoothly with no signs of wear or damage.

c. To replace, remove the snap ring in each end of the idler gear and slide out each bearing.

d. Replace the bearing(s) and install a new snap ring(s).

(148)

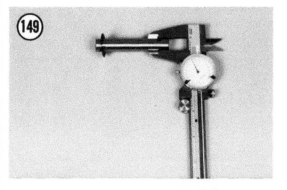
(149)

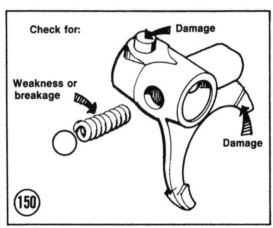

Check for:
Damage

Weakness or breakage

Damage

(150)

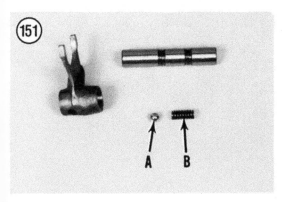
(151)

A   B

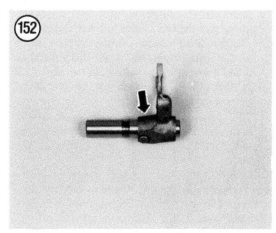
(152)

5

8. On 125 cc models, inspect both ends of the idler gear assembly (**Figure 148**) where they ride on the bearings. Check for wear or damage; replace the assembly if necessary.

9. Measure the outside diameter of the shift fork shaft with a micrometer or a vernier caliper (**Figure 149**). Replace if worn to the service limit dimensions listed in **Table 4**.

10. Move the shift fork back and forth on the shaft and make sure the ball detent locks the shift fork in position in each groove in the shaft. The shift fork must be held tightly in place when the ball detent moves into the groove.

NOTE
In the next step do not lose the small ball detent and spring located within the shift fork.

11. Hold the shift fork/shaft assembly over and down close to a work bench. Slide the shift fork off of either end of the shift fork shaft. Catch the small ball detent and spring that will come out of the recess in the shift fork.

12. Check the shift fork (**Figure 150**) for signs of wear or cracking. Check for bending and make sure the shift fork slides smoothly on the shift fork shaft. Replace as necessary.

13. Check the ball detent (A, **Figure 151**) for wear or distortion; replace as necessary.

14. Check the ball detent spring (B, **Figure 151**) for sagging or breakage; replace as necessary.

15. Reassemble the shift fork onto the shaft as follows:

    a. Hold the shift fork shaft so the end with 2 grooves is on the left-hand side with the long section toward the right-hand side.

    b. Partially install the shift fork (long side of the boss on first) (**Figure 152**) onto the left-hand end of the shaft (**Figure 153**).

c. Through the hole in the shift fork, insert the spring and the ball detent into the shift fork.

d. Using a small-bladed screwdriver, push down on the ball detent and push the shift fork completely onto the shaft. Push the shift fork on until the ball detent indexes into one of the grooves in the shaft.

e. Move the shift fork back and forth on the shaft and make sure the ball detent locks the shift fork in position in each groove in the shaft.

16. Inspect the shaft support bearing in the subtransmission cover. On 90-110 cc models, refer to **Figure 154**. On 125 cc models, refer to **Figure 155** and **Figure 156**. Check for roughness, pitting, galling and play by rotating it slowly with your fingers. It should rotate smoothly. If the bearing(s) require replacing, refer to *Bearing Replacement* in this chapter.

Bearing Replacement

1A. On 90-110 cc models, if bearing replacement is necessary, turn the case with the open side down and tap it on a piece of soft wood. The bearing should fall out. Install the bearing with the sealed side facing out as shown in **Figure 154**.

1B. On 125 cc models, if bearing replacement is necessary perform the following:

a. Remove each bearing from the cover with Honda bearing remover (part No. 07936-KC10000) and remover weight (part No. 07936-3710200 or 07741-0010201).

b. Install each bearing with Honda bearing driver (part No. 07749-0010000), 32×35 mm attachment (part No. 07746-0010100) and 15 mm pilot (part No. 07746-0040300).

2. On 125 cc models, there is an additional bearing located in the left-hand crankcase spacer (**Figure 155**). If replacement is necessary, perform the following:

a. Remove the left-hand crankcase cover and spacer as described in Chapter Four.

b. Remove the bearing from the crankcase cover with Honda 12 mm bearing remover (part No. 07936-1660100) and remover weight (part No. 07936-3710200 or 07741-0010201).

c. Install the bearing with Honda bearing driver (part No. 07749-0010000), 32×35 mm attachment (part No. 07746-0010100) and 12 mm pilot (part No. 07746-0040200).

Assembly/Installation

1. Install a new gasket (A, **Figure 157**).

2. Make sure the locating dowel (B, **Figure 157**) is in place.

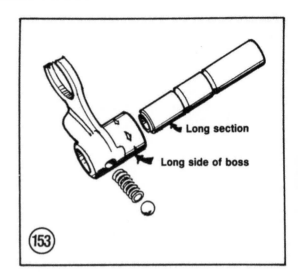

Long section

Long side of boss

(153)

(154)

(155)

3. If removed, install the drive sprocket bushing (**Figure 144**).

4. On 125 cc models, install the splined thrust washer (**Figure 143**) onto the transmission countershaft.

5A. On 90 cc models, install the high speed gear and splined washer.

5B. On 110-125 cc models, install the high speed gear (A, **Figure 158**) and the splined washer (B, **Figure 158**).

6. Install the circlip (C, **Figure 158**). Make sure it seats correctly in the groove in the main transmission countershaft.

7. Position the shift lever plate as shown in **Figure 159**.

8. Install the shift fork shaft, shift fork and low speed gear as an assembly (**Figure 160**). Index the dowel in the shift fork into the groove in the shift lever plate.

9. On 110 cc models, make sure the dowel pin (A, **Figure 161**) in place in the idler gear shaft and install the washer (B, **Figure 161**).

10. Slide on the idler gear with the smaller diameter gear end on first (C, **Figure 161**).

11. On 110 cc models, align the dowel pin (A, **Figure 161**) with the locating groove (**Figure 162**) in the left-hand crankcase cover.

5

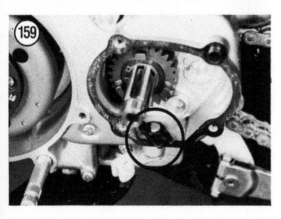

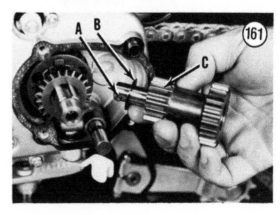

12. Install the idler gear assembly and push it on until it seats completely (**Figure 140**).

13. On 110 cc models, install the washer on the idler gear shaft (**Figure 139**).

14. Position the shift lever on the cover as shown in **Figure 163** so that it will engage with the dowel pin on the shift fork. As you push the cover into place, the shift lever will move from one gear selection to the other. This is okay; it means that the lever is properly engaged with the shift drum dowel pin.

15. Install the subtransmission cover and tighten the screws securely.

16. Refill the engine with the recommended type and quantity of engine oil; refer to Chapter Three.

Shifter Mechanism
Removal/Inspection/Installation

Refer to **Figure 164** (90-110 cc) or **Figure 165** (125 cc) for this procedure.

1. Remove all subtransmission components as described in this chapter.

2. Remove the clip and the shift lever plate.

3. Slide the shift lever out of the crankcase cover.

4. Check the O-ring on the shift lever for wear or damage. Replace as necessary.

5. Install by reversing these removal steps, noting the following.

6. Be sure to install the clip onto the shift lever as shown in **Figure 166**.

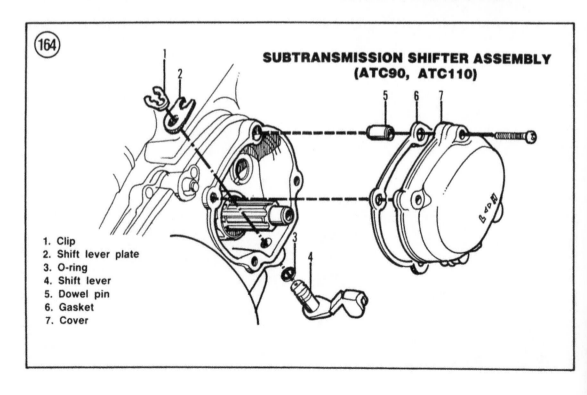

SUBTRANSMISSION SHIFTER ASSEMBLY
(ATC90, ATC110)

1. Clip
2. Shift lever plate
3. O-ring
4. Shift lever
5. Dowel pin
6. Gasket
7. Cover

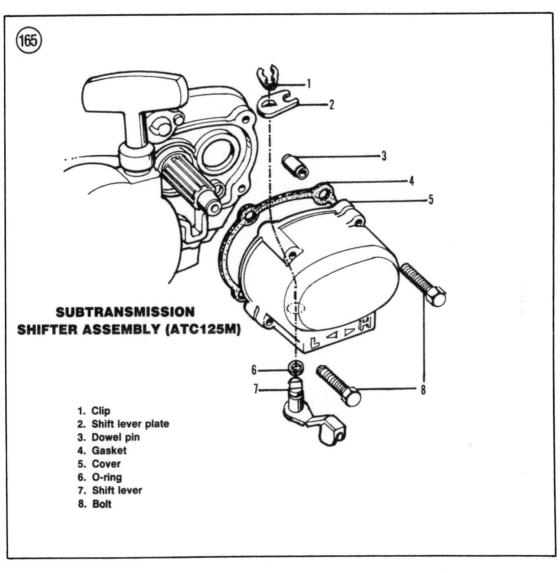

**SUBTRANSMISSION
SHIFTER ASSEMBLY (ATC125M)**

1. Clip
2. Shift lever plate
3. Dowel pin
4. Gasket
5. Cover
6. O-ring
7. Shift lever
8. Bolt

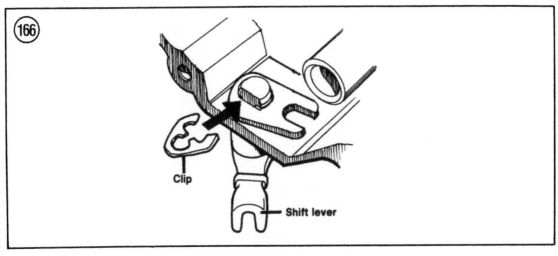

Clip

Shift lever

Table 1 CENTRIFUGAL CLUTCH SPECIFICATIONS

Item	Standard	Wear limit
Friction disc thickness		
ATC70	3.5 mm (0.136 in.)	3.15 mm (0.124 in.)
ATC90	2.8-2.9 mm (0.110-0.114 in.)	2.4 mm (0.094 in.)
ATC110, ATC125M	2.65-2.75 mm (0.104-0.108 in.)	2.5 mm (0.098 in.)
Clutch plate and disc warpage (all models)	–	0.20 mm (0.008 in.)
Clutch springs free length		
ATC70	20.0 mm (0.787 in.)	19.0 mm (0.748 in.)
ATC90	27.0 mm (1.063 in.)	26.0 mm (1.023 in.)
ATC110	24.5 mm (0.965 in.)	23.5 mm (0.925 in.)
ATC125	21.1 mm (0.83 in.)	20.2 mm (0.80 in.)

Table 2 SHIFT FORK AND SHAFT SPECIFICATIONS

Item	Specifications	Wear limit
Shift fork ID		
ATC70	34.0-34.025 mm (1.338-1.339 in.)	34.2 mm (1.347 in.)
ATC90, ATC110, ATC125M	42.0-42.025 mm (1.6535-1.6545 in.)	42.1 mm (1.657 in.)
Shift drum OD		
ATC70	33.95-33.98 mm (1.336-1.337 in.)	33.9 mm (1.335 in.)
ATC90, ATC110, ATC125M	41.95-41.975 mm (1.6516-1.6526 in.)	41.8 mm (1.645 in.)
Shift fork finger thickness		
ATC70		
Left shift fork	4.50-5.30 mm (0.177-0.209 in.)	4.3 mm (0.169 in.)
Right shift fork	5.50-6.30 mm (0.217-0.248 in.)	5.3 mm (0.209 in.)
ATC90, ATC110, ATC125M	5.96-6.04 mm (0.2346-0.2378 in.)	5.70 mm (0.2244 in.)

Table 3 TRANSMISSION SPECIFICATIONS
(1981-ON ATC110 AND ATC125M)*

Item	Standard	Service limit
Transmission gears ID		
Main shaft		
2nd gear	18.000-18.018 mm (0.7087-0.7094 in.)	18.08 mm (0.712 in.)
4th gear	20.000-20.0212 mm (0.7874-0.7882 in.)	20.10 mm (0.791 in.)
Countershaft		
1st gear, 3rd gear	14.000-14.027 mm (0.5512-0.5522 in.)	14.10 mm (0.555 in.)

* Honda provides service information for this transmission only.

Table 4 SUBTRANSMISSION SPECIFICATIONS*

Item	Standard	Service limit
ATC90		
Idler gear ID	13.000-13.018 mm (0.5200-0.5207 in.)	13.10 mm (0.5157 in.)
Idler gear shaft OD	12.966-12.984 mm (0.5200-0.5207 in.)	12.85 mm (0.5140 in.)
ATC110		
Idler gear shaft OD	13.000-13.011 mm (0.5118-0.5122 in.)	12.95 mm (0.510 in.)

* Honda does not provide service specifications for the ATC125M.

5

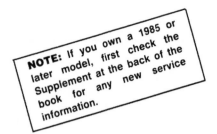

NOTE: If you own a 1985 or later model, first check the Supplement at the back of the book for any new service information.

CHAPTER SIX

FUEL AND EXHAUST SYSTEMS

The fuel system consists of the fuel tank, the shutoff valve, a single carburetor and the air cleaner.

The exhaust system consists of an exhaust pipe and a muffler.

This chapter includes service procedures for all parts of the fuel system and exhaust system. Air cleaner service is covered in Chapter Three. **Table 1** and **Table 2** are at the end of this chapter.

CARBURETOR OPERATION

For proper operation a gasoline engine must be supplied with fuel and air mixed in proper proportions by weight. A mixture in which there is an excess of fuel is said to be rich. A lean mixture is one which contains insufficient fuel. A properly adjusted carburetor supplies the proper mixture to the engine under all operating conditions.

The carburetor consists of several major systems. A float and float valve mechanism maintain a constant fuel level in the float bowl. The pilot system supplies fuel at low speeds. The main fuel system supplies fuel at medium and high speeds. A starter (choke) system supplies the very rich mixture needed to start a cold engine.

CARBURETOR SERVICE

Major carburetor service (removal and cleaning) should be performed at the intervals indicated in Chapter Three or when poor engine performance, hesitation and little or no response to mixture adjustment is observed. Alterations in jet size and throttle slide cutaway, and changes in jet needle position, etc., should be attempted only if you're experienced in this type of "tuning" work; a bad guess could result in costly engine damage or, at least, poor performance. If, after servicing the carburetor and making the adjustments described in this chapter, the ATC does not perform correctly (and assuming that other factors affecting performance are correct, such as valve clearance, ignition timing and condition, etc.), the vehicle should be checked by a dealer or a qualified performance tuning specialist.

Two different carburetor designs are used, depending on the year and model. Be sure to use the correct procedure for your specific ATC.

Carburetor specifications are in **Table 1** at the end of this chapter.

Removal/Installation

This procedure represents a typical carburetor removal and installation sequence. Minor variations exist among the different models and years. Pay particular attention to the location and routing of the fuel lines to the carburetor and the overflow and vent tubes from the carburetor through the clips on the side of the engine.

1. Place the ATC on level ground and set the parking brake or block the wheels so the vehicle will not roll in either direction.
2. Remove the seat/rear fender assembly.

3. Remove the fuel lines to the carburetor (**Figure 1**). Plug the ends of the fuel lines with golf tees to prevent the discharge of fuel (**Figure 2**).

4. Remove the fuel tank as described in this chapter.

5. Remove the bolts (**Figure 3**) securing the intake tube to the cylinder head.

6A. On ATC90 models, move the wire retaining clamp (**Figure 4**) off the carburetor and slide it back onto the air cleaner.

6B. On all other models, loosen the clamping screw (A, **Figure 5**) on the intake tube from the air cleaner.

NOTE
Before removing the top cap, thoroughly clean the area around it so no dirt will fall into the carburetor.

7. Unscrew the carburetor top cap (B, **Figure 5**) and pull the throttle valve assembly up and out of the carburetor.

NOTE
If the top cap and throttle valve assembly are not going to be removed from the throttle cable for cleaning, wrap them in a clean shop cloth or place them in a plastic bag to help keep them clean.

8. To remove the throttle valve from the throttle cable (**Figure 6**), depress the throttle spring away from the throttle valve. Push the throttle cable end down and out along the groove in the side of the throttle valve and remove the throttle valve and needle jet assembly.

NOTE
Do not lose the spring clip that will come out when the needle is removed.

9. On ATC125M models, loosen the clamping band (C, **Figure 5**) and unhook the choke cable end (D, **Figure 5**) from the carburetor.

10. Note the routing of the carburetor overflow and vent tubes through the clips on the side of the engine. Carefully pull the tubes free from the clips; leave them attached to the carburetor.

11. Take the carburetor to a workbench for disassembly and cleaning.

12. Install by reversing these removal steps, noting the following.

13. Make sure the mounting bolts on the intake tube are tight to avoid a vacuum loss and possible valve damage.

Disassembly/Assembly (Type I)

The Type I carburetor (**Figure 7**) is used on the following models:

    a. 1973-1974 ATC70.

    b. ATC90.

Refer to the exploded view drawing when disassembling and assembling this carburetor. After assembly, adjust the carburetor as described in this chapter.

Disassembly/Assembly (Type II)

The Type II carburetor (**Figure 8**) is used on the following models:

    a. 1978-on ATC70.

    b. ATC110.

    c. ATC125M.

1. On 1984 ATC110 and ATC125M models, perform the following:

    a. Unscrew the fuel strainer cup from the float bowl (**Figure 9**).

    b. Withdraw the fuel strainer (**Figure 10**).

    c. Remove the O-ring seal (A, **Figure 11**).

2. Remove the drain tube (B, **Figure 11**).

3. Remove the screws (**Figure 12**) securing the float bowl and remove the float bowl.

4. Remove the float pivot pin (**Figure 13**) and remove the float.

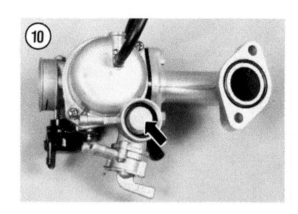

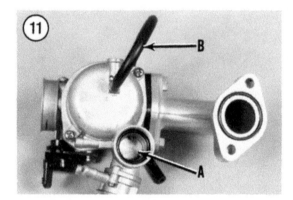

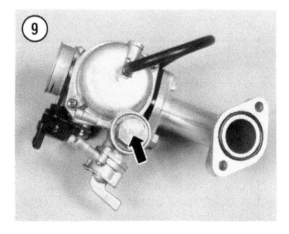

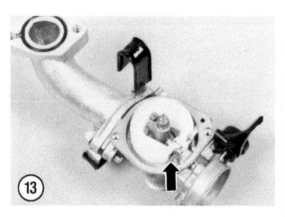

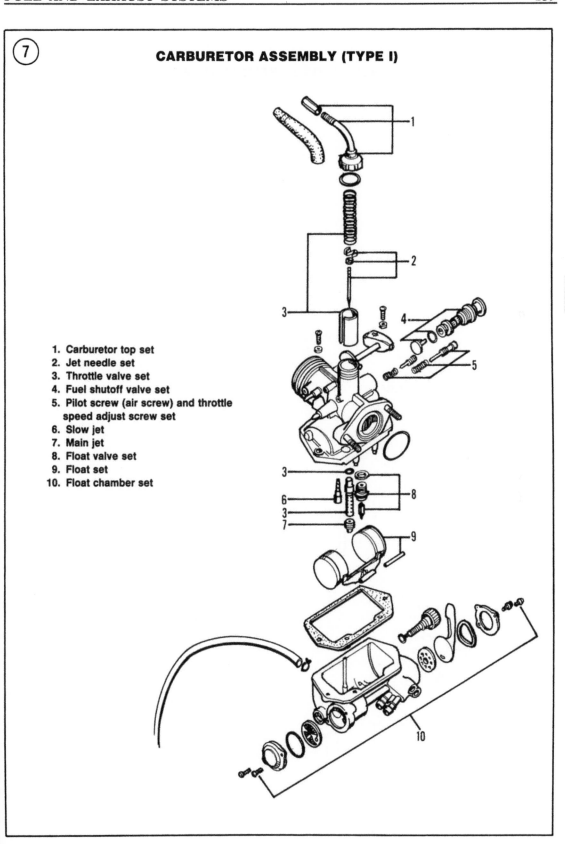

⑦   **CARBURETOR ASSEMBLY (TYPE I)**

1. Carburetor top set
2. Jet needle set
3. Throttle valve set
4. Fuel shutoff valve set
5. Pilot screw (air screw) and throttle
   speed adjust screw set
6. Slow jet
7. Main jet
8. Float valve set
9. Float set
10. Float chamber set

⑧

CARBURETOR ASSEMBLY (TYPE II)

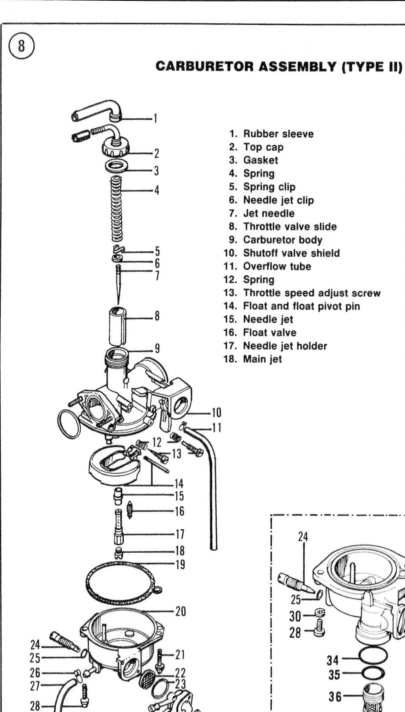

1. Rubber sleeve
2. Top cap
3. Gasket
4. Spring
5. Spring clip
6. Needle jet clip
7. Jet needle
8. Throttle valve slide
9. Carburetor body
10. Shutoff valve shield
11. Overflow tube
12. Spring
13. Throttle speed adjust screw
14. Float and float pivot pin
15. Needle jet
16. Float valve
17. Needle jet holder
18. Main jet

19. Gasket
20. Float bowl
21. Screw
22. Screen
23. O-ring
24. Drain screw
25. O-ring
26. Clip
27. Drain tube
28. Screw
29. Fuel shutoff valve
30. Washer
31. Screw
32. Washer
33. Screw
34. O-ring
35. O-ring
36. Fuel strainer

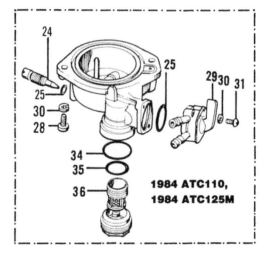

1984 ATC110,
1984 ATC125M

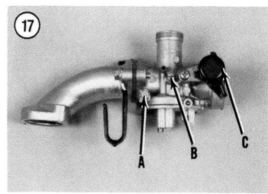

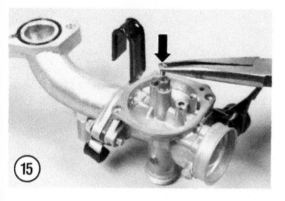

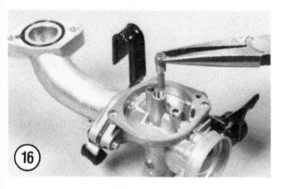

5. Remove the float valve from the float arm (**Figure 14**).

6. Remove the main jet (**Figure 15**) and the needle jet holder (**Figure 16**).

7. Turn the carburetor over and catch the needle jet as it falls out into your hand. If the needle jet does not fall out, use a plastic or fiber tool and gently push the needle jet out. Do not use any metal tool for this purpose.

8. Do not remove the slow jet (on some models, it is pressed in place).

NOTE
*Before removing the pilot screw, carefully screw it in until it **lightly** seats.*

Count and record the number of turns so it can be installed in the same position.

9. Unscrew the pilot screw and spring (A, **Figure 17**).

10. Unscrew the idle adjust screw and spring (B, **Figure 17**).

11. Remove the choke assembly from the carburetor body (C, **Figure 17**).

12. Remove the screws (**Figure 18**) securing the fuel shutoff valve and the fuel strainer assembly and remove them from the float bowl. Remove the O-ring seal and filter (**Figure 19**) from the float bowl.

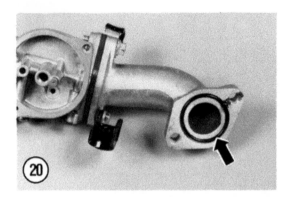

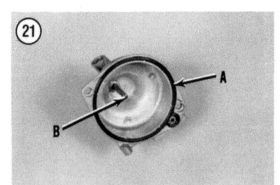

13. Remove the O-ring seal (**Figure 20**) from the carburetor mounting flange.

14. Remove the float bowl gasket (A, **Figure 21**) from the float bowl.

15. Unscrew the drain screw and O-ring seal (**Figure 22**) from the float bowl.

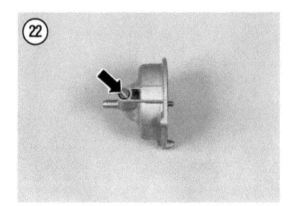

16. If not already removed, push the jet needle from the throttle slide. Do not lose the jet needle retaining clip.

> *NOTE*
> *Further disassembly is neither necessary nor recommended. If throttle or choke shafts or butterflies are damaged, take the carburetor body to a dealer for replacement.*

17. Clean and inspect all parts as described in this chapter.

18. Assembly is the reverse of these disassembly steps, noting the following.

19. Install the needle jet with the chamfered end facing out toward the needle jet holder (**Figure 23**).

20. On 1984 ATC110 and ATC125M models, inspect the O-ring seal (**Figure 24**) on the fuel strainer; replace if necessary.

21. Install the needle jet clip in the correct groove; refer to **Table 1** at the end of this chapter.

22. Check the float height and adjust if necessary as described in this chapter.

23. After the carburetor has been disassembled the pilot screw and the idle speed should be adjusted as described in this chapter.

Cleaning/Inspection

1. Clean all parts, except rubber or plastic parts, in a good grade of carburetor cleaner. This solution is available at most automotive or motorcycle supply stores in a small, resealable tank with a dip basket for just a few dollars. If it is tightly sealed when not in use, the solution will last for several cleanings. Follow the manufacturer's instructions for correct soak time (usually about 1/2 hour).

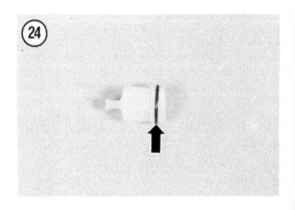

2. Remove all parts from the cleaner and blow dry with compressed air. Blow out the jets with compressed air. *Do not* use a piece of wire to clean them as minor gouges in the jet can alter flow rate and upset the fuel-air mixture.

3. Be sure to clean out the overflow tube in the float bowl from both ends (B, **Figure 21**).

4. Inspect the end of the float valve needle (**Figure 25**) for wear or damage; replace if necessary.

5. Inspect the condition of all O-ring seals. O-ring seals tend to become hardened after prolonged use and heat and therefore lose their ability to seal properly.

6. On models so equipped, clean the filter screen with a medium soft toothbrush and solvent. Thoroughly dry with compressed air. Replace the filter screen if it is broken or damaged.

CARBURETOR ADJUSTMENTS

Float Adjustment

The carburetor assembly has to be removed and partially disassembled for this adjustment.

1. Remove the carburetor as described in this chapter.

2. Remove the float bowl from the main body.

3. Hold the carburetor so the float arm is just touching the float needle, not pushing it down. Use a float level gauge, vernier caliper or small ruler (**Figure 26**) and measure the distance from the carburetor body to the float. The correct height is listed in **Table 1**.

4A. On models equipped with a plastic float the float assembly must be replaced if float height is incorrect. The float tang cannot be adjusted as it will break off.

4B. On models with a metal float assembly, adjust by carefully bending the tang on the float arm (**Figure 27**). If the float level is set too high, the result will be a rich fuel-air mixture. If it is set too low the mixture will be too lean.

5. Reassemble and install the carburetor.

Needle Jet Adjustment

The position of the needle jet can be adjusted to affect the fuel-air mixture for medium throttle openings. It is not necessary to remove the carburetor body but the top of the carburetor must be removed for this adjustment.

NOTE
Honda does not provide specifications for all models and years. Some late models have a needle jet with a fixed clip position (non-adjustable). Refer to **Table 1** *before starting this procedure.*

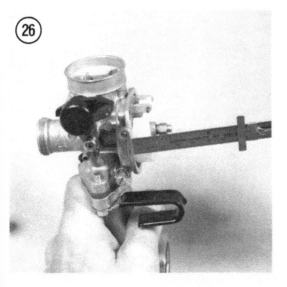

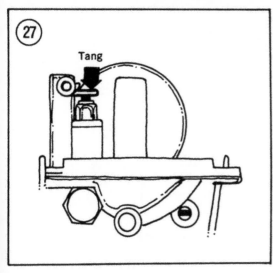

Tang

1. Place the ATC on level ground and set the parking brake or block the wheel so the vehicle will not roll in either direction.

2. Remove the seat/rear fender assembly.

3. Remove the fuel tank as described in this chapter.

> *NOTE*
> *Before removing the top cap, thoroughly clean the area around it so no dirt will fall into the carburetor.*

4. Unscrew the carburetor top cap (**Figure 28**) and pull the throttle valve assembly up and out of the carburetor.

5. Depress the throttle valve spring and remove the throttle cable from the throttle valve (**Figure 29**).

> *NOTE*
> *Record the clip position prior to removal.*

6. Remove the needle clip retainer and remove the jet needle.

7. Raising the needle (lowering the clip) will enrich the mixture during mid-throttle opening, while lowering the needle (raising the clip) will lean the mixture. Refer to **Figure 30**.

8. Refer to **Table 1** for standard clip position.

9. Reassemble and install the carburetor top cap.

Idle Speed Adjustment

Refer to Chapter Three for this procedure.

Pilot Screw Adjustment
(ATC70; ATC90; 1979-1980 ATC110)

1. Place the ATC on level ground and set the parking brake or block the wheel so the vehicle will not roll in either direction.

2. Start the engine and let it reach normal operating temperature. If you are in an area where you can ride the ATC, approximately 5-10 minutes of stop and go riding is usually sufficient. Shut off the engine.

3. Connect a portable tachometer following the manufacturer's instructions. Restart the engine.

4A. On 1973-1974 ATC70 models, turn the idle adjust screw (A, **Figure 31**) to obtain the idle speed listed in **Table 1**.

4B. On 1978-on ATC70, all ATC90 and 1979-1980 ATC110 models, turn the idle adjust screw (A, **Figure 31**) to obtain the lowest stable idle speed.

5. Turn the air screw (B, **Figure 31**) *clockwise* until the engine speed decreases or begins to miss. Note the location of the air screw.

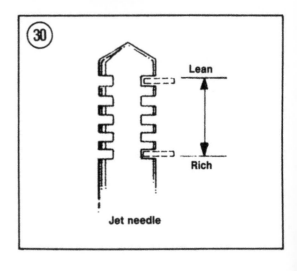

Jet needle

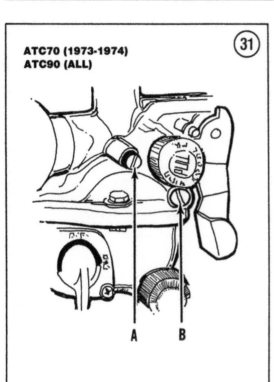

ATC70 (1973-1974)
ATC90 (ALL)

(31)

A   B

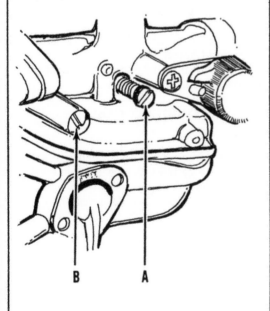

ATC70 (1978-ON)
ATC110
ATC125M

B   A

A. Idle screw
B. Air screw (or pilot screw)

6. Turn the air screw *counterclockwise* until the engine speed decreases or begins to miss. Note the location of the air screw.

7. Turn the air screw to a point midway between the locations noted in Step 5 and Step 6.

8. Check the engine idle speed and readjust if necessary to the idle speed listed in **Table 1**.

9. Open and close the throttle a couple of times and check for variations in idle speed. Readjust if necessary.

10. Disconnect the portable tachometer.

Pilot Screw Adjustment
(1981-on ATC110; ATC125M)

The pilot jet is pre-set at the factory and adjustment is not necessary unless the carburetor has been overhauled or someone has misadjusted it.

1. Place the ATC on level ground and set the parking brake.

2. For the preliminary adjustment, carefully turn the pilot screw (B, **Figure 31**) in until it seats *lightly* and then back it out the following number of turns:

   a. ATC110: 1 1/8 turns out.

   b. ATC125M: 1 3/8 turns out.

CAUTION
The pilot screw seat can be damaged if the pilot screw is tightened too hard.

3. Start the engine and let it reach normal operating temperature. If you are in an area where you can ride the ATC, approximately 5-10 minutes of stop and go riding is usually sufficient. Shut off the engine.

4. Connect a portable tachometer following the manufacturer's instructions. Restart the engine.

5. Turn the idle speed adjust screw (A, **Figure 31**) to obtain the idle speed listed in **Table 1**.

6. Turn the pilot screw (B, **Figure 31**) in slowly until the engine stops running, then stop. Back the pilot screw out 1 full turn.

7. Restart the engine and check the engine idle speed. Readjust if necessary as described in Step 5.

8. Open and close the throttle a couple of times and check for variations in idle speed. Readjust if necessary.

WARNING
With the engine idling, move the handlebar from side to side. If idle speed increases during this movement, the throttle cable needs adjustment or it may be incorrectly routed through the frame. Correct this problem immediately. Do not ride the ATC in this unsafe condition.

9. Disconnect the portable tachometer.

6

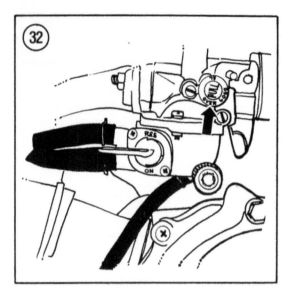

**High-elevation Adjustment
(1973-1974 ATC70)**

If the ATC is going to be ridden for any sustained period at high elevation (above 5,000 ft./1,500 m), the high elevation compensator knob (**Figure 32**), located on the left-hand side of the carburetor, must be pulled *out*.

> *CAUTION*
> *If the carburetor has been adjusted for high-elevation operation, the high elevation adjuster knob must be pushed* ***in*** *to the standard setting when ridden at elevations below 5,000 ft. (1,500 m). Engine overheating and piston seizure will occur if the engine runs too lean.*

**High-elevation Adjustment
(All Other Models)**

If the ATC is going to be ridden for any sustained period at high elevations (above 5,000 ft./1,500 m), the main jet should be changed to a one-step smaller jet. Never change the jet by more than one size at a time without test riding the bike and running a spark plug test. Refer to Chapter Three.

> *CAUTION*
> *If the carburetor has been adjusted for high-elevation operation, it must be changed back to standard settings when ridden at elevations below 5,000 ft. (1,500 m). Engine overheating and piston seizure will occur if the engine runs too lean with the smaller jet installed.*

1. Remove the carburetor as described in this chapter.
2. Remove the screws securing the float bowl and remove the float bowl.
3. Remove the main jet (**Figure 33**) and replace it with the factory recommended high elevation size. Refer to **Table 2**.
4. Install the float bowl.
5. Reinstall the carburetor as described in this chapter. Be sure to route the drain tube correctly.
6. Turn the pilot screw *in* 1/2 turn.
7. Start the engine and adjust the idle speed as described in Chapter Three.
8. Test ride the bike and perform a spark plug test, refer to Chapter Three.

THROTTLE CABLE

Removal

1. Place the ATC on level ground and set the parking brake or block the wheels so the vehicle will not roll in either direction.
2. Remove the seat/rear fender assembly.
3. Remove the fuel tank as described in this chapter.

> *NOTE*
> *Before removing the top cap, thoroughly clean the area around it so no dirt will fall into the carburetor.*

4. Unscrew the carburetor top cap and pull the throttle valve assembly up and out of the carburetor.
5. Depress the throttle valve spring and remove the throttle cable from the throttle valve.

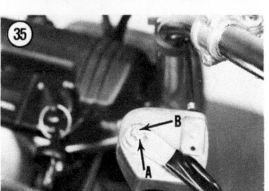

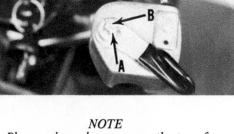

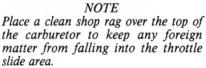

6

NOTE
Place a clean shop rag over the top of the carburetor to keep any foreign matter from falling into the throttle slide area.

6. Disassemble the throttle lever assembly as follows:

   a. Remove the screws (**Figure 34**) securing the throttle cover and separate the 2 halves of the throttle lever assembly.

   b. Remove the assembly from the handlebar.

   c. On models so equipped, pull the engine stop switch from the top of the throttle lever cover.

   d. On models so equipped, withdraw the electrical cable from the rubber grommet in the cover.

   e. Turn the throttle lever base upside down and straighten the locking tabs on the lockplate (A, **Figure 35**).

   f. Remove the bolt (B, **Figure 35**) securing the throttle lever to the base and remove the throttle lever and spring.

   g. Remove the throttle cable end from the throttle lever (**Figure 36**).

7. Disconnect the throttle cable from any clips holding the cable to the frame.

NOTE
The piece of string attached in the next step will be used to pull the new throttle cable back through the frame so it will be routed in the exact same position as the old one.

8. Tie a piece of heavy string or cord (approximately 6-8 ft./2-3 m long) to the carburetor end of the throttle cable. Wrap this end with masking or duct tape. Do not use an excessive amount of tape as it must be pulled through the frame (and, on some models, a rubber grommet) during removal. Tie the other end of the string to the frame.

9. At the throttle lever end of the cable, carefully pull the cable (and attached string) out through the frame (**Figure 37**). Make sure the attached string follows the same path of the cable through the frame.

10. Remove the tape and untie the string from the old cable.

Installation

1. Lubricate the new cable as described in Chapter Three.

2. Tie the string (used during removal) to the new throttle cable and wrap it with tape.

3. Carefully pull the string back through the frame routing the new cable through the same path as the old cable.

4. Remove the tape and untie the string from the cable and the frame.

5. Reverse Steps 1-7 of *Removal*, noting the following.

6. Apply grease to the pivot bushing in the throttle lever cover and to the throttle lever.

7. Install the throttle lever, spring and rubber seal as shown in **Figure 38**.

8. Operate the throttle lever and make sure the carburetor throttle linkage is operating correctly and with no binding. If operation is incorrect or there is binding carefully check that the cable is attached correctly and there are no tight bends in the cable.

9. Adjust the throttle cable as described in Chapter Three.

10. Test ride the ATC and make sure the throttle is operating correctly.

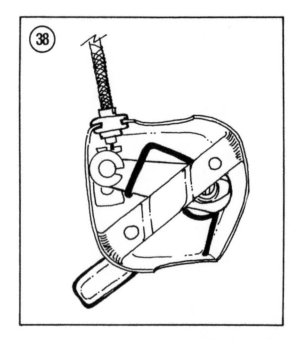

CHOKE CABLE
(ATC125M)

Removal/Installation

1. Place the ATC on level ground and set the parking brake.

2. Remove the seat/rear fender assembly.

3. Remove the fuel tank as described in this chapter.

4. Loosen the choke cable nut (**Figure 39**) securing the choke knob assembly to the handlebar upper holder and remove the cable from the holder.

5. Remove the clamping screw and clamp (A, **Figure 40**) securing the choke cable to the carburetor body.

6. Unhook the cable end (B, **Figure 40**) from the lever on the carburetor body.

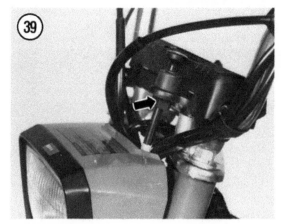

> *NOTE*
> *The piece of string attached in the next step will be used to pull the new choke cable back through the frame so it will be routed in the same position as the old cable (Figure 41).*

7. Tie a piece of heavy string or cord (approximately 6-8 ft./2-3 m long) to the carburetor end of the choke cable. Wrap this end with masking or duct tape. Do not use an excessive amount of tape as it will be pulled through the rubber grommet during removal. Tie the other end of the string to the frame.

8. At the handlebar end of the cable, carefully pull the cable (and attached string) out through the

frame (**Figure 41**). Make sure the attached string follows the same path that the cable does through the frame.

9. Remove the tape and untie the string from the old cable.

10. Lubricate the new cable as described in Chapter Three.

11. Tie the string to the new choke cable and wrap it with tape.

12. Carefully pull the string back through the frame routing the new cable through the same path as the old cable.

13. Remove the tape and untie the string from the cable and the frame.

14. Attach the choke cable to the carburetor choke lever.

15. Attach the choke cable to the handlebar upper holder and tighten the nut.

16. Operate the choke lever and make sure the carburetor choke linkage is operating correctly and with no binding. If operation is incorrect or there is binding carefully check that the cable is attached correctly and there are no tight bends in the cable.

17. Install the fuel tank and seat/rear fender assembly.

FUEL TANK

Removal/Installation

1. Place the ATC on level ground and set the parking brake or block the wheels so the vehicle will not roll in either direction.

2. Remove the seat/rear fender assembly.

3. Disconnect one fuel line (**Figure 42**) at a time from the fuel shutoff valve and plug with a golf tee (**Figure 43**). Perform this step on both fuel lines.

4A. On ATC90 models, unhook the rubber strap securing the rear of the fuel tank. Pull the tank up and toward the rear and remove the tank.

4B. On all other models, remove the bolt(s) securing the rear of the fuel tank (**Figure 44**). Pull the tank up and toward the rear and remove the tank.

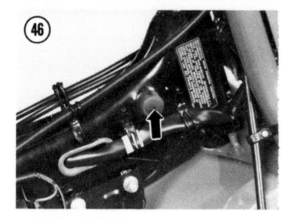

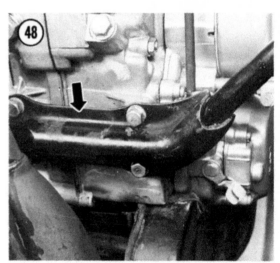

5. Inspect the rubber cushions (**Figure 45** and **Figure 46**) on the frame where the fuel tank is held in place. Replace as a set if either is damaged or starting to deteriorate.

6. Install by reversing these removal steps.

EXHAUST SYSTEM

The exhaust system is a vital performance component and frequently, because of its design, it is a vulnerable piece of equipment. Check the exhaust system for deep dents and fractures and repair them or replace parts immediately. Check the muffler frame mounting flanges for fractures and loose bolts or nuts. Check the cylinder head mounting flange for tightness. A loose exhaust pipe connection will not only rob the engine of power, it could also damage the piston and cylinder.

The exhaust system consists of a one-piece exhaust pipe, muffler and tailpipe assembly.

The following procedure represents a typical exhaust sytem removal and installation. Minor variations exist among the different models and years. Pay particular attention to the location of bolts, washers and nuts not shown in this procedure. Make sure all mounting hardware is installed and attached correctly.

Removal/Installation
(1973-1974 ATC70; All ATC90 and ATC110)

1. Place the ATC on level ground and set the parking brake or block the wheels so the vehicle will not roll in either direction.

2. Remove the seat/fender assembly.

3. For ease of removal, set the ATC up on end. Wrap the rear chrome handle with a shop cloth to protect the finish.

4. Remove the bolts securing the lower frame guard and remove the frame guard (**Figure 47**).

5. On ATC70 models, remove the bolts securing the footpeg assembly and remove the footpeg assembly (**Figure 48**).

6. Set the ATC back down on its wheels.

7A. On ATC70 models, perform the following:

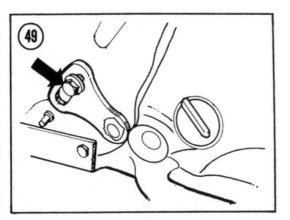

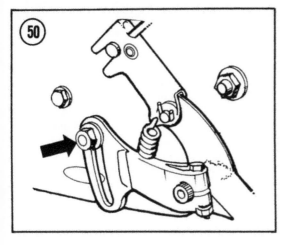

a. Remove the rear wheels and the rear axle as described in Chapter Eight.

b. Loosen the drive chain tensioner locknut (**Figure 49**).

7B. On ATC90 and ATC110 models, loosen the drive chain tensioner locknut (**Figure 50**).

8. Remove the bolts and washers securing the muffler to the frame.

9. On 1981-on ATC110 models, on the right-hand side, remove the long bolt located at the front of the rear brake drum cover. This bolt also holds the muffler in place.

10. Remove the nuts securing the exhaust pipe to the cylinder head.

11. Move the rear hub so it will not interfere with the muffler.

12. Move the exhaust system toward the front of the ATC and remove it from the frame.

13. Install by reversing these removal steps, noting the following.

NOTE
The 1974 ATC70 (frame No. 1100001-on) uses a slightly different

exhaust system than the 1973 ATC70 (frame No. 1000001 to 1100000). The 1974 ATC70 exhaust system will fit on the older 1973 model if the muffler attachment holes on the frame are elongated slightly with an electric drill or round metal file.

14. Tighten the nuts on the cylinder head first then tighten the nuts on the frame. This will minimize the chances of an exhaust leak at the cylinder head.

15. Make sure the cylinder head exhaust port gasket is in place.

16. Adjust the drive chain and rear brake as described in Chapter Three.

17. After installation is complete, start the engine and make sure there are no exhaust leaks.

Removal/Installation
(1978-on ATC70 and ATC125M)

1. Place the ATC on level ground and set the parking brake or block the wheels so the vehicle will not roll in either direction.

2. Remove the seat/fender assembly.

3. Remove the right-hand rear wheel as described in Chapter Eight.

4A. On ATC70 models, perform the following:

a. For ease of removal, set the ATC up on end. Wrap the rear chrome handle with a shop cloth to protect the finish.

b. Remove the nuts and washers (A, **Figure 51**) securing the exhaust pipe to the cylinder head.

c. Remove the bolts and washers (B, **Figure 51**) securing the muffler to the frame.

4B. On ATC125M models, perform the following:

a. Remove the nuts and washers (**Figure 52**) securing the exhaust pipe to the cylinder head.

b. Remove the bolts and washers (**Figure 53**) securing the muffler to the frame.

5. Remove the muffler assembly from within the frame.

6. Install by reversing these removal steps, noting the following.

7. Tighten the nuts on the cylinder head first then tighten the nuts on the frame. This will minimize the chances of an exhaust leak at the cylinder head.

8. Make sure the cylinder head exhaust port gasket is in place.

9. After installation is complete, start the engine and make sure there are no exhaust leaks.

Table 1 CARBURETOR SPECIFICATIONS

Item	1973-1974 ATC70	1978-on ATC70
Model No.	NA	PB38A
Main jet No.	60	58
Slow air jet	35	38
Initial pilot screw opening	1 1/8 turns out	1 3/4 turns out
Needle jet clip position	3nd groove	4th groove
Float level	20.0 mm (0.787 in.)	20.0 mm (0.787 in.)
Idle speed	1,500 ±100 rpm	1,500 ±100 rpm
Item	**ATC90**	**ATC110**
Model No.	U9B	PB20A
Main jet No.	65	85
Slow air jet	35	35
Initial pilot	1 turn out	1 1/8 turns out
Needle jet clip position	3rd groove	3rd groove
Float level	20.0 mm (0.787 in.)	10.7 mm (0.43 in.)
Idle speed	1,300 ±100 rpm	1,700 ±100 rpm
Item	**ATC125M**	
Model No.	PB20A	
Main jet No.	92	
Slow jet No.	38	
Initial pilot screw opening	1 3/8 turns out	
Needle jet clip position	2nd groove	
Float level	10.7 mm (0.43 in.)	
Idle speed	1,700 ±100 rpm	

NA—Honda does not provide information for all models.

Table 2 HIGH ELEVATION JET SIZE

Model	Jet size
ATC70	
1973-1974	NA
1978-on	NA
ATC90	NA
ATC110	No. 78
ATC125M	No. 88

NA—Does not apply (some models have a high-elevation adjust knob built into the carburetor) or Honda does not provide jet specifications.

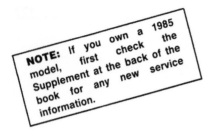

NOTE: If you own a 1985 model, first check the Supplement at the back of the book for any new service information.

CHAPTER SEVEN

ELECTRICAL SYSTEM

This chapter contains operating principles and service and test procedures for all electrical and ignition components. Information on the battery and spark plugs is covered in Chapter Three.

The electrical system includes the following systems:

a. Charging system (models with a battery).
b. Ignition system.
c. Starting system (models so equipped).
d. Lighting system.

Tables 1-4 are at the end of this chapter. Wiring diagrams are at the end of the book.

CHARGING SYSTEM (MODELS SO EQUIPPED)

The charging system consists of the battery, alternator and a solid-state voltage regulator/rectifier. **Figure 1** shows a typical charging system.

Alternating current generated by the alternator is rectified to direct current. The voltage regulator maintains the voltage to the electrical load (lights, ignition, etc.) at a constant voltage regardless of variations in engine speed and load.

Charging System Output Test

Whenever a charging system trouble is suspected, make sure the battery is fully charged and in good condition before going any further. Clean and test the battery as described in Chapter Three.

1. Start the ATC and let it reach normal operating temperature; shut off the engine.
2. Place the ATC on level ground and set the parking brake.
3. Remove the seat/rear fender assembly.
4. Remove the screw securing the starter relay cover and remove the cover (**Figure 2**).

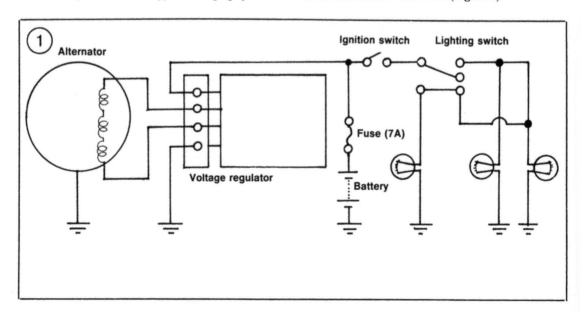

① Alternator

Ignition switch   Lighting switch

Fuse (7A)

Voltage regulator

Battery

5. Remove the wing nut (**Figure 3**) securing the battery holder and cover. Remove the battery cover.

6. Disconnect the red battery wire at the main fuse (**Figure 4**).

7. Leave the battery wires connected to the battery and connect a 0-15 *DC* voltmeter between the battery terminals (**Figure 5**).

8. At the main fuse connect a 0-10 *DC* ammeter to each end of the red wires as shown in **Figure 5**.

NOTE
During the test, if the needle of the ammeter reads in the opposite direction on the scale, reverse the polarity of the test leads.

9. Start the engine with the recoil starter and let it idle. Increase engine speed to 5,000 rpm. At this engine speed the meters should read 4.5 amps and 14 volts. If the charging current is considerably lower than specified, check the alternator and/or the regulator. Less likely is the possibility that the voltage is too high; in that case the voltage regulator is probably at fault.

10. Test the separate charging system components as described under the appropriate headings in this chapter.

11. After the test is completed, disconnect the voltmeter and ammeter.

12. Reconnect the red battery wire at the main fuse.

13. Install all items removed.

ALTERNATOR

The alternator is a form of electrical generator in which a magnetized field called a rotor revolves within a set of stationary coils called a stator. As the rotor revolves, alternating currect is induced in the stator. The current is then rectified and used to

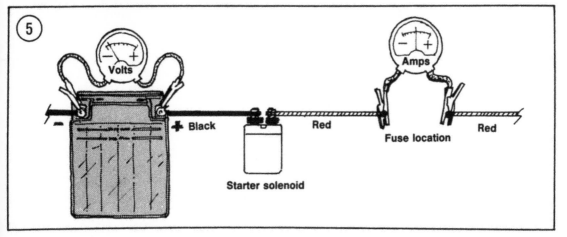

operate the electrical accessories on the ATC and to charge the battery (on models so equipped). The rotor is permanently magnetized.

There are 4 different alternators used among the different models. Some have an outer rotor and others have an inner rotor. The stator coils of the outer rotor type are either attached to the engine or to the alternator cover.

ALTERNATOR (OUTER ROTOR TYPE)

The outer rotor type alternators used among the various models are shown in the following illustrations:

a. ATC70—**Figure 6**.
b. 1981-on ATC110—**Figure 7**.
c. ATC125M—**Figure 8**.

Rotor Removal/Installation (All ATC70, 1981-on ATC110)

The following procedure represents a typical outer rotor removal and installation. Minor variations exist among the different models and years. Pay particular attention to the location of washers, rubber grommets, electrical connectors, etc. Make sure they are installed or attached in the correct location.

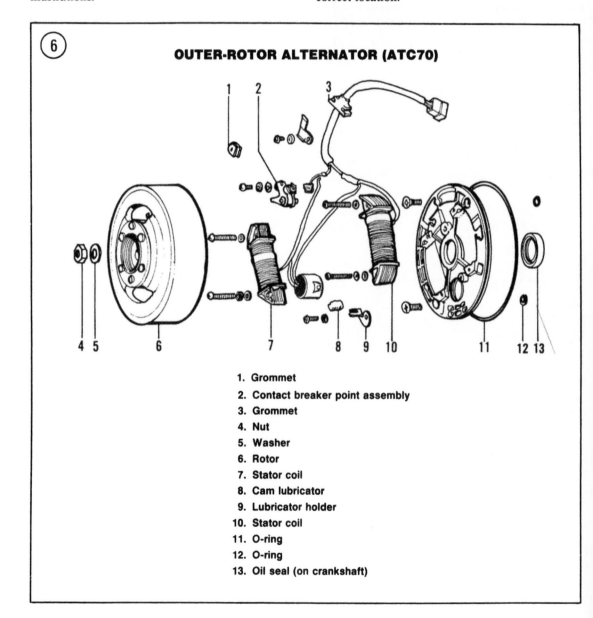

OUTER-ROTOR ALTERNATOR (ATC70)

1. Grommet
2. Contact breaker point assembly
3. Grommet
4. Nut
5. Washer
6. Rotor
7. Stator coil
8. Cam lubricator
9. Lubricator holder
10. Stator coil
11. O-ring
12. O-ring
13. Oil seal (on crankshaft)

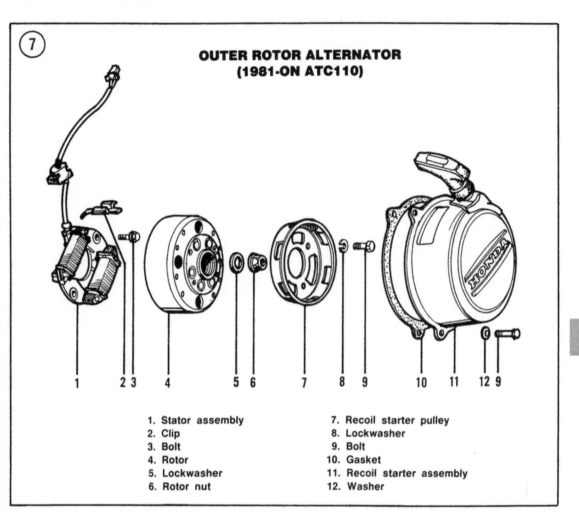

OUTER ROTOR ALTERNATOR
(1981-ON ATC110)

1. Stator assembly
2. Clip
3. Bolt
4. Rotor
5. Lockwasher
6. Rotor nut
7. Recoil starter pulley
8. Lockwasher
9. Bolt
10. Gasket
11. Recoil starter assembly
12. Washer

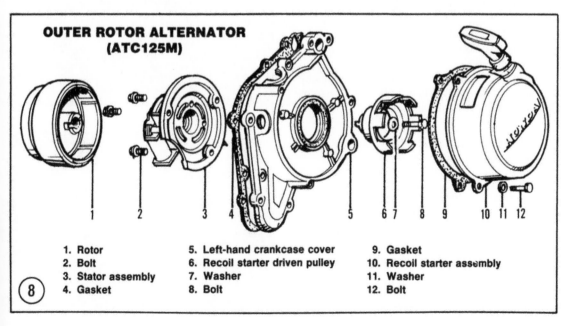

OUTER ROTOR ALTERNATOR
(ATC125M)

1. Rotor
2. Bolt
3. Stator assembly
4. Gasket
5. Left-hand crankcase cover
6. Recoil starter driven pulley
7. Washer
8. Bolt
9. Gasket
10. Recoil starter assembly
11. Washer
12. Bolt

1. Place the ATC on level ground and set the parking brake or block the wheels so the vehicle will not roll in either direction.

2. Remove the seat/rear fender assembly.

3. Remove the fuel tank as described in Chapter Six.

4. Remove the gearshift pedal.

5. Remove the recoil starter assembly as described in Chapter Four.

6. On ATC70 models, remove the bolts securing the left-hand crankcase cover and remove the cover and gasket.

7. Remove the nut (**Figure 9**) securing the rotor. On models so equipped, remove the lockwasher.

8. To keep the rotor from turning while removing the nut, install a long screwdriver or drift and prop it against the footpeg assembly as shown in **Figure 10**.

> *CAUTION*
> *Don't try to remove the rotor without a puller; any attempt to do so will ultimately lead to some form of damage to the engine and/or rotor. Many aftermarket pullers are available from most motorcycle dealers or mail order houses. The cost of one of these pullers is low and it makes an excellent addition to any mechanic's tool box. If you can't buy or borrow one, have a dealer remove the rotor.*

9. Screw in a flywheel puller (**Figure 11**) until it stops. Use the following flywheel puller:

   a. ATC70: Honda flywheel puller part No. 07933-0010000, K & N puller part No. 82-015 or equivalent.

   b. ATC110: Honda flywheel puller part No. 07733-0010000, K & N puller part No. 82-010 or equivalent.

10. Hold the puller with a wrench and gradually tighten the center bolt (**Figure 12**) until the rotor disengages from the crankshaft.

> *CAUTION*
> *If normal rotor removal attempts fail, do not force the puller as the threads may be stripped out of the rotor causing expensive damage. Take it to a dealer and have it removed.*

> *NOTE*
> *If the rotor is difficult to remove, strike the puller with a hammer a few times. This will usually break it loose. Do not hit the rotor.*

11. Remove the rotor and puller. Don't lose the Woodruff key on the crankshaft.

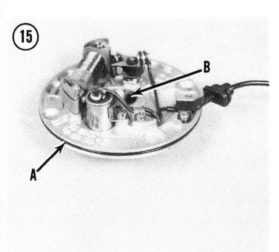

CAUTION
Carefully inspect the inside of the rotor for small bolts, washers or other metal "trash" that may have been picked up by the magnets. These small metal bits can cause severe damage to the alternator stator plate components.

12. Install by reversing these removal steps, noting the following.

13. Make sure the Woodruff key is in place on the crankshaft and align the keyway in the rotor with the key when installing the rotor.

14. On models so equipped, be sure to install the washer (**Figure 13**) prior to installing the rotor nut. Install the rotor nut.

15. Tighten the rotor nut or bolt to the following torque specifications:

    a. ATC70: 33-38 N•m (24-27 ft.-lb.).
    b. ATC110: 60-70 N•m (43-51 ft.-lb.).

Stator Removal/Installation
(ATC70, 1981-on ATC110)

1. Remove the alternator rotor as described in this chapter.

2. Disconnect the electrical connector from the alternator stator assembly to the wiring harness.

3. On models so equipped, slide out the clip (A, **Figure 14**) securing the electrical harness to the crankcase.

4. Remove the bolts (B, **Figure 14**) securing the stator assembly to the left-hand crankcase.

5. Pull the grommet and electrical harness out of the left-hand crankcase.

6. Remove the stator assembly.

7. Install by reversing these removal steps, noting the following.

8. Make sure the large perimeter O-ring seal (A, **Figure 15**) and the crankshaft oil seal (B, **Figure 15**) are in place and in good condition. Replace either if necessary.

9. On models so equipped, install the electrical wire clip and all bolts. Tighten the bolts securely.

10. Route the electrical harness the same way it was before removal.

Rotor Removal
(ATC125M)

1. Place the ATC on level ground and set the parking brake.

2. Remove the seat/rear fender assembly.

3. Drain the engine oil as described in Chapter Three.

4. Remove the fuel tank as described in Chapter Six.

5. Remove the gearshift pedal.

6. Remove the recoil starter assembly (**Figure 16**) as described in Chapter Four.

7. Remove the E-clip (**Figure 17**) on the neutral indicator and remove the neutral indicator.

8. Remove the bolt, O-ring seal and washer (**Figure 18**) securing the recoil starter driven pulley and remove the pulley. To keep the driven pulley from turning, hold it with a long screwdriver as shown in **Figure 19**.

9. Disconnect the electrical connector (**Figure 20**) from the stator assembly to the wiring harness.

10. Remove the bolts securing the left-hand crankcase cover (A, **Figure 21**) and remove the cover and gasket. Don't lose the locating dowels.

> *CAUTION*
> *Don't try to remove the rotor without a puller; any attempt to do so will ultimately lead to some form of damage to the engine and/or rotor. Many aftermarket pullers are available from most motorcycle dealers or mail order houses. The cost of one of these pullers is low and it makes an excellent addition to any mechanic's tool box. If you can't buy or borrow one, have a dealer remove the rotor.*

11. Screw in a flywheel puller (**Figure 22**) until it stops. Use Honda flywheel puller part No. 07733-0010000 or equivalent.

12. To prevent the rotor from rotating, hold the rotor with a strap wrench (**Figure 23**).

13. Using a wrench, gradually tighten the puller until the rotor disengages from the crankshaft.

> *CAUTION*
> *If normal rotor removal attempts fail, do not force the puller as the threads*

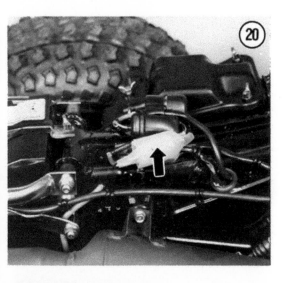

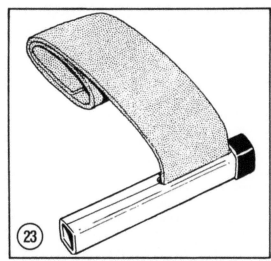

may be stripped out of the rotor causing expensive damage. Take it to a dealer and have it removed.

NOTE
If the rotor is difficult to remove, strike the puller with a hammer a few times. This will usually break it loose. Do not hit the rotor.

14. Remove the rotor and puller. Don't lose the Woodruff key on the crankshaft.

CAUTION
Carefully inspect the inside of the rotor for small bolts, washers or other metal "trash" that may have been picked up by the magnets. These small metal bits can cause severe damage to the alternator stator plate components.

Rotor Installation (ATC125M)

1. Make sure the Woodruff key (**Figure 24**) is in place on the crankshaft.

2. Slightly rotate the rotor/starter clutch assembly *clockwise* in order to install the rotor onto the shoulder on the starter driven gear. Align the keyway in the rotor with the Woodruff key when installing the rotor.
3. Make sure the locating dowels are in place and install a new gasket (**Figure 25**).
4. Install the left-hand crankcase cover.
5. Shift the transmission into NEUTRAL and install the neutral indicator and the E-clip.
6. Connect the electrical connector from the stator assembly.
7. Apply a light coat of grease to the oil seal (B, **Figure 21**) in the left-hand crankcase cover.
8. Align the flats on the recoil starter driven pulley with the notches in the alternator rotor. Then install the recoil starter driven pulley. Make sure the pulley is properly engaged with the rotor.
9. Install the washer, O-ring seal and the bolt securing· the recoil starter driven pulley. Tighten the rotor bolt to 40-45 N•m (29-33 ft.-lb.).
10. To keep the driven pulley from turning, hold it with a long screwdriver as shown in **Figure 19**.

Stator Removal/Installation (ATC125M)

1. Perform Steps 1-10 of *Rotor Removal (ATC125M)* in this chapter.
2. Remove the bolts (A, **Figure 26**) securing the stator assembly to the left-hand crankcase cover.
3. Pull the grommet (B, **Figure 26**) and electrical harness out of the left-hand crankcase cover.
4. Remove the stator assembly.
5. Install by reversing these removal steps, noting the following.
6. Make sure the smaller O-ring seals (A, **Figure 27**) and the crankshaft oil seal (B, **Figure 27**) are in place and in good condition. Replace if necessary.

ALTERNATOR (INNER ROTOR TYPE)

The inner rotor type alternator used on all ATC90 and 1979-1980 ATC110 models is shown in **Figure 28**.

Rotor Removal/Installation

1. Place the ATC on level ground and set the parking brake.
2. Remove the seat/rear fender assembly.
3. Remove the fuel tank as described in Chapter Six.
4. Remove the gearshift pedal.
5. Remove the recoil starter assembly as described in Chapter Four.

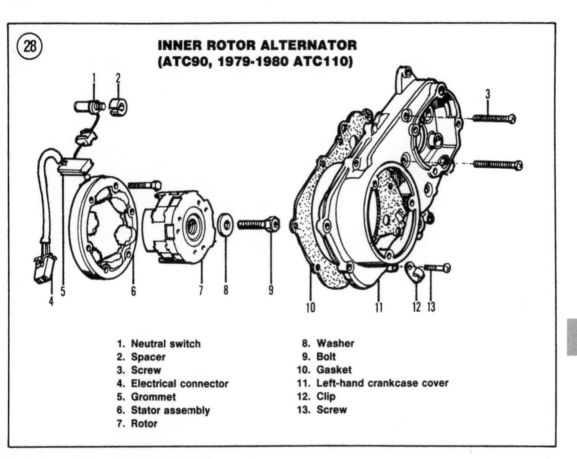

(28)

**INNER ROTOR ALTERNATOR
(ATC90, 1979-1980 ATC110)**

1. Neutral switch
2. Spacer
3. Screw
4. Electrical connector
5. Grommet
6. Stator assembly
7. Rotor
8. Washer
9. Bolt
10. Gasket
11. Left-hand crankcase cover
12. Clip
13. Screw

(29)

6. Insert a long drift or metal rod through the openings in the recoil starter pulley and remove the bolt (**Figure 29**) securing the rotor. On models so equipped, remove the lockwasher.

> *CAUTION*
> *Don't try to remove the rotor without a puller; any attempt to do so will ultimately lead to some form of damage to the engine and/or rotor. Many aftermarket pullers are available from most motorcycle dealers or mail*

order houses. *The cost of one of these pullers is low and it makes an excellent addition to any mechanic's tool box. If you can't buy or borrow one, have a dealer remove the rotor.*

7. Screw in a flywheel puller until it stops. Use the Honda flywheel puller (part No. 07933-2160000) or equivalent.

8. Hold the puller and tap on the cross bar with a rubber mallet until the rotor disengages from the crankshaft.

> *CAUTION*
> *If normal rotor removal attempts fail, do not force the puller as the threads may be stripped out of the rotor causing expensive damage. Take it to a dealer and have it removed.*

> *NOTE*
> *If the rotor is difficult to remove, strike the puller with a hammer a few times. This will usually break it loose. Do not hit the rotor.*

9. Remove the rotor and puller. Don't lose the Woodruff key on the crankshaft.

> *CAUTION*
> *Carefully inspect the outside of the rotor for small bolts, washers or other metal "trash" that may have been picked up by the magnets. These small metal bits can cause severe damage to the alternator stator plate components.*

10. Install by reversing these removal steps, noting the following.

11. Make sure the Woodruff key is in place on the crankshaft and align the keyway in the rotor with the key when installing the rotor.

12. On models so equipped, be sure to install the washer (**Figure 30**) prior to installing the rotor bolt. Install the rotor nut.

13. To keep the rotor from turning, use the same tool set-up (**Figure 31**) used during removal.

14. Tighten the rotor bolt to 26-32 N•m (19-23 ft.-lb.).

Stator Removal/Installation

1. Remove the rotor as described in this chapter.

2. Disconnnect the electrical connector from the stator assembly to the wiring harness.

3. Remove the bolts (**Figure 32**) securing the stator assembly to the left-hand crankcase cover.

4. Pull the grommet and electrical harness out of the left-hand crankcase cover.

5. Remove the stator assembly.

6. Install by reversing these removal steps.

ROTOR TESTING

The rotor is permanently magnetized and cannot be tested except by replacement with a rotor known to be good. A rotor can lose magnetism from old age or a sharp blow. If defective, the rotor must be replaced; it cannot be remagnetized.

STATOR COIL TESTING

Honda does not provide continuity nor resistance specifications for all models. Specifications are available for the following models only:

  a. 1981-on ATC110.
  b. ATC125M.

It is not necessary to remove the stator assembly to perform the following tests. It is shown removed in the following procedures for clarity. All tests are performed at the electrical connector (**Figure 20**). Tests points are either between the different pins within the connector or between the different pins and ground.

In order to get accurate resistance measurements the stator assembly and coil must be warm (minimum temperature is 68° F/20° C). If necessary, start the engine and let it warm up to normal operating temperature.

1981-on ATC110

To check the lighting coil, use an ohmmeter set at R×1 and check for continuity between the white/yellow terminal and ground. If there is no continuity (infinite resistance), the stator assembly must be replaced (the individual coil cannot be replaced).

To check the exciter coil, use an ohmmeter set at R×1 and check for continuity between the black/red terminal and ground. If there is no continuity (infinite resistance), the stator assembly must be replaced (the individual coil cannot be replaced).

ATC125M

To check the exciter coil, use an ohmmeter set at R×1 and check the resistance between the black/red terminal and ground. There should be continuity (specified resistance of 100-400 ohms). If there is no continuity (infinite resistance) or the resistance value is not within these limits, the stator assembly must be replaced (the individual coil cannot be replaced).

To check the charging coil, use an ohmmeter set at R×1 and check the resistance between both yellow terminals within the connector. There should be continuity (specified resistance of 0.5-1.5 ohms). If there is no continuity (infinite resistance) or the resistance value is not within these limits, the stator assembly must be replaced (the individual coil cannot be replaced). Also check for continuity between each yellow terminal and ground. If there is continuity (low resistance), the coil is shorted and the stator assembly must be replaced (the individual coil cannot be replaced).

NOTE
There is no lighting coil on this model.

**VOLTAGE REGULATOR/RECTIFIER
(MODELS SO EQUIPPED)**

Removal/Installation

1. Remove the seat/rear fender assembly.
2. Disconnect the battery negative lead.
3. Remove the screws securing the starter solenoid cover and remove the cover (**Figure 33**).
3. Disconnect the electrical connector to the voltage regulator/rectifier (**Figure 34**) from the wiring harness.
4. Remove the bolts (**Figure 35**) securing the voltage regulator/rectifier to the frame.

7

5. Remove the voltage regulator/rectifier, electrical connector and wires.

6. Install by reversing these removal steps. Make sure all electrical connectors are tight.

Testing

To test the voltage regulator/rectifier, disconnect the electrical connector from the wiring harness (**Figure 34**).

> *NOTE*
> *Tests must be made with a quality ohmmeter or the test readings may be false.*

Make the test measurements using a quality ohmmeter. Refer to **Table 1** for ohmmeter positive (+) and negative (-) test lead placement and specified resistance values.

If the voltage regulator/rectifier unit fails *any one* of the tests, the unit is faulty and must be replaced.

Voltage Regulator
Performance Test

1. Remove the seat/rear fender assembly.
2. Remove the wing nuts securing the battery cover (**Figure 36**) and remove the battery cover.
3. Leave the battery cables attached and connect a DC voltmeter to the battery as shown in **Figure 37**.
4. Start the engine and let it idle.
5. Increase engine speed until the voltage going to the battery reaches 14.0-15.0 volts.
6. At this point, the voltage regulator/rectifier should prevent any further increase in voltage. If this does not happen and the voltage increases above specification, the voltage regulator/rectifier is faulty and must be replaced.

CONTACT BREAKER POINT IGNITION

Contact breaker point ignition is used on all models except the 1981-on ATC110 and the ATC125M. These are equipped with an electronic ignition system that is covered separately in this chapter.

As the rotor of the alternator turns, magnets located in it move past a stationary ignition source coil on the stator, inducing a current in the coil. A contact breaker assembly that is actuated by a cam (attached either to the crankshaft or camshaft), opens at the precise instant the piston reaches its firing position. The energy produced in the source coil is then discharged to the primary side of the ignition coil where the voltage is stepped up on the secondary circuit to a value sufficient to fire the spark plug.

Figure 38 shows a typical contact breaker point ignition system. For a specific model, refer to the electrical diagrams at the end of this book.

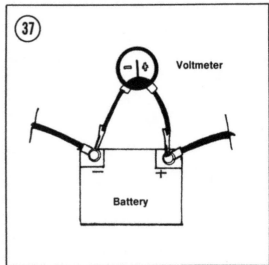

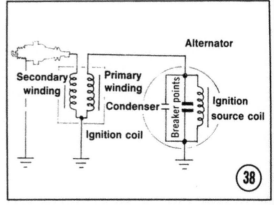

**Breaker Point
Inspection and Cleaning**

NOTE
*The contact breaker point assembly is
mounted on the left-hand side of the
crankshaft on all 70 cc engines. On
90-110 cc engines, the assembly is
mounted on the left-hand side of the
camshaft in the cylinder head.*

During normal operation, the contact surfaces of
the points gradually pit and burn. If the points are
not too badly pitted, they can be dressed with a few
strokes of a clean point file or Flexstone (available at
most auto supply stores). Do not use emery cloth or
sandpaper, as particles will remain on the points

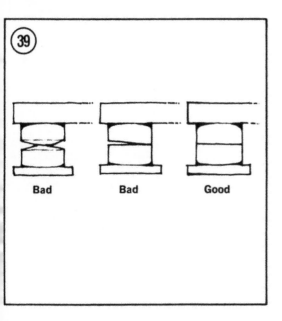

Bad   Bad   Good

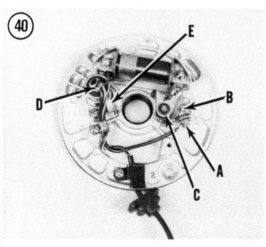

and cause arcing and burning. If a few strokes of the
file do not smooth the points completely, replace
them with a new set. If the points are still
serviceable after filing, remove all residue with
electrical contact cleaner or lacquer thinner. Close
the points on a piece of white paper such as a
business card. Continue to pull the card through the
closed points until no particles or discoloration are
transferred to the card. Finally, rotate the engine
and observe the points as they open and close. If
they do not meet squarely (**Figure 39**) replace them
as described in this chapter.

Oil or dirt may get on the points, creating
electrical resistance in them or resulting in their
failure. These conditions can be caused by a
defective crankshaft or camshaft seal (depending
on model), incorrect breaker cam lubricant or (on
ATC70 engines) dirt getting into the alternator
when the crankcase cover is removed. To correct
these conditions, remove the contact breaker
assembly and dress the points, clean the assembly
in lacquer thinner and lubricate the breaker cam
with contact breaker lubricant. Never use oil or
common grease; they break down under high
temperature and frictional load and are likely to
find their way to the point surface.

A weak return spring will allow the points to
bounce at high engine speeds and cause misfiring.
Usually the spring will last for the life of the
contact breaker assembly.

**Point Set
Removal/Installation
(ATC70)**

1. Remove the alternator rotor as described in this
chapter.
2. Loosen the nut (A, **Figure 40**) securing the
electrical wire to the contact breaker point
assembly and slide the electrical wire out of the
assembly.

NOTE
***Figure 40** is shown with the contact
breaker point assembly and alternator
stator assembly removed for clarity. It is
not necessary to remove the assembly
for this procedure.*

3. Remove the screw (B, **Figure 40**) and E-clip (C,
Figure 40) which hold the contact breaker assembly
in place and remove the breaker point assembly.
4. Install by reversing these removal steps, noting
the following.
5. If the contact breaker points were removed
from the base plate for cleaning, make sure that the

bakelite washers are reinstalled on the mounting post of the contact breaker point assembly (**Figure 41**). These washers insulate the condensor and alternator electrical wires from ground. If the washers are not installed, there will be a dead short in the ignition circuit.

6. When the contact breaker point assembly is replaced the condenser (D, **Figure 40**) should also be replaced. Apply breaker point lubricant to the contact breaker point wick (E, **Figure 40**) and coat the breaker cam.

7. Adjust the timing as described in Chapter Three.

Point Set
Removal/Installation
(ATC90 and ATC110)

1. Remove the screws (**Figure 42**) securing the contact breaker point cover and remove the cover and the gasket.

2. Loosen the nut (A, **Figure 43**) securing the electrical wires to the contact breaker point assembly and slide the wire out of the assembly.

> *NOTE*
> *Figure 43 is shown with the contact breaker point assembly removed for clarity. It is not necessary to remove the assembly for this procedure.*

3. Remove the screws (B, **Figure 43**) which hold the contact breaker assembly in place and remove the breaker point assembly.

4. Install by reversing these removal steps, noting the following.

5. If the contact breaker point assembly and the base plate were replaced, align the circle on the base plate with the index mark on the base casting (**Figure 44**). Install the screws.

6. If the contact breaker points were removed from the base plate for cleaning, make sure that the bakelite washers are reinstalled on the mounting post of the contact breaker points (**Figure 41**). These washers insulate the condensor and alternator electrical wires from ground. If the washers are not installed, there will be a dead short in the ignition circuit.

7. When the contact breaker point assembly is replaced the condenser should also be replaced. Apply breaker point lubricant to the contact breaker point wick (C, **Figure 43**) and coat the breaker cam.

> *NOTE*
> *The condenser is located next to the ignition coil.*

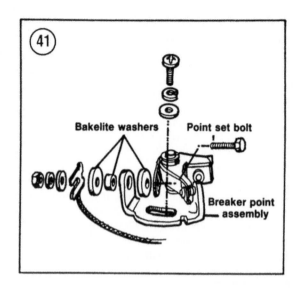

Bakelite washers   Point set bolt

Breaker point assembly

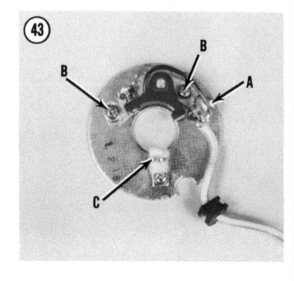

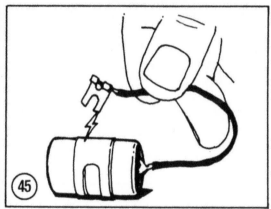

8. Adjust the timing as described in Chapter Three.

Condenser (All Models)

The condenser requires no service other than checking to see that its connections is clean and tight. It should be routinely replaced each time the contact breaker assembly is replaced as described in this chapter.

To test the condenser, remove it from the breaker point (or ignition coil) assembly and connect it to a 6-volt battery. Connect the battery negative lead (-) to the condenser lead and the battery positive lead (+) to the condenser case. Allow it to charge for a few seconds. Then, quickly disconnect it and touch the lead to the condenser case (**Figure 45**). If there is a spark as the lead touches the case, you may assume that the condenser is good. If not, replace the condenser.

Ignition Advance Mechanism
Removal/Inspection/Installation

The ignition advance mechanism advances the ignition (fires the spark plug sooner) as engine speed increases. If it does not advance properly and smoothly, the ignition will be incorrect at high engine rpm. It must be inspected periodically to make certain it operates smoothly.

The ignition advance mechanism is used on all ATC90 and ATC110 engines. ATC70 engines are not equipped with an ignition advance mechanism.

1. Remove the contact breaker point assembly as described in this chapter.
2. Remove the bolt and washer (**Figure 46**) securing the ignition advance unit to the camshaft and remove the unit.
3. Inspect the pivot points (A, **Figure 47**) of each weight. The arms must rotate freely to maintain proper ignition advance.

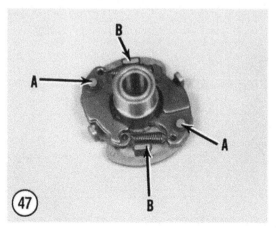

4. Inspect the return springs (B, **Figure 47**). Make sure they are taut and they completely return the arms to their fully retarded position.

5. If the unit fails any of these inspections it must be replaced.

6. Install by reversing these removal steps, noting the following.

7. Index the dowel pin on the camshaft (**Figure 48**) with the notch on the backside of the ignition advance unit. Install the bolt and washer and tighten the bolt to 9-12 N•m (7-9 ft.-lb.).

CAPACITOR DISCHARGE IGNITION

The capacitor discharge ignition is used on the 1981-on ATC110 and ATC125M models. The capacitor discharge ignition (CDI) system is a solid-state system that uses no breaker points. **Figure 49** shows a typical CDI ignition system.

Alternating current from the alternator flows to the CDI unit where it is rectified to direct current and is used to charge the capacitor. At the same time the ignition current is produced, another current pulse is produced by the alternator and a secondary signal coil. This secondary current is timed precisely to coinside with the engine's firing point and can be regarded as the timing signal.

This timing signal is sent to an electronic switch called a thyristor which is connected between the discharge side of the capacitor and the primary side of the ignition coil. In its normal condition, a thyristor blocks the flow of electricity. When the signal reaches the thyristor, it opens, or conducts, permitting the energy stored in the capacitor to discharge to the primary side of the ignition coil where it is stepped up in the secondary circuit to a value sufficient to fire the spark plug.

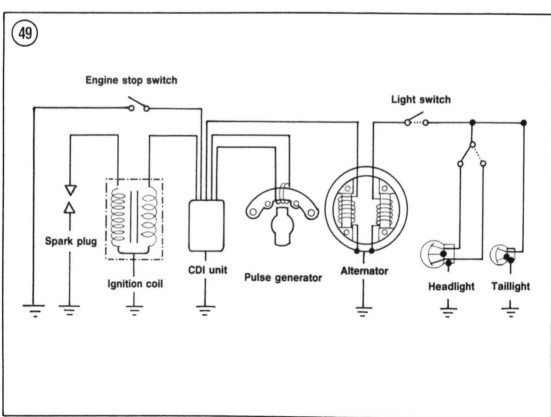

Precautions

Certain measures must be taken to protect the capacitor discharge system. Damage to the semiconductors in the system may occur if the following precautions are not observed.

1. Never disconnect any of the electrical connections while the engine is running.

2. Keep all connections between the various units clean and tight. Be sure that the wiring connectors are pushed together firmly to help keep out moisture.

3. Do not substitute another type of ignition coil.

4. The CDI unit is mounted within a rubber vibration isolator. Always be sure that the isolator is in place when installing the unit.

5. On models so equipped, never connect the battery backwards. If the battery polarity is wrong, damage will occur to the rectifier and to the alternator.

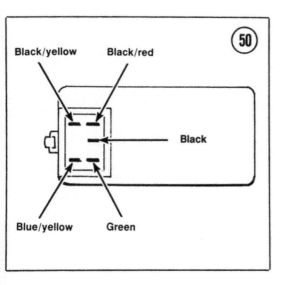

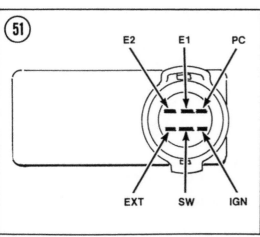

Troubleshooting

Problems with the capacitor discharge system are usually the production of a weak spark or no spark at all.

Check all connections to make sure they are tight and free of corrosion or rust.

Check that the ignition coil is not damaged or cracked. If the case is damaged in any way or the spark plug lead is damaged the coil should be replaced.

Testing

To test the CDI unit, remove the unit from the frame as described in this chapter.

CAUTION
Tests may be performed on the CDI unit but a good one may be damaged by someone unfamiliar with the test equipment. If you feel unqualified to perform the test, have the test made by a Honda dealer or substitute a known good unit for a suspected one.

NOTE
Tests must be made with a good quality ohmmeter or the test readings may be false.

Refer to **Table 2** for ohmmeter positive (+) and negative (-) test lead placement and specified resistance values.

On all models the electrical wire harness connector disconnects from the CDI unit. The tests are made directly to the terminals within the CDI unit. For terminal color designation refer to **Figure 50** (ATC110) or **Figure 51** (ATC125M).

If the CDI unit fails *any one* of the tests, the unit is faulty and must be replaced.

CDI Unit Replacement

1. Remove the seat/rear fender assembly.
2. Remove the fuel tank as described in Chapter Six.
3. Pull the CDI unit and its rubber isolator (A, **Figure 52**) off of the bracket on the frame.
4. Disconnect the electrical connector (B, **Figure 52**) going from the CDI unit to the electrical harness.
5. Install a new CDI unit and attach the electrical connector to it. Make sure all electrical connections are tight.
6. Reinstall the fuel tank, rear fender and seat.

Ignition Pulse Generator
Inspection/Replacement

Refer to **Figure 53** for this procedure.

The ignition pulse generator is mounted on the end of the camshaft on the left-hand side of the cylinder head.

NOTE
In order to get accurate resistance measurements the unit must be at approximately 68° F (20° C).

1. Disconnect the electrical connector (containing 2 wires, one green and one blue/yellow) from the ignition pulse generator (**Figure 54**).

2. Use an ohmmeter set at R×10 and check resistance between the blue/yellow and green wires. The specified resistance is as follows:
   a. ATC110: 20-60 ohms.
   b. ATC125M: 90 ohms.
If the reading falls within these values the ignition pulse generator is good. If there is no continuity (infinite resistance) the unit is faulty and must be replaced.

3. To remove the ignition pulse generator assembly, remove the screws securing the ignition cover (**Figure 55**) and remove the cover.

NOTE
Prior to removing the pulse generator assembly, make a mark on the base plate that lines up with the centerline of one of the attachment screws. This will

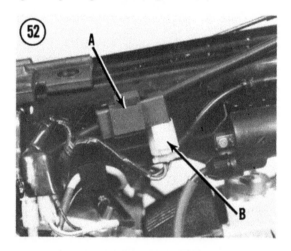

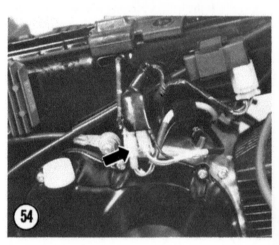

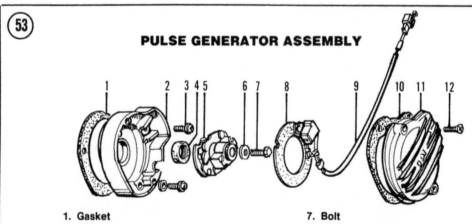

PULSE GENERATOR ASSEMBLY

1. Gasket
2. Pulse base
3. Screw
4. Oil seal
5. Pulse rotor and ignition advance unit
6. Washer
7. Bolt
8. Pulse generator assembly
9. Electrical wire and connector
10. Gasket
11. Ignition cover
12. Screw

assure correct ignition timing when the assembly is installed (providing it was correct prior to removal).

4. Pull the electrical wire (disconnected in Step 1) (A, **Figure 56**) free and remove the screw (B, **Figure 56**) securing the electrical cable to the cylinder head.

5. Remove the screws (**Figure 57**) securing the pulse generator assembly and remove the assembly.

6. Install by reversing these removal steps. Adjust the ignition timing as described in Chapter Three.

Ignition Advance Mechanism
Removal/Inspection/Installation

The ignition advance mechanism advances the ignition (fires the spark plug sooner) as engine

speed increases. If it does not advance properly and smoothly, the ignition will be incorrect at high engine rpm. It must be inspected periodically to make certain it operates freely.

1. Remove the ignition pulse generator as described in this chapter.

2. Remove the bolt and washer (**Figure 58**) securing the pulse rotor and the ignition advance mechanism and remove the assembly.

3. Don't lose the dowel pin (A, **Figure 59**) on the camshaft.

4. If necessary, remove the bolts (B, **Figure 59**) securing the pulse base and remove the pulse base and gasket.

5. Inspect the rotor pivot points (**Figure 60**) of each weight. The rotor must pivot freely to maintain proper ignition advance. Apply lightweight grease to the pivot pins.

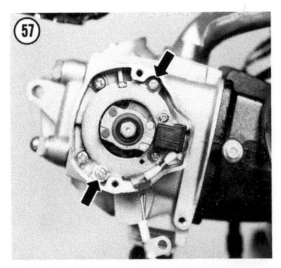

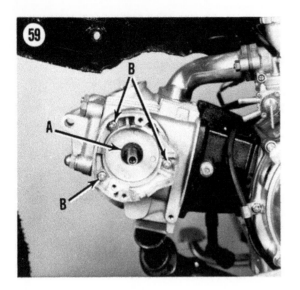

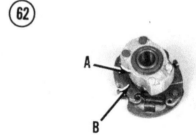

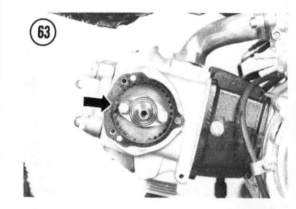

6. Inspect the rotor return springs (**Figure 61**). Make sure they are taut and completely return the rotor to its fully retarded position.

7. If the unit fails either of these inspections it must be replaced.

8. If the rotor was removed from the base, install it, aligning the punch mark (A, **Figure 62**) with the index mark on the base (B, **Figure 62**).

9. If removed, install the pulse base and gasket (**Figure 63**).

10. Make sure the dowel pin is in place on the camshaft.

11. When installing the pulse rotor and ignition advance mechanism, index the notch on the backside of the advance unit with the pin in the end of the camshaft (**Figure 64**).

12. Install the bolt and washer securing the pulse generator and ignition advance mechanism and tighten to 12 N•m (9 ft.-lb.).

13. Install the pulse generator assembly as described in this chapter.

14. Adjust the ignition timing as described in Chapter Three.

IGNITION COIL

The ignition coil is located on the backbone of the frame.

Removal/Installation

1. Remove the seat/rear fender assembly.

2. Remove the fuel tank as described in Chapter Six.

3. Disconnect the high voltage lead from the spark plug (A, **Figure 65**).

4. Remove the nuts and lockwashers (B, **Figure 65**) securing the ignition coil to the frame.

5. Disconnect the primary electrical connector (C, **Figure 65**) going to the ignition coil and remove the coil.

6. Install by reversing these removal steps. Make sure all electrical connections are tight and free of corrosion.

Testing

The ignition coil is a form of transformer which develops the high voltage required to jump the spark plug gap. The only maintenance required is that of keeping the electrical connections clean and tight and occasionally checking to see that the coil is mounted securely.

If the condition of the coil is doubtful, there are several checks which may be made.

Dynamic test

First, as a quick check of coil condition, disconnect the high voltage lead from the spark plug. Remove the spark plug from the cylinder head. Connect a new or known good spark plug to the high voltage lead and place the spark plug base on a good ground such as the engine cylinder head (**Figure 66**). Position the spark plug so you can see the electrodes.

> *WARNING*
> *On models with a CDI ignition system, if it is necessary to hold the high voltage lead, do so with an insulated pair of pliers. The high voltage generated by the CDI could produce serious or fatal shocks.*

Turn the engine over with the recoil starter. If a fat blue spark occurs, the coil is in good condition; if not, proceed as follows. Make sure that you are using a known good spark plug for this test. If the spark plug used is defective the test results will be incorrect.

Reinstall the spark plug in the cylinder head.

Static test

Honda does not provide resistance specifications for all models. Refer to **Figure 67** for this procedure.

> *NOTE*
> *In order to get accurate resistance measurements the coil must be at approximately 68° F (20° C).*

1. Disconnect all ignition coil wires before testing.

2. Measure the coil primary resistance using an ohmmeter set at R × 1. Measure between the primary terminal and the mounting flange. The reading should be as follows:

   a. All ATC70: 0.2-0.3 ohms.

   b. 1981-on ATC110: 0.2-0.8 ohms.

   c. ATC125M: 10-18 K ohms.

   d. All others–continuity should exist.

7

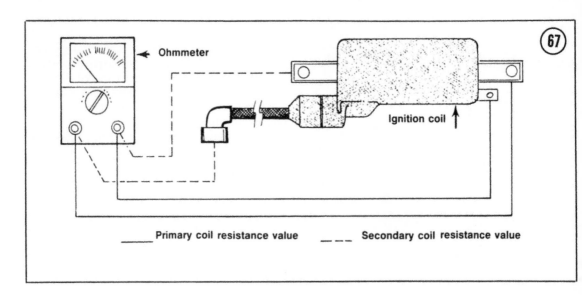

Primary coil resistance value _ _ _ _ Secondary coil resistance value

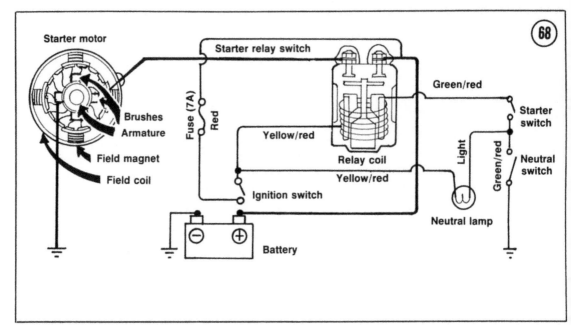

3. Measure the secondary resistance using an ohmmeter set at R×100 or R×1,000. Measure between the secondary lead (spark plug lead) and the mounting flange or green ground wire. The reading should be as follows:

   a. All ATC70: 9-11 ohms.
   b. 1981-on ATC110: 8-15 ohms.
   c. ATC125M: 3-5 K ohms.
   d. All others—continuity should exist.

4. If the coil resistance does not meet either of these specifications, the coil must be replaced. If the coil exhibits visible damage, it should be replaced.

STARTING SYSTEM (MODELS SO EQUIPPED)

The starting system consists of the starter motor, starter gears, solenoid and the starter button.

The layout of the starting system is shown in **Figure 68**. When the starter button is pressed, it engages the starter solenoid switch that completes the circuit allowing electricity to flow from the battery to the starter motor.

CAUTION
Do not operate the starter for more than 5 seconds at a time. Let it rest

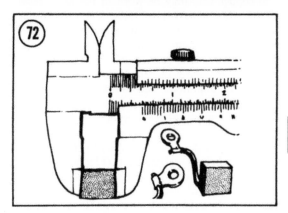

approximately 10 seconds, then use it again.

Table 3, at the end of the chapter, lists possible starter problems, probable causes and most common remedies.

STARTER

The overhaul of a starter motor is best left to an expert. The disassembly/inspection/assembly procedure shows how to detect a defective starter.

The starter gears are covered in Chapter Four.

Removal/Installation

1. Remove the seat/rear fender assembly.
2. Unscrew the wing bolts securing the battery cover and remove the cover (**Figure 36**).
3. Disconnect the battery negative lead.
4. Remove the bolts (**Figure 69**) on the left-hand crankcase spacer cover.
5. Remove bolts (**Figure 70**) securing the starter bracket on the right-hand side.
6. Pull back the rubber cap and disconnect the black electric starter cable from the starter (**Figure 71**).
7. Pull the starter to the right and disengage the splines of the starter from the starter idler gear.
8. Install by reversing these removal steps.

Disassembly/Inspection/Assembly

1. Remove the bolts and remove the end cap from the motor assembly.

NOTE
Write down the number of shims used on the shaft next to the commutator. Be sure to install the same number when reassembling the starter.

2. Clean all grease, dirt and carbon from the armature and the end cap.

CAUTION
Do not immerse brushes or the wire windings in solvent as the insulation may be damaged. Wipe the windings with a cloth lightly moistened with solvent and dry thoroughly.

3. Move the tension spring out from the backside of each brush and pull the brush out of its receptacle in the brush plate. Measure the length of each brush with a vernier caliper (**Figure 72**). Standard new brush length is 12-13 mm (0.47-0.51 in.). If the length of either brush is 6.5 mm (0.26 in.) or less, replace both brushes as a set.

4. To replace the brushes, remove the screw securing each brush to the brush plate and remove each brush assembly.

5. Reinstall each brush and tighten the mounting screws securely.

6. When reinstalling the brush into its receptacle in the brush plate, make sure the tension spring is properly located within the notch in the end of each brush.

7. Inspect the condition of the commutator. The mica in a good commutator is below the surface of the copper bars. On a worn commutator the mica and copper bars may be worn to the same level (**Figure 73**). If necessary, have the commutator serviced by a dealer or electrical repair shop.

8. Inspect the commutator copper bars for discoloration. If a pair of bars are discolored, grounded armature coils are indicated.

9. Use an ohmmeter and check for continuity between the commutator bars (**Figure 74**); there should be continuity (low resistance) between pairs of bars.

10. Also check for continuity between the commutator bars and the shaft (**Figure 75**); there should be no continuity (infinite resistance). If the unit fails either of these tests the armature is faulty and must be replaced.

11. Use an ohmmeter and check for continuity between the starter cable terminal and the starter case; there should be no continuity. Also check continuity between the starter cable terminal and each brush wire terminal; there should be continuity. If the unit fails either of these tests the starter motor assembly must be replaced.

12. Assemble the case as follows:

    a. Align the pin on the brush plate with the notch in the starter case and push the brush plate all the way down until it seats completely in the case.

    b. Be sure to install all shims on the shaft next to the commutator.

    c. Align the pin on the brush plate with the notch in the end cap and install the end cap.

    d. Install the case bolts and tighten securely.

STARTER SOLENOID

Removal/Installation

1. Remove the seat/rear fender assembly.

2. Unscrew the wing bolts securing the battery cover and remove the cover (**Figure 36**).

3. Disconnect the battery positive and negative leads.

4. Remove the screws securing the solenoid cover and remove the cover (**Figure 33**).

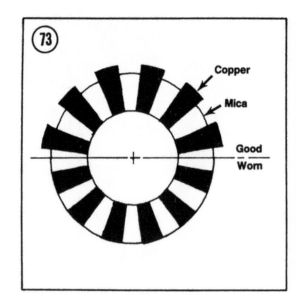

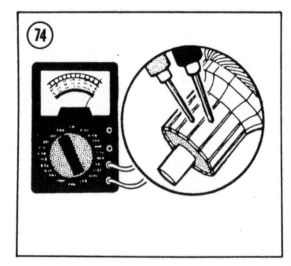

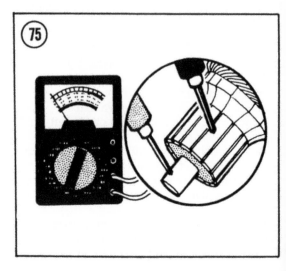

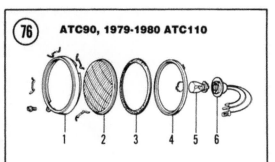

ATC90, 1979-1980 ATC110

1 2 3 4 5 6

1981-ON ATC110, ATC125M

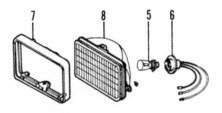

7   8   5   6

HEADLIGHT ASSEMBLY

1. Trim bezel
2. Lens
3. Gasket
4. Inner rim
5. Headlight bulb
6. Bulb socket
7. Trim bezel
8. Headlight lens unit

5. Slide off the rubber protective boot.

6. Remove the nuts and washers and disconnect both electrical wires from the top terminals of the solenoid.

7. Remove the solenoid from the rubber mount on the frame.

8. Replace by reversing these removal steps. Make sure all electrical connections are tight.

Testing

1. Disconnect the electrical connectors going to the starter solenoid.

2. Connect a 12 volt battery to the electrical connector containing 2 wires (one green/red and one yellow/red).

3. Check for continuity using an ohmmeter set at R×1. Measure between the connector bolts on top of the solenoid. There should be continuity (low resistance).

4. If there is no continuity, the solenoid is faulty and must be replaced.

LIGHTING SYSTEM
(MODELS SO EQUIPPED)

The lighting system consists of a headlight and a taillight. **Table 4** lists replacement bulbs for these components.

Always use the correct wattage bulb as indicated in this section. A larger wattage bulb will give a dim light and a smaller wattage bulb will burn out prematurely.

Headlight Replacement

Refer to **Figure 76** for this procedure.

1. Remove the screw(s) (**Figure 77**) securing the headlight assembly to the case.

2. Pull out on the bottom of the headlight assembly and disengage it from the locating tab on top of the headlight housing.

3. Pull back the rubber boot (**Figure 78**).

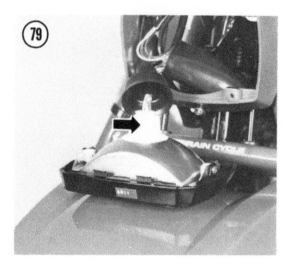

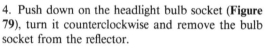

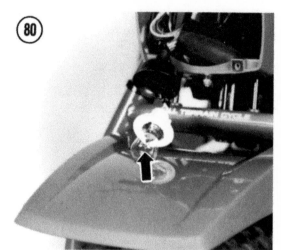

4. Push down on the headlight bulb socket (**Figure 79**), turn it counterclockwise and remove the bulb socket from the reflector.

5. Remove the light bulb (**Figure 80**) from the bulb socket.

6A. On ATC90 and ATC110 models, remove the retaining clips securing the lens units to the trim bezel.

6B. On ATC125M models, remove the adjusting components and remove the screws and nuts on each side of the lens unit securing the lens unit to the trim bezel.

7. Remove the lens unit from the trim bezel.

8. If the lens unit is dirty, wash out the inside and outside with a mild detergent and wipe dry. Blow out the inside with compressed air or let it sit until it is completely dry before installing the bulb.

9. Assemble by reversing this sequence.

10. Install by reversing these removal steps.

11. On ATC125M models, adjust the headlight as described in this chapter.

Headlight Adjustment (ATC125M)

Adjustment is limited to vertical changes. Adjust to your own personal preference. Turn the screw (**Figure 81**) at the base of the headlight trim bezel. There are as yet no regulations on headlight adjustment for off-road use.

Taillight Replacement

1. Remove the screws securing the lens (**Figure 82**) and remove the lens.

2. Wash out the inside and outside of the lens with a mild detergent and wipe dry. Wipe off the reflective base surrounding the bulb with a soft cloth.

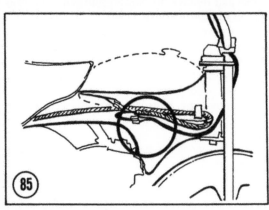

3. Inspect the condition of the lens gasket and replace if it is damaged or deteriorated.
4. Replace the bulb and install the lens; do not overtighten the screws as the lens may crack.

Neutral Indicator Light Replacement (ATC125M)

1. Carefully pull the neutral indicator light/socket assembly out of the bottom left-hand side of the handlebar upper holder.

2. Replace the defective bulb.
3. Install by reversing these removal steps.

SWITCHES

Engine Kill Switch, Light Switch and Starter Switch Removal/Installation (1982-on ATC110 and ATC125M)

1. Remove the headlight lens unit as described in this chapter.

> *NOTE*
> *Follow the electrical wires from the switch housing into the backside of the headlight case. Gently pull on the wire outside of the headlight case and watch which one moves within the headlight case. Disconnect those wires and continue until all wires going to the switch assembly are disconnected.*

2. Within the headlight housing, disconnect from the wiring harness all electrical wire connectors (**Figure 83**) going to the combination engine kill switch/light switch/starter switch (starter on ATC125M only).
3. Pull the wires out through the rear of the headlight case.
4. Remove the screws securing the combination switch (**Figure 84**) to the handlebar and remove the switch assembly.
5. Install a new switch assembly by reversing these removal steps. Make sure all electrical wires are tight.

Engine Kill Switch Removal/Installation (All Other Models)

1A. On models equipped with a headlight, perform the following:
   a. Remove the headlight lens as described in this chapter.
   b. Within the headlight housing, disconnect from the wiring harness the 2 electrical wire connectors going to the engine kill switch.
   c. Remove the engine kill switch electrical wires from the headlight housing.
1B. On models without a headlight, perform the following:
   a. Remove the fuel tank as described in Chapter Six.
   b. Disconnect from the wiring harness the 2 electrical wire connectors (**Figure 85**) going to the engine kill switch.

7

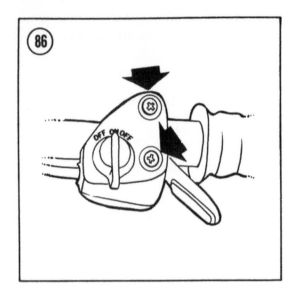

backside of the headlight case. Gently pull on the wire outside of the headlight case and watch which one moves within the-headlight case. Disconnect those wires and continue until all wires going to the ignition switch assembly are disconnected.

2. Within the headlight housing, disconnect from the wiring harness all electrical wire connectors (**Figure 83**) going to the ignition switch.

3. Pull the wires out through the rear of the headlight case.

4. Remove the small nameplate with a screwdriver.

5. Remove the screws securing the handlebar upper cover and remove the cover.

6. Loosen the locknut (**Figure 88**) on the choke cable and remove the choke cable and knob from the handlebar upper holder.

7. Carefully pull the neutral indicator light/socket assembly out of the bottom left-hand side of the handlebar upper holder.

8. Cover the fuel tank with a soft cloth to protect it from the handlebar.

9. Remove the bolts (**Figure 89**) securing the handlebar upper holder and remove the upper holder.

10. Let the handlebar assembly swing down until it stops.

11. Remove the rubber boot from the backside of the ignition switch.

12. Push in on the retaining tabs of the holder and push the ignition switch and holder out from the backside of the handlebar upper holder.

13. Install a new switch assembly by reversing these removal steps, noting the following.

14. Swing the handlebar up into position. Align the punch mark on the handlebar with the upper surface of the handlebar lower holders (**Figure 90**).

15. Install the handlebar upper holder and tighten the bolts finger-tight. Tighten the forward bolts first and then the rear to 18-30 N•m (13-22 ft.-lb.).

16. Make sure all electrical wires are tight.

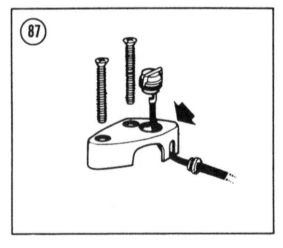

2. Remove the screws (**Figure 86**) securing the throttle lever assembly together and to the handlebar.

3. Separate the throttle lever assembly and remove the engine kill switch (**Figure 87**) from the upper case half.

4. Install a new switch assembly by reversing these removal steps. Make sure all electrical connectors are tight.

Ignition Switch
Removal/Installation
(ATC125M)

1. Remove the headlight lens unit as described in this chapter.

NOTE
Follow the electrical wires from the ignition switch housing into the

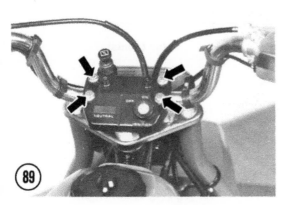

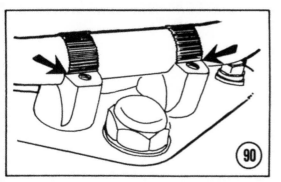

4. Install a new switch assembly by reversing these removal steps. Make sure all electrical connectors are tight.

FUSE

Only models that are equipped with a starter have a fuse.

Remove the screws securing the starter relay cover and remove the cover (**Figure 33**). The fuse is located next to the starter solenoid (**Figure 91**) and its capacity is 7 amps.

NOTE
Always carry a spare fuse.

Whenever a fuse blows, find out the reason for the failure before replacing the fuse. Usually the trouble is a short circuit in the wiring. This may be caused by worn-through insulation or a disconnected wire shorted to ground.

CAUTION
Never substitute aluminum foil or wire for a fuse. Never use a higher amperage fuse than specified. An overload could cause a fire and complete loss of the ATC.

Headlight Switch
Removal/Installation
(ATC90 and 1979-1980 ATC110)

1. Remove the headlight lens as described in this chapter.

2. Within the headlight housing, disconnect from the wiring harness all electrical wire connectors going to the light switch.

3. Remove the switch assembly and electrical wires from the headlight housing.

Table 1 VOLTAGE REGULATOR/RECTIFIER TEST POINTS

Test probe		
Positive	Negative	Value (ohms)
Yellow	yellow	1-50
Yellow	green	0.1-10
Yellow	red	infinity
Yellow	yellow	1-50
Yellow	green	0.1-10
Yellow	red	infinity
Green	yellow	0.5-50
Green	yellow	0.5-10
Green	red	infinity
Red	yellow	0.1-10
Red	yellow	0.1-10
Red	green	0.2-30

Table 2 CDI UNIT TEST POINTS

Test probe		
Positive	Negative	Value (ohms)
ATC110		
Black	green	0.2-60K
Black	black/red	0.1-20K
Black	blue/yellow	0.5-200K
Black	black/yellow	infinity
Green	black	infinity
Green	black/red	infinity
Green	blue/yellow	1-5K
Green	black/yellow	infinity
Black/red	black	infinity
Black/red	green	0.1-20K
Black/red	blue/yellow	0.5-100K
Black/red	black/yellow	infinity
Blue/yellow	black	infinity
Blue/yellow	green	infinity
Blue/yellow	black/red	infinity
Blue/yellow	black/yellow	infinity
Black/yellow	black	infinity
Black/yellow	green	infinity
Black/yellow	black/red	infinity
Black/yellow	blue/yellow	infinity
ATC125M		
SW	EXT	0.1-20
SW	PC	0.5-200
SW	E1	0.2-60
SW	E2	0.2-60
SW	IGN	infinity
EXT	SW	infinity
EXT	PC	0.5-100
EXT	E1	0.1-2.0
EXT	E2	0.1-2.0
EXT	IGN	infinity
PC	SW	infinity
PC	EXT	infinity
PC	E1	infinity
PC	E2	infinity
PC	IGN	infinity
E1	SW	infinity
E1	EXT	infinity
E1	PC	1-5
E1	IGN	infinity
E2	SW	infinity
E2	EXT	infinity
E2	PC	1-5
E2	IGN	infinity
IGN	SW	infinity
IGN	EXT	infinity
IGN	PC	infinity
IGN	E1	infinity
IGN	E2	infinity

Table 3 STARTER TROUBLESHOOTING

Symptom	Probable Cause	Remedy
Starter does not work	Low battery	Recharge battery
	Worn brushes	Replace brushes
	Defective relay	Repair or replace
	Defective switch	Repair or replace
	Defective wiring or connection	Repair wire or clean connection
	Internal short circuit	Repair or replace defective component
Starter action is weak	Low battery	Recharge battery
	Pitted relay contacts	Clean or replace
	Worn brushes	Replace brushes
	Defective connection	Clean and tighten
	Short circuit in commutator	Replace armature
Starter runs continuously	Stuck relay	Replace relay
Starter turns; does not turn engine	Defective starter clutch	Replace starter clutch

Table 4 REPLACEMENT BULBS

Item	Voltage/wattage
Headlight	
ATC90	6V 15W
ATC110	
1978-1980	6V 25W
1981-on	12V 45/45W
ATC125M	12V 45/45W
Taillight	
ATC90	6V 3W
ATC110	
1978-1980	6V 3W
1981-on	12V 3.4W
ATC125M	12V 5W

7

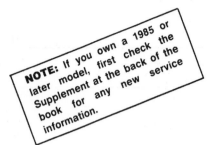

NOTE: If you own a 1985 or later model, first check the Supplement at the back of the book for any new service information.

CHAPTER EIGHT

STEERING, SUSPENSION AND FRAME

This chapter describes repair and maintenance of the front and rear wheels, front forks, steering components and rear axle.

Refer to **Table 1** for torque specifications for both the front and rear suspension components. **Table 1** and **Table 2** are located at the end of this chapter.

FRONT WHEEL

Removal/Installatiton

1. Place the ATC on level ground and set the parking brake. Block the rear wheels so the vehicle will not roll in either direction.
2. Jack up the front of the vehicle with a small hydraulic jack or place wood blocks under the engine. If a small jack is used, perform the following:
   a. Place the jack either under the frame or the engine crankcase.
   b. Place a piece of wood between the jack and the engine crankcase if this location is used.
   c. Apply just enough jack pressure to take any weight off the front wheel.
3. On models equipped with a front brake, perform the following:
   a. Completely unscrew the front brake cable adjusting nut (A, **Figure 1**).
   b. Withdraw the brake cable from the pivot pin in the brake lever.
   c. Remove the brake cable from the receptacle on the brake panel (B, **Figure 1**).
4A. On ATC70 models, remove the cotter pin and axle nut on the left-hand side.

NOTE
The 1970-1974 ATC90 models are also equipped with a lockwasher between the axle nut and the collar on each end. Remove the lockwasher after the axle nut is removed.

4B. On all other models, remove the cotter pin and axle nut (**Figure 2**) on either the right-hand or the left-hand side.
5. On the side from which the nut was removed, slide the collar (**Figure 3**) off the axle.
6. Withdraw the front axle from the wheel and the fork legs.

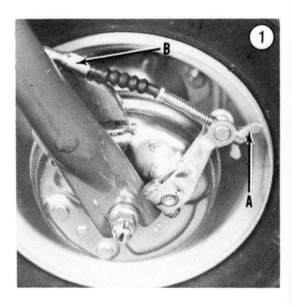

2

3

4

7A. On models equipped with a front brake, remove the spacer collar from the right-hand side.

7B. On all other models, remove the spacer collars on each side of the hub.

8. Roll the wheel forward and remove it.

9. Install by reversing these removal steps, noting the following.

10. On models equipped with a front brake, perform the following:

   a. Position the brake panel correctly when lowering the front fork down onto the axle. Once the forks are down and in position the brake panel cannot be rotated into the correct location.

   b. Make sure that the notch in the brake panel is properly indexed onto the stud on the inside surface of the left-hand fork leg (**Figure 4**).

11. Tighten the axle nuts to the torque specification listed in **Table 1**. Install new cotter pin(s) and bend the ends over completely.

> *NOTE*
> *Always install new cotter pins. Never reuse an old one as it may break and fall out.*

12. On models equipped with a front brake, adjust the front brake as described in Chapter Three.

8

FRONT HUB

Refer to **Figures 5-9** for this procedure. This procedure is shown on a model equipped with a front brake. The service procedures are the same for models without an integral brake drum on the front hub.

The front wheel and hub on the 1970-1974 ATC90 looks different from all other models, but service is the same.

Inspection

Inspect each wheel bearing prior to removing it from the wheel hub.

> *CAUTION*
> *Do not remove the wheel bearings for inspection as they will be damaged during the removal process. Remove the wheel bearings only if they are to be replaced.*

1. Perform Steps 1-4 of *Disassembly* in this chapter.

2. Turn each bearing by hand. Make sure each bearing turns smoothly.

> *NOTE*
> *Some axial play is normal, but radial play should be negligible. The bearing should turn smoothly.*

⑤

FRONT AXLE (ATC70)

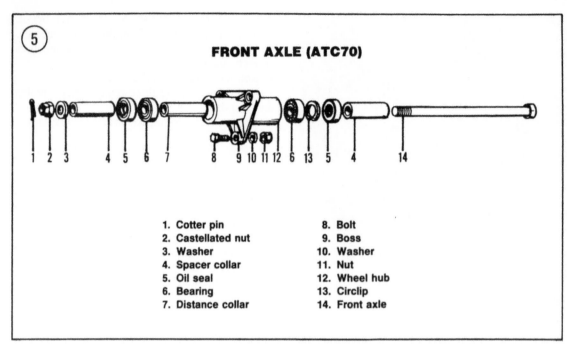

1. Cotter pin
2. Castellated nut
3. Washer
4. Spacer collar
5. Oil seal
6. Bearing
7. Distance collar
8. Bolt
9. Boss
10. Washer
11. Nut
12. Wheel hub
13. Circlip
14. Front axle

⑥

FRONT AXLE (1970-1974 ATC90)

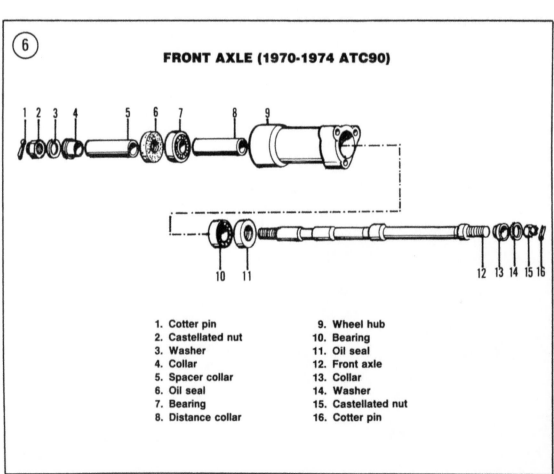

1. Cotter pin
2. Castellated nut
3. Washer
4. Collar
5. Spacer collar
6. Oil seal
7. Bearing
8. Distance collar
9. Wheel hub
10. Bearing
11. Oil seal
12. Front axle
13. Collar
14. Washer
15. Castellated nut
16. Cotter pin

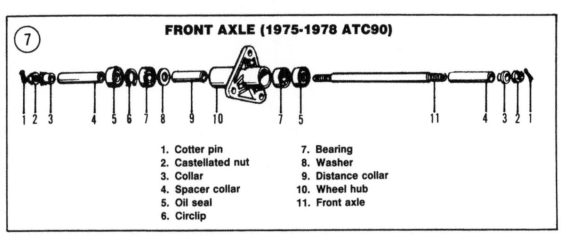

FRONT AXLE (1975-1978 ATC90)

1. Cotter pin
2. Castellated nut
3. Collar
4. Spacer collar
5. Oil seal
6. Circlip
7. Bearing
8. Washer
9. Distance collar
10. Wheel hub
11. Front axle

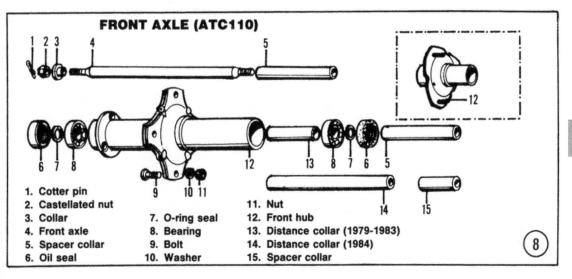

FRONT AXLE (ATC110)

1. Cotter pin
2. Castellated nut
3. Collar
4. Front axle
5. Spacer collar
6. Oil seal
7. O-ring seal
8. Bearing
9. Bolt
10. Washer
11. Nut
12. Front hub
13. Distance collar (1979-1983)
14. Distance collar (1984)
15. Spacer collar

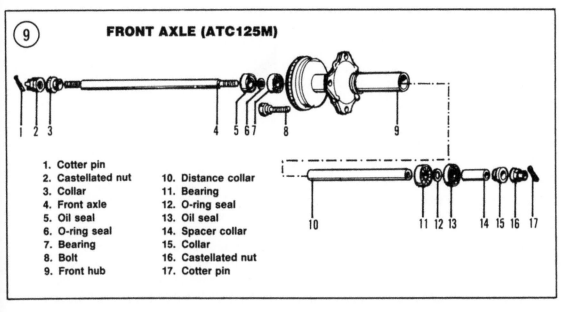

FRONT AXLE (ATC125M)

1. Cotter pin
2. Castellated nut
3. Collar
4. Front axle
5. Oil seal
6. O-ring seal
7. Bearing
8. Bolt
9. Front hub
10. Distance collar
11. Bearing
12. O-ring seal
13. Oil seal
14. Spacer collar
15. Collar
16. Castellated nut
17. Cotter pin

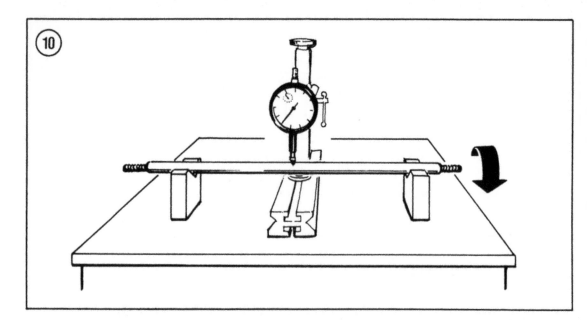

3. On non-sealed bearings, check the balls for evidence of wear, pitting or excessive heat (bluish tint). Replace bearings if necessary; always replace as a complete set. When replacing, be sure to take your old bearings along to ensure a perfect matchup.

> *NOTE*
> *Fully sealed bearings are available from many good bearing specialty shops. Fully sealed bearings provide better protection from dirt and moisture that may get into the hub.*

4. Check the axle for signs of fatigue, fractures and straightness. Use V-blocks and a dial indicator as shown in **Figure 10**. If the runout is 0.5 mm (0.02 in.) or greater, the axle should be replaced.

5. Check the hole in both ends of the axle where the cotter pins fit in. Make sure there are no fractures or cracks leading out toward the end of the axle. If any are found, replace the axle immediately.

6. Inspect the grease seals and O-ring seals. Replace if they are deteriorating or starting to harden.

Disassembly

1. Remove the front wheel as described in this chapter.

> *NOTE*
> *Do not remove the hub assembly from the tire/wheel assembly as the tire/wheel assembly is an ideal holding fixture.*

2. On models so equipped, remove the brake assembly.

3. On the left-hand side, remove the grease seal (**Figure 11**). On 1979-on ATC110 and ATC125M, also remove the O-ring seal.

4. On the right-hand side, remove the grease seal (**Figure 12**). On 1979-on ATC110 and ATC125M, also remove the O-ring seal.

5. Befor proceeding any further, inspect the wheel bearings as described in this chapter.

6. On 1973-1974 ATC70 and 1975-1978 ATC90 models, remove the circlip from the right-hand side of the hub next to the right-hand bearing.

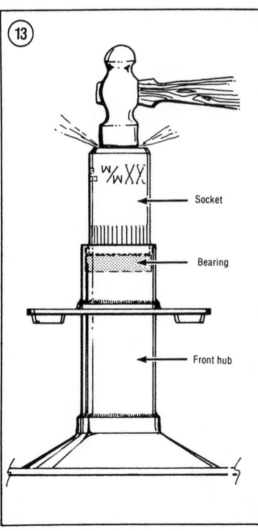

Socket

Bearing

Front hub

7. To remove the left- and right-hand bearings and distance collar, insert a soft aluminum or brass drift into one side of the hub. Push the distance collar over to one side and place the drift on the inner race of the lower bearing. Tap the bearing out of the hub with a hammer working around the perimeter of the inner race.

8. Remove the distance collar and tap out the opposite bearing.

9. Thoroughly clean out the inside of the hub with solvent and dry with compressed air or a shop cloth.

10. Do not clean sealed bearings. If non-sealed bearings are installed, thoroughly clean them in solvent and thoroughly dry with compressed air. Do not let the bearing spin while drying.

Assembly

1. On non-sealed bearings, pack the bearings with a good quality bearing grease. Work the grease in between the balls thoroughly. Turn the bearing by hand a couple of times to make sure the grease is distributed evenly inside the bearing.

2. Pack the wheel hub and distance collar with multipurpose grease.

> *CAUTION*
> *Install the wheel bearings with the sealed side facing out. During installation, tap the bearings squarely into place and tap on the outer race only. Use a socket (**Figure 13**) that matches the outer race diameter. Do not tap on the inner race or the bearing may be damaged. Be sure that the bearings are completely seated.*

3A. On 1973-1974 ATC70 and 1975-1978 ATC90 models, perform the following:
   a. Install the circlip into the hub assembly. Make sure it is completely seated.
   b. Install the right-hand bearing.
   c. Install the distance collar and the left-hand bearing.

3B. On all other models, perform the following:
   a. Install the left-hand bearing.
   b. Install the distance collar and the right-hand bearing.

4. On 1979-on ATC110 and ATC125M models, apply a light coat of multipurpose grease to the O-ring seals and install one onto the center race of the bearing.

5. Apply a light coat of multipurpose grease to the grease seals and install one on each side of the hub. Push the grease seal in until it is flush with the outside surface of the hub.

8

CAUTION
On models so equipped, make sure the
O-ring seal is aligned with the inner
opening of both the bearing and the
grease seal on each side. If alignment is
not correct the O-ring will be damaged
when the front axle is inserted through
the front hub.

6. On models so equipped, install the front brake
panel into the brake drum.
7. Install the front wheel as described in this
chapter.

HANDLEBAR

Removal

1. On models so equipped, remove the plastic
band (A, **Figure 14**) holding the throttle cable and
engine stop switch wire to the handlebar.
2. On models so equipped, remove the screw
(**Figure 15**) securing the end guard and remove the
end guard and right-hand grip.

NOTE
In the following steps carefully lay the
throttle assembly and brake cables over
the front fender or back over the fuel
tank. Be careful that the cables do not
get crimped or damaged.

3. On 1982-on ATC110 and ATC125M models,
perform the following:
  a. Remove the screws securing the combination
    engine kill/headlight/starter switch to the
    handlebar and remove the switch assembly (A,
    Figure 16).
  b. Remove the plastic band holding the
    electrical wires to the handlebar.
4. Remove the screws (B, **Figure 14**) securing the
throttle and (on some models) engine stop switch
assembly to the handlebar and remove the
assembly.
5. On models equipped with a front brake, loosen
the clamping bolts (**Figure 17**) on the right-hand
brake lever assembly and slide the assembly off the
handlebar.
6. Remove the screw securing the end guard and
remove the end guard and left-hand grip (B, **Figure
16**).
7A. On ATC70 models, remove the pivot bolt
(**Figure 18**) and remove the brake hand lever from
the handlebar.
7B. On all other models, loosen the clamping bolts
(C, **Figure 16**) on the left-hand brake lever
assembly and slide the assembly off the handlebar.

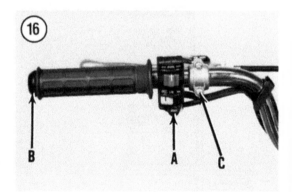

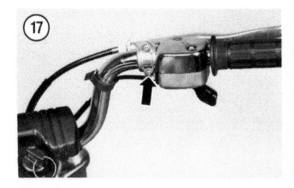

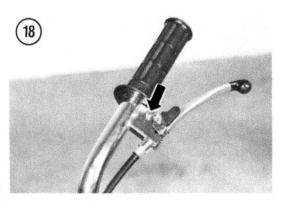

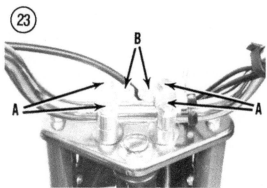

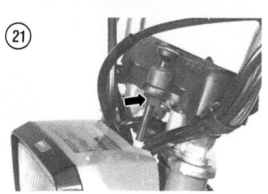

8. On all 1982-on models, perform the following:
   a. Using a small screwdriver, remove the small insert nameplate (**Figure 19**).
   b. Remove the screws (**Figure 20**) securing the handlebar upper cover and remove the cover.
9A. On ATC125M models, perform the following:
   a. Loosen the locknut (**Figure 21**) on the choke cable and remove the choke cable from the handlebar upper holder.
   b. Carefully pull the neutral indicator light/socket assembly out of the bottom left-hand side of the handlebar upper holder.
   c. Remove the bolts (**Figure 22**) securing the upper holder and remove the upper holder assembly. Carefully lay the upper holder and ignition switch assembly over the fuel tank or front fender.
   d. Remove the handlebar.
9B. On all other models, perform the following:
   a. Remove the bolts and washers (A, **Figure 23**) securing the handlebar holders and remove the holders.
   b. Remove the handlebar.
10. To maintain a good grip on the handlebar and to prevent it from slipping down, clean the knurled section of the handlebar with a wire brush. It should be kept rough so it will be held securely by

the holders. The holders should also be kept clean and free of any metal that may have been gouged loose by handlebar slippage.

Installation

1. Position the handlebar on the lower handlebar holders so the punch mark on the handlebar is aligned with the top surface of the lower handlebar holders (**Figure 24**).
2A. On ATC125M models, perform the following:
  a. Install the upper holder assembly.
  b. Install the bolts and tighten the bolts finger-tight.
  c. Tighten the forward bolts first and then the rear bolts to the torque specification listed in **Table 1**.
  d. Install the neutral indicator bulb/socket assembly into the bottom left-hand side of the handlebar upper holder.
  e. Install the choke cable into the receptacle in the handlebar upper holder and tighten the locknut.
2B. On all 1982-on models, install the upper holders with the "L" (left-hand side) or "R" (right-hand side) mark on the tabs (B, **Figure 23**) to the correct side. The correct placement is necessary so the cover can be attached.
2C. On all other models, install the upper handlebar holders with the punch mark (**Figure 25**) facing toward the front.
3. Install the handlebar washers and bolts. Tighten the forward bolts first and then the rear bolts to the torque specification listed in **Table 1**.
4. After installation is complete, recheck the alignment of the punch mark on the handlebar (**Figure 24**). Readjust if necessary.
5. On all 1982-on models, install the handlebar upper cover and install the screws. Install the small insert nameplate.
6A. On ATC70 models, install the brake hand lever and install the pivot bolt.
6B. On all other models, slide on the left-hand brake lever assembly. Do not tighten the bolt at this time.
7. Slide on the left-hand grip and install the end guard and screw. Tighten the screw securely.
8. On 1982-on ATC110 and ATC125M models, install the combination engine kill/headlight/starter switch onto the left-hand handlebar. Tighten the screws.
9. On all models except the ATC70 and ATC125M, after the left-hand grip has been installed, slide the left-hand brake assembly to within 15 mm (0.6 in.) of the end of the hand grip.

10. On all models except the ATC70, position the left-hand brake lever approximately 20° down from true horizontal (**Figure 26**). Tighten the clamping bolt(s).
11. On models equipped with a front brake, slide on the right-hand brake lever assembly. Do not tighten the bolts at this time.
12. Slide on the right-hand grip and install the end guard and screw. Tighten the screw securely.
13. Install the throttle and (on some models) the engine stop switch assembly onto the handlebar. Slide it to within 10 mm (0.4 in.) of the end of the hand grip. Tighten the screws.
14. After the right-hand grip and throttle and engine stop switch assembly have been installed,

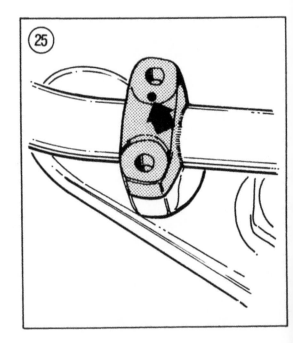

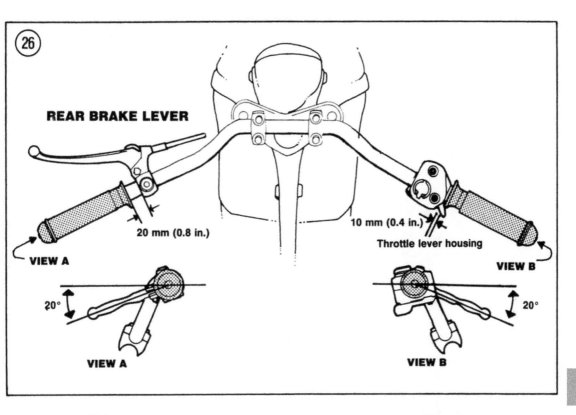

REAR BRAKE LEVER

20 mm (0.8 in.)

10 mm (0.4 in.)

Throttle lever housing

VIEW A

VIEW B

20°

20°

VIEW A

VIEW B

8

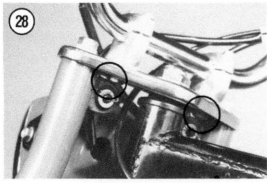

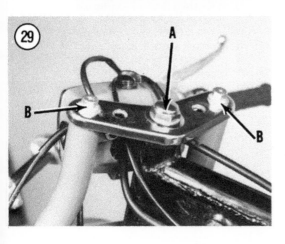

A

B

B

slide the right-hand brake assembly directly against the throttle and (on some models) the engine stop switch assembly and position it apparoximately 20° down from true horizontal (**Figure 26**). Tighten the clamping bolt.

15. On models so equipped, install the plastic bands holding the throttle and engine stop switch wires to the handlebar.

FRONT FORK AND STEERING HEAD

The front fork and steering stem are one integral unit and are removed as an assembly. The front fork is rigid without the assist of hydraulics or springs.

Removal

Refer to **Figure 27** for this procedure.

1. Remove the front wheel as described in this chapter.
2. Remove the front fender.
3. Remove the nut and lockwashers securing the lower handlebar holders (**Figure 28**) and remove the handlebar assembly.
4. Disconnect the electrical wires to the headlight assembly. If so desired the headlight assembly can be removed as described in Chapter Seven.
5. Remove the steering stem nut and washer (A, **Figure 29**).

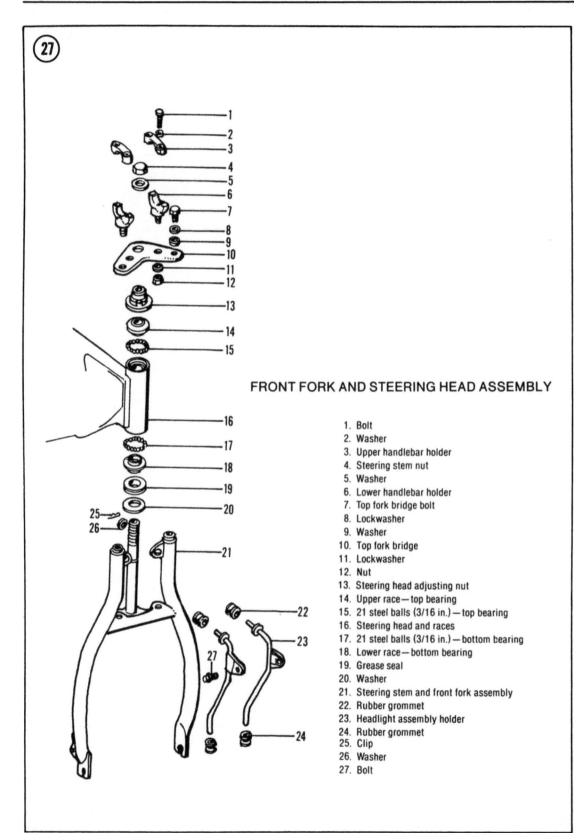

FRONT FORK AND STEERING HEAD ASSEMBLY

1. Bolt
2. Washer
3. Upper handlebar holder
4. Steering stem nut
5. Washer
6. Lower handlebar holder
7. Top fork bridge bolt
8. Lockwasher
9. Washer
10. Top fork bridge
11. Lockwasher
12. Nut
13. Steering head adjusting nut
14. Upper race—top bearing
15. 21 steel balls (3/16 in.)—top bearing
16. Steering head and races
17. 21 steel balls (3/16 in.)—bottom bearing
18. Lower race—bottom bearing
19. Grease seal
20. Washer
21. Steering stem and front fork assembly
22. Rubber grommet
23. Headlight assembly holder
24. Rubber grommet
25. Clip
26. Washer
27. Bolt

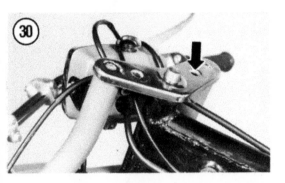

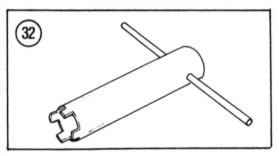

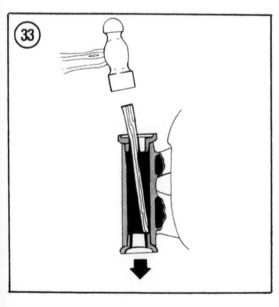

6. Remove the top fork bridge bolts, washers and lockwashers (B, **Figure 29**).

7. Remove the top fork bridge (**Figure 30**).

8. Remove the steering head adjusting nut (**Figure 31**). Use a large drift and hammer or use the easily improvised tool shown in **Figure 32**.

NOTE
Have an assistant hold a large pan under the steering stem to catch the loose ball bearings while you carefully lower the steering stem. All models are equipped with 21 ball bearings in both the upper and lower race.

9. Lower the front fork and steering stem assembly down and out of the steering head. Remove the 21 ball bearings from the lower race.

10. Remove the 21 ball bearings from the upper race in the steering head.

Inspection

1. Clean the bearing races in the steering head, the steering stem races and the steel balls with solvent.

2. Check the welds around the steering head for cracks and fractures. If any are found, have them repaired by a competent frame shop or welding service.

3. Check the balls for pitting, scratches or discoloration indicating wear or corrosion. Replace them in sets if any are bad.

4. Check the races for pitting, galling and corrosion. If any of these conditions exist, replace the races as described in this chapter.

5. Check the steering stem for cracks and check its race for damage or wear. If this race or any race is damaged, the bearings should be replaced as a complete bearing set. Take the old races and bearings to your dealer to ensure accurate replacement.

6. Check the front forks for signs of wear or damage. Also check the fork legs for straightness. If bent or severely dented, the assembly should be replaced.

Steering Head
Bearing Race Replacement

The headset and steering stem bearing races are pressed into place. Because they are easily bent, do not remove them unless they are worn and require replacement.

Headset bearing race
removal/installation

To remove the headset race, insert a hardwood stick or soft punch into the head tube (**Figure 33**)

8

and carefully tap the race out from the inside. After it is started, tap around the race so that neither the race nor the head tube is damaged.

To install the headset race, tap it in slowly with a block of wood, a suitable size socket or piece of pipe (**Figure 34**). Make sure that the race is squarely seated in the headset race bore before tapping it into place. Tap the race in until it is flush with the steering head surface.

Steering stem bearing race and grease seal removal/installation

To remove the steering stem race, try twisting and pulling it up by hand. If it will not come off, carefully pry it up with a screwdriver; work around in a circle, prying a little at a time. Remove the race, the grease seal and washer.

Install the washer and new grease seal. Slide the lower race over the steering stem with the bearing surface pointing up. Tap the race down with a piece of hardwood; work around in a circle so the race will not be bent. Make sure it is seated squarely and is all the way down.

Installation

Refer to **Figure 27** for this procedure.
1. Make sure the steering head and stem races are properly seated.
2. Apply a coat of cold grease to the upper bearing race cone and fit 21 ball bearings around it (A, **Figure 35**).
3. Apply a coat of cold grease to the lower bearing race cone and fit 21 ball bearings around it.
4. Install the front fork and steering stem assembly into the head tube and hold it firmly in place (B, **Figure 35**).
5. Install the upper race of the top bearing (**Figure 36**).
6. Install the steering stem adjusting nut (**Figure 31**) and tighten it until it is snug against the upper race, then back it off 1/8 turn.

NOTE
The adjusting nut should be just tight enough to remove both horizontal and vertical play, yet loose enough so that the assembly will turn to both lock positions under its own weight after an assist.

7. Install the top fork bridge and steering stem nut and washer. Tighten the steering stem nut to the torque specification listed in **Table 1**.
8. Install the top fork bridge washers, lockwashers and bolts. Tighten the bolts to the torque specification listed in **Table 1**.

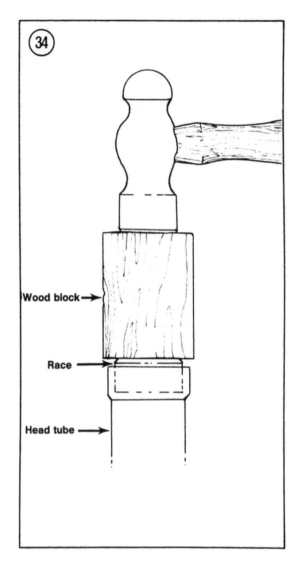

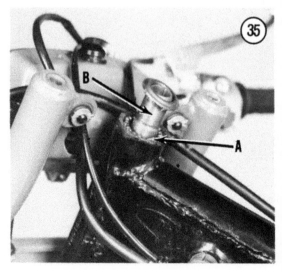

9. Attach the electrical wires to the headlight assembly or install the headlight assembly, if removed.
10. Install the handlebar assembly and install the lockwasher and nuts to the lower handlebar holder studs (**Figure 28**). Tighten the nuts to the torque specification listed in **Table 1**.
11. Install the front wheel as described in this chapter.

12. Install the front fender.
13. After a few hours of riding, the bearings have had a chance to seat; readjust the free play in the steering stem with the steering stem adjusting nut. Refer to Step 6.

Steering Stem Adjustment

If play develops in the steering system, it may only require adjustment. However, don't take a chance on it. Disassemble the stem and look for possible damage. Then reassemble and adjust as described in Step 6 of the installation procedure.

REAR WHEEL

Removal/Installation

1. Set the ATC on level ground and set the parking brake. Also block the front wheel so the vehicle will not roll in either direction.
2. Jack up the rear of the vehicle with a small hydraulic jack. Place wood blocks under the engine; release jack pressure and securely support the vehicle on the wood blocks.
3A. On 1970-1974 ATC90 models, perform the following:
   a. Remove the axle cap.
   b. Remove the cotter pin and discard it.
   c. Remove the axle nut and washer.
3B. On all other models, remove the wheel nuts (**Figure 37**) securing the wheel to the hub and remove the wheel.

> *NOTE*
> *The number of wheel nuts varies with the different models.*

4. Install by reversing these removal steps; note the following.
5. On 1970-1974 ATC90 models, when installing the right-hand wheel, make sure the spacer collar is in place on the axle prior to installing the wheel.
6. Tighten the axle nut or wheel nuts to torque specifications listed in **Table 1**.

REAR AXLE AND DRIVEN SPROCKET (ATC70)

Removal/Installation (1973-1975)

1. Remove the seat/rear fender assembly.
2. Remove the bolts securing the skid plate and remove the skid plate.
3. Remove both rear wheels as described in this chapter.
4. Remove the cotter pin, castellated nut and lockwasher securing the rear hub (**Figure 38**).
5. Remove both the left- and right-hand hubs and the axle spacers.

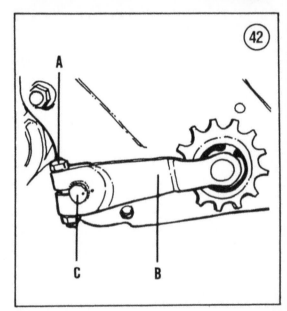

6. Remove the rear cover, step bar and the lower skid plate.

7. Remove the left-hand crankcase cover and the recoil starter as an assembly (**Figure 39**).

8. Loosen the drive chain tensioner lock bolt.

9. Remove the master link (**Figure 40**) on the drive chain.

10. Remove the bolts and washers (**Figure 41**) securing the drive sprocket and remove the drive sprocket and drive chain.

11. Remove the lockbolt (A, **Figure 42**) and remove the drive chain tensioner (B, **Figure 42**) from the shaft (C, **Figure 42**). Remove the shaft from the frame.

12. Loosen the brake adjust nut (A, **Figure 43**) and disconnect the brake cable (B, **Figure 43**) from the brake arm.

13. Remove the brake arm locking bolt (C, **Figure 43**) and remove the brake arm from the camshaft along with the return spring. Disconnect the brake cable from the right-hand panel clamp (D, **Figure 43**).

14. Remove the bolts (E, **Figure 43**) securing the right-hand panel and remove the panel and the internal collar.

15. Remove the bolts securing the left-hand panel and remove the panel and the internal collar (**Figure 44**).

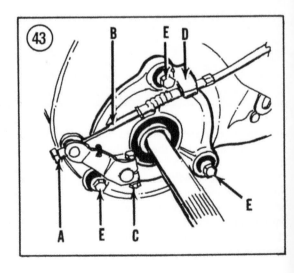

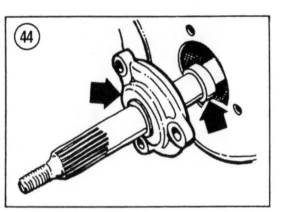

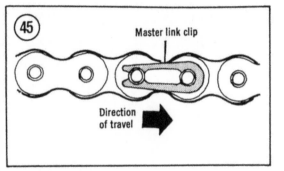

Master link clip

Direction
of travel

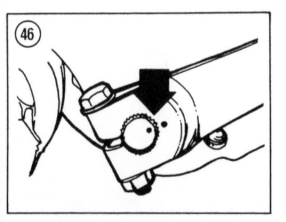

16. Have a helper securely hold the rear axle hub.
17. Place a wood block on the right-hand end of the axle and tap on it until the axle splines are free from the axle hub.
18. Remove the axle.
19. Remove the hub/driven sprocket assembly from the frame.
20. Inspect the rear axle and hubs as described in this chapter.
21. Perform *Disassembly/Inspection/Assembly* in this chapter.
22. Install by reversing these removal steps, noting the following.
23. Be sure to install the drive chain master link with the closed end facing in the direction of travel (**Figure 45**).
24. Align the punch marks on the drive chain tensioner arm and shaft (**Figure 46**) and tighten the lockbolt securely.

Removal/Installation (1978-on)

1. Remove the seat/rear fender assembly.
2. Remove the bolts securing the skid plate (**Figure 47**) and remove the skid plate.
3. Remove both rear wheels as described in this chapter.
4. Remove the cotter pin, castellated nut and lockwasher securing the rear hub (**Figure 38**).
5. Remove both the left- and right-hand hubs and the axle spacers.
6. Remove the left-hand crankcase cover and the recoil starter as an assembly (A, **Figure 48**).
7. Remove the bolts securing the chain cover and remove the chain cover (B, **Figure 48**).
8. Loosen the drive chain tensioner nuts (**Figure 49**).

9. Remove the master link (**Figure 40**) on the drive chain.

10. Remove the bolts and washers (**Figure 50**) securing the drive sprocket and remove the drive sprocket and drive chain.

11. Slide off the drive sprocket (**Figure 51**) and the sprocket retainer (**Figure 52**).

12. Remove the bolts and washers (**Figure 53**) securing the brake cover and remove it.

13. Slide off the brake drum (**Figure 54**).

14. Withdraw the axle from the left-hand side.

15. Inspect the rear axle and hubs as described in this chapter.

16. Perform *Disassembly/Inspection/Assembly* in this chapter.

17. Install by reversing these removal steps, noting the following.

18. Be sure to install the drive chain master link with the closed end facing in the direction of travel (**Figure 45**).

19. Be sure to install the sprocket retainer (**Figure 52**).

20. Install the axle from the left-hand side (**Figure 55**).

21. Install the drive chain protector (**Figure 56**) onto the axle prior to installing the left-hand hub.

Disassembly/Inspection/Assembly

Refer to **Figure 57** and **Figure 58** for this procedure.

1. Remove the rear axle and driven sprocket assembly as described in this chapter.

2A. On 1973-1974 models, perform the following:
  a. Remove the circlip securing the driven sprocket to the rear wheel hub.
  b. Tap around the perimeter of the driven sprocket with a plastic mallet and remove the driven sprocket from the rear wheel hub.
  c. Remove the damper cover.
  d. Remove the rubber dampers from the rear wheel hub.

2B. On 1978-on models, perform the following:
  a. Slide the driven sprocket assembly off the axle.
  b. Remove the driven sprocket, damper cover and the rubber dampers from the damper case.

3. Inspect all components (**Figure 59**) for wear or damage.

4. Replace all rubber dampers as a set even if only one shows signs of deterioration or damage.

5. Inspect the driven sprocket. Compare to **Figure 60**. If it is worn or distorted, replace the sprocket.

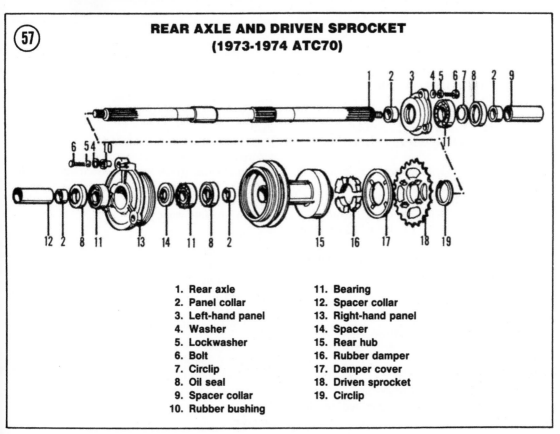

REAR AXLE AND DRIVEN SPROCKET
(1973-1974 ATC70)

1. Rear axle
2. Panel collar
3. Left-hand panel
4. Washer
5. Lockwasher
6. Bolt
7. Circlip
8. Oil seal
9. Spacer collar
10. Rubber bushing
11. Bearing
12. Spacer collar
13. Right-hand panel
14. Spacer
15. Rear hub
16. Rubber damper
17. Damper cover
18. Driven sprocket
19. Circlip

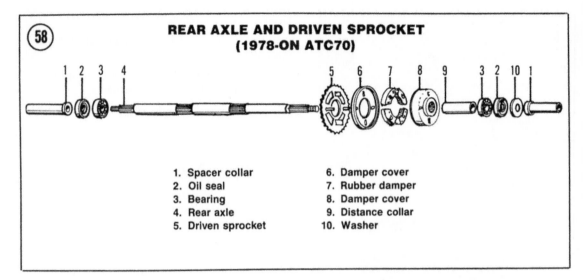

**REAR AXLE AND DRIVEN SPROCKET
(1978-ON ATC70)**

1. Spacer collar
2. Oil seal
3. Bearing
4. Rear axle
5. Driven sprocket
6. Damper cover
7. Rubber damper
8. Damper cover
9. Distance collar
10. Washer

NOTE
If the driven sprocket is worn or damaged and must be replaced, also inspect the drive chain and drive sprocket for damage. Never replace just one of these 3 components without a thorough inspection of all the rest. If one is replaced, the other 2 should also be replaced. If not, the new component will wear out prematurely.

6. Assemble by reversing these disassembly steps.

REAR AXLE AND DRIVEN SPROCKET (1970-1974 ATC90)

Removal/Installation

1. Remove the seat/rear fender assembly.
2. Remove both rear wheels as described in this chapter.
3. Remove the bolts securing the drive chain case.
4. On the left-hand side, remove the bolts securing the rear axle to the driven sprocket assembly.
5. Withdraw the rear axle from the left-hand side.
6. Inspect the rear axle as described in this chapter.
7. Install by reversing these removal steps, noting the following.
8. When installing the rear axle, carefully align the splines on the axle with the splines inside the driven sprocket assembly.
9. Tighten the bolts to the torque specification listed in **Table 1**.

Disassembly/Inspection/Assembly

Refer to **Figure 61** for this procedure.
1. Remove the rear axle as described in this chapter.

2. On the right-hand side, remove the brake drum nut, seal washer and the brake drum.
3. Remove the driven sprocket/wheel shaft assembly from the left-hand side.
4. Remove the wheel shaft collar from the wheel shaft/sprocket assembly.
5. Remove the nuts, lockwasher and washers securing the driven sprocket to the wheel shaft.
6. Remove the driven sprocket assembly from the wheel shaft.
7. To separate the driven sprocket assembly, perform the following:

   a. Remove the nuts, lockwashers and lockwashers holding the driven sprocket together.
   b. Separate the damper holders from each side of the driven sprocket and remove the rubber dampers.
   c. On 1974 models, remove the sprocket ring.

8. Inspect all components for wear or damage.
9. Replace all rubber dampers as a set even if only one shows signs of deterioration or damage.
10. Inspect the driven sprocket. Compare to **Figure 60**. If it is worn or distorted, replace the sprocket.

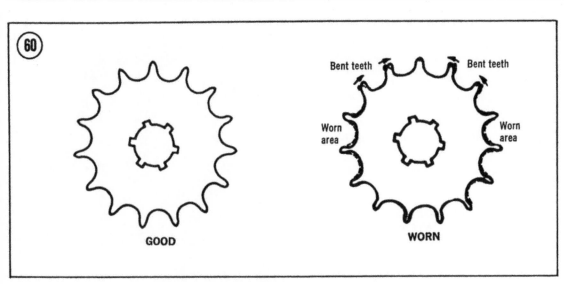

GOOD   WORN

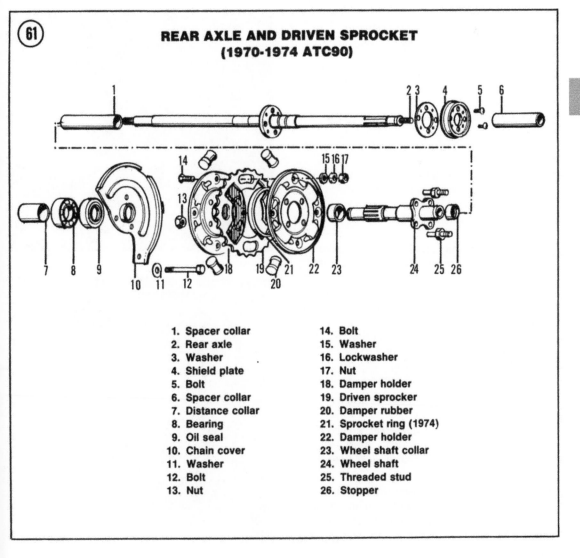

REAR AXLE AND DRIVEN SPROCKET
(1970-1974 ATC90)

8

1. Spacer collar
2. Rear axle
3. Washer
4. Shield plate
5. Bolt
6. Spacer collar
7. Distance collar
8. Bearing
9. Oil seal
10. Chain cover
11. Washer
12. Bolt
13. Nut
14. Bolt
15. Washer
16. Lockwasher
17. Nut
18. Damper holder
19. Driven sprocker
20. Damper rubber
21. Sprocket ring (1974)
22. Damper holder
23. Wheel shaft collar
24. Wheel shaft
25. Threaded stud
26. Stopper

NOTE
If the driven sprocket is worn or damaged and must be replaced, also inspect the drive chain and drive sprocket for damage. Never replace just one of these 3 components without a thorough inspection of all the rest. If one is replaced, the other 2 should also be replaced. If not, the new component will wear out prematurely.

11. Assemble by reversing these disassembly steps.

REAR AXLE AND DRIVEN SPROCKET (1975-1978 ATC90 AND 1979-1983 ATC110)

Removal/Installation

1. Place the ATC on level ground and set the parking brake.
2. Remove the seat/rear fender assembly.
3. Remove the bolts securing the skid plate and remove the skid plate.
4. Remove both rear wheels as described in this chapter.
5. To remove the hubs, perform the following:
   a. Remove the cotter pin and castellated nut securing the rear hub.
   b. Remove the lockwasher and the hub (A, **Figure 62**).
   c. Remove both the left- and right-hand hubs.
   d. Remove the spacer collar(s) from the axle.
6. On the left-hand side, remove the bolts securing the cover plate and slide off the cover plate (B, **Figure 62**).
7. On the left-hand side, remove the bolts securing the drive chain cover and slide off the cover (C, **Figure 62**).
8. On the right-hand side, perform the following:
   a. Remove the chain tensioner locknut (A, **Figure 63**).
   b. Remove the bolt and nut securing the drive chain tensioner arm (B, **Figure 63**).
   c. Remove the tensioner arm.
9. Use a 41 mm wrench and remove the locknut (**Figure 64**) securing the brake drum.

NOTE
*The special 41 mm flame cut wrench (**Figure 65**) is available from a motorcycle dealer, Rocky or other mail order houses.*

10. If you are unable to loosen the locknut it will have to be chiseled off (**Figure 66**). Do not chisel all the way through into the threads on the axle (**Figure 67**).

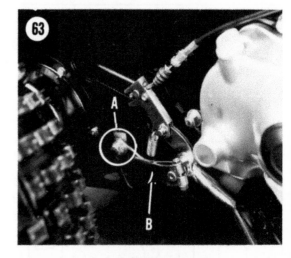

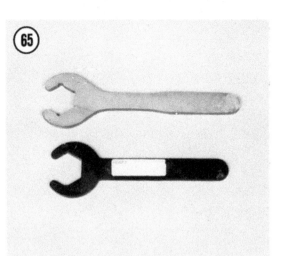

8

NOTE
The inner nut does not have Loctite
applied to it and is easier to remove.

11. Remove the inner nut (**Figure 68**).

12. Slide off the small cover plate.

13. Remove the bolts securing the brake drum
cover (**Figure 69**) and slide off the cover.

14. Release the parking brake.

15. Slide off the brake drum (**Figure 70**).

16. Loosen the rear axle bearing holder bolts.
There are 2 on each side. Loosen the drive chain
adjuster and push the rear axle assembly forward
to allow slack in the drive chain.

17A. On models with a master link equipped drive chain, perform the following:
  a. Remove the master link (**Figure 71**) and remove the drive chain from the driven sprocket.
  b. Withdraw the rear axle from the bearing holder from the left-hand side.

NOTE
On 1981-1983 ATC110 models, the original equipment drive chain can be broken with a chain breaker (Figure 72) and then replaced with an aftermarket drive chain with a master link. Do not add a master link to the continuous loop Honda drive chain.

17B. On models with a continuous loop drive chain, perform the following:
  a. Remove the recoil starter assembly as described in Chapter Seven.
  b. Remove the alternator assembly as described in Chapter Seven.
  c. Remove the subtransmission as described in Chapter Five.
  d. Remove the left-hand crankcase cover as described in Chapter Four.
  e. Disconnect the rear brake cable from the brake pedal assembly and completely unscrew the brake pedal adjustment nut (**Figure 73**).
  f. Unhook the brake pedal return spring and remove the brake pedal.
  g. Withdraw the drive chain tensioner from the left-hand side.
  h. Withdraw the rear axle, drive chain and drive sprocket as an assembly from the left-hand side.

18. Install by reversing these steps, noting the following.
19. Install the brake drum and push it on all the way until it is completely seated.
20. Install the axle inner nut. Have an assistant hold the left-hand wheel while you tighten the inner nut enough to seat the brake drum.
21. Apply the parking brake and completely tighten the inner nut to the torque specification listed in **Table 1**.
22. Thoroughly clean all grease from the axle threads prior to applying the Loctite in the next step.
23. Apply Loctite Lock N' Seal to the axle shaft threads and install the axle locknut. Hold onto the inner nut and tighten the locknut to the torque specification listed in **Table 1**.

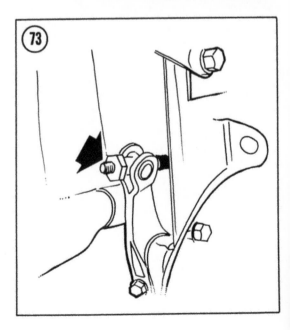

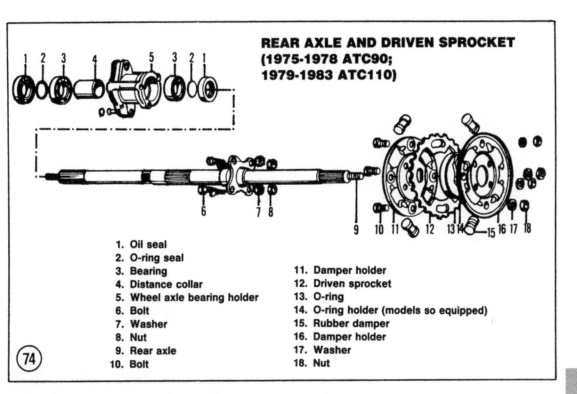

**REAR AXLE AND DRIVEN SPROCKET
(1975-1978 ATC90;
1979-1983 ATC110)**

1. Oil seal
2. O-ring seal
3. Bearing
4. Distance collar
5. Wheel axle bearing holder
6. Bolt
7. Washer
8. Nut
9. Rear axle
10. Bolt
11. Damper holder
12. Driven sprocket
13. O-ring
14. O-ring holder (models so equipped)
15. Rubber damper
16. Damper holder
17. Washer
18. Nut

(74)

8

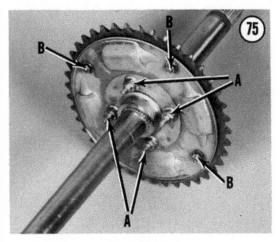

(75)

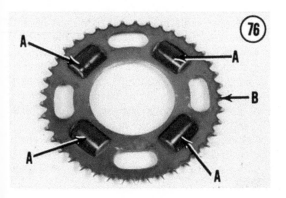

(76)

24. On models equipped with a drive chain master link, install the master link so that the closed end of the clip is facing in the direction of travel (**Figure 45**).

25 Adjust the drive chain as described in Chapter Three.

26. Adjust the rear brake as described in Chapter Three.

Disassembly/Inspection

Refer to **Figure 74** for this procedure.

1. Remove the rear axle as described in this chapter.

2. Remove the nuts (A, **Figure 75**) securing the driven sprocket assembly to the axle.

3. Slide the driven sprocket assembly off the rear axle.

4. Remove the bolts (B, **Figure 75**) holding the driven sprocket assembly together and separate the assembly.

5. Inspect the rubber dampers (A, **Figure 76**) for signs of damage or deterioration. Replace all if any are damaged.

6. Replace all rubber dampers as a set even if only one shows signs of deterioration or damage.

7. Inspect the O-ring (**Figure 77**) for signs of deterioration. Replace if necessary.

8. Inspect both damper holders (**Figure 78**) for damage, especially in the area where the rubber

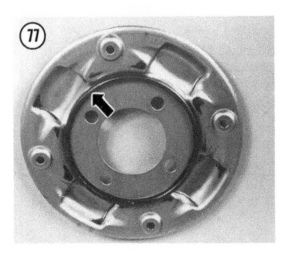

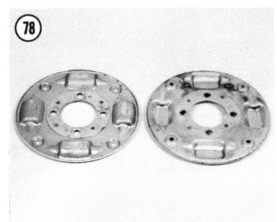

dampers ride. These areas should be free of burrs, dents and corrosion. Replace if necessary.

9. Inspect the driven sprocket (B, **Figure 76**). Compare to **Figure 60**. If it is worn or distorted, replace the sprocket.

> *NOTE*
> *If the driven sprocket is worn or damaged and must be replaced, also inspect the drive chain and drive sprocket for damage. Never replace just one of these 3 components without a thorough inspection of all the rest. If one is replaced, the other 2 should also be replaced. If not, the new component will wear out prematurely.*

Assembly

1. Apply a light coat of multipurpose grease to the pockets of the damper holder where the rubber dampers ride and to the center flange area.

2. Make sure the rubber dampers and O-ring seal are installed in one of the damper holders.

3. Place the driven sprocket onto this assembly and install the other damper holder.

4. Align the holes in the 2 damper holders, install the bolts (B, **Figure 75**) and tighten securely.

5. Slide the driven sprocket assembly onto the left-hand end of the rear axle.

6. Install the nuts (A, **Figure 75**) securing the driven sprocket assembly to the axle and tighten to the torque specification listed in **Table 1**.

7. Install the rear axle as described in this chapter.

REAR AXLE AND DRIVEN SPROCKET (1984 ATC110 AND ATC125M)

Removal/Installation

1. Place the ATC on level ground and set the parking brake.

2. Remove the seat/rear fender assembly.

3. Remove both rear wheels as described in this chapter.

4. To remove the hubs, perform the following:
   a. Remove the cotter pin and castellated nut securing the rear hub (**Figure 79**).
   b. Remove the lockwasher and the hub (**Figure 80**).
   c. Remove both the left- and right-hand hubs.
   d. Remove the spacer collar(s) from the axle.

5. On the left-hand side, perform the following:
   a. Remove the crankcase breather, carburetor and (on ATC125M) the battery overflow tubes (A, **Figure 81**) from the drive chain cover.
   b. Remove the bolts securing the cover plate and slide off the cover plate (B, **Figure 81**).
   c. Remove the bolts securing the drive chain cover and slide off the cover (C, **Figure 81**). There is one additional bolt at the rear (**Figure 82**).

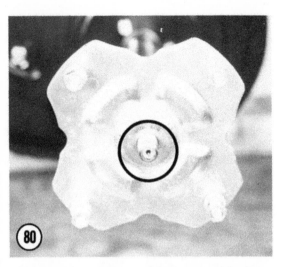

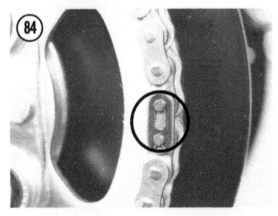

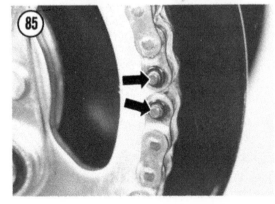

6. Loosen the rear brake adjust nut (**Figure 83**).
7. Loosen the drive chain adjust nut.
8. Loosen the rear axle bearing holder bolts (there are 2 on each side). Push the rear axle assembly forward to allow slack in the drive chain.
9. Remove the drive chain master link (**Figure 84**). Don't lose the rubber O-ring seals (**Figure 85**) on the master link pins. Remove the drive chain from the driven sprocket.
10. If the driven sprocket is going to be removed, perform the following steps at this time:

a. Remove the nuts (**Figure 86**) securing the damper cover and remove the cover.

b. Slide the driven sprocket assembly from the axle (**Figure 87**).

11. Use a 41 mm wrench and remove the locknut (**Figure 88**) securing the brake drum. It may be necessary to tap on the end of the wrench with a soft-faced mallet to break the locknut loose (**Figure 89**).

> *CAUTION*
> *The locknut has had Loctite applied during assembly and is tightened to 120-140 N•m (87-101 ft.-lb.). It is very hard to remove even with the correct size tool and a lot of force. **Do not apply heat** to the area in order to try to loosen the locknut as this would ruin the axle.*

> *NOTE*
> *The special 41 mm flame cut wrench (**Figure 65**) is available from a motorcycle dealer, Rocky or other mail order houses.*

12. If you are unable to loosen the locknut it will have to be chiseled off (**Figure 66**). Do not chisel all the way through into the threads on the axle (**Figure 67**).

> *NOTE*
> *The inner nut does not have Loctite applied to it and is easier to remove.*

13. Remove the inner nut (**Figure 90**).

14. On models so equipped, slide off the dished washer (**Figure 91**).

15. Remove the bolts (**Figure 92**) securing the brake drum cover and slide off the cover.

16. Release the parking brake.

17. Slide off the brake drum (**Figure 93**).

18. On the right-hand side, remove the O-ring seal (**Figure 94**) on the axle next to the rear axle bearing holder oil seal.

19. Using a soft-faced mallet, tap on the right-hand end of the axle and withdraw the rear axle from the bearing holder from the left-hand side.

20. Install by reversing these steps, noting the following.

21. Install the brake drum and push it on all the way until it is completely seated.

22. On models so equipped, install the dished washer with the dished side facing toward the outside.

23. Install the axle inner nut. Have an assistant hold the left-hand wheel while you tighten the inner nut (**Figure 95**) enough to seat the brake drum.

8

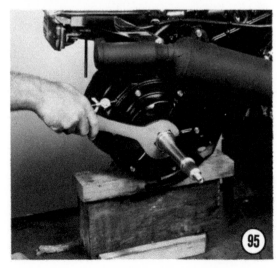

24. Apply the parking brake and completely tighten the inner nut to the torque specification listed in **Table 1**.

25. Thoroughly clean all grease from the axle threads prior to applying the Loctite in the next step.

26. Apply Loctite Lock N' Seal to the axle shaft threads and install the axle locknut. Hold onto the inner nut and tighten the locknut to the torque specification listed in **Table 1**.

27. Inspect the dust seal in the brake cover **(Figure 96)**. Replace the seal if necessary. Apply a light coat of grease to the dust seal prior to installation.

28. Inspect the rubber seal on the backside of the brake cover **(Figure 97)**. Replace the seal if necessary.

29. Make sure the O-ring seals **(Figure 85)** are in place on the master link prior to installing the plate and clip.

30. Install the master link so that the closed end of the clip is facing in the direction of travel **(Figure 98)**.

31. Make sure to install the washer on the hub with the "OUTSIDE" mark **(Figure 80)** facing toward the outside.

32. Adjust the drive chain as described in Chapter Three.

33. Adjust the rear brake as described in Chapter Three.

Disassembly/Inspection/Assembly

Refer to **Figure 99** for this procedure.

1A. If the entire axle is to be serviced, remove the axle as described in this chapter.

1B. If only the driven sprocket is to be removed, perform Steps 1-10 of *Removal/Installation* in this chapter.

2. Remove the snap ring **(Figure 100)** securing the driven sprocket to the rear axle.

3. Slide the driven sprocket assembly off the rear axle.

4. Inspect the rubber dampers **(Figure 101)** for signs of damage or deterioration. If they are damaged the entire driven sprocket must be replaced as the rubber dampers are an integral part of the component.

5. Inspect the driven sprocket **(Figure 102)**. Compare to **Figure 60**. If it is worn or distorted, replace the sprocket.

NOTE
If the driven sprocket is worn or damaged and must be replaced, also inspect the drive chain and drive sprocket for damage. Never replace just one of these 3 components without a thorough inspection of all the rest. If one is replaced, the other 2 should also be replaced. If not, the new component will wear out prematurely.

6. Inspect the bolt holes and threaded holes in the damper cover **(Figure 103)** for wear or elongation; replace if necessary.

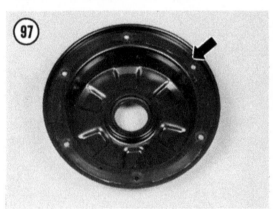

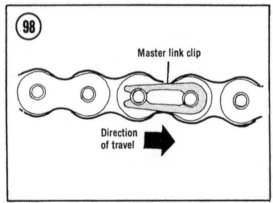

Master link clip

Direction
of travel

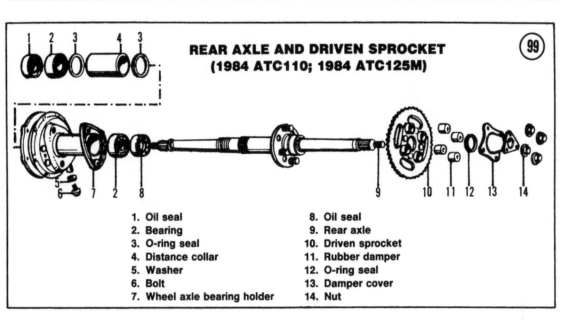

REAR AXLE AND DRIVEN SPROCKET
(1984 ATC110; 1984 ATC125M)

1. Oil seal
2. Bearing
3. O-ring seal
4. Distance collar
5. Washer
6. Bolt
7. Wheel axle bearing holder
8. Oil seal
9. Rear axle
10. Driven sprocket
11. Rubber damper
12. O-ring seal
13. Damper cover
14. Nut

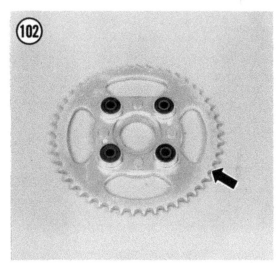

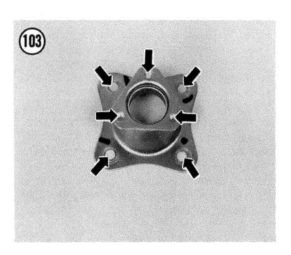

8

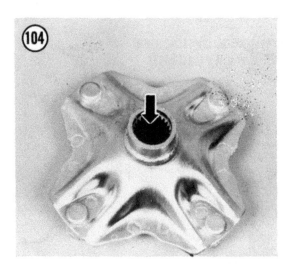

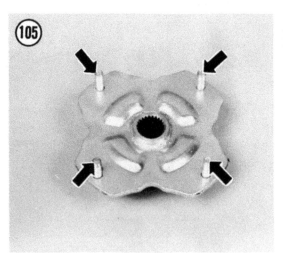

7. Assemble by reversing these disassembly steps.
8. If removed, install the rear axle as described in this chapter.

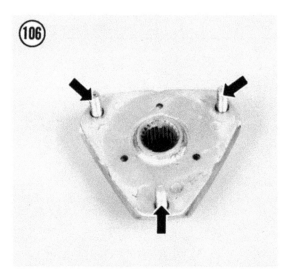

REAR HUB INSPECTION
(ALL MODELS)

Inspect the hub splines (**Figure 104**) for wear or damage. Replace the hub if necessary.

Inspect the threads on the lug nut studs for wear or damage. Refer to **Figure 105** or **Figure 106**. Replace the hub if necesary.

NOTE
The number of lug nut studs varies among the different models.

REAR AXLE INSPECTION
(ALL MODELS)

1. Inspect the axle for signs of fatigue, fractures or damage.
2. Inspect all of the splines (**Figure 107**) for wear or damage. `
3. Inspect the flange where the driven sprocket attaches. Make sure there are no cracks or damage. Depending on the model, make sure the holes (**Figure 108**) are not elongated or that the threaded studs (**Figure 109**) are not bent or stripped. Replace the axle if necessary.
4. Check the hole at each end of the axle (**Figure 110**) where the cotter pin fits in. Make sure there are no fractures or cracks leading out toward the end of the axle. If any are found, replace the axle.
5. Check the axle for straightness. Use V-blocks and a dial indicator as shown in **Figure 111**. Check the runout in the center of the axle (remember that the actual runout is 1/2 of the total indicator reading). If the runout is 3.0 mm (0.12 in.) or greater, the axle must be replaced.

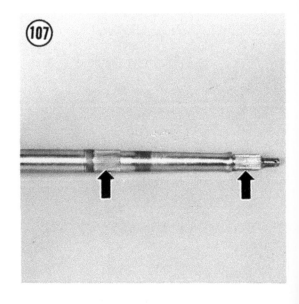

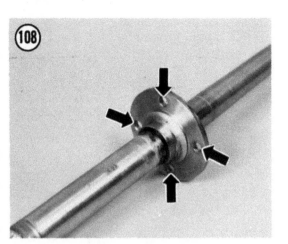

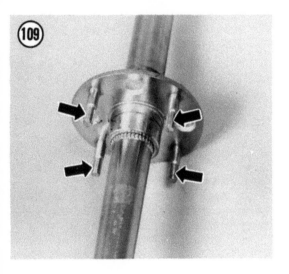

DRIVE CHAIN

Removal/Installation

1. Place the ATC on level ground and set the parking brake or block the wheel so the vehicle will not roll in either direction.

2. Remove the seat/rear fender assembly.

3. Remove the left-hand rear wheel as described in this chapter.

4. Remove the cotter pin and castellated nut securing the left-hand rear hub. Remove the lockwasher and hub.

5. On 1973-1975 ATC70 models, remove the rear cover, step bar and the lower skid plate.

6. On all models except the ATC70, remove the bolts securing the cover plate and slide off the cover plate.

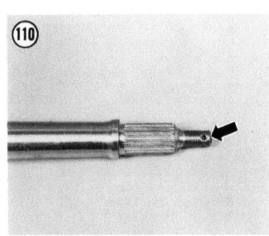

8

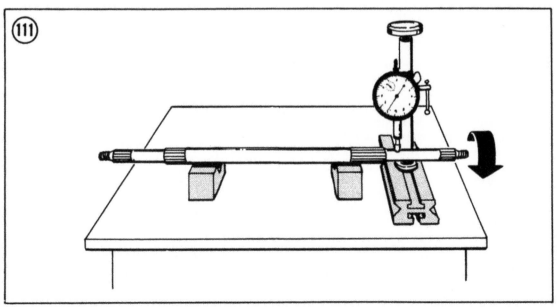

7. Remove the bolts securing the drive chain cover in place and remove the drive chain cover.

8. Loosen the rear axle bearing holder bolts. There are 2 on each side. Loosen the drive chain adjuster and push the rear axle assembly forward to allow slack in the drive chain.

9A. On ATC70 models, perform the following:
    a. Remove the left-hand crankcase cover and the recoil starter as an assembly.
    b. Remove the master link (**Figure 112**) on the drive chain and remove the drive chain.

> *NOTE*
> *On models equipped with a subtransmission, the drive sprocket is located under the left-hand crankcase cover.*

9B. On 1981-1983 ATC110 models with the original equipment continuous loop drive chain, perform the following:
    a. Remove the recoil starter as described in Chapter Seven.
    b. Remove the alternator as described in Chapter Seven.
    c. Remove the subtransmission as decribed in Chapter Five.
    d. Remove the left-hand crankcase cover and spacer as described in Chapter Four.
    e. Remove the rear axle and the drive sprocket as described in this chapter.

> *NOTE*
> *Step 9C is designed to avoid the time-consuming procedure of having to remove the recoil starter, alternator and the subtransmission.*

9C. On all models with a subtransmission and a drive chain with a master link, perform the following:
    a. Attach a piece of soft wire to one end of the drive chain next to the master link.
    b. Attach this wire to either the new drive chain (if a new drive chain is to be installed) or to a piece of old drive chain (if the existing drive chain is to be reinstalled).
    c. As the existing drive chain is removed, it will thread the new chain (or piece of old chain) onto the drive sprocket.

> *NOTE*
> *If the piece of old chain is used, leave it installed on the drive sprocket. Repeat Step 9C when the drive chain has been*

cleaned and lubricated and is ready for installation.

10. On models with an O-ring drive chain and master link, remove the master link (**Figure 84**). Don't lose the rubber O-rings on the master link pins (**Figure 85**).

11. Install by reversing these removal steps, noting the following.

12. On models with an O-ring drive chain and master link, be sure to install the O-rings on the master link pins.

13. On models equipped with a master link, install the drive chain and the master link. Install a new clip in the master link so that the closed end of the clip is facing the direction of chain travel (**Figure 98**).

14. Clean out the drive chain cover. Remove any accumulation of drive chain lubricant, sand, gravel and other trail dirt.

15. Make sure the rubber seal is in good condition and in place on the drive chain cover. Install the drive chain cover and secure it with the bolts.

16. Install the hub washer with the side marked "OUTSIDE" facing toward the outside.

17. Install the axle nut and tighten to the torque specification listed in **Table 1**.

18. Install a new cotter pin and bend it over completely. Never reuse an old cotter pin as it may break and fall out.

19. Adjust the drive chain as described in Chapter Three.

20. Adjust the rear brake as described in Chapter Three.

Cleaning/Inspection/Lubrication

> *CAUTION*
> *Some models are equipped with an O-ring type drive chain. These rubber*

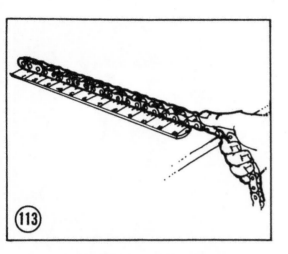

O-rings can easily be damaged. Do not use a steam cleaner, a high-pressure washer or any solvent that may damage the rubber O-rings.

1. Remove the drive chain as described in this chapter.
2. Immerse the chain in a pan of kerosene or non-flammable solvent and allow it to soak for about half an hour. Move it around and flex it during this period so that the dirt between the links, pins and rollers may work its way out.

CAUTION
In the next step, on O-ring type chains do not use a wire brush or the O-rings will be damaged and the drive chain must be replaced.

3A. On O-ring type chains, scrub the rollers and side plates with a medium soft brush and rinse away loosened dirt. Do not scrub hard as the O-rings may be damaged. Rinse it a couple of times to make sure all dirt and grit are washed out. Dry the chain with a shop cloth then hang it up and allow the chain to thoroughly dry.
3B. On chains without O-rings, scrub the rollers and side plates with a stiff brush and rinse away loosened dirt. Rinse it a couple of times to make sure all dirt and grit are washed out. Dry the chain with a shop cloth then hang it up and allow the chain to thoroughly dry.
4. After cleaning the chain, examine it carefully for wear or damage. If any signs are visible, replace the chain.
5. Lay the chain alongside a ruler (**Figure 113**) and compress the links together. Then stretch them apart. If more than 0.6 mm (1/4 in.) of movement within 30.5 mm (12 in.) of chain is possible, replace the drive chain as it is too worn to be used again.

NOTE
Honda does not provide drive chain description numbers nor number of links. If the chain must be replaced, take the old chain to a dealer and purchase one identical to it.

NOTE
Always check both sprockets every time the chain is removed. If any wear is visible on the teeth, replace the sprocket(s). Never install a new chain over worn sprockets or a worn chain over new sprockets.

6A. On O-ring type chains, lubricate the chain with SAE 80W-90 gear oil or a good grade of chain lubricant (specifically formulated for O-ring chains), following the manufacturer's instructions.
6B. On chains without O-rings, lubricate the chain with a good grade of chain lubricant, following the manufacturer's instructions. If a chain lubricant isn't available use SAE 10W-30 motor oil.
7. Reinstall the chain as described in this chapter.

REAR AXLE BEARING HOLDER

The rear axle bearing holder is attached to the frame at the rear and contains the rear axle bearings and grease seals. On some models, it is also part of the rear brake.

**Removal/Installation And
Bearing Replacement
(1973-1974 ATC70)**

Refer to **Figure 57** for this procedure.
1. Remove the axle as described in this chapter.

NOTE
On these models only, when the axle is removed, the 2 bearing holders (or panels) that contain the axle bearings are removed at the same time.

2. On the left-hand panel, perform the following:
   a. Remove the short panel collar from each side of the panel.
   b. Remove the oil seal and discard it.
   c. Remove the circlip.
   d. Using your fingers, press the bearing out of the panel.
   e. Turn the bearing by hand and make sure it turns smoothly.

NOTE
Some axial play is normal, but radial play should be negligible. The bearing should turn smoothly.

f. Check the balls for evidence of wear, pitting or excessive heat (bluish tint). Replace the bearing if necessary. When replacing, be sure to take your old bearings along to ensure a perfect matchup.

g. Install the bearing with the sealed surface facing toward the outside. Press the bearing in with your fingers until it bottoms.

h. Install the circlip and make sure it completely seats in the groove.

i. Apply a light coat of multipurpose grease to the lips of the new oil seal. Tap the oil seal in until it is flush with the surface of the left-hand panel.

j. Install the short panel collar into each side of the panel.

3. On the right-hand panel, perform the following:

a. Remove the short panel collar from each side of the panel.

b. Remove the mounting bolt rubber cushions.

c. Remove the brake arm dust seal.

d. Remove the brake shoes and return springs.

e. Remove the brake camshaft.

f. Remove the oil seal from each side and discard them.

g. Using your fingers, press the 2 bearings out. The panel spacer that is between the 2 bearings will also come out.

h. Turn each bearing by hand and make sure it turns smoothly.

NOTE
Some axial play is normal, but radial play should be negligible. The bearing should turn smoothly.

i. Check the balls for evidence of wear, pitting or excessive heat (bluish tint). Replace the bearing if necessary. When replacing, be sure to take your old bearings along to ensure a perfect matchup.

j. Apply a light coat of multipurpose grease to the lips of the new oil seal. Tap the outer oil seal in until it is flush with the outer surface of the right-hand panel.

k. Place the panel spacer in between the 2 bearings (with their sealed surfaces facing toward the outside). Press this assembly into the right-hand panel until it touches the already installed oil seal.

l. Apply a light coat of multipurpose grease to the lips of the new oil seal. Tap the oil seal in until it is flush with the surface of the right-hand panel.

m. Install the brake camshaft and apply a light coat of multipurpose grease to the camshaft

and anchor pin. Do not allow any grease to come in contact with the brake shoes.

n. Install the brake shoes, return springs and the dust seal.

o. Install the mounting bolt rubber cushions.

p. Install the short panel collar into each side of the panel.

4. Install the rear axle as described in this chapter.

Removal/Installation
(1978-on ATC70, All ATC90
and 1981-1983 ATC110)

NOTE
On 1978-on ATC70 models, the rear axle bearing holder is permanently attached to the frame and cannot be removed. Use this procedure for oil seal and bearing replacement.

Refer to **Figure 74** for this procedure.

1. Remove the rear axle as described in this chapter.

2. Completely unscrew the brake adjust nut.

3. Remove the bolt and nut securing the brake arm. Remove the brake arm, return spring, washer and felt seal from the camshaft.

4. On 1970-1974 ATC90 models, perform the following:

a. Remove the nut securing the brake drum and the sealing washer.

b. Slide off the brake drum.

5. Remove the cotter pin and washer (A, **Figure 114**) from the anchor pin.

6. Remove the brake shoes, return springs and the camshaft as an assembly (B, **Figure 114**).

7A. On 1978-on ATC70 models, perform the following:

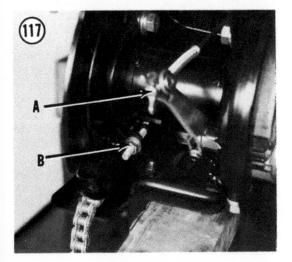

a. Remove the bolts securing the brake anchor and brake cam holder.
b. Remove the anchor and the cam holder.
c. Remove the oil seals and bearings as described in this chapter.

7B. On 1974-1978 ATC90 and ATC110 models, perform the following:
a. On the right-hand side, remove the nut and washers securing the brake drum outer panel and remove the panel.
b. Withdraw the bolts from the left-hand side and rotate the bearing holder housing down and out of the frame as shown in **Figure 115**.
c. Remove the oil seals and bearings as described in this chapter.

8. Install by reversing these removal steps, noting the following.

9. Adjust the rear brake and drive chain as described in Chapter Three.

Removal/Installation (1984 ATC110 and ATC125M)

Refer to **Figure 99** for this procedure.

1. Remove the rear axle (**Figure 116**) as described in this chapter.

2. Completely unscrew the brake adjust nut (A, **Figure 117**) and disconnect the brake rod from the brake arm.

3. Completely unscrew the drive chain adjust nut (B, **Figure 117**).

4. Remove the bolts securing the drive chain rear cover and remove the cover.

5. Remove the brake shoes and return springs (**Figure 118**) as an assembly.

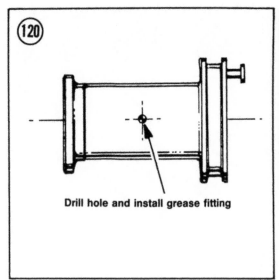

Drill hole and install grease fitting

6. Remove the bolts (**Figure 119**) securing the rear axle bearing housing to the frame and remove the housing.

7. Install by reversing these removal steps, noting the following.

8. Adjust the rear brake and drive chain as described in Chapter Three.

Bearing Removal
(Except 1973-1974 ATC70)

1. Remove the rear axle and bearing housing as described in this chapter.

2. Remove the oil seal and the O-ring seal (models so equipped) from each side of the bearing holder.

3. To remove the left- and right-hand bearings and distance collar, insert a soft aluminum or brass drift into one side of the hub. Push the center collar over to one side and place the drift on the inner race of the opposite bearing. Tap the bearing out of the hub with a hammer, working around the perimeter of the inner race.

4. Remove that bearing and the distance collar.

5. Repeat Step 3 for the other bearing.

Bearing Inspection
(Except 1973-1974 ATC70)

1. Thoroughly clean the inside of the bearing holder with solvent and dry with compressed air or a shop cloth.

2. Do not clean sealed bearings. If non-sealed bearings are installed, thoroughly clean them in solvent and thoroughly dry with compressed air. Do not let the bearing spin while drying.

3. Turn each bearing by hand. Make sure the bearings turn smoothly.

NOTE
Some axial play is normal, but radial play should be negligible. The bearing should turn smoothly.

4. On non-sealed bearings, check the balls for evidence of wear, pitting or excessive heat (bluish tint). Replace bearings if necessary; always replace as a complete set. When replacing, be sure to take your old bearings along to ensure a perfect matchup.

NOTE
Fully sealed bearings are available from many good bearing specialty shops. Fully sealed bearings provide better protection from dirt and moisture that may get into the hub.

5. Inspect the grease seals and O-ring seals. Replace if they are deteriorating or starting to harden. If the ATC is ridden in a lot of water or mud the water will enter the housing and wash the grease away from the bearings. To help prevent bearing damage, install a grease fitting to the bearing housing and keep the housing packed with grease. Drill a hole in the bottom of the housing in the center and press in a 3/16 in. automotive type Zerk fitting as shown in **Figure 120**. After reinstalling the bearing housing in the frame and installing the rear axle, fill the bearing housing with multipurpose grease using a small hand-held grease gun.

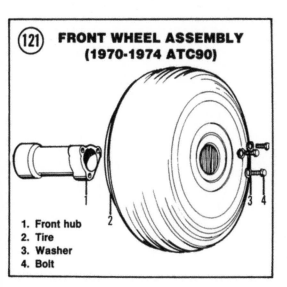

**FRONT WHEEL ASSEMBLY
(1970-1974 ATC90)**

1. Front hub
2. Tire
3. Washer
4. Bolt

Bearing Installation
(Except 1973-1974 ATC70)

NOTE
Install the Honda bearings with their markings facing toward the outside of the housing.

1. On non-sealed bearings, pack the bearings with a good quality bearing grease. Work the grease in between the balls thoroughly. Turn the bearing by hand a couple of times to make sure the grease is distributed evenly inside the bearing.
2. Coat the inside of the bearing holder and the center collar with multipurpose grease.

CAUTION
During installation, tap the bearings squarely into place and tap on the outer race only. Use a socket that matches the outer race diameter. Do not tap on the inner race or the bearing may be damaged. Be sure that the bearings are completely seated.

3. Install the right-hand bearing.
4. Install the center collar and the left-hand bearing.
5. Apply a light coat of multipurpose grease to the grease seals (and O-ring seals, if so equipped) and install one on each side of the bearing holder.
6. Install the bearing holder and the rear axle as described in this chapter.

TIRES AND WHEELS

The ATC is equipped with tubeless, low pressure tires designed specifically for off-road use only. Rapid tire wear will occur if the ATC is ridden on paved surfaces. Due to their low pressure

requirements, they should be inflated only with a hand-operated air pump instead of using an air compressor or the air available at service stations.

CAUTION
*Do not overinflate the stock tires as they will be permanently distorted and damaged. If overinflated they will bulge out similar to an inner tube that is not within the constraints of a tire and **will not** return to their original contour.*

NOTE
Additional inflation pressure in the stock tires will not improve the ride or the handling characteristics of the ATC. For improved handling, aftermarket tires will have to be installed.

To guard against punctures from *small objects*, install a commercially available liquid tire sealer into all 3 tires though the valve stem. It's a good idea to carry a cold patch tire repair kit and hand held pump in the tow vehicle. Its also a good idea to carry the tire pump, some chewing gum and a small strip of cater).

Removing the tire from the special rims is different than on a motorcycle or automobile wheel. Due to the different types of rims used on the various models, tire removal procedures are separated into different groups.

CAUTION
***Do not use conventional motorcycle tire irons** for tire removal as the tire sealing bead will be damaged when forced away from the rim flange.*

Tire Changing
(1970-1974 ATC90)

The front and rear tires on these models are of the one-piece type (similar to an inner tube) and have no rim. Refer to **Figure 121** for the front wheel and **Figure 122** for the rear wheel. After the tire is removed from the axle all you have is a large tire with a very small hole in the center where the wheel boss is attached.

Tire Changing
(All ATC70, 1975-1978 ATC90,
1979-1983 ATC110)

Refer to **Figure 123** for this procedure.
To make tire changing easier, special tools are available. The one from Honda is the Tire Disassembly Tool, Honda part No. 07772-0010000. See **Figure 124**. A variety of aftermarket tire removal tools are available at most dealers, mail order houses or motorcycle

8

supply stores. The one shown in this procedure is only an example from one manufacturer. Most tools fit different size rims, but make sure you purchase the correct one for your specific wheel size.

NOTE
On the front wheel it is necessary to remove the front hub from the wheel. Remove the bolts and nuts securing the hub to the wheel and remove the hub.

1. Remove the valve stem cap and core and deflate the tire. Do not reinstall the core at this time.

2. Lubricate the tire bead and rim flanges with water and liquid dish detergent, Armor All or any rubber lubricant.

CAUTION
If you are running aftermarket aluminum wheels, special care must be taken when changing tires to avoid scratches and gouges to the outer rim surface.

3. After the air pressure is released from the tire, use one of the previously mentioned tire removal

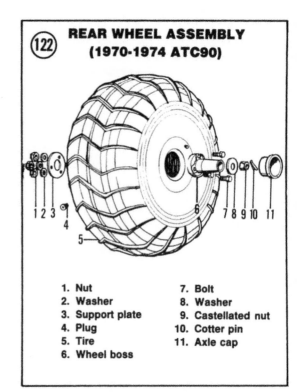

**REAR WHEEL ASSEMBLY
(1970-1974 ATC90)**

1. Nut
2. Washer
3. Support plate
4. Plug
5. Tire
6. Wheel boss
7. Bolt
8. Washer
9. Castellated nut
10. Cotter pin
11. Axle cap

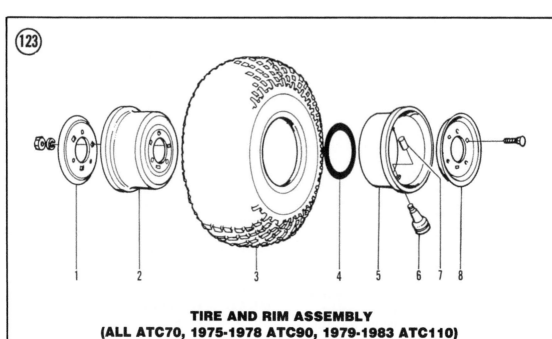

**TIRE AND RIM ASSEMBLY
(ALL ATC70, 1975-1978 ATC90, 1979-1983 ATC110)**

1. Support plate
2. Inner rim
3. Tire
4. O-ring
5. Outer rim
6. Valve stem
7. Cap
8. Support plate

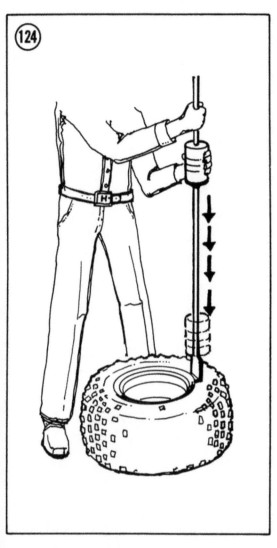

tools (**Figure 125**) or stand on the tire with the heel of your shoe, close to the wheel rim. Exert as much downward pressure as possible to break the tire bead loose. If you are unable to break it loose this way, place a wooden 2×4 next to the rim and hit the 2×4 with a hammer (**Figure 126**).

4. Continue to work your way around the tire until it is completely loose on one side (**Figure 127**). Turn the tire over and repeat for the other side.

5. Remove the rim bolts, lockwashers and nuts.

6. Remove the rim, the large O-ring and, on models so equipped, the rim plate(s).

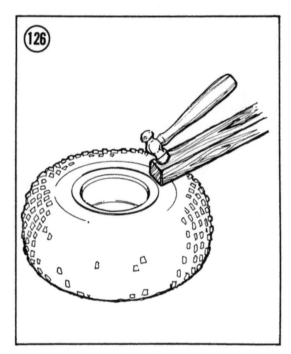

8

7. Inspect the rim sealing surface on both rims. If the rim has been severely hit it will probably cause an air leak. Either repair or replace any damaged rim. On stock rims, remove any rust on the rim sealing surface area and repaint if necessary.

8. Inspect the tire for cuts, tears, abrasions or any other defects.

9. Wipe the tire beads and rims free from any lubricating agent used in Step 2.

NOTE
Make sure that the beads are up on the bead seats and are uniformly seated all around (Figure 128).

10. Apply clean water to the rim flanges, tire rim beads and the outer rim.

NOTE
Use only clean water and make sure the rim flange is clean. Wipe with a lint-free cloth prior to wetting down.

11. On ATC90 and ATC110 models, lay the outer rim flange on the floor upside down.

12. Place the outer rim (the one with the valve stem) on the floor with the outside rim facing down. Place it directly over the outer rim flange already on the floor.

13. Set the tire into position on the outer rim (**Figure 129**).

14. Inspect the large O-ring seal. If it is starting to harden or deteriorate, replace with a new one.

15. Apply a light coat of grease to the large O-ring seal and place it in the groove in the outer rim (**Figure 130**).

16. Install the inner rim into the tire and onto the outer rim. Align the bolt holes (**Figure 131**).

17. On ATC90 and ATC110 models, install the inner rim plate.

18. Reach down through the opening in the rim and pull the outer rim up into position (on models so equipped). Align the bolt holes.

19. Insert the bolts from the outer rim side and install the lockwasher and nuts (**Figure 132**). Tighten the nuts to the torque specification listed in **Table 1**.

20. Install the valve stem core.

21. Apply tire mounting lubricant or a liquid dish detergent to the tire bead and inflate the tire to the recommended tire pressure.

22. Deflate the tire and let it sit for about one hour.

23. Inflate the tire to the recommended air pressure; refer to **Table 3**. Also check the tire circumference with a tape measure (**Figure 133**) and compare to dimension given in **Table 3**.

24. Check for air leaks and install the valve cap.

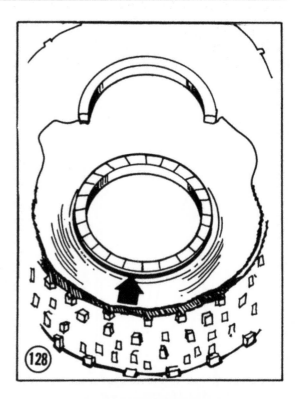

Tire Changing
(1984 ATC110 and ATC125M)

Refer to **Figure 134** for this procedure.

The rims used on these models have a very deep built-in ridge to keep the tire bead seated on the rim under severe riding conditions. Unfortunately it also tends to keep the tire on the rim during tire removal as well.

A special tool is *required* for tire changing on these models and is shown in use in this procedure. The special tool from Honda is the Universal Bead

8

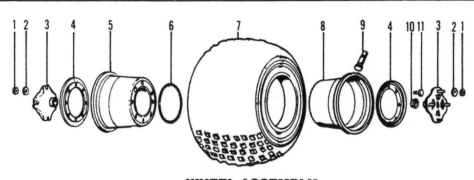

**WHEEL ASSEMBLY
(1984 ATC110, ATC125M)**

1. Nut
2. Washer
3. Hub—rear wheel only
4. Inner rim plate
   Outer rim plate
5. Inner rim

6. O-ring
7. Tire
8. Outer rim
9. Valve rim
10. Collar
11. Bolt

Breaker, Honda part No. GN-AH-958-BB1. The use of this specific tool is necessary as it exerts all of the applied pressure to a very small séction of the tire bead at a time. Most other aftermarket bead breakers spread out the applied pressure over a larger section of the tire bead and therefore are unable to break the bead loose from this type of rim.

If you are going to purchase this bead breaker and also have other ATCs with different rim sizes, the blade length (**Figure 135**) is important. The following blades are recommended:

a. Short blade for 7 in. and 8 in. rims.
b. Long blade for 9 in. and 11 in. rims.

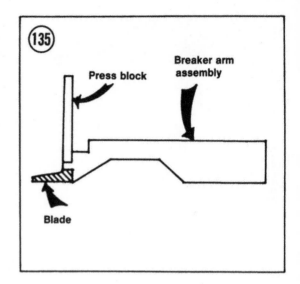

> *CAUTION*
> *The use of the improper size blade may damage the rim, tire or the blade.*

> *NOTE*
> *On the front wheel it is necessary to remove the front hub from the wheel. Remove the bolts and nuts securing the hub to the wheel and remove the hub.*

1. Remove the valve stem cap and core and deflate the tire. Do not reinstall the core at this time.
2. Install the correct size adapter onto the threaded shaft and place the wheel over this assembly (**Figure 136**).
3. Lubricate the tire bead and rim flanges with a liquid dish detergent, Armor All or any rubber lubricant. Press the tire sidewall/bead down to allow the liquid to run into and around the bead area. Also apply lubricant to the area where the bead breaker arm will come in contact with the tire sidewall.
4. Hold the breaker arm at about 45° to the tire and insert the blade between the tire bead and the rim.
5. Push the breaker arm inward and downward until it is horizontal with the press block against the rim outer surface (**Figure 136**).

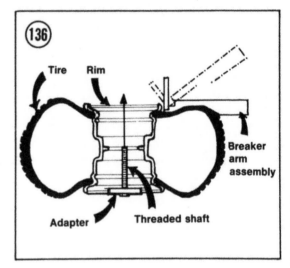

> *NOTE*
> *To completely seat the breaker arm, hold it horizontal and tap the end of the breaker arm with soft-faced mallet to position the press block **completely** against the rim outer surface. This is necessary for the tool to work properly.*

6. With the breaker arm positioned correctly, place the breaker press head assembly over the press block of the breaker arm. Make sure the press head bolt is backed out all the way (**Figure 137**).

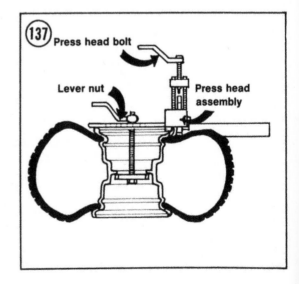

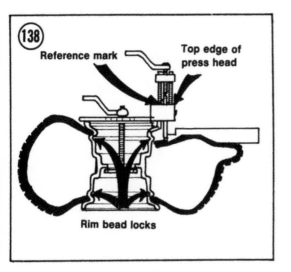

(138)

Reference mark

Top edge of press head

Rim bead locks

7. Position the nylon buttons on the press head against the inside edge of the rim.

8. Pull the threaded shaft and adapter assembly up and insert it into the breaker press head assembly. Install the bolts through the rim holes and the adapter to correctly position the adapter assembly to the center of the rim.

9. Slowly tighten the lever nut until both ends of the breaker press head assembly are in firm contact with the rim.

10. Slowly tighten the press head bolt until the reference mark on the press block is aligned with the top edge of the press head (**Figure 138**). At this point the tire bead *should* break away from the rim.

11. Using your hands, press down on the tire on either side of the breaker arm assembly and try to break the rest of the bead free from the rim.

12. If the rest of the tire bead cannot be broken loose, loosen the press head bolt and lever nut. Rotate the press head assembly about 1/8 to 1/4 of the circumference of the rim.

13. Repeat Steps 4-11 until the entire bead is broken loose from the rim.

14. Remove the tool assembly from the rim assembly. Turn the wheel over and repeat Steps 2-13 for the other rim flange.

15. Remove the rim bolts, lockwashers and nuts.

16. Remove the rim, the large O-ring and the rim plates.

17. Inspect the rim sealing surface on both rims. If the rim has been severely hit it will probably cause an air leak. Either repair or replace any damaged rim. On stock rims, remove any rust on the rim sealing surface area and repaint if necessary.

18. Inspect the tire for cuts, tears, abrasions or any other defects.

19. Wipe the tire beads and rims free from any lubricating agent used in Step 3.

20. Apply clean water to the rim flanges, tire rim beads and onto the outer rim.

NOTE
Use only clean water and make sure the rim flange is clean. Wipe with a lint-free cloth prior to wetting down.

21. Lay the outer rim flange on the floor upside down.

22. Place the outer rim (the one with the valve stem) on the floor with the outside rim facing down. Place it directly over the outer rim flange already on the floor.

23. Set the tire into position on the outer rim (**Figure 129**).

24. Inspect the large O-ring seal. If it is starting to harden or deteriorate, replace with a new one.

25. Apply a light coat of grease to the large O-ring seal and place it in the groove in the outer rim (**Figure 130**).

26. Install the inner rim into the tire and onto the outer rim. Align the bolt holes (**Figure 131**) and install the inner rim plate.

27. Reach down through the opening in the rim and pull the outer rim up into position. Align the bolt holes.

28. Insert the bolts from the outer rim side and install the lockwasher and nuts (**Figure 132**). Tighten the nuts to the torque specification listed in **Table 1**.

29. Install the valve stem core.

30. Apply tire mounting lubricant or a liquid dish detergent to the tire bead and inflate the tire to the recommended tire pressure.

31. Deflate the tire and let it sit for about one hour.

32. Inflate the tire to the recommended air pressure; refer to **Table 3**. Also check the tire circumference with a tape measure (**Figure 133**) and compare to dimension given in **Table 3**.

33. Check for air leaks and install the valve cap.

Cold Patch Repair

This is the method that Honda recommends for patching a tire. The rubber plug type of repair is recommended only for an emergency repair or until the tire can be patched correctly with the cold patch method.

NOTE
If you get caught out in the boonies without any means of patching a tire, you can try the following method. Chew

8

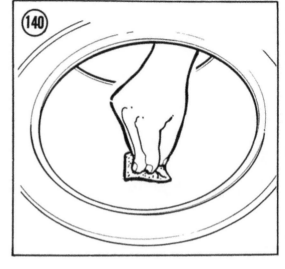

some gum (preferably the soft bubble-gum type) and then knead it into a small strip of cloth. Stuff this gum/cloth into the hole in the tire, pump up the tire and it just may get you back to camp.

1. Remove the tire as described in this chapter.

2. Prior to removing the object that punctured the tire, mark the location of the puncture with chalk or crayon on the outside of the tire. Remove the object (**Figure 139**).

3A. On 1970-1974 ATC90 models, on the *outside* of the tire, roughen the area around the hole slightly larger than the patch. Use the cap from the tire repair kit or pocket knife. Do not scrape too vigorously or you may cause additional damage.

3B. On all other models, on the inside of the tire, roughen the area around the hole slightly larger than the patch (**Figure 140**). Use the cap from the tire repair kit or pocket knife. Do not scrape too vigorously or you may cause additional damage.

4. Clean the area with a non-flamable solvent. Do not use an oil base solvent as it will leave a residue rendering the patch useless.

NOTE
In the following steps, the patch is applied to the outside surface of the tire on 1970-1974 ATC90 models, not the inside as on all other models.

5. Apply a small amount of special cement to the puncture and spread it with your finger.

6. Allow the cement to dry until tacky—usually 30 seconds or so is sufficient.

7. Remove the backing from the patch.

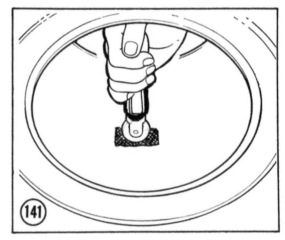

CAUTION
Do not touch the newly exposed rubber with your fingers or the patch will not stick firmly.

8. Center the patch over the hole. Hold the patch firmly in place for about 30 seconds to allow the cement to dry. If you have a roller use it to help press the patch into place (**Figure 141**).

9. Dust the area with talcum powder.

FRAME

The frame does not require routine maintenance. However, it should be inspected immediately after any accident or spill.

Component Removal/Installation

1. Remove the seat, fenders and fuel tank.

2. Remove the engine as described in Chapter Four.

3. Remove the front wheel, front fender, handlebar assembly and front fork/steering stem assembly as described in this Chapter.

4. Remove the rear wheels and rear axle as described in this chapter.

5. Remove the lighting and ignition equipment and the wiring harness as described in Chapter Seven.

6. Remove the footpeg assembly.

7. Inspect the frame for bends, cracks or other damage, especially around welded joints and areas that are rusted.

8. Assemble by reversing these steps.

Stripping and Painting

Remove all components from the frame. Thoroughly strip off all old paint. The best way is to have it sandblasted down to bare metal. If this is not possible, you can use a liquid paint remover and steel wool and a fine, hard wire brush.

CAUTION
The headlight housing and both the front and rear fenders are molded plastic. If you wish to change the color of these parts, consult an automotive paint supplier for the proper procedure. Do not use any liquid paint remover on these components as it will damage the surface. The color is an integral part of some of these components and cannot be removed.

When the frame is down to bare metal, have it inspected for hairline and internal cracks. Magnafluxing is the most common and complete process.

Make sure that the primer is compatible with the type of paint you are going to use for the final coat. Spray on one or two coats of primer as smoothly as possible. Let it dry thoroughly and use a fine grade of wet sandpaper (400-600 grit) to remove any flaws. Carefully wipe the surface clean and then spray the final coat. Use either lacquer or enamel base paint and follow the manufacturer's instructions.

A shop specializing in painting will probably do the best job. However, you can do a surprisingly good job with a good grade of spray paint. Spend a few extra dollars and get a good grade of paint as it will make a difference in how well it looks and how long it will stand up. It's a good idea to shake the can and make sure the ball inside the can is loose when you purchase the can of paint. Shake the can as long as is stated on the can. Then immerse the can *upright* in a pot or bucket of *warm water (not hot—not over 120° F).*

WARNING
Higher temperatures could cause the can to burst. Do not place the can in direct contact with any flame or heat source.

Leave the can in the water for several minutes. When thoroughly warmed, shake the can again and spray the frame. Be sure to get into all the crevices where there may be rust problems. Several light mist coats are better than one heavy coat. Spray painting is best done in temperatures of 70-80° F (21-26° C); any temperature above or below this will give you problems.

After the final coat has dried completely, at least 48 hours, any overspray or orange peel may be removed with a *light application* of Dupont rubbing compound (red color) and finished with Dupont polishing compound (white color). Be careful not to rub too hard or you will go through the finish.

Finish off with a couple coats of good wax prior to reassembling all the components.

It's a good idea to keep the frame touched up with fresh paint if any minor rust spots or scratches appear.

8

Tables are on the following page.

Table 1 FRAME TORQUE SPECIFICATIONS

Item	N·m	ft.-lb.
Front axle nut		
ATC70	60-80	43-57
ATC90	NA	NA
ATC110, ATC125M	50-70	36-51
Handlebar upper holder bolts		
ATC70	6-9	4-6
ATC90	NA	NA
ATC110, ATC125M	18-30	13-22
Handlebar lower holder nuts	40-48	29-34
Steering stem nut	50-70	36-51
Front fork bridge bolt		
ATC70	40-48	29-34
ATC90	NA	NA
ATC110, ATC125M	50-70	36-51
Rear axle nut	60-80	43-58
Rear brake drum nut		
ATC70	NA	NA
ATC90	40-45	29-32
ATC110	40-60	29-43
ATC125M		
Inner	35-45	25-33
Outer	120-140	87-101
Rear bearing holder		
ATC70 (right- and left-hand)	20-24	14-17
ATC90	20-24	14-17
ATC110	NA	NA
ATC125M	50-70	36-51
Driven sprocket to axle		
ATC70	NA	NA
ATC90	40-48	29-35
ATC110	44-52	32-38
ATC125M	21-27	15-20
Wheel rim bolts and nuts	19-25	14-18

NA—Does not apply to this model or Honda does not provide specifications for all models.

Table 2 TIRE INFLATION PRESSURE AND CIRCUMFERENCE MEASUREMENTS

Model	Tire size (Front and rear)	Tire pressure kg/cm²	psi	Circumference mm	in.
ATC70	16×8-7	0.2	2.8	1,520	60
ATC90					
1970-1974	NA	NA	NA	NA	NA
1975-1978	22×11-8 ATV	0.15	2.2	1,742	68.6
ATC110	22×11-8 ATV	0.15	2.2	1,742	68.6
ATC125	22×11-8 ATV	0.15	2.2	1,742	68.6

NA—Honda does not provide service information for all models.

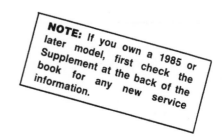
NOTE: If you own a 1985 or later model, first check the Supplement at the back of the book for any new service information.

CHAPTER NINE

BRAKES

Both the front (if so equipped) and rear brakes are drum type. **Figure 1** illustrates the major components of the brake assembly. Activating the brake hand lever or foot pedal pulls the cable and/or rod which in turn rotates the camshaft. This forces the brake shoes out into contact with the brake drum. The rear brake can be activated either by the lever on the left-hand side of the handlebar or by a foot pedal.

All models except the ATC70 are equipped with a parking brake. This is the rear brake that is activated by the hand lever. Pulling the brake lever on all the way and flipping the lock into position will hold the rear brake on.

Lever and pedal free play must be maintained on both brakes to minimize brake drag and premature brake wear and maximize braking effectiveness. Refer to Chapter Three for complete adjustment procedures.

Both front and rear brake cables must be inspected and replaced periodically as they will stretch with use until they can no longer be properly adjusted.

Table 1 is at the end of this chapter.

FRONT BRAKE

Disassembly

Refer to **Figure 2** for this procedure.
1. Remove the front wheel as described in Chapter Eight.
2. Pull the brake assembly straight up and out of the brake drum.
3. Remove the brake shoes from the backing plate by firmly pulling up on the center of each shoe.

NOTE
Place a clean shop rag on the linings to protect them from oil and grease during removal.

4. Remove the return springs and separate the shoes.
5. Loosen the bolt (**Figure 3**) securing the brake lever to the cam.
6. From the outside surface of the brake panel, remove the lever, wear indicator and cam outer dust seal from the camshaft.
7. From the inside surface of the brake panel, remove the return spring and withdraw the camshaft and washer.

Inspection

1. Thoroughly clean and dry all parts except the linings.
2. Check the contact surface of the drum (**Figure 4**) for scoring. If there are grooves deep enough to snag a fingernail, the drum should be turned and

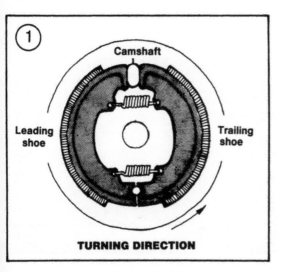

1

Camshaft

Leading shoe

Trailing shoe

TURNING DIRECTION

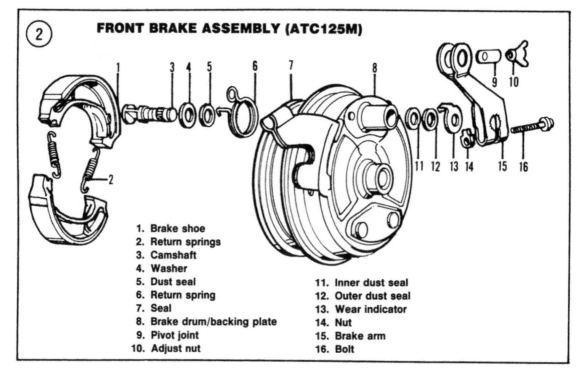

② **FRONT BRAKE ASSEMBLY (ATC125M)**

1. Brake shoe
2. Return springs
3. Camshaft
4. Washer
5. Dust seal
6. Return spring
7. Seal
8. Brake drum/backing plate
9. Pivot joint
10. Adjust nut
11. Inner dust seal
12. Outer dust seal
13. Wear indicator
14. Nut
15. Brake arm
16. Bolt

new shoes fitted. This type of wear can be avoided to a great extent if the brakes are disassembled and thoroughly cleaned after riding the vehicle in water, mud or deep sand.

NOTE
If oil or grease is on the drum surface, clean it off with a clean rag soaked in lacquer thinner—do not use any solvent that may leave an oil residue.

3. Use a vernier caliper (**Figure 5**) and check the inside diameter of the drum for out-of-round or excessive wear. The standard new brake drum ID and the service limit are listed in **Table 1**. Turn or replace the drum as necessary.

4. If the drum is turned, the linings will have to be replaced and the new linings arced to the new drum contour.

5. Inspect the linings for imbedded foreign material. Dirt can be removed with a stiff wire brush. Check for traces of oil or grease. If they are contaminated, they must be replaced.

6. Use a vernier caliper (**Figure 6**) and measure the thickness of the brake linings from the metal shoe. They should be replaced if worn to the service limit listed in **Table 1** or less.

7. Inspect the cam lobe (**Figure 7**) and the pivot pin area of the shaft (A, **Figure 8**) for wear and corrosion. Minor roughness can be removed with fine emery cloth.

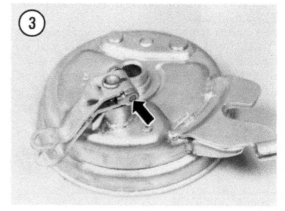

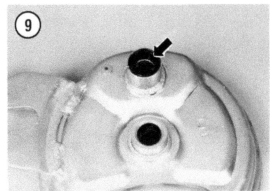

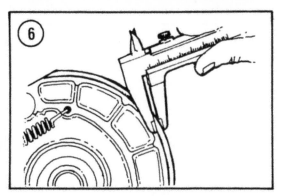

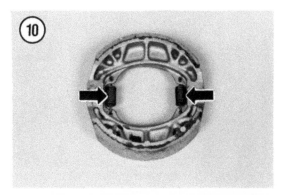

9

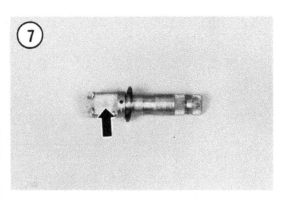

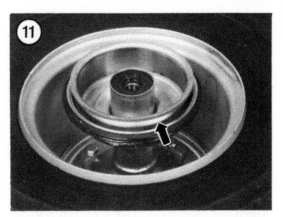

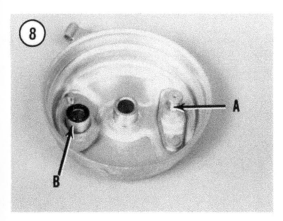

8. Check the dust seal (B, **Figure 8**) on the inside surface and the inner dust seal (**Figure 9**) on the outside surface of the brake panel. Replace if damaged or torn.

9. Inspect the brake shoe return springs for wear (**Figure 10**). If they are stretched, they will not fully retract the brake shoes from the drum, resulting in a power-robbing drag on the drums and premature wear of the linings. Replace as necessary and always replace as a pair.

10. Inspect the outer perimeter seal (**Figure 11**) on the brake drum. Replace it if torn or deteriorated.

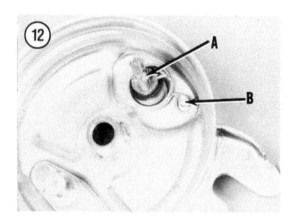

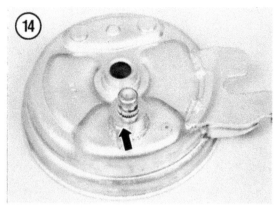

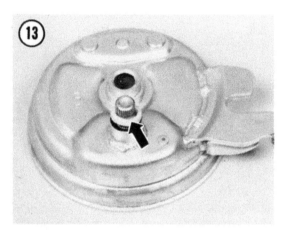

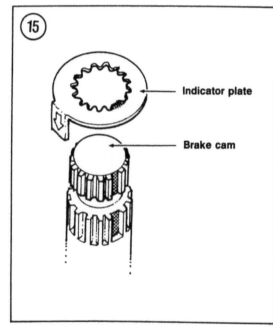

Indicator plate

Brake cam

Assembly

1. Apply a light coat of molybdenum disulfide grease to the cam prior to installation and to the pivot post in the brake panel (A, **Figure 8**). Avoid getting any grease on the brake plate where the linings come in contact with it.

3. Install the washer onto the cam and insert the cam into the brake panel. Make sure the cam seals are still in position in the brake panel.

4. Install the hook on the return spring into the hole in the camshaft (A, **Figure 12**) and place the loop onto the locating pin (B, **Figure 12**) on the brake panel.

5. Install the outer dust seal (**Figure 13**) onto the camshaft.

6. Install the wear indicator (**Figure 14**) correctly onto the cam as shown in **Figure 15**.

7. When installing the brake lever onto the brake cam, be sure to align the punch marks (**Figure 16**) on the two parts.

8. Hold the brake shoes in a "V" formation with the return springs attached and snap them in place on the brake backing plate. Make sure they are firmly seated on it (**Figure 17**).

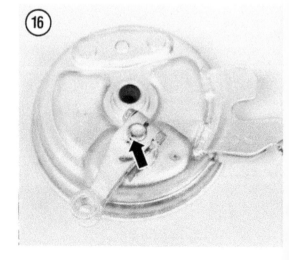

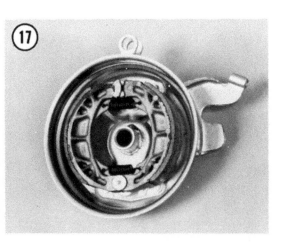

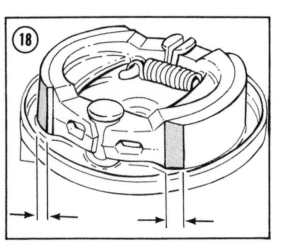

NOTE
If new linings are being installed, file off the leading edge of each shoe a little (Figure 18) so that the brake will not grab when applied.

9. Install the brake panel assembly into the brake drum.

10. Install the front wheel as described in this chapter.

NOTE
When installing the front wheel, be sure that the brake panel is indexed onto the locating pin on the right-hand fork leg. This is necessary for proper brake operation.

11. Adjust the front brake as described in Chapter Three.

REAR BRAKE

The rear brake is a single-leading shoe type. In order to service the rear brake, the majority of the rear axle components must be removed from the frame in order to gain access to the brake parts.

Removal/Disassembly/Installation (70 cc)

Refer to **Figure 19** and **Figure 20** for this procedure.

1A. On 1973-1974 models, perform the following:
   a. Remove the rear axle as described in Chapter Eight.

9

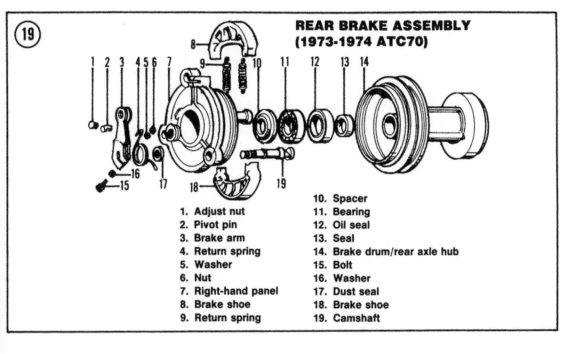

REAR BRAKE ASSEMBLY (1973-1974 ATC70)

1. Adjust nut
2. Pivot pin
3. Brake arm
4. Return spring
5. Washer
6. Nut
7. Right-hand panel
8. Brake shoe
9. Return spring
10. Spacer
11. Bearing
12. Oil seal
13. Seal
14. Brake drum/rear axle hub
15. Bolt
16. Washer
17. Dust seal
18. Brake shoe
19. Camshaft

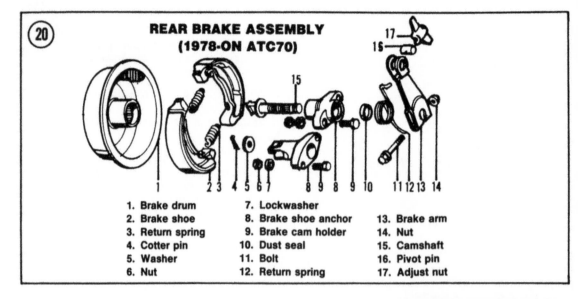

**REAR BRAKE ASSEMBLY
(1978-ON ATC70)**

1. Brake drum
2. Brake shoe
3. Return spring
4. Cotter pin
5. Washer
6. Nut
7. Lockwasher
8. Brake shoe anchor
9. Brake cam holder
10. Dust seal
11. Bolt
12. Return spring
13. Brake arm
14. Nut
15. Camshaft
16. Pivot pin
17. Adjust nut

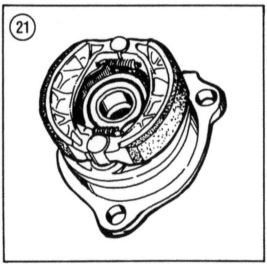

b. Wrap the linings with a clean shop cloth, pull up on the center of the linings and remove the linings and return springs from the right-hand panel (**Figure 21**).

1B. On 1978-on models, perform the following:
  a. Remove the rear axle as described in Chapter Eight.
  b. Remove the cotter pin and washer (**Figure 22**) on the brake anchor.
  c. Wrap the linings with a clean shop cloth, pull up on the center of the linings and remove the linings and return springs.

2. Remove the springs and separate the shoes.
3. Inspect all brake components as described in this chapter.

4. Install by reversing these removal steps, noting the following.
5. Grease the cam and pivot post with a light coat of molybdenum disulfide grease; avoid getting any grease on the brake plate where the linings come in contact with it.
6. Attach the return springs to the brake shoes.
7. Hold the brake shoes in a "V" formation with the return springs attached and snap them in place on the right-hand panel or brake backing plate. Make sure they are firmly seated on it.

NOTE
If new linings are being installed, file off the leading edge of each shoe a little (Figure 18) so that the brake will not grab when applied.

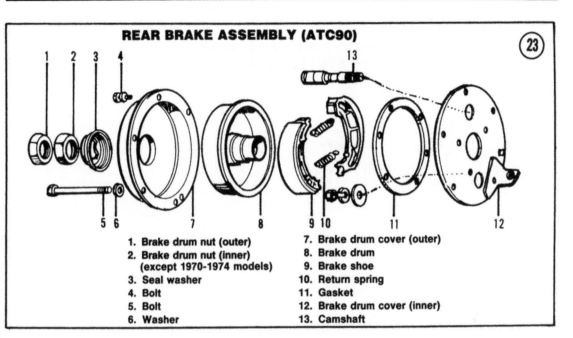

REAR BRAKE ASSEMBLY (ATC90) (23)

1. Brake drum nut (outer)
2. Brake drum nut (inner) (except 1970-1974 models)
3. Seal washer
4. Bolt
5. Bolt
6. Washer
7. Brake drum cover (outer)
8. Brake drum
9. Brake shoe
10. Return spring
11. Gasket
12. Brake drum cover (inner)
13. Camshaft

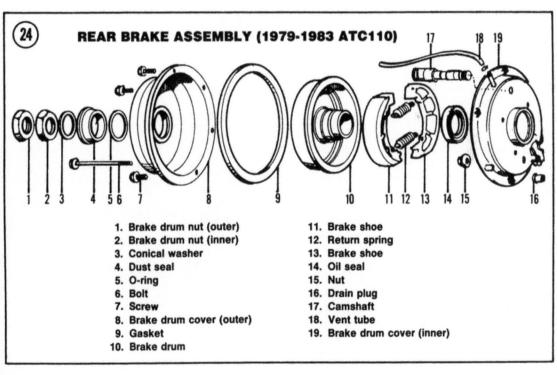

(24) **REAR BRAKE ASSEMBLY (1979-1983 ATC110)**

1. Brake drum nut (outer)
2. Brake drum nut (inner)
3. Conical washer
4. Dust seal
5. O-ring
6. Bolt
7. Screw
8. Brake drum cover (outer)
9. Gasket
10. Brake drum
11. Brake shoe
12. Return spring
13. Brake shoe
14. Oil seal
15. Nut
16. Drain plug
17. Camshaft
18. Vent tube
19. Brake drum cover (inner)

Removal/Disassembly (90-125 cc)

Refer to **Figures 23-25** for this procedure.

1A. On 1970-1974 ATC90 models, perform the following:

   a. Remove the rear axle as described in Chapter Eight.

   b. Remove the nut securing the brake drum and the sealing washer.

   c. Slide off the brake drum.

1B. On 1975-on ATC90 and 1979-1983 ATC110 models, perform Steps 1-15 of *Rear Axle and Driven Sprocket Removal/Installation* in Chapter Eight.

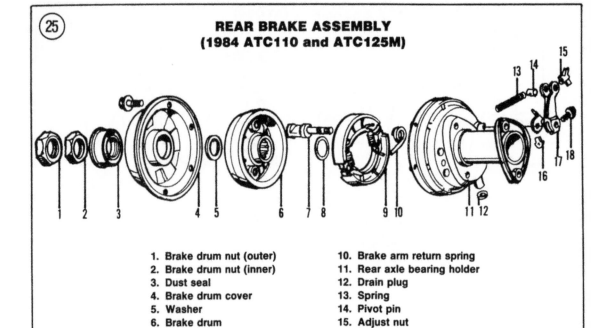

**REAR BRAKE ASSEMBLY
(1984 ATC110 and ATC125M)**

1. Brake drum nut (outer)
2. Brake drum nut (inner)
3. Dust seal
4. Brake drum cover
5. Washer
6. Brake drum
7. Camshaft
8. O-ring seal
9. Brake shoe
10. Brake arm return spring
11. Rear axle bearing holder
12. Drain plug
13. Spring
14. Pivot pin
15. Adjust nut
16. Nut
17. Brake arm
18. Bolt

1C. On 1984 ATC110 and ATC125M models, perform Steps 1-17 of *Rear Axle and Driven Sprocket Removal/Installation* in Chapter Eight.

2. Slide off the brake drum.

3. Wrap the linings with a clean shop cloth, pull up on the center of the linings and remove the linings and return springs (**Figure 26**).

4. Remove the springs and separate the shoes.

5. Inspect all brake components as described in this chapter.

6. Install by reversing these removal steps, noting the following.

7. Grease the cam and pivot post with a light coat of molybdenum disulfide grease; avoid getting any grease on the brake plate where the linings come in contact with it.

8. Attach the return springs to the brake shoes.

9. Hold the brake shoes in a "V" formation with the return springs attached and snap them in place on the brake backing plate. Make sure they are firmly seated on it.

NOTE
*If new linings are being installed, file off the leading edge of each shoe a little (**Figure 18**) so that the brake will not grab when applied.*

**Inspection
(All Models)**

1. Thoroughly clean and dry all parts except the linings.

2. Check the contact surface of the drum (**Figure 27**) for scoring. If there are grooves deep enough to snag a fingernail, the drum should be reground and new shoes fitted. This type of wear can be avoided to a great extent if the brakes are disassembled and thoroughly cleaned after riding the ATC in water, mud or deep sand.

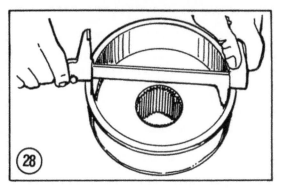

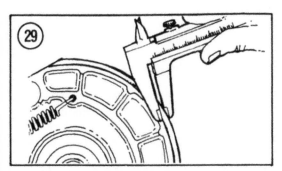

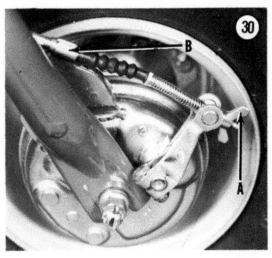

NOTE
If oil or grease is on the drum surface,
clean it off with a clean rag soaked in
lacquer thinner—do not use any solvent
that may leave an oil residue.

3. Use a vernier caliper (**Figure 28**) and check the inside diameter of the drum for out-of-round or excessive wear. The standard new brake drum inside diameter and service limit dimenson is listed in **Table 1**. Replace any drum that is worn to the service limit or greater.

4. If the drum is turned, the linings will have to be replaced and the new linings arced to the new drum contour.

5. Inspect the linings for imbedded foreign material. Dirt can be removed with a stiff wire brush. Check for traces of oil or grease. If they are contaminated, they must be replaced.

6. Use a vernier caliper and measure the brake linings (**Figure 29**). They should be replaced if worn to the service limit listed in **Table 1** or less.

7. Inspect the cam lobe and the pivot pin for wear and corrosion. Minor roughness can be removed with fine emery cloth.

8. Inspect the brake shoe return springs. If they are stretched, they will not fully retract the brake shoes from the drum, resulting in a power-robbing drag on the drums and premature wear of the linings. Replace as necessary and always replace as a pair.

BRAKE CABLE

Brake cable adjustment should be checked periodically as the cable stretches with use and increases brake lever free play. Free play is the distance that the brake lever travels between the released position and the point when the brake shoes come in contact with the drum.

If the brake adjustment as described in Chapter Three can no longer be achieved, the cable must be replaced.

Remember that the rear brake can be activated either by the brake lever on the left-hand side of the handlebar or the foot pedal (except ATC70 models).

Front Brake Cable Replacement

1. Place the ATC on level ground and set the parking brake or block the wheels so the vehicle will not roll in either direction.

2. At the brake assembly completely unscrew the adjusting nut (A, **Figure 30**).

3. Pull the brake cable out of the pivot pin in the brake lever.

4. Disconnect the cable from the receptacle on the backing plate (B, **Figure 30**).

5. Pull the right-hand brake lever all the way to the grip, remove the cable nipple (A, **Figure 31**) from the lever and remove the cable.

> *NOTE*
> *Prior to removing the cable, make a drawing (or take a Polaroid picture) of the cable routing through the frame. It is very easy to forget once it has been removed. Replace it exactly as it was, avoiding any sharp turns.*

6. Withdraw the cable from the holders on the front fork (B, **Figure 31**) and from behind the headlight housing.
7. Install by reversing these removal steps, noting the following.
8. Lubricate the new cable as described in Chapter Three.
9. Adjust the brake as described in Chapter Three.

Rear Brake Cable Replacement

1. Place the ATC on level ground and block the wheels so the vehicle will not roll in either direction.
2. Remove the seat/rear fender assembly.
3. Remove the fuel tank as described in Chapter Six.
4A. On ATC70 models, perform the following:
   a. Completely unscrew the brake adjust nut at the brake lever at the rear brake panel.
   b. Pull the cable out of the pivot pin in the brake lever.
   c. Pull the brake cable out of the receptacle on the frame.
4B. On all other models, perform the following:
   a. At the brake pedal assembly, loosen the locknut and the adjust nut (**Figure 32**) on the brake cable.

   b. Pull the cable out of the receptacle on the frame.
   c. Remove the cable end from the lever on the brake pedal arm.
5. Pull the left-hand brake lever all the way to the grip, remove the cable nipple from the lever and remove the cable.
6. Open any frame-mounted clips that hold the brake cable to the frame.

> *NOTE*
> *The piece of string attached in the next step will be used to pull the new brake cable back through the frame so it will be routed in the exact same position.*

7. Tie a piece of heavy string or cord (approximately 6-8 ft./2-3 m long) to the rear end of the brake cable. Wrap this end with masking or duct tape. Do not use an excessive amount of tape as it must be pulled through the frame loops during removal. Tie the other end of the string to the frame or rear axle.
8. At the handlebar end of the cable, carefully pull the cable (and attached string) out from behind the headlight housing. Make sure the attached string follows the same path of the cable through the frame and behind the headlight.
9. Remove the tape and untie the string from the old cable.
10. Lubricate the new cable as described in Chapter Three.
11. Tie the string to the brake mechanism end of the new clutch cable and wrap it with tape.
12. Carefully pull the string back through the frame, routing the new cable through the same path as the old cable.
13. Remove the tape and untie the string from the cable and the frame or rear axle.

14. Attach the cable to the left-hand brake lever.
15. Attach the other end of the cable to the lever on the brake pedal or brake lever (ATC70 models).
16. Install the cable into the receptacle on the frame.
17. Install the fuel tank and the seat/rear fender assembly.
18. Adjust the rear brake as described in Chapter Three.

REAR BRAKE PEDAL

NOTE
The ATC70 model does not have a brake pedal. The rear brake is actuated by the left-hand brake lever only.

Removal/Installation
(ATC90 and ATC110)

1. Set the ATC on level ground and block the front wheel so the vehicle will not roll in either direction.
2. Remove the drive chain adjust nut (A, **Figure 33**) from the chain tensioner arm.
3. Remove the clamping bolt and nut (B, **Figure 33**) on the chain tensioner arm and remove the tensioner arm (C, **Figure 33**).
4. Remove the return spring (D, **Figure 33**) from the brake pedal.
5. Loosen the locknut and the adjust nut (**Figure 32**) on the brake cable.
6. Pull the cable out of the receptacle on the frame.
7. Remove the cable end (E, **Figure 33**) from the lever on the brake pedal arm.
8. Slide the brake pedal off the pivot shaft on the frame. Note the location of any washers, as they must be reinstalled in the same position.

9. Install by reversing these removal steps, noting the following.
10. Apply grease to the pivot shaft prior to installing the brake pedal. Be sure that the return spring is properly attached.
11. Adjust the rear brake as described in Chapter Three.

Removal/Installation
(ATC125M)

1. Set the ATC on level ground and set the parking brake.
2. Remove the seat/rear fender assembly.
3. Completely unscrew the adjust nut on the brake rod at the brake lever (**Figure 34**).
4. Pull the brake rod out of the pivot pin in the brake lever.
5. At the brake pedal assembly, loosen the locknut and the adjust nut (**Figure 32**) on the brake cable.
6. Pull the cable out of the receptacle on the frame.
7. Remove the cable end from the lever on the brake pedal arm.
8. Remove the return spring from the brake pedal.
9. Remove the cotter pin, washer and dust seal from the pivot shaft on the frame.
10. Slide the brake pedal and dust seal off the pivot shaft on the frame.
11. Install by reversing these removal steps, noting the following.
12. Apply grease to the pivot shaft prior to installing the brake pedal. Be sure that the return spring is properly attached.
13. Adjust the rear brake as described in Chapter Three.

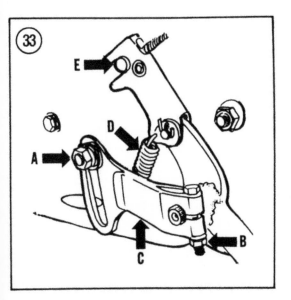

Table 1 BRAKE SPECIFICATIONS

	New	Service limit
Brake drum		
ATC70		
1973-1974	NA	NA
1978-on	130.0-130.02 mm (5.122-1.125 in.)	131 mm (5.161 in.)
ATC90	NA	140.6 mm (5.54 in.)
ATC110	139.9-140.1 mm (5.51-5.52 in.)	141 mm (5.55 in.)
ATC125M		
Front	110 mm (4.3 in.)	111 mm (4.4 in.)
Rear	140 mm (5.5 in.)	141 mm (5.55 in.)
Brake shoe lining		
ATC90	NA	1.5 mm (0.06 in.)
All other models	NA	2.0 mm (0.1 in.)

NA—Honda does not provide specifications for all models.

SUPPLEMENT

1985 AND LATER SERVICE INFORMATION

The following supplement provides procedures unique to all models since 1985. All other service procedures are identical to earlier models.

The Fourtrax 70, TRX125 and Fourtrax 125 are essentially 4-wheeled versions of their 3-wheeled counterparts of the same engine displacement. The engine, clutch and transmission assemblies have only the usual yearly minor updates and are covered in their respective sections in this supplement. The major changes relate to the front end of the vehicles which have an additional wheel, new steering assemblies and brake systems.

On all 4-wheel models, refer to the latest year of the same displacement engine (i.e. 70 cc or 125 cc) for *all* maintenance and service procedures that are not covered in this supplement.

The chapter headings in this supplement correspond to those in the main body of this book. If a chapter is not included in the supplement, there are no changes affecting models since 1984.

CHAPTER ONE

MANUAL ORGANIZATION

Table 1 contains model designation information.

Table 1 MODEL, YEAR AND FRAME NUMBER

Model and year	Engine serial No.	Frame serial No.
ATC70 1985*	TB03E-3000001-on	TB030-FK000001-on
ATC110 1985*	TB02E-2700001-on	TB020-FC600001-on
ATC125M 1985**	TE01E-2100001-on	TE010-FC100001-on
Fourtrax 70		
1986	TE10E-2000001-on	TE100-GC000001-on
	TE10E-2046642	TE100-GC045787
1987	TE10E-2100001-on	TE100-HC000001-on
TRX125 1985*	TE05E-2000034-on	TE050-FC000005-on
Fourtrax 125 1986**	TE05E-2100001-on	TE050-GC100001-on

* Last year of production.
** Last year covered in this book.

CHAPTER TWO

TROUBLESHOOTING

**EMERGENCY
TROUBLESHOOTING**

If the engine will not start, follow the procedures in Chater Two in the main body of this book. On models equipped with an ignition switch, make sure the ignition switch is in the ON position.

CHAPTER THREE

LUBRICATION, MAINTENANCE AND TUNE-UP

SERVICE INTERVALS

The service intervals indicated in **Table 2** are recommended by the factory. Strict adherence to these recommendations will ensure long service from your Honda ATV. However, if the the vehicle is run in an area of high humidity, the lubrication and services must be done more frequently to prevent possible rust damage. This is especially true if you have run the ATV through water (especially salt water).

TIRES AND WHEELS

**Tire Pressure
(4-Wheel Models)**

The tire pressure service procedure is the same as on 3-wheel models with the exception of tire size and the recommended tire inflation pressure. Refer to **Table 3** for tire size, recommended tire inflation pressure and tire circumference.

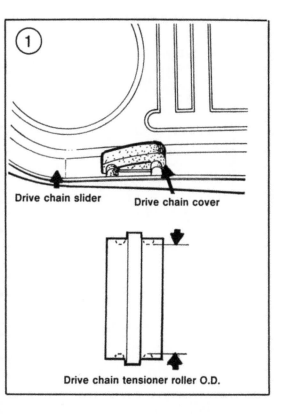

Drive chain slider   Drive chain cover

Drive chain tensioner roller O.D.

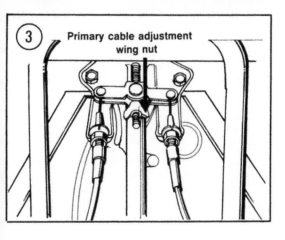

Primary cable adjustment
wing nut

PERIODIC LUBRICATION

Drive Chain

The drive chain on the TRX125 and Fourtrax 125 is an O-ring type chain. Lubricate the drive chain as described under *Drive Chain Lubrication, With O-rings* in Chapter Three in the main body of this book.

PERIODIC MAINTENANCE

Drive Chain Adjustment
(TRX125 and Fourtrax 125)

The drive chain adjustment is the same as on 1984 ATC125M models, described in Chapter Three in the main body of this book, with the exception of the tightening torque for the rear axle bearing holder bolts. Tighten these bolts to 70-80 N•m (51-58 ft.-lb.).

Drive Chain Slider
(Fourtrax 70)

1. Remove the drive chain cover as described under *Drive Chain Removal/Installation* in Chapter Eight in the main body of this book.
2. Inspect the chain slider and roller (**Figure 1**) for wear or damage.
3. Measure the outside diameter of the roller. If worn to 37.0 mm (1.46 in.) or less, replace the roller.
4. There are no wear limit specifications on the chain slider. If a groove is worn half way through the slider, replace the slider.
5. Install the drive chain cover as described under *Drive Chain Removal/Installation* in Chapter Eight in the main body of this book.

Front Brake Adjustment

The front brake lever should be checked at the interval indicated in **Table 2** and adjusted if necessary to maintain the proper amount of free play. The brake lever should travel about 15-20 mm (5/8-3/4 in.) (**Figure 2**) before the brake shoes come in contact with the brake drums, but must not be adjusted so closely that the brake shoes contact the brake drums with the lever relaxed.

Fourtrax 70

If adjustment is necessary, perform the following.
1. Place the ATV on level ground and set the parking brake.
2. Turn the primary cable adjustment wing nut (**Figure 3**) until the correct amount of free play is achieved.

10

NOTE
Make sure the cut-out relief in the adjustment wing nut is properly seated on the brake arm pivot pin.

3. Jack up the front of the vehicle with a small hydraulic jack or place wood blocks under the frame and lift the front wheels off the ground.
4. Spin both front wheels at the same speed and apply the front brake lighty. Make sure both wheels slow down and stop at the same time. If braking action is uneven, loosen the locknuts and turn the secondary cable adjustment nuts (**Figure 4**) on either or both cables as required to equalize the braking action.
5. Re-spin both front wheels at the same speed and apply the front brake lighty. Make sure both wheels slow down and stop at the same time. If braking action is uneven, repeat Step 4 until braking action is equal.
6. If the equalizer arm (**Figure 4**) is inclined to one side after equal braking action is achieved, inspect the brake cable, the brake shoes and drum on that side for excessive wear as described in this supplement.
7. Tighten the secondary brake cable locknuts and repeat Step 2.
8. Remove the wood blocks or jack from under the vehicle.

TRX125 and Fourtrax 125

If adjustment is necessary, perform the following.
1. Place the ATV on level ground and set the parking brake.
2. Turn the adjustment wing nut (**Figure 5**) on both the right- and left-hand brake arms an equal number of turns alternately until the correct amount of free play is achieved.

NOTE
Make sure the cut-out relief in each adjustment wing nut is properly seated on the brake arm pivot pin.

3. Jack up the front of the vehicle with a small hydraulic jack or place wood blocks under the frame and lift the front wheels off the ground.
4. Spin both front wheels at the same speed and apply the front brake lighty. Make sure both wheels slow down and stop at the same time. If braking action is uneven, loosen or tighten one or both of the adjustment wing nuts as required to equalize the braking action.
5. Re-spin both front wheels at the same speed and apply the front brake lighty. Make sure both wheels slow down and stop at the same time. If

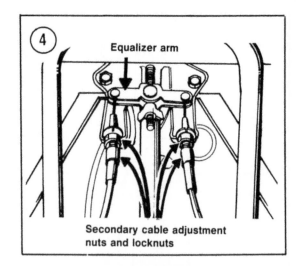
Equalizer arm

Secondary cable adjustment nuts and locknuts

braking action is uneven, repeat Step 4 until braking action is equal.
6. If either brake arm at the front wheel brake panel does *not* have any free play, after the brake lever free play is achieved, the individual brake cables within the cable's front junction box must be adjusted. Refer to *Front Brake Cable Replacement, TRX125 and Fourtrax 125* in this supplement.
7. Remove the wood blocks or jack from under the vehicle.

Rear Brake Pedal and Lever Adjustment (1987 Fourtrax 70)

A foot operated rear brake pedal has been added to activate the rear brake as well as the brake lever on the handlebar.

The rear brake pedal and lever should be inspected every 30 days of operation and adjusted, if necessary, to maintain the proper amount of free play. The brake lever should travel the specified amount of travel before the brake shoes come in contact with the brake drum, but should not be

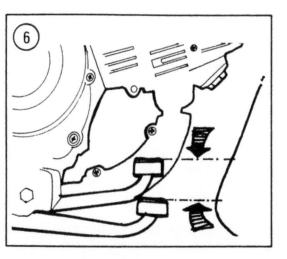

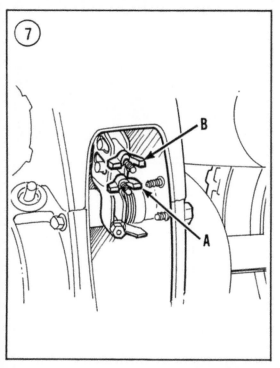

adjusted so closely that the brake shoes contact the brake drum with the pedal relaxed.

1. Set the ATV on level ground and block the wheels so the vehicle will not roll in either direction.

2. Depress the brake pedal until the brake shoes come in contact with the brake drum. The correct amount of free play is 15-20 mm (5/8-3/4 in.) as shown in **Figure 6**.

3. If adjustment is necessary, turn the *lower* adjustment nut (A, **Figure 7**) on the end of the rear brake cable in or out to achieve the correct amount of free play.

NOTE
Make sure the cut-out relief in the adjustment nut is properly seated on the brake arm pivot pin.

4. The rear brake lever free play must be adjusted after the rear brake pedal has been adjusted. Adjust the rear brake lever as follows:

   a. Pull on the brake lever until the brake shoes come in contact with the brake drum. The correct amount of free play is 15-20 mm (5/8-3/4 in.).

   b. If adjustment is necessary, turn the *upper* adjustment nut (B, **Figure 7**) on the end of the rear brake cable in or out to achieve the correct amount of free play.

NOTE
Make sure the cut-out relief in the adjustment nut is properly seated on the brake arm pivot pin.

Clutch Adjustment
(Fourtrax 70)

The clutch adjustment should be checked at the interval indicated in **Table 2**. The adjustment procedure is the same as described in Chapter Three in the main body of this book with the exception of the torque value for the Fourtrax 70. After clutch adjustment is completed, tighten the locknut to 8-12 N•m (6-9 ft.-lb.).

No torque specifications are given by Honda for any other models.

Reverse Gear Selection
Cable Adjustment
(TRX125 and Fourtrax 125)

The reverse gear selector cable lever should be inspected at the interval indicated in **Table 2** and adjusted if necessary to maintain the proper amount of free play. The reverse gear selector cable lever (**Figure 8**) should have about 2-4 mm

(1/16-1/8 in.) of free play at the lever end of the cable.

If adjustment is necessary, perform the following.

1. Place the ATV on level ground and set the parking brake.
2. Remove the rear fender as described in this supplement.
3. Loosen the locknut (A, **Figure 9**) and turn the adjustment nut (B, **Figure 9**) until the correct amount of free play is achieved.
4. Tighten the cable locknut securely and install the rear fender.

Front Wheel Toe-in
Inspection and Adjustment
(4-Wheel Models)

The front wheel toe-in alignment should be checked at the interval indicated in **Table 2**.

1. Inflate the front tires to the recommended tire pressure; refer to **Table 3**.
2. Place the ATV on level ground and set the parking brake. Block the rear wheels so the vehicle will not roll in either direction.
3. Place wood block(s) under the frame so the front wheels are off the ground.

4. Turn the handlebar so the wheels are at the straight ahead position.
5. Use a tape measure and measure or hold a scribe (**Figure 10**), white crayon or white tire marker against the center of the front tire and spin the wheel slowly. Make sure the line is visible at both the front and rear of the tire. Repeat for the other tire.
6. Carefully measure the distance between the center line of both front tires at the front and rear as shown in **Figure 11**. The difference between the front dimension "A" and the rear dimension "B" is listed in **Table 4**. This amount of toe-in is

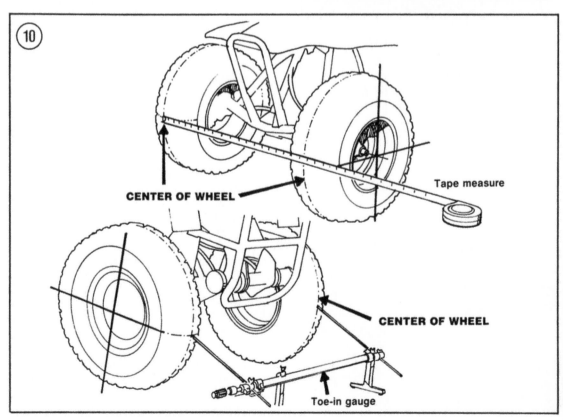

Tape measure

CENTER OF WHEEL

CENTER OF WHEEL

Toe-in gauge

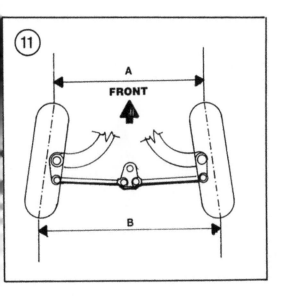

necessary for proper steering. Too much toe-in can cause excessive tire wear and hard steering. Too little toe-in will allow the front end to wander.

7. If the toe-in is incorrect, perform the following:
   a. Loosen the locknuts securing each tie rod end (**Figure 12**). The inside locknuts (**Figure 13**) have *left-hand threads*.
   b. Use a wrench on the flat (**Figure 14**) on the tie rod and slowly rotate one or both tie rods until the dimensions are correct. Recheck each measurement after each adjustment. Turn the tie rods only a small amount each time. It takes very little adjustment of the tie rod to move each tire a large amount.
   c. When the adjustments are correct, hold each tie rod in place and tighten the locknuts securing each tie rod end to the following torque specification:
   Fourtrax 70:-35-43 N•m (25-31 ft.-lb.);
   TRX125 and Fourtrax 125: 25-31 N•m (18-22 ft.-lb.).

Fuel Filter Cleaning (4-Wheel Models)

The fuel filter screen is attached to the carburetor at the base of the fuel shutoff valve and is cleaned as described under *Fuel Filter Cleaning, 1978-on ATC70; ATC110; ATC125M* in Chapter Three in the main body of this book.

Spark Arrester Cleaning

The spark arrester should be cleaned at the interval indicated in **Table 2**.

> *WARNING*
> *To avoid burning your hands, do not perform this operation with the exhaust system hot. Work in a well ventilated area (outside your garage) that is free of any fire hazards. Be sure to protect your eyes with safety glasses or goggles.*

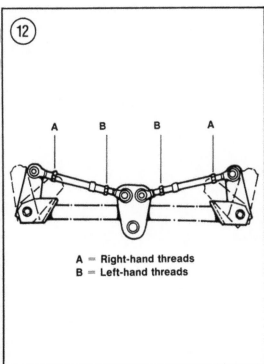

A = Right-hand threads
B = Left-hand threads

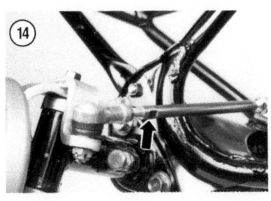

10

1. Place the ATV on level ground and set the parking brake.

2A. On 70 cc models, remove the bolt (**Figure 15**) securing the spark arrester to the tailpipe. Slide the unit out of the tailpipe.

2B. On 110 cc models, remove the bolt (A, **Figure 16**) securing the spark arrester and slide the unit out of the tailpipe (B, **Figure 16**).

2C. .On 125 cc models, remove the bolt (**Figure 17**) and sealing washer at the base of the spark arrester. The spark arrester does not come out of the tailpipe on this model.

3A. On 70 cc and 110 cc models, perform the following:

   a. Clean off accumulated carbon from the spark arrester with a scraper and wash off with solvent. Thoroughly dry with compressed air.

   b. Start the engine and rev it up a couple of times to blow out accumulated carbon from the tail section of the muffler. Continue until the carbon stops coming out.

   c. Turn the engine off and let the exhaust system cool down.

   d. Install the spark arrester and install the bolt. Tighten the bolt securely.

3B. On 125 cc models, perform the following:

   a. Start the engine and rev it up a couple of times to blow out accumulated carbon from the opening at the base of the muffler. Continue until the carbon stops coming out.

   b. Turn the engine off and let the exhaust system cool down.

   c. Inspect the sealing washer on the bolt. Replace if necesary.

   d. Install the bolt and sealing washer. Tighten to 30-40 N•m (22-29 ft.-lb.)

ENGINE TUNE-UP

A tune-up is general adjustment and maintenance to ensure peak engine performance. A complete tune-up should be performed every 30 operating days with normal riding. More frequent tune-ups may be required if the ATV is ridden hard or raced.

Table 5 summarizes tune-up specifications.

VALVE CLEARANCE ADJUSTMENT

Fourtrax 70

Valve clearance adjustment is the same as on ATC70 models with the exception of the location of the timing mark on the alternator rotor. Remove the timing inspection cap on the left-hand crankcase cover in order to see the timing mark (**Figure 18**).

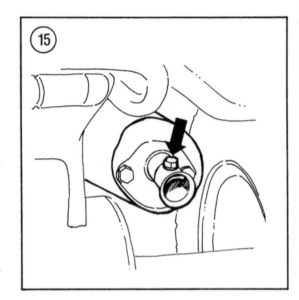

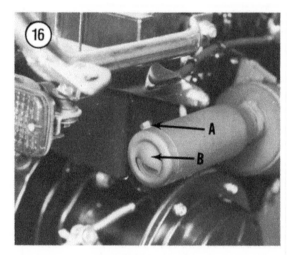

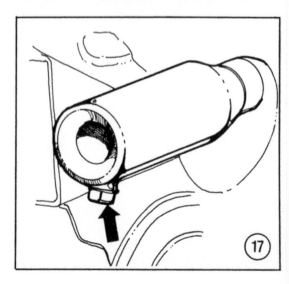

TRX125 and Fourtrax 125

Valve clearance adjustment is the same as on ATC125M models except that the skid plate must be removed to gain access to the exhaust valve adjustment cover.

Remove the bolts securing the skid plate and remove the skid plate.

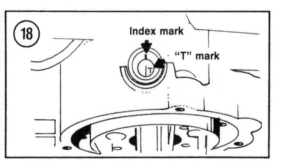

SOLID STATE IGNITION

(Fourtrax 70)

The Fourtrax 70 is equipped with a solid state ignition system. Follow the procedure for the 1981-on ATC110 as described in Chapter Three in the main body of this book with the exception of the idle speed. The correct idle speed is 1,700 ± 100 rpm.

CAMSHAFT CHAIN TENSIONER ADJUSTMENT

The cam chain tensioner on all models since 1985 is automatic and requires no routine adjustment. There are no provisions for adjusting the tensioner mechanism.

Table 2 MAINTENANCE SCHEDULE*

Every 30 days of operation	
	• Change engine oil
	• Clean oil filter and filter rotor
	• Clean and oil air filter element (perform sooner if used in wet or dusty terrain)
	• Inspect spark plug, regap if necessary
	• Inspect valve clearance, adjust if necessary
	• Check and adjust the carburetor
	• Check ignition timing (CDI ignition)
	• Check and adjust ignition timing (contact breaker point ignition)
	• Inspect fuel lines for chafed, cracked or swollen ends, replace if necessary
	• Clean fuel strainer, replace if necessary
	• Check throttle operation, adjust if necessary
	• Clean spark arrester
	• Lubricate drive chain
	• Inspect drive chain slider (models so equipped)
	• Adjust drive chain tension
	• Check and adjust clutch free play
	• Check and adjust reverse gear selector lever free play (models so equipped)
	• Check and adjust brake(s)
	• Check brake lining wear indicator(s)
	• Check and adjust rear brake pedal height and free play
	• Lubricate rear brake pedal and shift lever
	• Check tire and wheel condition
	• Check and adjust front wheel toe-in (4-wheel models)
	• Inspect front steering for looseness
	• Check wheel bearings for smooth operation
	• Check engine mounting bolts for tightness

* This Honda factory maintenance schedule should be considered as a guide to general maintenance and lubrication intervals. Harder than normal use (racing) and exposure to mud, water, sand, high humidity, etc. will naturally dictate more frequent attention to most maintenance items.

10

Table 3 TIRE INFLATION PRESSURE
AND CIRCUMFERENCE MEASUREMENTS (4-WHEEL MODELS)

Model	Tire size	Tire pressure		Circumference	
		kg/cm²	psi	mm	in.
Fourtrax 70 Front and rear	16×8.00-7	0.15	2.2	1,285	50.6
TRX125 and Fourtrax 125	20×7.0-8 22×11.0-8	0.2 0.15	2.9 2.2	1,585 1,742	62.4 68.2

Table 4 FRONT SUSPENSION TOE-IN DIMENSION

Fourtrax 70	0 ±7.5 mm (0 ±0.30 in.)
TRX125 and Fourtrax	5 ±10 mm (0.2 ±0.4 in.)

Table 5 TUNE-UP SPECIFICATIONS

Valve clearance (intake and exhaust)	
Fourtrax 70	0.05 mm (0.002 in.)
TRX125 and Fourtrax 125	0.07 mm (0.003 in.)
Compression pressure (at sea level)	
Fourtrax 70	10.5-13.5 kg/cm² (149-191 psi)
TRX125 and Fourtrax 125	11.0-14.0 kg/cm² (156.5-199 psi)
Spark plug type	
Fourtrax 70	NGK CR7HS, ND U22FSR-L
TRX125 and Fourtrax 125	NGK DR8ES-L, ND X24ESR-U
Spark plug gap	0.6-0.7 mm (0.024-0.028 in.)
Ignition timing at idle	Timing mark "F"
Idle speed	1,700 ±100 rpm

CHAPTER FOUR

ENGINE

ENGINE

Removal/Installation
(1987 Fourtrax 70)

The engine removal and installation procedures are the same as on previous years with the exception of the added rear brake pedal assembly.

Remove the rear brake pedal assembly as described in this supplement.

Removal/Installation
(All Other 4-Wheel Models)

The engine removal and installation procedures are the same as on late model ATC70s and ATC125Ms as described in Chapter Four in the main body of this book with the following exceptions:

1. Remove the front fender and fuel tank as described in this supplement.
2. Remove the seat/rear fender as described in this supplement.
3. On TRX125 and Fourtrax 125 models, perform the following:
   a. Remove the bolts (**Figure 19**) securing the inner fenders and remove both inner fenders.
   b. Remove the bolts (**Figure 20**) securing the engine mounting front pipe and remove the front pipe.
4. During installation, tighten the engine mounting bolts to the torque specifications listed in **Table 6**.

All models that have new parts installed are identified by an "X" mark stamped directly under the engine serial number on the crankcase.

The models that are affected by this problem are as follows:

    a. 1985 ATC110: Frame serial No. 600001-627729.

    b. 1985 ATC125M: Frame serial No. 100001-138210.

Installation
(1985 ATC110 and 1985 ATC125)

In order to gain the maximum amount of cam chain slack when installing the cylinder head, remove the cam chain tensioner bolt, spring and pushrod as described in this supplement. After the cylinder head is installed, install the cam chain tensioner parts that were removed as described in this supplement.

Installation
(Fourtrax 70)

Cylinder head and camshaft installation is the same as on ATC70 models except for the location of the timing mark on the alternator rotor. Remove the timing inspection cap on the left-hand crankcase cover to see the timing mark (**Figure 18**).

Installation
(TRX125 and Fourtrax 125)

Cylinder head and camshaft installation is the same as on ATC125M models except for the torque specification for the cylinder head cover nuts. Tighten the nuts to 20-22 N•m (14-16 ft.-lb.).

10

CYLINDER HEAD
AND CAMSHAFT

Removal (1985 ATC110
and 1985 ATC125)

Damage to the valves and cylinder head can be caused by overreving of the engine on 1985 ATC110 and 1985 ATC125M models. In order to eliminate this problem, Honda has developed a new CDI unit with a built-in rpm limiter. If your ATC is still covered by the factory warranty, take it to the Honda dealer and have this modification performed under the conditions of your warranty. If your ATC is out of the warranty period, this modification should still be performed to eliminate the possibility of engine damage.

CAMSHAFT CHAIN
AND TENSIONER

Removal/Installation
(70 cc Engines)

This procedure is shown with the engine removed from the frame for clarity. All components can be removed with the engine in the frame.

Refer to **Figure 21** for this procedure.

1. Remove the cylinder head and cylinder as described in Chapter Four in the main body of this book.

2. Remove the alternator rotor and stator assembly as described in Chapter Seven in the main body of this book.

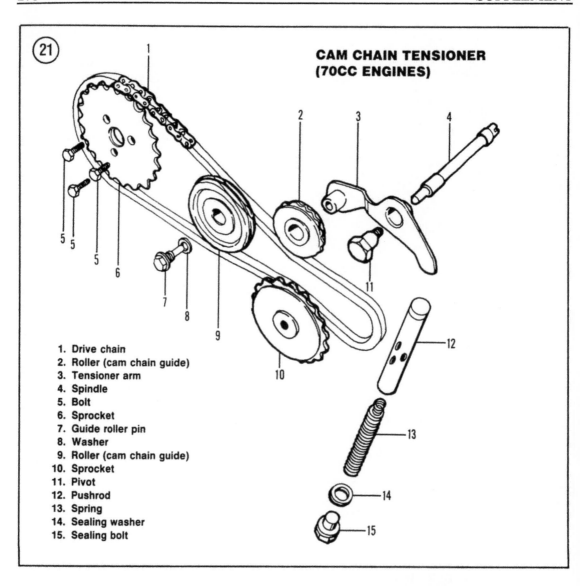

CAM CHAIN TENSIONER (70CC ENGINES)

1. Drive chain
2. Roller (cam chain guide)
3. Tensioner arm
4. Spindle
5. Bolt
6. Sprocket
7. Guide roller pin
8. Washer
9. Roller (cam chain guide)
10. Sprocket
11. Pivot
12. Pushrod
13. Spring
14. Sealing washer
15. Sealing bolt

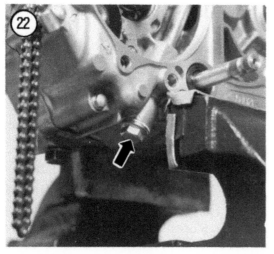

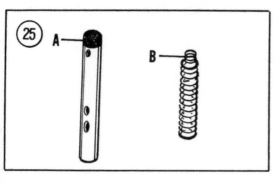

3. Unscrew the sealing bolt and washer (**Figure 22**).

4. Remove the spring and pushrod (**Figure 23**).

5. Remove the bolt (A, **Figure 24**) securing the tensioner arm and remove the tensioner arm and roller.

6. Remove the cam chain (B, **Figure 24**).

7. Inspect all components as described in this supplement.

8. Install by reversing these removal steps, noting the following.

9. Apply fresh engine oil to all components prior to installation.

10. Position the pushrod with the head end (A, **Figure 25**) going into the crankcase first.

11. Position the spring so the tapered end (B, **Figure 25**) fits into the recess in the end of the pushrod.

12. Install the sealing bolt and washer and tighten to 20-25 N•m (15-18 ft.-lb.).

Removal/Installation
(110-125 cc Engines)

This procedure is shown with the engine removed from the frame for clarity. All components can be removed with the engine in the frame.

Refer to **Figure 26** for this procedure.

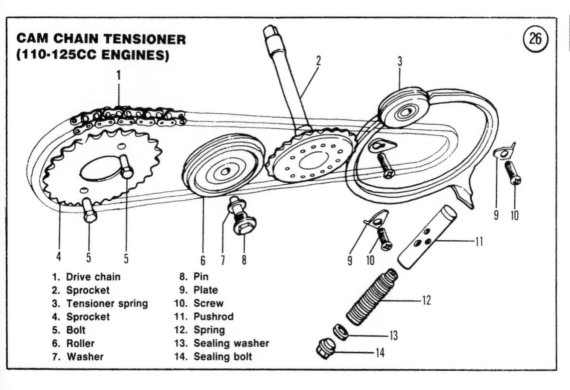

CAM CHAIN TENSIONER
(110-125CC ENGINES)

1. Drive chain
2. Sprocket
3. Tensioner spring
4. Sprocket
5. Bolt
6. Roller
7. Washer
8. Pin
9. Plate
10. Screw
11. Pushrod
12. Spring
13. Sealing washer
14. Sealing bolt

1. Remove the cylinder head and cylinder as described in Chapter Four in the main body of this book.

2. Remove the alternator rotor and stator assembly as described in Chapter Seven in the main body of this book.

3. Unscrew the sealing bolt and washer (A, **Figure 27**).

4. Remove the left-hand crankcase cover as described for your specific model in Chapter Four in the main body of this book.

5. Remove the spring and pushrod (**Figure 28**).

6. Remove the chain guide sprocket (**Figure 29**).

7. Remove the cam chain (A, **Figure 30**).

8. Remove the screw securing the set plates (B, **Figure 30**) and remove the tensioner assembly (C, **Figure 30**).

9. Inspect all components as described in this supplement.

10. Install by reversing these removal steps, noting the following.

11. Apply fresh engine oil to all components prior to installation.

12. Slightly rotate the chain guide sprocket assembly so the notch in the shaft will mesh with the raised tab on the oil pump rotor shaft (located within the crankcase on the opposite side of the engine).

13. Position the pushhrod with the head end (A, **Figure 25**) going into the crankcase first.

14. Position the spring so the tapered end (B, **Figure 25**) fits into the recess in the end of the pushrod.

15. Install the sealing bolt and washer and tighten to the following torque specifications:
   a. ATC110: 30-40 N•m (22-29 ft.-lb.)
   b. ATC125: 20-25 N•m (15-18 ft.-lb.)

16. Remove the oil bolt (B, **Figure 27**) and sealing washer. Using a "pumper type" oil can, fill the cavity with clean engine oil until the oil starts to run out of the hole.

CAUTION
Do not install a bolt longer than 6 mm as a longer bolt would interfere with the action of the pushrod.

17. Install the oil bolt and sealing washer and tighten securely.

Inspection

1. Clean all parts in solvent and thoroughly dry with compressed air.

2. Inspect the roller, tensioner assembly and the chain guide sprocket.

3. If any of the components are worn or any rubber-coated parts are starting to disintegrate,

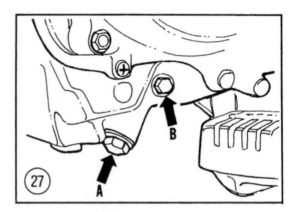

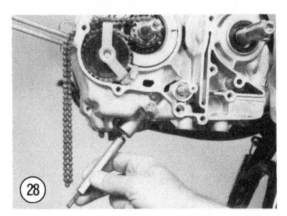

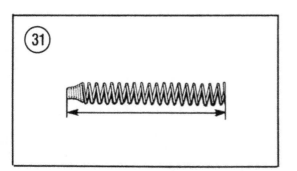

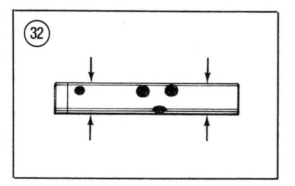

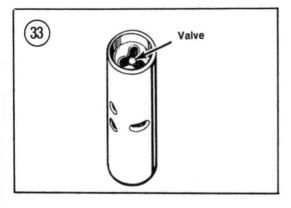

Valve

they must be replaced. If the cam chain is replaced it is a good idea to replace the sprocket at the same time and vice versa.

4. Measure the length of the spring (**Figure 31**). If it has sagged to 77 mm (3.0 in.) or less it must be replaced.

5. Measure the outside diameter of the pushrod (**Figure 32**). If it is worn to 11.90 mm (0.469 in.) or less it must be replaced.

6. Check the operation of the valve (**Figure 33**) in the end of the pushrod. If the valve does not move freely, replace the pushrod.

7. Inspect the pushrod for cracks or other damage. Replace if necessary.

OIL PUMP

All service procedures for the oil pump on all models are the same as on previous models except for one additional inspection procedure.

Inspection
(70-110 cc Engines)

1. Install the gasket onto the oil pump body.
2. Inspect the rotor side clearance with a straightedge and a flat feeler gauge (**Figure 34**). The side clearance service limit between the rotors and the body is as follows:

   a. 70 cc engine: 0.12 mm (0.005 in.)
   b. 110 cc engine: 0.15 mm (0.006 in.)

If the clearance is this dimension or greater replace the worn parts.

10

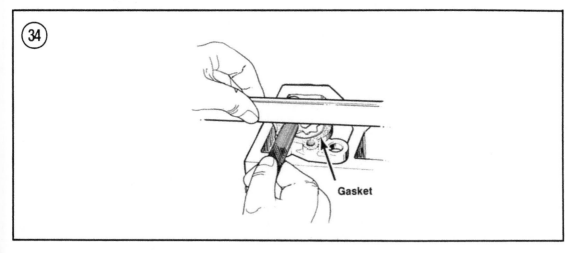

Gasket

RIGHT-HAND CRANKCASE COVER
(1987 FOURTRAX 70)

Removal/Installation

1. Drain the engine oil as described in Chapter Three in the main body of this book.
2. Remove the rear brake pedal and brake cable guard as described in this supplement.
3. Remove the exhaust pipe as described in this supplement.
4. Remove the bolts securing the step guard and remove the step guard.
5. Remove the bolts securing the foot peg assembly and remove the foot peg assembly.
6. Remove the bolts securing the right-hand crankcase cover and remove the cover and gasket. Don't lose the locating dowels.
7. Install by reversing these removal steps, noting the following.
8. Install a new gasket and make sure the locating dowels are in place.
9. Fill the crankcase with the recommended type and quantity of engine oil as described in·Chapter Three in the main body of this book.

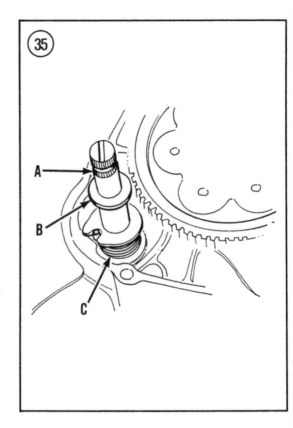

REAR BRAKE PEDAL PIVOT SHAFT
(1987 FOURTRAX 70)

Removal/Installation

The rear brake pedal pivot shaft is integrated into the crankcase.
1. Remove the right-hand crankcase cover as described in this section of the supplement.
2. Withdraw the brake pedal pivot shaft (A, **Figure 35**), washer (B) and spring (C) from the left-hand crankcase half.
3. Inspect the pivot shaft for wear, damage or bending. Replace if necessary.
4. Install the spring into the crankcase with the raised end point up.
5. Install the pivot shaft and align the raised end of the spring (A, **Figure 36**) with the notch (B, **Figure 36**) in the pivot shaft plate. Push the pivot shaft in until it bottoms out.
6. Make sure the washer (B, **Figure 35**) is in place on the pivot shaft.
7. Install the right-hand crankcase cover as described in this section of the supplement.   ·

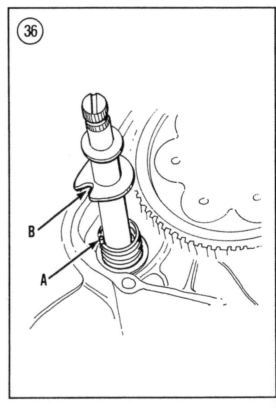

**LEFT-HAND CRANKCASE COVER
(TRX125 AND FOURTRAX 125)**

Removal/Installation

1. Drain the engine oil as described in Chapter Three in the main body of this book.
2. Remove the recoil starter as described in this supplement.
3. Remove the alternator as described in Chapter Seven in the main body of this book.

4. Loosen the clamping screws on the air cleaner connecting tube bands (A, **Figure 37**) and remove the connecting tube (B, **Figure 37**).
5. Disconnect the electrical connector (**Figure 38**) on the alternator stator assembly and the reverse switch wire from the wiring harness.
6. Remove the sub-transmission (A, **Figure 39**) as described in this supplement.
7. Remove the bolts securing the left-hand crankcase cover (B, **Figure 39**) and remove the cover and gasket. Don't lose the locating dowels.
8. Install by reversing these removal steps, noting the following.
9. Install a new gasket and reinstall the locating dowels.
10. Make sure the oil seals in the crankcase cover for the starter driven pulley (part of the recoil starter and alternator rotor) and the shift shaft are in place.

CRANKCASE AND CRANKSHAFT

**Crankcase Disassembly/Assembly
(TRX125 and Fourtrax 125)**

The crankcase disassembly and assembly procedure is the same as on previous 90-125 cc engines except that there is no longer a neutral indicator shaft to remove or install.

RECOIL STARTER

**(Fourtrax 70)
Removal/Installation**

1. Place the ATV on level ground and set the parking brake.
2. Remove the bolts securing the recoil starter assembly and remove the assembly and gasket.
3. Install by reversing these removal steps. Make sure to install a new gasket on the assembly prior to installation.

**Disassembly and
Starter Rope Removal**

NOTE
If you have been stranded with a broken starter rope, consider replacing the Honda starter rope with an aftermarket vinyl coated flexible wire cable. These cables are available from many dealers and mail order houses and will outlast the rope.

Refer to **Figure 40** for this procedure

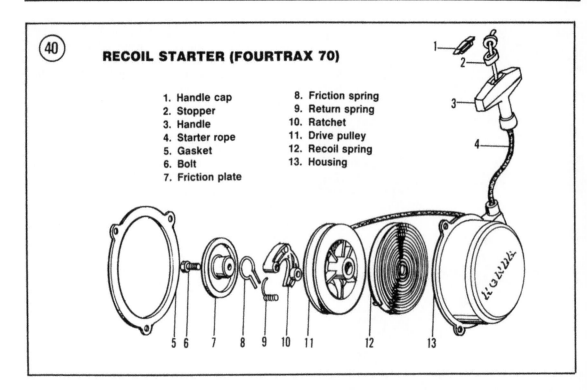

RECOIL STARTER (FOURTRAX 70)

1. Handle cap
2. Stopper
3. Handle
4. Starter rope
5. Gasket
6. Bolt
7. Friction plate
8. Friction spring
9. Return spring
10. Ratchet
11. Drive pulley
12. Recoil spring
13. Housing

WARNING

The return spring is under pressure and may jump out during the disassembly procedure. It is a very strong spring and may cut fingers or cause eye injury. Wear safety glasses and gloves during the disassembly and assembly procedure.

1. Remove the cover from the starter handle and untie the knot in the starter rope or cut the rope if it is going to be replaced.
2. Hold the starter rope with Vise Grips and remove the starter handle (A, **Figure 41**) from the rope.
3. Remove and discard the gasket.
4. Remove the bolt (B, **Figure 41**) and friction plate (C, **Figure 41**).
5. Remove the friction spring, return spring and the ratchet from the drive pulley.
6. Hold onto the starter rope and remove the Vise Grips. Release the starter rope slowly into the housing.

WARNING
The recoil spring may jump out at this time—protect yourself accordingly.

7. Remove the drive pulley and the recoil spring.
8. Untie and remove the starter rope from the drive pulley.

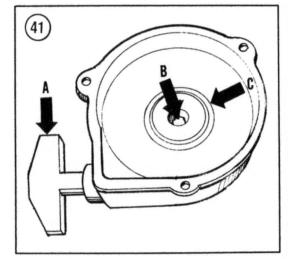

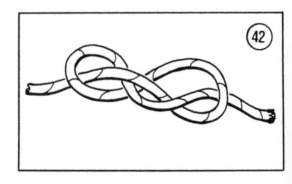

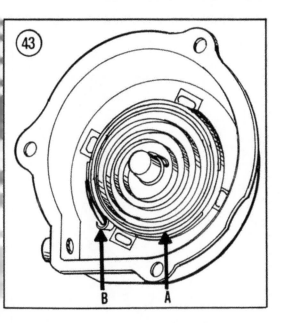

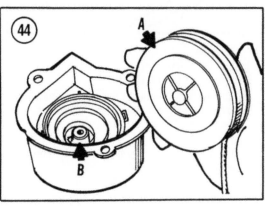

3. As viewed from the ratchet side, coil the rope onto the drive pulley in a *clockwise* direction.

4. Position the end of the rope in the drive pulley so the starter grip end is located within the notch in the drive pulley.

WARNING
*This step requires an assistant as it is very dangerous, and almost impossible, to try to install the spring by yourself. Both of you must wear eye and hand protection as the recoil spring could jump out at any time—**protect yourself accordingly**.*

5. Install the recoil spring into the housing as follows:

   a. Have the assistant hold onto the housing so it will not rotate.

   b. Hook the end of the spring (A, **Figure 43**) onto the outer hook in the housing (B, **Figure 43**).

   c. Hold the end of the spring in place and start feeding the spring into the housing in a clockwise direction.

   d. As you feed the spring into the housing, have the assistant hold the spring down after each loop is installed. The spring must be continually held in place or it will jump out.

   e. Continue to feed the spring in and hold it down until the entire spring is installed.

   f. After the spring is completely installed, do not move the housing and spring assembly, as at this point the spring is under a lot of pressure and could jump out at any time. *Protect yourself and your assistant accordingly.*

6. Install the drive pulley into the housing and spring assembly while rotating it in a *clockwise* direction. Make sure the rope is positioned up through the notch in the drive pulley. The tab (A, **Figure 44**) on the bottom of the drive pulley must engage with the hook (B, **Figure 44**) in the end of the recoil spring. If they engage, proceed to Step 9. If the two parts will not engage, *carefully* remove the drive pulley as the spring could jump out at this point. Use the procedure in Step 7 and Step 8.

7. Make a *soft* wire hook (do not use stiff wire) and hook it onto the inner end of the recoil spring as shown in **Figure 45**. The other end of the hook must lay flat on top of the spring coils to allow the drive pulley to drop into position. The wire must be long enough so it can be pulled on.

8. Reinstall the drive pulley into the housing while rotating it in a *clockwise* direction. Make sure the rope is positioned up through the notch in the drive pulley. When the drive pulley comes into contact with the recoil spring, pull sideways on the

NOTE
It is a good idea to replace the starter rope every time the recoil starter is disassembled.

9. Clean all parts in solvent and thoroughly dry.

10. Inspect all moving parts for wear or damage and replace as necessary.

11. Check the recoil spring and housing for wear or damage. Replace as necessary.

**Assembly and
Starter Rope Installation**

1. Install a new starter rope in the drive pulley. If a stock Honda nylon rope is used, tie a special knot at the end (**Figure 42**). Apply heat to the knot (a match is sufficient) and *slightly* melt the nylon rope. This will hold the knot securely.

2. Apply multipurpose grease to the housing shaft where the drive pulley rides.

10

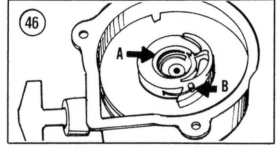

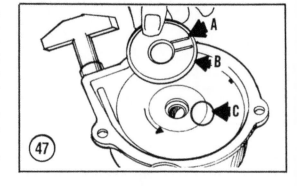

hook to bring the inner end of the recoil spring away from the shaft in the housing. Continue to rotate the drive pulley and push it the rest of the way down until it seats and engages with the spring hook. Hold the drive pulley down and pull the soft wire hook out from between the drive pulley and the spring.

9. Make sure the end of the rope in the drive pulley is located within the notch in the drive pulley.

10. To pre-load the recoil spring, rotate the drive pulley *clockwise* 2 complete turns.

11. Have the assistant hold the drive pulley in this position and feed the free end of the starter rope through the opening in the housing. Attach a pair of Vise Grips to the rope where it exits the housing.

12. Install the rope through the starter handle and move the handle all the way down until it touches the Vise Grips. If a stock Honda nylon rope is used, tie the end using the same special knot as shown in **Figure 42**. Apply heat to the knot (a match is usually sufficient) and *slightly* melt the nylon rope. This will hold the knot securely. Install the handle cover.

13. Apply a light coat of multipurpose grease to the ratchet and install the ratchet (A, **Figure 46**).

14. Install the return spring (B, **Figure 46**) onto the ratchet and drive pulley.

15. Install the spring, spring housing and ratchet guide.

16. Install the friction spring (A, **Figure 47**) onto the friction plate (B, **Figure 47**).

17. Align the friction spring with the raised hook (C, **Figure 47**) on the ratchet. These two parts must align correctly or the recoil starter will not function properly.

18. Install the bolt, (B, **Figure 41**) and tighten to 8-12 N•m (6-9 ft.-lb.).

19. After assembly is complete, check the operation of the recoil starter by pulling on the starter handle. Make sure the drive pulley rotates freely and returns completly. Also make sure the ratchet moves out and in correctly. If either does not operate correctly, disassemble and correct the problem.

20. Inspect the slots in the starter driven pulley. If they are damaged it should be replaced.

Table 6 ENGINE MOUNTING BOLT TORQUE SPECIFICATIONS

Item	N•m	ft.-lb.
Fourtrax 70		
Engine hanger bolts and nuts	24-30	17-22
TRX125 and Fourtrax 125		
Engine hanger bolts and nuts		
Front	24-30	17-22
Rear	50-60	36-43
Engine mount pipe bolts		
8 mm	30-40	22-29
10 mm	40-48	29-35

CHAPTER FIVE

CLUTCH AND TRANSMISSION

CENTRIFUGAL CLUTCH

**Removal/Disassembly/Assembly/
Installation (1987 Fourtrax 70)**

The centrifugal clutch removal, disassembly, assembly and installation are the same as on previous models with the exception of the right-hand crankcase cover.

Remove and install the right-hand crankcase cover as described in this supplement.

4-SPEED TRANSMISSION AND INTERNAL SHIFT MECHANISM (FOURTRAX 70)

Removal/Installation

The removal and installation procedures are the same as the 70 cc models described in Chapter Five in the main body of this book.

Main Shaft
Disassembly/Inspection/Assembly

Refer to **Figure 48** for this procedure

NOTE
A helpful "tool" that should be used for transmission disassembly is a large egg flat (the type restaurants get their eggs in). As you remove a part from the shaft, set it in one of the depressions in the same position from which it was removed. This is an easy way to remember the correct relationship of all parts.

1. Clean the shaft as described under *Preliminary Transmission Inspection, All Models* in Chapter Five in the main body of this book.

10

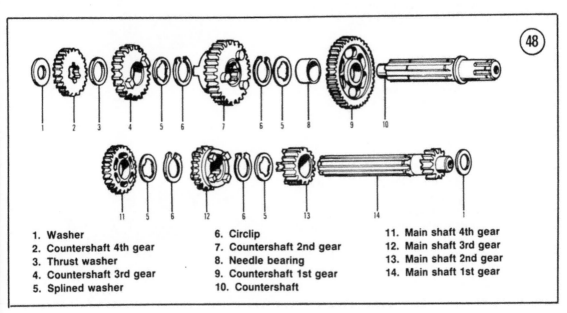

1. Washer
2. Countershaft 4th gear
3. Thrust washer
4. Countershaft 3rd gear
5. Splined washer
6. Circlip
7. Countershaft 2nd gear
8. Needle bearing
9. Countershaft 1st gear
10. Countershaft
11. Main shaft 4th gear
12. Main shaft 3rd gear
13. Main shaft 2nd gear
14. Main shaft 1st gear

2. Slide off the 4th gear.
3. Slide off the splined washer and remove the circlip.
4. Slide off the 3rd gear.
5. Remove the circlip and slide off the splined washer.
6. Slide off the 2nd gear.
7. From the other end of the shaft, remove the thrust washer.
8. Check each gear for excessive wear, burrs, pitting or chipped or missing teeth. Make sure the lugs on the gears are in good condition.

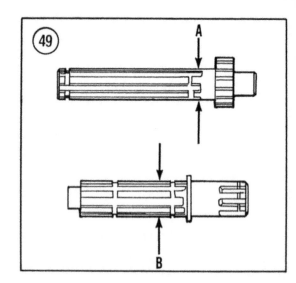

NOTE
Defective gears should be replaced. It is a good idea to replace the mating gear on the countershaft even though it may not show as much wear or damage.

NOTE
The 1st gear is part of the shaft. If the gear is defective the shaft must be replaced.

9. Make sure that all gears slide smoothly on the main shaft splines.
10. Measure the outside diameter of the raised portion of the splines at location "A" shown in **Figure 49**. Refer to the dimension listed in **Table 7**. If the shaft is worn to the service limit, the shaft must be replaced.
11. Measure the inside diameter of the 2nd and 4th gears. Refer to dimensions listed in **Table 7**. If the gear(s) are worn to the service limit dimension (or greater) the gear(s) must be replaced.

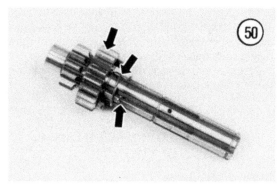

NOTE
It's a good idea to replace all circlips every other time the transmission is disassembled to ensure proper gear alignment.

12. Slide on the 2nd gear and install the splined washer and circlip (**Figure 50**).
13. Slide on the 3rd gear and install the circlip and splined washer (**Figure 51**).
14. Slide on the 4th gear (**Figure 52**).
15. Slide the thrust washer onto the other end of the main shaft.
16. Before installation, double check the placement of all gears (**Figure 53**). Make sure the circlips are seated correctly in the countershaft grooves.

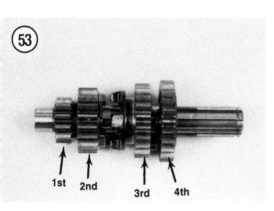

1st 2nd 3rd 4th

Countershaft
Disassembly/Inspection/Assembly

Refer to **Figure 48** for this procedure.

NOTE
Use the same large egg flat (used on the main shaft · disassembly) during the countershaft disassembly. This is an easy way to remember the correct relationship of all parts.

1. Clean the shaft as described under *Preliminary Transmission Inspection, All Models* in Chapter Five in the main body of this book.

2. Remove the thrust washer and slide off the 4th gear.

3. Slide off the thrust washer and the 3rd gear.

4. Slide off the splined washer and remove the circlip.

5. Slide off the 2nd gear.

6. Remove the circlip and splined washer and slide off the 1st gear and 1st gear bushing.

7. Check each gear for excessive wear, burrs, pitting or chipped or missing teeth. Make sure the lugs on the gears are in good condition.

NOTE
Defective gears should be replaced. It is a good idea to replace the mating gear on the main shaft even though it may not show as much wear or damage.

8. Make sure that all gears slide smoothly on the countershaft splines.

9. Measure the outside diameter of the raised portion of the splines at location "B" shown in **Figure 49**. Refer to the dimension listed in **Table 7**. If the shaft is worn to the service limit, the shaft must be replaced.

10. Measure the inside diameter of the 1st and 3rd gears. Refer to dimensions listed in **Table 7**. If the gear(s) are worn to the service limit dimension (or greater) the gear(s) must be replaced.

11. Measure the inside diameter and outside diameter of the 1st gear bushing. Refer to dimensions listed in **Table 7**. If the bushing is worn to the service limit dimension (or greater or less) the bushing must be replaced.

NOTE
It's a good idea to replace all circlips every other time the transmission is disassembled to ensure proper gear alignment.

12. Slide on the 1st gear bushing, the 1st gear and splined washer and install the circlip (**Figure 54**).

13. Slide on the 2nd gear, circlip and splined washer (**Figure 55**).

14. Slide on the 3rd gear and the thrust washer (**Figure 56**).

10

15. Slide on the 4th gear and the thrust washer (**Figure 57**).

16. Before installation, double check the placement of all gears (**Figure 58**). Make sure the circlips are seated correctly in the countershaft grooves.

NOTE
After both transmission shafts have been assembled, mesh the 2 assemblies together in the correct position. Check that all gears meet correctly. This is your last chance prior to installing the assemblies into the cranckcase; make sure they are correctly assembled.

TRANSMISSION AND INTERNAL SHIFT MECHANISM (ALL OTHER MODELS)

All service procedures for the transmission on all models are the same as on previous models with the exception of the inside dimensions for some of the transmission gears. Refer to **Table 7** for standard and service limit dimensions.

INTERNAL SHIFT MECHANISM (TRX125 AND FOURTRAX 125)

The internal shift mechanism is the same as that used on the prior 90-125 cc engines with the following exceptions.

1. A collar has been added to the shift drum as shown in **Figure 59**.

2. The clearance between the shift drum and the shift forks is different than on previous models and is listed in **Table 8**.

SUBTRANSMISSION (TRX125 AND FOURTRAX 125)

The dual-range subtransmission consists of 2 reduction gears and a reverse gear. The unit is driven by the countershaft of the main transmission. It offers 3 different riding ranges or ratios—a low or high forward range and reverse. The low range is just that—*low* as it gears the engine down for low-end pulling power for use when pulling a trailer or heavy load.

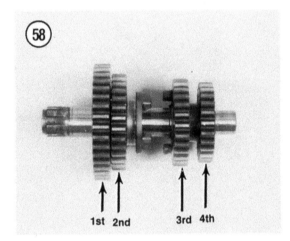

1st 2nd   3rd 4th

NOTE
*On some 1985 TRX125 models, damage to the high speed gear, the super low drive gear and the right-hand shift fork may occur due to improper gear engagement. To solve this problem, Honda has replacement parts available. If your ATV is still covered by the factory warranty, take it to a Honda dealer and have the new parts installed. The models effected by this problem have these **engine serial numbers: 2000001-2026374**. Models that have had the new parts installed, are identified by a **blue mark** on the subtransmission chrome cover.*

Removal/Disassembly

Refer to **Figure 60** for this procedure.

1. Place the ATV on level ground and set the parking brake.

2. Remove the seat and rear fender as described in this supplement.

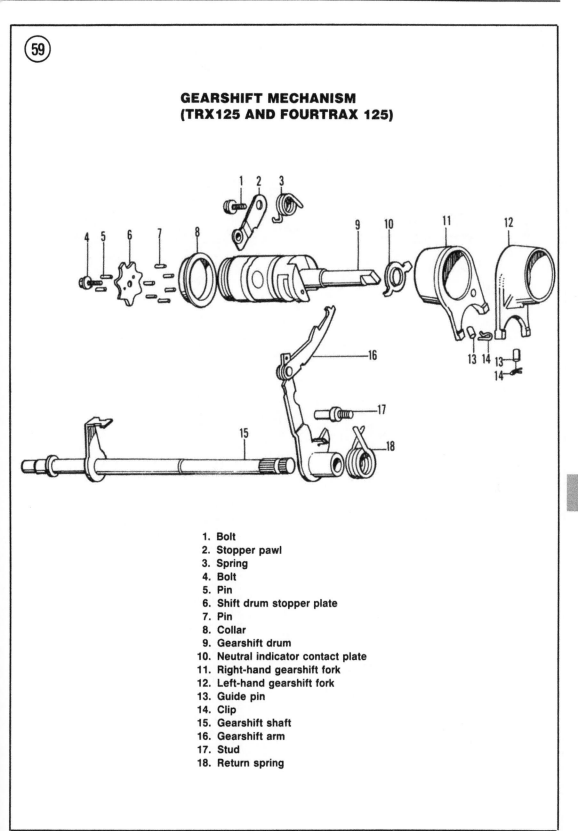

59

GEARSHIFT MECHANISM
(TRX125 AND FOURTRAX 125)

1. Bolt
2. Stopper pawl
3. Spring
4. Bolt
5. Pin
6. Shift drum stopper plate
7. Pin
8. Collar
9. Gearshift drum
10. Neutral indicator contact plate
11. Right-hand gearshift fork
12. Left-hand gearshift fork
13. Guide pin
14. Clip
15. Gearshift shaft
16. Gearshift arm
17. Stud
18. Return spring

10

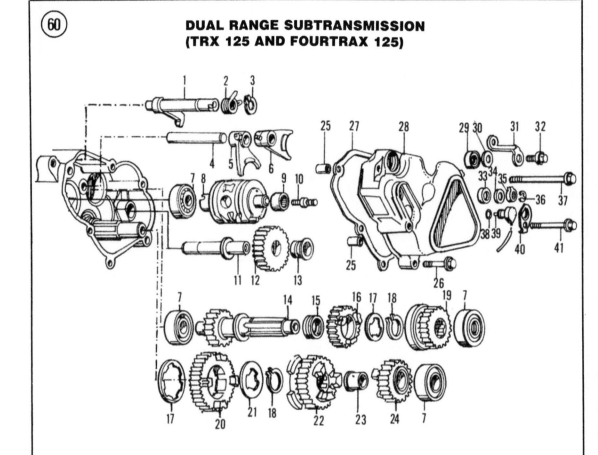

DUAL RANGE SUBTRANSMISSION (TRX 125 AND FOURTRAX 125)

1. Reverse stopper shaft
2. Spring
3. Circlip
4. Shift fork shaft
5. Right-hand shift fork
6. Left-hand shift fork
7. Bearing
8. Shift drum
9. Needle bearing
10. Bolt
11. Reverse idle gear shaft
12. Reverse idle gear
13. Reverse idle gear bushing
14. Reduction shaft
15. Super low driven gear bushing
16. Super low driven gear
17. Splined washer
18. Circlip
19. Reverse driven gear
20. High speed drive gear
21. Splined washer

22. Super low drive gear
23. Reverse drive low gear bushing
24. Reverse drive low gear
25. Locating dowel
26. Bolt
27. Gasket
28. Cover
29. Oil seal
30. Washer
31. Bracket
32. Bolt
33. Oil seal
34. Washer
35. Neutral indicator
36. E-clip
37. Bolt
38. O-ring
39. Reverse switch
40. Reverse switch contact plate
41. Bolt

3. Shift the transmission into NEUTRAL.

4. Drain the engine oil as described in Chapter Three in the main body of this book.

5. Loosen the locknut and adjust nut (A, **Figure 61**) on the reverse cable at the subtransmission to allow slack in the cable.

6. Remove the bolt (B, **Figure 61**) securing the reverse stopper arm shaft lever to the shaft and remove the lever (C, **Figure 61**) and washer.

7. Remove the bolt (D, **Figure 61**) securing the reverse cable mounting bracket and remove the bracket (E, **Figure 61**).

8. Loosen the clamping screws on the air cleaner tube and remove the tube (A, **Figure 62**).

9. Disconnect the reverse switch electrical connector.

10. Remove the E-clip, neutral indicator and washer (B, **Figure 62**).

11. Remove the bolts securing the subtransmission cover and remove the cover and gasket (C, **Figure 62**). Don't lose the locating dowels.

NOTE
When the cover is removed some of the components may come off with it. The following steps present a sequence where all components stayed in place during cover removal.

10

12. Slide off the reverse idle gear and bushing (A, **Figure 63**).

13. Withdraw the shift fork shaft (B, **Figure 63**) and the left-hand shift fork.

14. Slide off the reverse drive low gear (C, **Figure 63**) and the right-hand shift fork.

15. Slide off the super low gear (D, **Figure 63**) from the main transmission's countershaft.

16. Remove the reverse driven gear (E, **Figure 63**) and the reduction shaft (F, **Figure 63**).

17. Remove the circlip (A, **Figure 64**) and slide off the high speed drive gear (B, **Figure 64**) from the main transmission's countershaft.

18. Withdraw the reverse stopper shaft (C, **Figure 64**) and the shift drum (D, **Figure 64**).

19. Withdraw the reverse idle gear shaft (E, **Figure 64**).

20. Clean all parts in solvent and dry with compressed air.

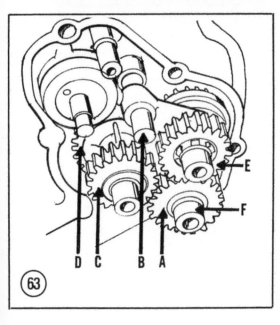

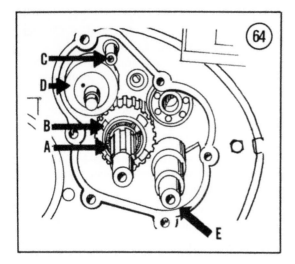

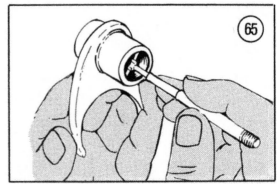

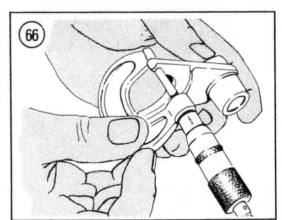

Inspection

1. Inspect each shift fork for signs of wear or cracking. Check for bending and make sure each shift fork slides smoothly on the shaft.

2. Check for any arc-shaped wear or burn marks on the shift forks. This indicates that the shift fork has come in contact with the gear. The fork fingers may have become excessively worn and the fork must be replaced.

3. Measure the outside diameter of the shift fork shaft and the inside diameter of the shift forks (**Figure 65**) with a micrometer or a vernier caliper. Replace if worn to the service limit (or less or greater) listed in **Table 9**.

4. Measure the width of the shift fork fingers with a micrometer or a vernier caliper (**Figure 66**). Replace if worn to the service limit (or less) listed in **Table 9**.

5. Inspect the grooves in the shift drum for wear or roughness. If the groove profiles have excessive wear or damage, replace the shift drum.

6. Measure the inside diameter of the reverse idle gear bushing (A, **Figure 67**), the reverse drive low gear and the super low driven gear. Refer to dimensions listed in **Table 9**. If the bushing is worn to the service limit dimension (or greater) the bushing must be replaced.

7. Measure the outside diameter of the reverse idle gear shaft at location shown in B, **Figure 67**. Refer to the dimension listed in **Table 9**. If the shaft is worn to the service limit (or less), the shaft must be replaced.

8. Check each gear for excessive wear, burrs, pitting or chipped or missing teeth.

9. Check that the engagement lugs on the gears are in good shape. If worn or damaged the gear should be replaced.

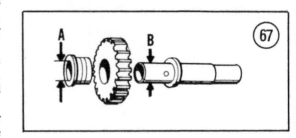

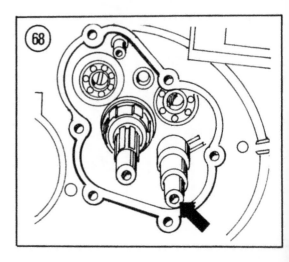

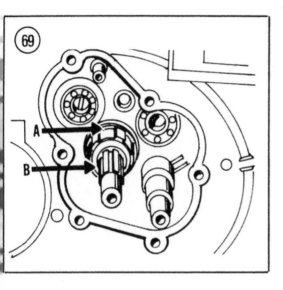

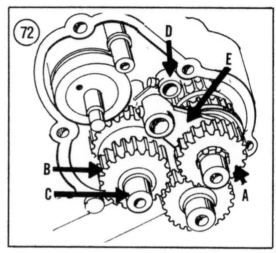

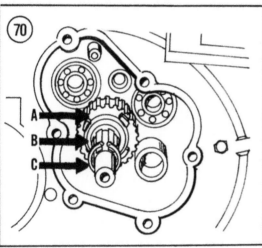

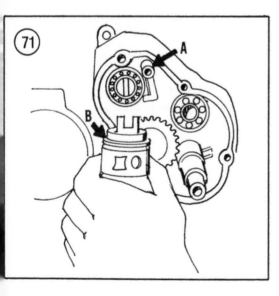

10. Inspect the shaft support bearings in the subtransmission cover. Check for roughness, pitting, galling and play by rotating them slowly with your fingers. They should rotate smoothly. If replacement is necessary, refer to *Cover Bearing Replacement* in this supplement.

Assembly/Installation

1. Install the reverse idle gear shaft (**Figure 68**).
2. Make sure the thrust washer (A, **Figure 69**) is in place on the drive sprocket bushing (B, **Figure 69**).
3. Slide on the high speed drive gear (A, **Figure 70**) and the splined washer (B, **Figure 70**).
4. Install the circlip (C, **Figure 70**).
5. Install the reverse stopper shaft.
6. Move the pawl on the reverse stopper shaft (A, **Figure 71**) out of the way and install the shift drum (B, **Figure 71**). Align the groove in the shift drum with the guide on the neutral indicator shaft.
7. Assemble the reduction shaft on the work bench as follows:
   a. Slide on the super low driven gear bushing and the super low driven gear.
   b. Slide on the splined washer and install the circlip.
   c. Install the reverse driven gear.
8. Install the reduction shaft assembly (A, **Figure 72**).
9. Slide the reverse drive low gear bushing and the reverse drive low gear (B, **Figure 72**) onto the main transmission's countershaft (C, **Figure 72**).

> *NOTE*
> *The right-hand shift fork is marked "V6R" and the left-hand shift fork is marked "V6L." The marks must face toward the outside of the engine when installed.*

10

10. Install the right-hand shift fork (D, **Figure** 72) then the left-hand shift fork (E, **Figure** 72). Make sure they are indexed properly into their respective gears.

11. Install the shift fork shaft (A, **Figure** 73).

12. Insert the reverse idle gear bushing into the reverse idle gear and install this assembly onto the idle gear shaft (B, **Figure** 73).

13. If removed, install the locating dowels (A, **Figure** 74). Install a new gasket (B, **Figure** 74).

14. Install the subtransmission cover and tighten the bolts securely.

15. Onto the neutral indicator shaft, install the washer. Align the flats on the neutral indicator with the flats on the shaft and install the neutral indicator and the E-clip (B, **Figure** 62).

16. Connect the reverse switch electrical connector.

17. Install the air cleaner tube and tighten the clamping screws at each end of the tube.

18. Install the reverse cable mounting bracket and bolt (D, **Figure** 61). Tighten the bolt securely.

19. Install the bolt, washer and the reverse stopper arm shaft lever onto the shaft (B, **Figure** 61).

20. Refill the engine with the recommended type and quantity of engine oil as described in Chapter Three in the main body of this book.

21. Adjust the reverse cable as described in the Chapter Three section of this supplement.

22. Install the seat and rear fender as described in this supplement.

Cover Bearing Replacement

Special tools are required for removal of both shaft support bearings in the cover.

Due to the number of special tools required, it may be less expensive to have the bearings replaced by a dealer. Considerable money can be saved by removing the cover yourself and taking it in for bearing replacement.

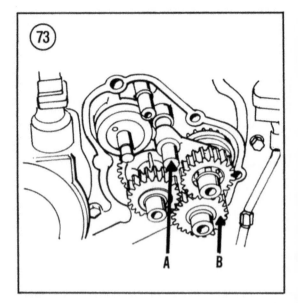

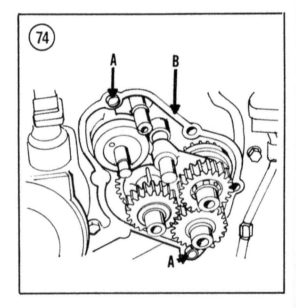

Table 7 TRANSMISSION SPECIFICATIONS

Item	Standard	Service limit
ATC70		
Transmission gears ID		
Main shaft		
2nd & 4th gear	17.016-17.043 mm (0.6699-0.6710 in.)	17.10 mm (0.673 in.)
Countershaft		
1st gear	17.006-17.018 mm (0.6695-0.6700 in.)	17.07 mm (0.672 in.)
3rd gear	17.016-17.043 mm (0.6699-0.6710 in.)	17.1. mm (0.673 in.)
	(continued)	

Table 7 TRANSMISSION SPECIFICATIONS (continued)

Item	Standard	Service limit
FOURTRAX 70		
Transmission gears ID		
Main shaft		
2nd & 4th gear	17.016-17.043 mm (0.6699-0.6710 in.)	17.10 mm (0.673 in.)
Countershaft		
1st gear	20.020-20.053 mm (0.7882-0.7895 in.)	20.10 mm (0.791 in.)
3rd gear	17.016-17.043 mm (0.6699-0.6710 in.)	17.1. mm (0.673 in.)
Countershaft 1st gear bushing		
ID	17.000-17.018 mm (0.6693-0.6700 in.)	17.04 mm (0.671 in.)
OD	19.979-20.000 mm (0.7866-0.7874 in.)	19.63 mm (0.773 in.)
Main shaft OD at location "A"	16.983-16.994 mm (0.6686-0.6691 in.)	16.95 mm (0.667 in.)
Countershaft OD at location "B"	16.966-16.984 mm (0.6680-0.6687 in.)	16.95 mm (0.667 in.)
ATC110, ATC125M, TRX125 and FOURTRAX 125		
Transmission gears ID		
Main shaft		
2nd gear	18.000-18.018 mm (0.7087-0.7094 in.)	18.08 mm (0.712 in.)
4th gear	20.000-20.021 mm (0.7874-0.7882 in.)	20.10 mm (0.791 in.)
Countershaft		
1st & 3rd gear	14.000-14.027 mm (0.5512-0.5522 in.)	14.10 mm (0.555 in.)

Table 8 SHIFT FORK AND SHAFT SPECIFICATIONS

Item	Standard	Wear limit
Shift fork ID		
Fourtrax 70	34.000-34.025 mm (1.3386-1.3396 in.)	34.07 mm (1.341 in.)
TRX125 and Fourtrax 125	42.075-42.100 mm (1.6565-1.6575 in.)	42.15 mm (1.659 in.)
Shift drum OD		
Fourtrax 70	33.950-33.975 mm (1.3366-1.3376 in.)	33.93 mm (1.336 in.)
TRX125 and Fourtrax 125	41.950-41.975 mm (1.6516-1.6526 in.)	41.80 mm (1.65 in.)
Shift fork finger thickness		
Fourtrax 70	4.86-4.94 mm (0.191-0.195 in.)	4.60 mm (0.18 in.)
TRX125 and Fourtrax 125	5.96-6.04 mm (0.234-0.238 in.)	5.70 mm (0.224 in.)
Shift fork-to-shift drum clearance		
Fourtrax 70	*	
TRX125 and Fourtrax 125	0.150-0.118 mm (0.0059-0.0046 in.)	0.155 mm (0.006 in.)

* Honda does not provide service specifications for this item.

10

Table 9 SUBTRANSMISSION SPECIFICATIONS

TRX125 AND FOURTRAX 125		
Item	Standard	Service limit
Gear bushing ID		
Reverse idle gear	15.000-15.018 mm (0.590-0.5913 in.)	15.1 mm (0.59 in.)
Reverse drive low gear	15.000-15.017 mm (0.590-0.5912 in.)	15.1 mm (0.59 in.)
Super low driven gear	20.000-20.021 mm (0.784-0.7882 in.)	20.1 mm (0.79 in.)
Reverse idle gear shaft	14.966-14.984 mm (0.5892-0.5899 in.)	14.93 mm (0.589 in.)
Shift fork ID	10.000-10.015 mm (0.394-0.3943 in.)	10.05 mm (0.396 in.)
Shift fork shaft OD	9.972-9.987 mm (0.3926-0.3932 in.)	9.95 mm (0.392 in.)
Shift fork finger thickness	5.93-6.00 mm (0.233-0.236 in.)	5.8 mm (0.23 in.)

CHAPTER SIX

FUEL AND EXHAUST CARBURETOR SERVICE

Refer to **Table 10** for carburetor specifications and model numbers.

Disassembly/Assembly (Fourtrax 70)

Follow the disassembly and assembly procedure as described under *Disassembly/Assembly Type II* in Chapter Six in the main body of this book. The fuel strainer on the float bowl is the same as the one used on the 1985 ATC125M. Refer to **Table 10** for jet needle clip position.

CARBURETOR ADJUSTMENTS

Float Adjustment (TRX125 and Fourtrax 125)

Perform the service procedure as described under *Float Adjustment* in Chapter Six in the main body of this book. Refer to **Table 10** for float height specification.

Needle Jet Adjustment (Fourtrax 70)

Perform the service procedure as described under *Needle Jet Adjustment* in Chapter Six in the main body of this book. Refer to **Table 10** for needle jet position.

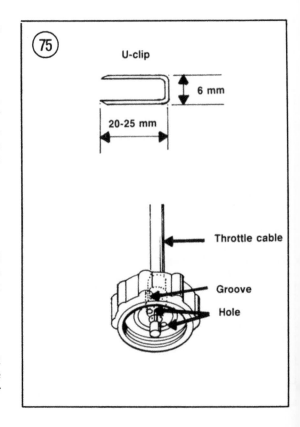

**Pilot Screw Adjustment
(ATC70, 1987 Fourtrax 70)**

Perform the service procedure as described in Chapter six of the main book with the exception of the preliminary adjustment and idle speed (**Table 10**). Follow the steps in the procedures specified for 1978-on ATC models.

**Pilot Screw Adjustment
(ATC110)**

Perform the service procedure for this model in Chapter Six in the main body of this book with the exception of the preliminary adjustment.

For preliminary adjustment, carefully turn the pilot screw in until it *lightly* seats and then back it out 1 1/4 turns.

**Pilot Screw Adjustment
(TRX125 and Fourtrax 125)**

Perform the service procedure as described under *Pilot Screw Adjustment, 1981-on ATC110 and ATC125M* in Chapter Six in the main body of this book with the exception of the preliminary adjustment.

For preliminary adjustment, carefully turn the pilot screw in until it *lightly* seats and then back it out the following number of turns:
a. 1985 models: 2 full turns.
b. 1986 models: 1 3/4 turns.

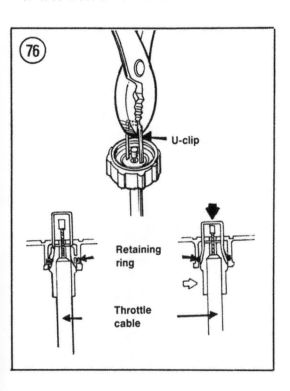

U-clip

Retaining
ring

Throttle
cable

**High-elevation Adjustment
(TRX125 and Fourtrax 125)**

Perform the service procedure as described under *High-elevation Adjustment, All Other Models* in Chapter Six in the main body of this book with the exception of the main jet size, jet needle clip position and pilot screw setting. For these specifications, refer to **Table 11**.

THROTTLE CABLE

**Removal/Installation
(1986 Fourtrax 125)**

Throttle cable removal and installation are the same as on previous ATC125M models with the exception of the way the throttle cable attaches to the carburetor top cap.

On 1986 models there are 2 different types of carburetor top caps and throttle cable assemblies. There is an integral type where the throttle cable and the carburetor top cap must be replaced as an assembly. The other type is the clip-on type and is covered in this procedure.
1. Remove the throttle cable from the ATV as described in Chapter Six in the main body of this book.
2. Using 1 mm (0.04 in.) diameter wire, make a U-clip as shown in **Figure 75**. Be sure to trim the ends of the U-clip as shown in **Figure 75**.
3. Rotate the carburetor top cap until the holes in the cap align with the grooves in the end of the throttle cable (**Figure 75**).
4. Insert the U-clip through the holes in the carburetor top cap and into the grooves in the cable end (**Figure 76**).
5. Press the U-clip in with a pair of pliers and expand the retaining ring to separate the throttle cable from the carburetor top cap (**Figure 76**).
6. Slowly withdraw the throttle cable from the carburetor top cap.
7. Check that the retaining ring is in the groove in the carburetor top cap.
8. Slide the new throttle cable through the hole in the carburetor top cap until the retaining ring seats in the cable end. Remove the clip.
9. Pull on the throttle cable to be sure it is secured by the retaining ring.

FUEL TANK

**Removal/Installation
(4-Wheel Models)**

1. Place the ATV on level ground and set the parking brake or block the wheels so the vehicle will not roll in either direction.

2A. On Fourtrax 70 models, remove the seat/rear fender assembly as described in this supplement.

2B. On TRX125 and Fourtrax 125 models, remove the seat.

3A. On Fourtrax 70 models, remove the bolts securing the front fender at the rear.

3B. On TRX125 and Fourtrax 125 models, remove the bolts and nuts (A, **Figure 77**) securing the rear portion of the front fender. Remove the nuts and tie bar (B, **Figure 77**) at the top of the fuel tank.

4A. On Fourtrax 70 models, cover the middle portion of the sides of the fuel tank with masking or duct tape to protect the paint during the next step.

4B. On TRX125 and Fourtrax 125 models, cover the rear portion of the sides of the fuel tank with a soft cloth to protect the paint during the next step.

5. Disconnect one fuel line (**Figure 78**) at a time from the fuel shutoff valve and plug with a golf tee. Perform this step on both fuel lines.

6. Lift up on the rear of the front fender assembly then pull the fuel tank toward the rear and out of the frame and front fender assembly.

7. On Fourtrax 70 models, remove the fuel filler cap and cover the tank opening with duct tape.

8. Remove the bolt securing the rear of the fuel tank (**Figure 79**).

9. Inspect the rubber cushions (**Figure 80**) on the frame where the fuel tank is held in place. Replace as a set if either is damaged or starting to deteriorate.

10. Install by reversing these removal steps, noting the following.

11. Make sure the fuel tanks' locating brackets at the front of the fuel tank are correctly positioned onto the rubber cushions on the frame.

12. Check for fuel leaks.

EXHAUST SYSTEM
(1987 FOURTRAX 70)

Removal/Installation

1. Place the ATV on level ground and set the parking brake or block the rear wheels so the vehicle will not roll in either direction.

2. Remove the seat/rear fender assembly.

3. Remove the right-hand rear wheel as described in Chapter Eight in the main body of this book.

4. Remove the bolts securing the rear brake cable guard and remove the guard.

5. Remove the screws securing the exhaust pipe protector next to the right-hand foot peg and remove the protector.

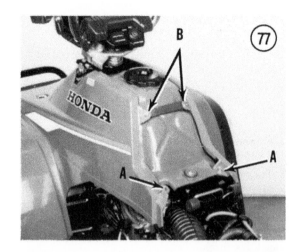

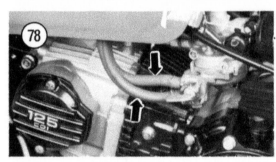

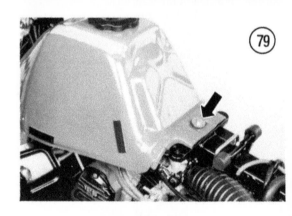

6. Remove the cap nuts and washers securing the exhaust pipe to the cylinder head.

7. Remove the bolts and washers securing the muffler to the frame.

8. Remove the exhaust pipe assembly from the frame.

9. Install by reversing these removal steps, noting the following.

10. Tighten the cap nuts on the cylinder head first then tighten the bolts on the frame. This will minimize the chances of an exhaust leak at the cylinder head.

11. Make sure the cylinder head gasket is in place.

12. Apply Loctite Lock N' Seal to the screw threads securing the protector before installation.

13. After installation is complete, start the engine and make sure there is no exhaust leak.

Table 10 CARBURETOR SPECIFICATIONS

FOURTRAX 70	
Model No.	PB86A
Main jet No.	62
Slow jet No.	38
Initial pilot screw opening	
1985-1986	1 3/8 turns out
1987	1 1/8 turns out
Needle jet clip position	3rd groove
Float level	10.7 mm (0.43 in.)
1985 ATC110	
Model No.	PD20A
Main jet No.	82
Slow jet No.	35
Initial pilot screw opening	1 1/4 turns out
Needle jet clip position	3rd groove
Float level	10.7 mm (0.43 in.)
TRX125 AND FOURTRAX 125	
Model No.	
1985	PB01B
1986*	PB01C
Main jet No.	95
Slow jet No.	38
Initial pilot screw opening	
1985	2 turns out
1986*	1 3/4 turns out
Needle jet clip position	3rd groove
Float level	10.5 mm (0.41 in.)

* Last year covered in this manual.

Table 11 HIGH ELEVATION JET SIZE

TRX125 AND FOURTRAX 125			
Altitude (feet)	Main jet	Jet needle clip position	Pilot screw
0-5,000	95	3rd groove	Factory preset*
4,500-6,000	90	3rd groove	7/8 turns out from factory preset
6,000-10,000	88	3rd groove	1 full turn out from factory preset

* See Table 10 for factory preset position.

10

CHAPTER SEVEN

ELECTRICAL SYSTEM

CHARGING SYSTEM
(TRX125 AND FOURTRAX 125)

The charging system consists of a battery, alternator and solid-state voltage regulator/rectifier. **Figure 81** shows the charging system.

Charging System Output Test

The output test is the same as on previous models with the exception of the amperage readings.

Perform the test as described in Chapter Seven in the main body of this book and compare the readings to the following:

    a. Minimum: 2.4 amps at 2,000 rpm (14 volts).
    b. Maximum: 7.5 amps at 10,000 rpm (14 volts).

ALTERNATOR
(OUTER ROTOR TYPE)

Removal/Installation
(TRX125 and Fourtrax 125)

The removal and installation procedure is the same as for the ATC125M as described in Chapter

Seven in the main body of this book. The only exception is the shape of the left-hand crankcase cover as shown in **Figure 82**.

STATOR COIL TESTING

It is not necessary to remove the stator assembly to perform the following tests. All tests are performed at the alternator stator electrical connector (**Figure 83**).

To get an accurate resistance measurement the stator assembly and coil must be warm (minimum temperature is 68° F/20° C). If necessary, start the engine and let it warm up to normal operating temperature.

Fourtrax 70
Exciter Coil Test

1. Place the ATV on level ground and set the parking brake.
2. Remove the seat/rear fender assembly as described in this supplement.
3. Disconnect the exciter coil electrical connector (black/red wire).

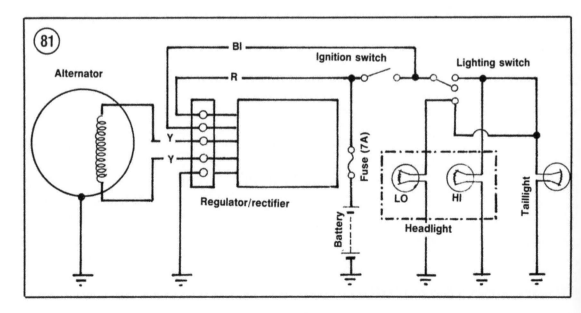

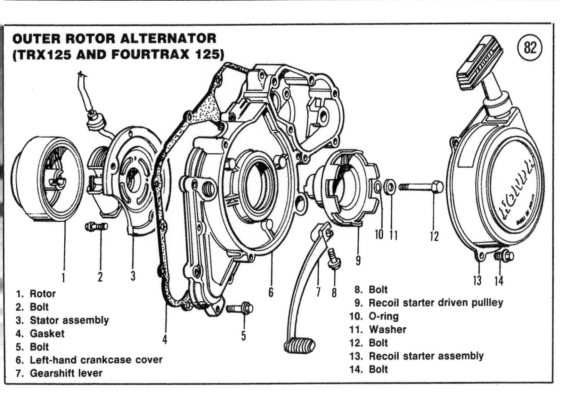

OUTER ROTOR ALTERNATOR (TRX125 AND FOURTRAX 125)

1. Rotor
2. Bolt
3. Stator assembly
4. Gasket
5. Bolt
6. Left-hand crankcase cover
7. Gearshift lever
8. Bolt
9. Recoil starter driven pulley
10. O-ring
11. Washer
12. Bolt
13. Recoil starter assembly
14. Bolt

4. Use an ohmmeter set at R×1 and check resistance between the black/red wire and ground. There should be continuity (specified resistance of 464-696 ohms). If there is no continuity (infinite resistance) or the resistance value is not within these limits, the stator assembly must be replaced (the individual coil cannot be replaced) as described in Chapter Seven in the main body of this book.

5. Reconnect the exciter coil electrical connector.

6. Install the seat/rear fender assembly.

TRX125 and Fourtrax 125
Charging Coil Test

1. Place the ATV on level ground and set the parking brake.

2. Remove the seat/rear fender assembly as described in this supplement.

3. Loosen the clamping screws (A, **Figure 84**) on the air cleaner tube and remove the air cleaner tube (B, **Figure 84**).

4. Disconnect the alternator 2-pin electrical connector (2 yellow wires) (**Figure 83**).

5. Use an ohmmeter set at R×1 and check resistance between both yellow terminals within the connector. There should be continuity (specified resistance of 0.1-1.0 ohms). If there is no continuity (infinite resistance) or the resistance value is not within these limits, the stator assembly

must be replaced (the individual coil cannot be replaced) as described in Chapter Seven in the main body of this book.

6. Reconnect the alternator 2-pin electrical connector.

7. Install the air cleaner tube and tighten the clamping screws on each end.

8. Install the seat/rear fender assembly.

Exciter Coil (ATC110)

1. Remove the seat/rear fender assembly.

2. To check the exciter coil, use an ohmmeter set at R×100.

3. Disconnect the black/red wire connector going to the alternator.

4. Check the resistance between the black/red wire and ground. The specified resistance is 110-400 ohms.

5. If the resistance value is not within these limits, the stator assembly must be replaced (the individual coil cannot be replaced) as described in Chapter Seven in the main body of this book.

6. Reconnect the black/red wire and install the seat/rear fender assembly.

Lighting Coil (ATC110)

1. Remove the seat/rear fender assembly.

2. To check the lighting coil, use an ohmmeter set at R×1.

3. Disconnect the yellow wire connector going to the alternator.

4. Check the resistance between the yellow wire and to ground. The specified resistance is 0.8 ohms.

5. If the resistance value is not as specified, the stator assembly must be replaced (the individual coil cannot be replaced) as described in Chapter Seven in the main body of this book.

6. Reconnect the yellow wire and install seat /rear fender assembly.

VOLTAGE REGULATOR/RECTIFIER

Testing (ATC125M, TRX125 and Fourtrax 125)

1. Remove the seat/rear fender assembly.

2. Disconnect the electrical connector from the wiring harness (**Figure 85**).

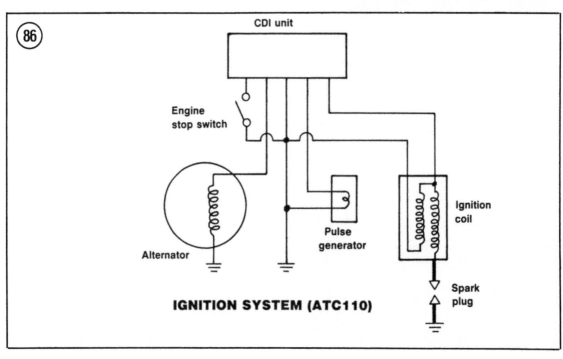

IGNITION SYSTEM (ATC110)

NOTE
Test must be made with a quality ohmmeter or the test readings may be false.

3. Make the test measurements using a quality ohmmeter. Refer to **Table 12** for ohmmeter positive and negative test lead placement and specified resistance values.

4. If the voltage regulator/rectifier fails *any one* of these tests, the unit must replaced as described in Chapter Seven in the main body of this book.

CAPACITOR DISCHARGE IGNITION

Refer to **Figure 86** for the ignition system used on the ATC110 or **Figure 87** for the Fourtrax 70. All other models are the same as on previous years.

CDI Testing
(ATC110, Fourtrax 70,
TRX 125 and Fourtrax 125)

To test the CDI unit, remove the unit from the frame as described in Chapter Seven in the main body of this book.

CAUTION
Test may be performed on the CDI unit but a good one may be damaged by someone unfamiliar with the test equipment. If you feel unqualified to perform this test, have the test made by a Honda dealer or substitute a known good one for a suspected one.

NOTE
Test must be made with a quality ohmmeter or the test readings may be false.

Refer to the following tables for ohmmeter positive and negative test lead placement and specified resistance values.
a. ATC110: **Table 13**.
b. Fourtrax 70: **Table 14**.
c. 1985 TRX125: **Table 15**.
d. 1986 Fourtrax 125: **Table 16**.

Disconnect the electrical connector from the CDI unit. The test connections are made directly to the terminals within the CDI unit. For terminal color designition refer to the following figures:
a. ATC110: **Figure 88**.
b. Fourtrax 70: **Figure 89**.

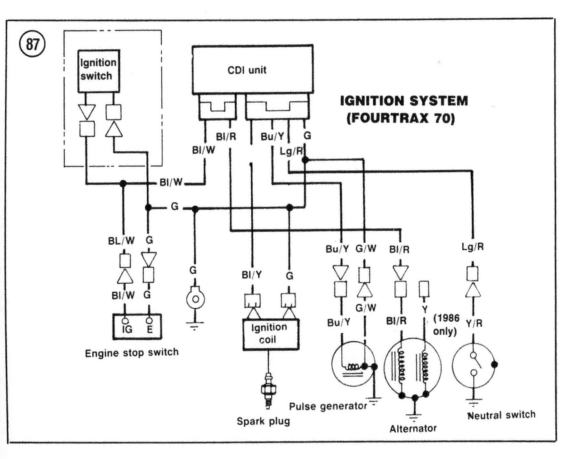

IGNITION SYSTEM (FOURTRAX 70)

    c. 1985 TRX125: **Figure 90**.

    d. 1986 Fourtrax 125: **Figure 91**.

    If the CDI unit fails *any one* of the tests, the unit is faulty and must be replaced.

Ignition Pulse Generator Inspection (TRX70 and ATC110)

> *NOTE*
> *In order to get accurate resistance measurements, the unit must be at approximately 68° F (20° C).*

1. Remove the seat/rear fender assembly.

2A. On TRX70 models, disconnect the electrical connector (containing 2 wires, one green/white and one blue/yellow) from the ignition pulse generator.

2B. On ATC110 models, disconnect the electrical connector (containing 2 wires, one green and one blue/yellow) from the ignition pulse generator (**Figure 92**).

3. Use an ohmmeter set at R × 10 and check resistance between the blue/yellow and green wires. The specified resistance is as follows:

a. TRX70: 80-120 ohms.

b. ATC110: 90 ohms.

If the reading is not as specified, the ignition pulse generator must be replaced as described in Chapter Seven in the main body of this book.

4. Reconnect the electrical connector and install the seat/rear fender assembly.

IGNITION COIL

Removal/Installation (TRX70, ATC110, ATC125M, TRX125, Fourtrax 125)

1. Remove the seat/rear fender assembly.

2. On ATC110 and ATC125M models, remove the fuel tank as described in Chapter Six in the main body of this book.

3. Disconnect the high voltage lead (A, **Figure 93**) from the spark plug.

4. Disconnect the primary electrical connectors from the ignition coil.

5. Carefully remove the ignition coil (B, **Figure 93**) and its rubber holder from the mounting tab on the frame.

6. Install by reversing these removal steps. Make sure all electrical connectors are tight and free of corrosion.

Testing

    Refer to **Figure 94** for this procedure.

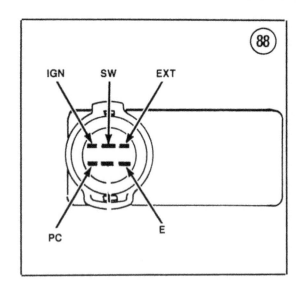

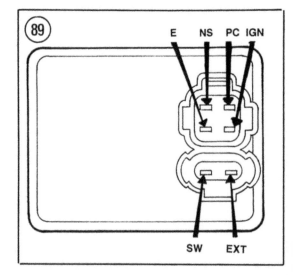

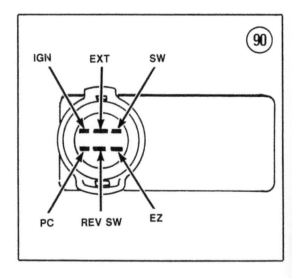

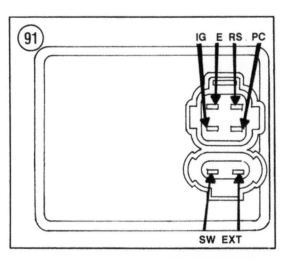

IG E RS PC

SW EXT

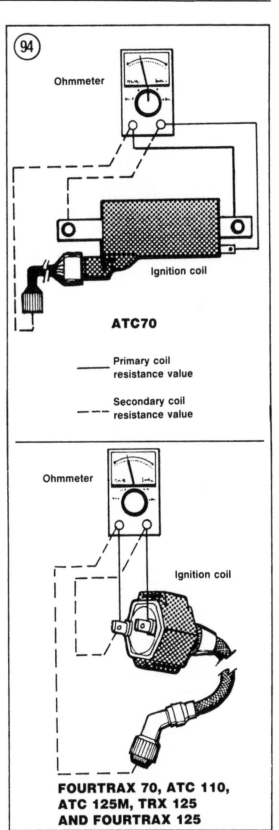

Ohmmeter

Ignition coil

ATC70

——— Primary coil resistance value

– – – Secondary coil resistance value

Ohmmeter

Ignition coil

FOURTRAX 70, ATC 110, ATC 125M, TRX 125 AND FOURTRAX 125

10

Static test (ATC70)

NOTE
In order to get accurate resistance measurements the unit must be at approximately 68° F (20° C).

1. Remove the fuel tank as described in Chapter Six in the main body of this book.
2. Disconnect all ignition coil wires before testing.
3. Measure the coil primary resistance using an ohmmeter set at R × 1. Measure between the primary terminal and the mounting flange. The specified resistance is 1.35-1.65 ohms.
4. Measure the coil secondary resistance using an ohmmeter set at R × 10. Measure between the primary terminal and the spark plug cap. The specified resistance is 7.65-9.35 ohms.
5. If the coil resistance does not meet either of these specifications, the ignition coil must be replaced. If the coil exhibits visible damage, it should be replaced. To replace the ignition coil refer to Chapter Seven in the main body of this book.
6. Reconnect all ignition coil wires and install the seat/rear fender assembly.

Static test (all other models)

NOTE
In order to get accurate resistance measurements the unit must be at approximately 68° F (20° C).

1. Disconnect all ignition coil wires before testing.
2. Measure the coil primary resistance using an ohmmeter set at R × 1. Measure between the primary terminal and the mounting flange. The specified resistance is as follows:
   a. TRX70: 0.16-0.198 ohms.
   b. ATC110: 0.16-0.20 ohms.
   c. ATC125M: 0.2-0.4 ohms.
   d. TRX125 and Fourtrax 125: 0.18-0.20 ohms.
3. Measure the coil secondary resistance using an ohmmeter set at R × 10. Remove the spark plug cap from the wire. Measure between the primary terminal and the end of the spark plug wire. The specified resistance is as follows:
   a. TRX70: 3.69-4.51 ohms.
   b. ATC110: 3.75-6.25 ohms.
   c. ATC125M: 3.7-4.5 ohms.
   d. TRX125 and Fourtrax 125: 3.7-4.5 ohms.

4. Measure the spark plug cap resistance using an ohmmeter set at R×10. Remove the spark plug cap from the wire. Measure between each end of the spark plug cap. The specified resistance is as follows:
   a. ATC110: 3.75-6.25 ohms.
   b. ATC125M: 3.7-4.5 ohms.
   c. TRX70, TRX125 and Fourtrax 125: no specifications given.
5. If the coil resistance does not meet any of these specifications, the ignition coil must be replaced. If the coil exhibits visible damage, it should be replaced as described in this supplement.
6. Reconnect all ignition coil wires.

SWITCHES

Ignition Switch (1987 Fourtrax 70)
Removal/Installation

1. Using a small screwdriver, remove the small insert nameplate (A, **Figure 95**) in the center of the handlebar upper cover.
2. Remove the screws (B, **Figure 95**) securing the handlebar upper cover.

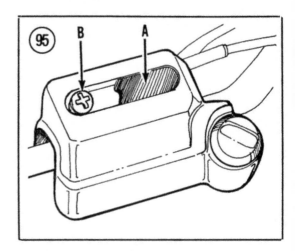

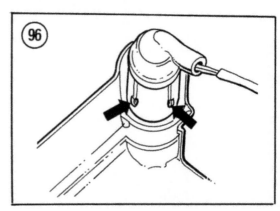

3. Partially pull the upper cover off the handlebar and disconnect the ignition switch electrical wires from the wiring harness.

4. Remove the handlebar upper cover and ignition switch assembly.

5. To remove the ignition switch from the handlebar upper cover, perform the following:

a. Turn the assembly over and set it on several shop cloths to protect the finish.

b. Push in on the locking lugs (**Figure 96**) on the ignition switch and remove the switch through the top surface of the upper cover.

6. Install by reversing these removal steps.

Table 12 VOLTAGE REGULATOR/RECTIFIER TEST POINTS

ATC125M, TRX125 and Fourtrax 125		
Positive	Negative	Value (ohms)
Yellow	yellow	infinity
Yellow	green	1-20
Yellow	red	infinity
Yellow	black	1-50
Yellow	yellow	infinity
Yellow	green	1-20
Yellow	red	infinity
Yellow	black	1-50
Green	yellow	infinity
Green	yellow	infinity
Green	red	infinity
Green	black	0.2-10
Red	yellow	1-20
Red	yellow	1-20
Red	green	3-100
Red	black	3-10
Black	yellow	infinity
Black	yellow	infinity
Black	green	0.20-20
Black	red	infinity

Table 13 CDI TEST POINTS (ATC110)

Positive	Negative	Value (ohms)
SW	EXT	0.1-20
SW	PC	0.5-200
SW	E	0.2-60
SW	IGN	infinity
EXT	SW	infinity
EXT	PC	0.5-100
EXT	E	0.1-1.0
EXT	IGN	infinity
PC	SW	infinity
PC	EXT	infinity
PC	E	infinity
PC	IGN	infinity
E	SW	infinity
E	EXT	infinity
E	PC	1-5
E	IGN	infinity
IGN	SW	infinity
IGN	EXT	infinity
IGN	PC	infinity
IGN	E	infinity

10

Table 14 CDI TEST POINTS (FOURTRAX 70)

Positive	Negative	Value (K-ohms)
SW	EXT	0.5-10
SW	PC	50-infinity
SW	E	1-30
SW	IGN	50-infinity
SW	NS	50-infinity
EXT	SW	50-infinity
EXT	PC	10-infinity
EXT	E	0.5-1.0
EXT	IGN	50-infinity
EXT	NS	50-infinity
PC	SW	50-infinity
PC	EXT	50-infinity
PC	E	1-15
PC	IGN	50-infinity
PC	NS	50-infinity
E	SW	50-infinity
E	EXT	50-infinity
E	PC	10-infinity
E	IGN	50-infinity
E	NS	50-infinity
IGN	SW	50-infinity
IGN	EXT	50-infinity
IGN	PC	50-infinity
IGN	E	50-infinity
IGN	NS	50-infinity
NS	SW	50-infinity
NS	EXT	30-200
NS	PC	50-infinity
NS	E	1-30
NS	IGN	50-infinity

Table 15 CDI TEST POINTS (1985 TRX125)

Positive	Negative	Value (ohms)
SW	EXT	0.5-9
SW	PC	20-200
SW	REV SW	infinity
SW	E	2-30
SW	IGN	infinity
EXT	SW	infinity
EXT	PC	10-50
EST	REV SW	infinity
EXT	E	0.5-9
EXT	IGN	infinity
PC	SW	infinity
PC	EXT	infinity
PC	REV SW	infinity
PC	E	infinity
PC	IGN	infinity
REV SW	SW	infinity
REV SW	EXT	5-500
REV SW	PC	10-50
REV SW	E	0.5-9
REV SW	IGN	infinity

(continued)

Table 15 CDI TEST POINTS (1985 TRX 125) (continued)

Positive	Negative	Value (ohms)
E	SW	infinity
E	EXT	5-500
E	PC	5-30
E	REV SW	infinity
E	IGN	infinity
IGN	SW	infinity
IGN	EXT	infinity
IGN	PC	infinity
IGN	REV SW	infinity
IGN	E	infinity

Table 16 CDI TEST POINTS (1986 FOURTRAX 125)

Positive	Negative	Value (ohms)
SW	EXT	0.5-10
SW	PC	50-infinity
SW	REV SW	infinity
SW	E	2-50
SW	IGN	infinity
EXT	SW	infinity
EXT	PC	40-infinity
EST	REV SW	infinity
EXT	E	0.5-10
EXT	IGN	infinity
PC	SW	infinity
PC	EXT	70-infinity
PC	REV SW	infinity
PC	E	1-15
PC	IGN	infinity
REV SW	SW	infinity
REV SW	EXT	20-100
REV SW	PC	100-infinity
REV SW	E	2-40
REV SW	IGN	infinity
E	SW	infinity
E	EXT	40-infinity
E	PC	20-100
E	REV SW	infinity
E	IGN	infinity
IGN	SW	infinity
IGN	EXT	infinity
IGN	PC	infinity
IGN	REV SW	infinity
IGN	E	infinity

10

CHAPTER EIGHT

STEERING, SUSPENSION AND FRAME

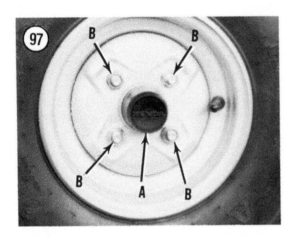

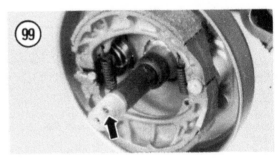

This section of the supplement describes repair and maintenance of the front wheels, suspension and steering components for all 4-wheel models.

Refer to **Table 17** for torque specifications for the front suspension components and **Table 18** for front suspension specifications.

FRONT WHEEL

Removal/Installation

1. Place the ATV on level ground and set the parking brake. Block the rear wheels so the vehicle will not roll in either direction.

2. Jack up the front of the vehicle with a small hydraulic or scissor jack. Place the jack under the frame with a piece of wood between the jack and the frame.

3. Place wood block(s) under the frame to support the ATV securely with the front wheels off the ground.

4. On models so equipped, remove the rubber hub cover (A, **Figure 97**).

5. Remove the lug nuts (B, **Figure 97**) securing the wheel to the hub/brake drum. Remove the front wheel.

6. Install by reversing these removal steps, noting the following.

7. Tighten the lug nuts to the torque specification listed in **Table 17**.

8. Install the rubber hub cover on models so equipped.

9. After the wheel is installed completely, rotate it; apply the brake several times to make sure that the wheel rotates freely and that the brake is operating correctly.

FRONT HUB

Removal/Inspection

Inspect each wheel bearing prior to removing it from the wheel hub.

> *CAUTION*
> *Do not remove the wheel bearings for inspection purposes as they will be damaged during the removal process. Remove the wheel bearings only if they are to be replaced.*

1. Remove the front wheel(s) as described in this supplement.

2. Remove the cotter pin and hub nut (**Figure 98**) securing the wheel and the hub/brake drum to the steering knuckle. Discard the cotter pin.

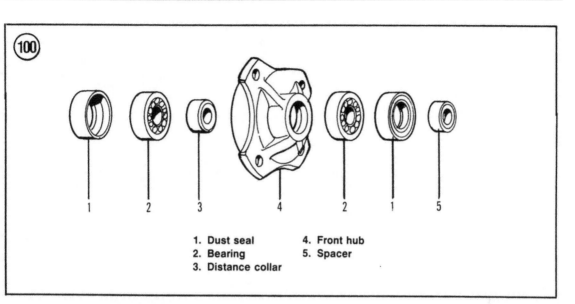

1. Dust seal
2. Bearing
3. Distance collar
4. Front hub
5. Spacer

3. Remove the front hub.
4. Turn each bearing by hand. Make sure each bearing turns smoothly.

NOTE
Some axial play is normal, but radial play should be negligible. The bearing should turn smoothly.

5. On non-sealed bearings, check the balls for evidence of wear, pitting or excessive heat (bluish tint). Replace bearings if necessary; always replace as a complete set. When replacing, be sure to take your old bearings along to ensure a perfect matchup.

NOTE
Fully sealed bearings are available from many good bearing specialty shops. Fully sealed bearings provide better protection from dirt and moisture that may get into the hub.

6. Check the hole (**Figure 99**) in the end of the steering knuckle where the cotter pins fit in. Make sure there are no fractures or cracks leading out toward the end of the steering knuckle. If any are found, replace the steering knuckle immediately.
7. Inspect the dust seals. Replace if they are deteriorating or starting to harden.
8. Inspect the threaded studs on the wheel hub. Replace if necessary.

Disassembly

Refer to **Figure 100** for this procedure.
1. Remove the front hub as described in this supplement.
2. Remove the spacer from the outside dust seal.
3. Remove the dust seal (**Figure 101**) from the outside surface of the hub/brake drum.
4. Remove the dust seal (**Figure 102**) from the inside surface of the hub/brake drum.
5. Before proceeding any further, inspect the wheel bearings as described in this chapter.
6. To remove the inner and outer bearings and distance collar, insert a soft aluminum or brass drift into one side of the hub. Push the distance collar over to one side and place the drift on the inner race of the outer bearing. Tap the bearing out of the hub with a hammer working around the perimeter of the inner race.
7. Remove the distance collar and tap out the inner bearing in the same manner.
8. Thoroughly clean out the inside of the hub with solvent and dry with compressed air or a shop cloth.

10

Assembly/Installation

1. On non-sealed bearings, pack the bearings with a good quality bearing grease. Work the grease in between the balls thoroughly. Turn the bearing by hand a couple of times to make sure the grease is distributed evenly inside the bearing.

2. Pack the wheel hub and distance collar with multipurpose grease.

CAUTION
*Install the wheel bearings with the sealed side facing out (**Figure 103**). During installation, tap the bearings squarely into place and tap on the outer race only. Use a socket that matches the outer race diameter. Do not tap on the inner race or the bearing may be damaged. Be sure that the bearings are completely seated.*

3. Install the inner bearing.

4. Install the distance collar and the outer bearing.

5. Apply a light coat of multipurpose grease to both dust seals.

6. Install the inner and outer dust seals.

7. Install the spacer into the outside dust seal.

8. Apply a light coat of silicone grease to the perimeter seal on the brake drum (**Figure 104**) prior to installation.

9. Install the hub onto the steering knuckle and install the hub nut. Tighten the hub nut to the torque specification listed in **Table 17**.

NOTE
Always install new cotter pins. Never reuse an old one as it may break and fall out.

10. Install a new cotter pin and bend the ends over completely.

11. Install the front wheel(s) as described in this supplement.

STEERING SYSTEM

Handlebar Removal (Fourtrax 70)

1. Remove the plastic bands holding the switch assembly electrical cable to the handlebar.

2. Remove the screws securing the throttle assembly to the handlebar and remove the assembly. Lay the assembly over the front fender or fuel tank. Be careful that the cable does not get crimped or damaged.

3. Remove the screw securing the front brake lever to the boss on the right-hand side of the handlebar and remove the front brake lever and cable assembly.

4. Remove the screw securing the rear brake lever to the boss on the left-hand side of the handlebar and remove the rear brake lever and cable assembly.

5. Remove the screws securing the engine stop switch assembly to the boss on the handlebar and remove the switch assembly.

6. Using a small screwdriver, remove the small insert nameplate (A, **Figure 95**) in the center of the handlebar upper cover.

7. Remove the screws (B, **Figure 95**) securing the handlebar upper cover.

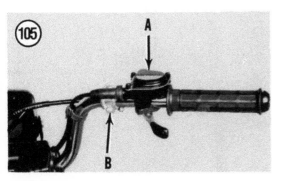

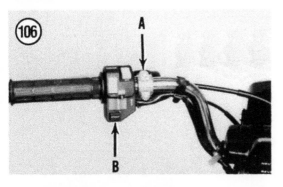

8. Partially pull the upper cover off the handlebar and disconnect the ignition switch electrical wires from the wiring harness.

9. Remove the handlebar upper cover and ignition switch assembly.

10. Remove the bolts securing the handlebar upper holders and remove the holders and the handlebar.

11. To maintain a good grip on the handlebar and to prevent it from slipping down, clean the knurled section of the handlebar with a wire brush. It should be kept rough so it will be held securely by the holders. The holders should also be kept clean and free of any metal that may have been gouged loose by handlebar slippage.

Handlebar Installation
(Fourtrax 70)

1. Position the handlebar on the handlebar lower holders so the punch mark on the handlebar is aligned with the top surface of the handlebar lower holders.

2. Install the upper holders with the "R" (right-hand side) or "L" (left-hand side) mark on the tabs to the correct side. The correct placement is necessary so the handlebar holder cover can be attached.

3. Install the handlebar holder bolts and tighten the forward bolts first and then the rear to the torque specification listed in **Table 17**. After installation is complete, recheck the alignment of the punch mark on the handlebar. Readjust if necessary.

4. Install the handlebar holder cover and screws. Tighten the screws securely.

5. Install the trim panel onto the center of the handlebar holder cover.

6. Install the engine stop switch assembly onto the boss on the handlebar. Install the screws and tighten securely.

7. Install the front and rear brake levers onto their respective bosses on the handlebar. Install the screws and tighten securely.

8. Install the throttle assembly onto the handlebar. Install the screws and tighten securely.

9. Install the plastic bands holding the switch electrical cable to the handlebar.

10

Handlebar Removal
(TRX125 and Fourtrax 125)

1. Remove the plastic bands holding the switch assembly electrical cables and control cables to the handlebar.

2. Remove the screws securing the throttle assembly (A, **Figure 105**) to the handlebar and remove the assembly. Lay the assembly over the front fender or fuel tank. Be careful that the cable does not get crimped or damaged.

3. Remove the clamping bolts securing the front brake lever (B, **Figure 105**) to the handlebar and remove the front brake lever assembly.

4. Remove the clamping bolts (A, **Figure 106**) securing the rear brake lever to the handlebar and remove the rear brake lever assembly.

5. Remove the screws securing the left-hand switch assembly (B, **Figure 106**) to the handlebar and remove the assembly.

6. Remove the trim panel (**Figure 107**) in the center of the handlebar holder cover.

7. Remove the screws (**Figure 108**) securing the handlebar holder cover and remove the holder cover.

8. Loosen the locknut on the choke cable and remove the choke cable (A, **Figure 109**) from the handlebar upper holder.

9. Remove the bolts (B, **Figure 109**) securing the handlebar upper holder. Remove the holder and the handlebar.

10. To maintain a good grip on the handlebar and to prevent it from slipping down, clean the knurled section of the handlebar with a wire brush. It should be kept rough so it will be held securely by the holders. The holders should also be kept clean and free of any metal that may have been gouged loose by handlebar slippage.

Handlebar Installation

1. Position the handlebar on the handlebar lower holders so the punch mark on the handlebar is aligned with the top surface of the handlebar lower holders.

2. Install the upper handlebar holder and holder bolts.

3. Install the handlebar holder bolts and tighten the forward bolts first and then the rear to the torque specification listed in **Table 17**. After installation is complete, recheck the alignment of the punch mark on the handlebar. Readjust if necessary.

4. Install the handlebar holder cover and screws. Tighten the screws securely and install the trim panel.

5. Install the left-hand switch assembly onto the handlebar and position the switch against the stopper plate on the handlebar. Install the screws and tighten securely.

6. Install the throttle assembly and position it against the right-hand handle grip. Install the screws and tighten securely.

7. Install the front and rear brake levers onto the handlebar as follows:

  a. Position the front brake lever assembly against the throttle assembly.

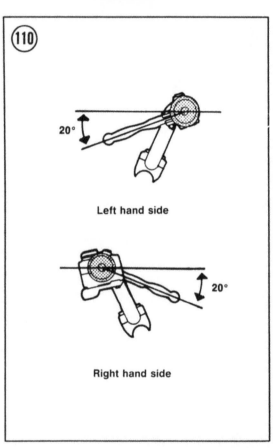

Left hand side

Right hand side

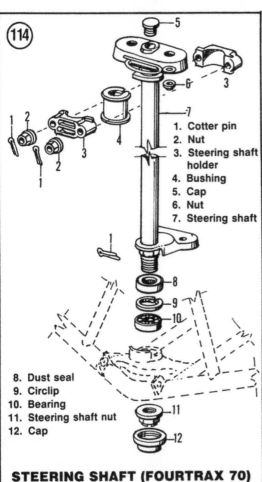

1. Cotter pin
2. Nut
3. Steering shaft holder
4. Bushing
5. Cap
6. Nut
7. Steering shaft
8. Dust seal
9. Circlip
10. Bearing
11. Steering shaft nut
12. Cap

STEERING SHAFT (FOURTRAX 70)

b. Position the rear brake lever assembly against the stopper plate on the handlebar.

c. Install the clamps with the punch mark toward the top and install the bolts. Tighten the bolts finger-tight at this time.

d. Position the brake levers so they are approximately 20° down from true horizontal as shown in **Figure 110**. Tighten the clamping bolts securely.

8. Install the plastic bands holding the switch electrical cable to the handlebar.

Throttle Lever
Disassembly/Assembly

1. Remove the screws securing the throttle lever cover (**Figure 111**) and remove the cover and gasket.

2. Disconnect the throttle cable (A, **Figure 112**) from the throttle lever arm.

3. Bend down the lockwasher tab and remove the bolt (1985 models) or nut (1986 models) and lockwasher (B, **Figure 112**).

4. Remove the throttle lever, arm and spring from the housing.

5. Assemble by reversing these disassembly steps, noting the following.

6. Apply a light coat of grease to all moving parts prior to assembly.

7. Bend the tab of the lockwasher up against one side of the bolt (1985 models) or nut (1986 models).

8. Install a new gasket (**Figure 113**) on the cover and install the cover and screws. Tighten the screw securely.

Steering Shaft and Bearing
Removal (Fourtrax 70)

Refer to **Figure 114** for this procedure.

1. Place the ATV on level ground and set the parking brake. Block the rear wheels so the vehicle will not roll in either direction.

2. Remove the seat and front fender as described in this supplement.

3. Remove both front wheels as described in this supplement.

4. Disconnect both tie rods from the steering shaft arm as described in this supplement.

5. Remove the handlebar as described in this supplement.

6. Remove the cap, the cotter pin and nut securing the lower end of the steering shaft to the frame.

7. Remove the cotter pins and nuts securing the steering shaft holders to the frame. Discard the cotter pins.

10

8. Remove both steering shaft holders. Note that the split in steering shaft bushing is positioned toward the rear of the steering shaft.
9. Pull the steering shaft up and out of the bearing in the lower portion of the frame and remove the steering shaft from the frame.
10. Remove the steering shaft bushing from the steering column.
11. To remove the steering shaft bearing, perform the following:
   a. Remove the dust seal and circlip from the top of the frame where the lower end of the steering shaft rides.
   b. From the underside of the frame, tap the bearing out of the frame.

Steering Shaft and Bearing Installation (Fourtrax 70)

1. To install the steering shaft bearing, perform the following:
   a. Apply a coat of waterproof grease to the bearing prior to installation.
   b. Tap the bearing squarely into place in the frame and tap on the outer race only. Use a socket that matches the outer race diameter. Do not tap on the inner race or the bearing may be damaged. Be sure that the bearing is completely seated.
   c. Install the circlip and make sure it is correctly seated.
   d. Apply a coat of waterproof grease to the grease seal and install the seal onto the receptacle in the frame.
2. Install the steering shaft into the frame.
3. Apply a coat of waterproof grease to the steering shaft bushing and install the bushing onto the steering shaft. Position the split toward the rear of the vehicle.
4. Install the inner and outer steering shaft holders onto the steering shaft bushing and steering shaft and then onto the threaded studs on the frame.
5. Install the nuts and tighten to the torque specification listed in **Table 17**. Install new cotter pins and bend the ends over completely.
6. Install the nut securing the lower end of the steering shaft to the frame and tighten to the torque specification listed in **Table 17**. Install a new cotter pin and bend the ends over completely. Install the cap.
7. Install the handlebar as described in this chapter.
8. Connect both tie rods to the steering shaft arm as described in this supplement.
9. Install both front wheels as described in this supplement.

115

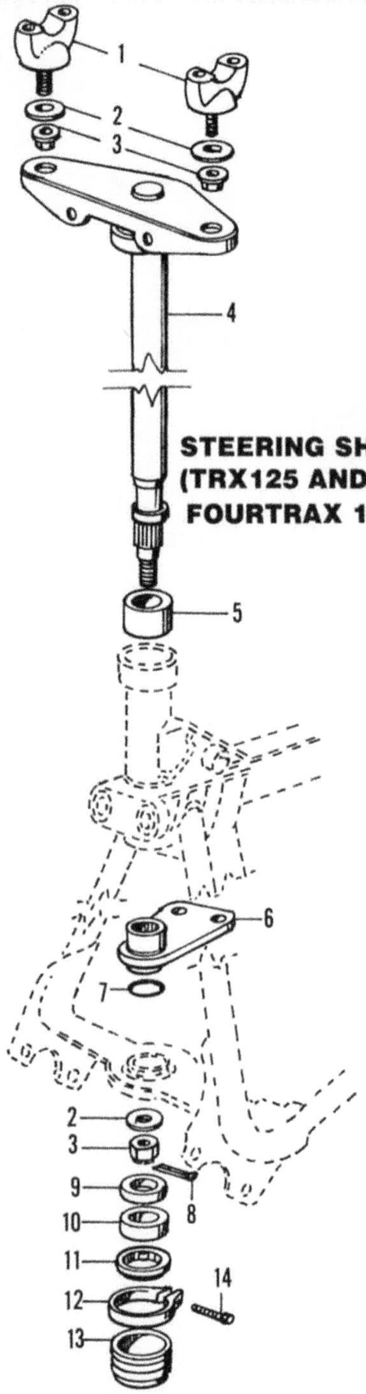

STEERING SHAFT (TRX125 AND FOURTRAX 125)

1. Handlebar lower holder
2. Washer
3. Nut
4. Steering shaft
5. Bushing
6. Steering shaft arm
7. O-ring
8. Cotter pin
9. Dust seal
10. Bearing
11. Bearing locknut
12. Clamp
13. Cover
14. Screw

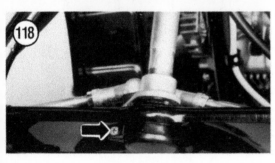

10. Install the seat and front fender as described in this supplement.

**Steering Shaft Inspection
(All 4-wheel Models)**

Refer to **Figure 115** for this procedure.

1. Place the ATV on level ground and set the parking brake. Block the rear wheels so the vehicle will not roll in either direction.

2. Remove both front wheels as described in this supplement.

3. Remove the handlebar (A, **Figure 116**) as described in this supplement.

4. Remove the bolts securing the headlight housing (B, **Figure 116**) to the steering shaft assembly. Move the headlight housing out of the

way. It is not necessary to remove the headlight assembly.

5. Remove the bolts securing the skid plate and remove the skid plate (A, **Figure 117**).

6. Disconnect both tie rods from the steering shaft arm as described in this supplement.

7. At the base of the steering shaft, loosen the clamp screw and remove the cap (**Figure 118**).

8. Remove the cotter pin, nut and washer (B, **Figure 117**) securing the lower end of the steering shaft to the frame.

9. Using a hammer and drift on the end of the steering shaft, partially drive the steering shaft up and out of the lower portion of the frame.

10. Remove the steering shaft arm and O-ring seal from the splines on the bottom of the steering shaft, then completely remove the steering shaft from the frame. Discard the O-ring seal.

NOTE
Steering shaft removal requires Honda special tools. They are the driver (part No. 07749-0010000), attachment (part No. 07746-0010100) and 17 mm pilot (part No. 07746-0040400).

11. To remove the steering shaft bearing from the lower portion of the frame, perform the following:

   a. Remove the dust seal from the top of the frame where the lower end of the steering shaft rides.

   b. From the underside of the frame, use the special tools and remove the locknut from the bottom of the frame.

   c. Drive the bearing out from the bottom of the frame.

**Steering Shaft Installation
(TRX125 and Fourtrax 125)**

1. To install the steering shaft bearing into the lower portion of the frame, perform the following:

   a. Apply a coat of waterproof grease to the bearing prior to installation.

   b. Tap the bearing squarely into place in the frame and tap on the outer race only. Use a socket that matches the outer race diameter. Do not tap on the inner race or the bearing may be damaged. Be sure that the bearing is completely seated.

   c. Install the locknut using the same special tool set-up used during removal. Tighten the locknut to the torque specification listed in **Table 17**.

   d. Apply a coat of waterproof grease to the grease seal and install the seal onto the receptacle in the frame.

10

2. Install the steering shaft partway into the frame.

3. Position the steering shaft arm with the larger diameter shoulder facing up.

4. Align the punch mark on the steering shaft arm with the one on the steering shaft and slide the arm into place.

5. Install a new O-ring seal into the lower recess of the shoulder on the steering shaft arm (**Figure 119**).

6. Install the steering stem the rest of the way into the lower portion of the frame.

7. Install the washer and the steering shaft nut and tighen to the torque specification listed in **Table 1**. Install a new cotter pin and bend the ends over completely.

8. Install the cap and tighten the clamp screw.

9. Connect both tie rods onto the steering shaft arm as described in this supplement.

10. Install the skid plate and tighten the bolts securely.

11. Install the headlight housing and tighten the bolts securely.

12. Install the handlebar as described in this supplement.

13. Install both front wheels as described in this supplement.

Steering Shaft Inspection
(All 4-wheel Models)

1. Carefully inspect the entire steering shaft assembly, especially if the vehicle has been involved in a collision or spill. If the shaft is bent or twisted in any way it must be replaced. If a damaged shaft is installed in the vehicle, it will cause rapid and excessive wear to the bushings as well as place undue stress on other components in the frame and steering system.

2. Inspect the lower bearing in the frame. If the bearing is worn or shows signs of wear due to lack of lubrication, it must be relaced as described in this supplement.

3. On Fourtrax 70 models, examine the steering shaft holders for wear or damage. Replace if necessary.

4A. On Fourtrax 70 models, measure the inside diameter of the bushing. If worn to the service limit dimension listed in **Table 18** or less, replace the bushing.

4B. On TRX125 and Fourtrax 125 models, perform the folllowing:

    a. Slide off the steering shaft bushing from the upper end of the steering shaft.

    b. Measure the outside diameter of the bushing. If worn to the service limit dimension listed in **Table 18** or less, replace the bushing.

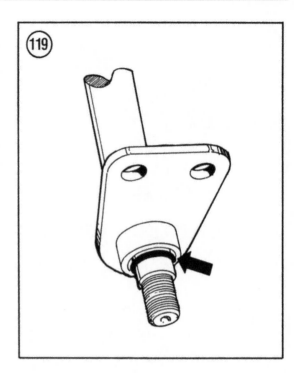

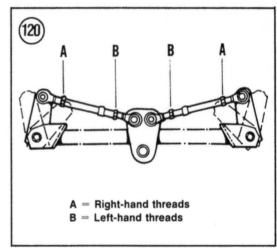

A = Right-hand threads
B = Left-hand threads

    c. Measure the inside diameter of the bushing. If worn to the service limit dimension listed in **Table 18** or less, replace the bushing.

5A. On Fourtrax 70 models, measure the outside diameter of the steering shaft where the shaft rides in the bushing. If worn to the service limit dimension listed in **Table 18** or less, replace the steering shaft.

5B. On TRX125 and Fourtrax 125 models, measure the outside diameter of the shaft where the shaft rides in the steering bushing. If worn to the service limit dimension listed in **Table 18** or less, replace the steering shaft.

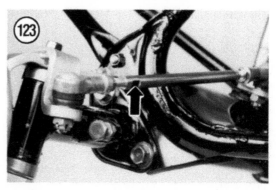

Tie Rod Removal
(All 4-wheel Models)

Both tie rod assemblies are the same. Refer to **Figure 120** for this procedure.

1. Place the ATV on level ground and set the parking brake. Block the rear wheels so the vehicle will not roll in either direction.
2. Remove the seat and front fender as described in this supplement.
3. On Fourtrax 70 models, remove the bolts securing the skid plate and remove the skid plate.
4. Remove both front wheels as described in this supplement.
5. Remove the cotter pin and nut **(Figure 121)** securing the tie rod end to the steering knuckle. Discard the cotter pin as a new pin must be installed.

CAUTION
If the tie rod is difficult to remove from the steering knuckle, do not attempt to pry it out as the tie rod seal may be damaged.

6. Carefully disconnect the tie rod from the steering knuckle. If the tie rod end is difficult to remove, install the nut just enough to cover the threads on tie rod end and tap the tie rod end out of the steering knuckle with a soft-faced mallet.
7. Remove the cotter pin and nut (A, **Figure 122**) securing the tie rod end to the steering shaft arm.

Discard the cotter pin as a new pin must be installed.
8. Carefully disconnect the tie rod (B, **Figure 122**) from the steering shaft arm and remove the tie rod assembly.
9. Repeat Steps 5-8 for the other tie rod.

Tie Rod Inspection/
Disassembly/Assembly

1. Inspect the rubber boot at each end of the tie rod end swivel joint. The swivel joints are permanently packed with grease. If the rubber boot is damaged, dirt and moisture can enter the swivel joint and destroy it. If the boot is damaged in any way, disassemble the tie rod assembly and replace the rod end(s) as they can be replaced separately.
2. Inspect the tie rod for bending or damage; replace if necesary.
3. If the tie rod ends (swivel joints) are to be replaced, refer to **Figure 120** and perform the following:

   a. Carefully measure and write down the overall length of the tie rod assembly before removing the worn tie rod ends.

   b. Loosen the locknuts securing the tie rod ends. The locknut securing the inside tie rod end has *left-hand* threads.

   c. Unscrew the damaged tie rod end(s).

   d. The notch (**Figure 123**) on the tie rod must be positioned toward the outside of the vehicle.

   e. The tie rod end with the "L" mark must be installed on the tie rod end next to the steering shaft arm.

   f. Thread the new tie rod end onto the tie rod until the groove in the rod threads enters the tie rod end.

   g. Turn the tie rod ends in or out until the overall length of the tie rod assembly is the same as that measured prior to disassembly in Step 3a. Leave the locknuts loose at this time. They will be tightened after the wheel alignment is adjusted.

10

Tie Rod Installation

1. Position the tie rod assembly so the notched end (**Figure 123**) is toward the outside or wheel side.

2. Attach the tie rod assembly onto the steering shaft end and onto the steering knuckle. Install the tie rod end nuts and tighten to the torque specification listed in **Table 17**.

3. Install a new cotter pin at each location and bend the ends over completely.

4. Install both front wheels as described in this supplement.

5. Align the toe-in adjustment of the front wheels as described in this supplement.

6. Tighten the tie rod end locknuts to the torque specification listed in **Table 17**.

7. Install the seat and front fender as described in this supplement.

Steering Knuckle
Removal/Installation

Refer to **Figure 124** for Fourtrax 70 models or **Figure 125** for TRX125 and Fourtrax 125 models for this procedure.

1. Place the ATV on level ground and set the parking brake. Block the rear wheels so the vehicle will not roll in either direction.

2. Remove the seat and front fender as described in this supplement.

3. Remove both front wheels as described in this supplement.

4. Disconnect the front brake cable (A, **Figure 126**) from the brake arm.

5. Remove the tie rod assemblies (B, **Figure 126**) from the steering knuckle as described in this supplement.

6A. On Fourtrax 70 models, perform the following:

  a. Remove the cap on top of the steering knuckle.

  b. Remove the cotter pin and loosen the nut on top of the steering knuckle. Discard the cotter pin as it is not to be reused.

  c. Hold onto the bottom of the steering knuckle and remove the nut and washer from the top of the steering knuckle. Remove the steering knuckle from the frame.

6B. On TRX125 and Fourtrax 125 models, perform the following:

  a. Remove the cotter pin, nut and washer (C, **Figure 126**) from the bottom of the kingpin bolt. Discard the cotter pin as it is not to be reused.

  b. Hold onto the bottom of the steering knuckle and remove the kingpin bolt from the top of

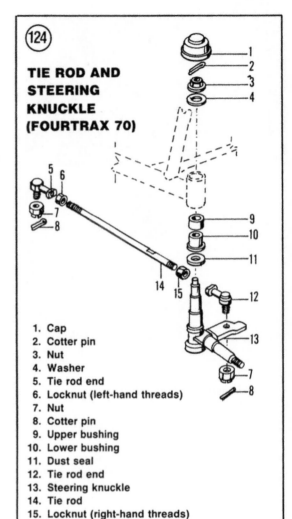

TIE ROD AND STEERING KNUCKLE (FOURTRAX 70)

1. Cap
2. Cotter pin
3. Nut
4. Washer
5. Tie rod end
6. Locknut (left-hand threads)
7. Nut
8. Cotter pin
9. Upper bushing
10. Lower bushing
11. Dust seal
12. Tie rod end
13. Steering knuckle
14. Tie rod
15. Locknut (right-hand threads)

the steering knuckle. Remove the steering knuckle from the front axle assembly.

  c. Remove the dust seal covers (D, **Figure 126**), the dust seals and the kingpin from the front axle assembly.

7. Install by reversing these removal steps, noting the following.

8. Apply a coat of waterproof grease to all pivot areas and dust seals prior to installing any components.

9. On Fourtrax 70 models, install the washer on top of the steering knuckle with the OUTSIDE mark facing up toward the nut.

10. On TRX125 and Fourtrax 125 models, hold onto the kingpin bolt with one wrench while tightening the nut to the torque specification listed in **Table 17**.

11. Tighten all bolts and nuts to the torque specification listed in **Table 17**.

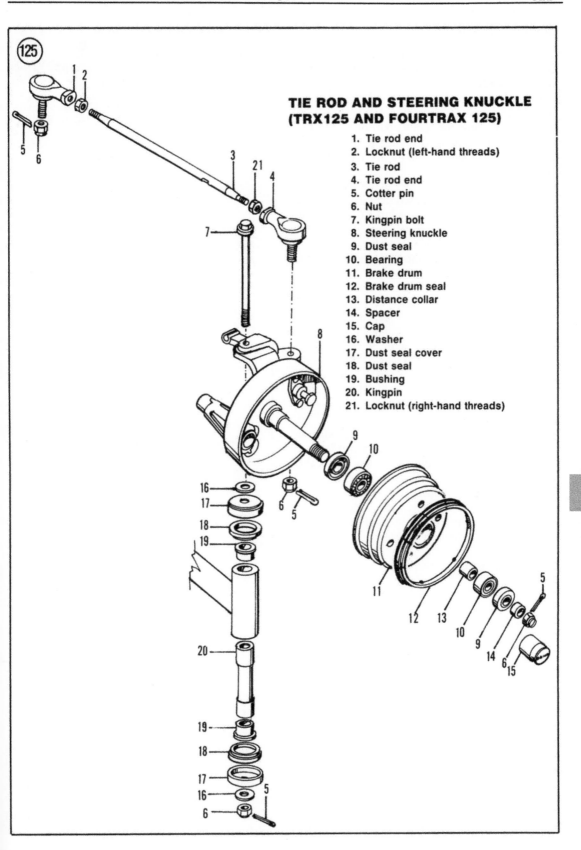

TIE ROD AND STEERING KNUCKLE (TRX125 AND FOURTRAX 125)

1. Tie rod end
2. Locknut (left-hand threads)
3. Tie rod
4. Tie rod end
5. Cotter pin
6. Nut
7. Kingpin bolt
8. Steering knuckle
9. Dust seal
10. Bearing
11. Brake drum
12. Brake drum seal
13. Distance collar
14. Spacer
15. Cap
16. Washer
17. Dust seal cover
18. Dust seal
19. Bushing
20. Kingpin
21. Locknut (right-hand threads)

10

Steering Knuckle Inspection

Refer to **Figure 124** for Fourtrax 70 models or **Figure 125** for TRX125 and Fourtrax 125 models for this procedure.

1. Inspect the spindle portion of the steering knuckle for wear or damage. A hard spill or collision may cause the spindle portion to bend or fracture. If the spindle is damaged in any way, replace the steering knuckle as described in this supplement.

2. Check the hole (**Figure 99**) at the end of the steering knuckle where the cotter pin fits. Make sure there are no fractures or cracks leading out toward the end of the steering knuckle. If any are present, replace the steering knuckle.

3A. On Fourtrax 70 models, perform the following:

   a. Measure the upper and lower pivot points on the steering knuckle (**Figure 127**). Replace the steering knuckle if it is worn to the service limit dimension listed in **Table 18** or less.

   b. Measure the upper and lower kingpin bushings in the frame (**Figure 128**). Replace the kingpin bushings if worn to the service limit dimension listed in **Table 18** or greater.

3B. On TRX125 and Fourtrax 125 models, perform the following:

   a. Measure the pivot points of the kingpin (**Figure 129**). Replace the kingpin if it is worn to the service limit dimension listed in **Table 18** or less.

   b. Measure the upper and lower kingpin bushings in the front axle (**Figure 130**). Replace the kingpin bushings if worn to the service limit dimension listed in **Table 18** or more.

4. Inspect all parts for wear or damage. Replace if necessary.

DRIVE CHAIN (4-WHEEL MODELS)

Cleaning/Inspection/Lubrication

The cleaning, inspection and lubrication procedures are the same as on previous models with the exception of the service limit length dimension.

1. Lay the drive chain alongside a ruler and pull the chain taut.

2. Measure the distance between the following number of pins and compare to the following service limit dimension "A" in **Figure 131**.

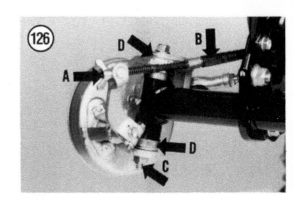

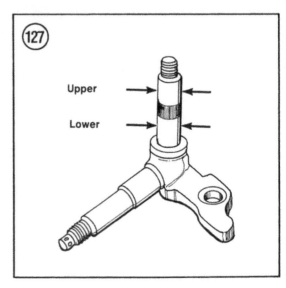

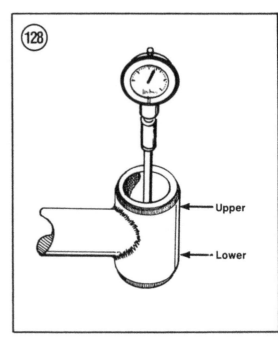

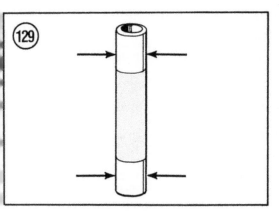

a. Fourtrax 70: 72 pins = 919.7 mm (36.21 in.).
b. TRX125 and Fourtrax 125: 41 pins = 513 mm (20.2 in.).

3. If the chain has stretched to the service limit dimension or greater, the drive chain must be replaced.

CAUTION
Always check both sprockets every time the drive chain is removed. If any wear is visible on the teeth, replace the sprockets. Never install a new drive chain over worn sprockets or worn chain over new sprockets.

TIRES AND WHEELS

Tire Changing
(TRX125 and Fourtrax 125)

The front wheel on these models is a one-piece type and does not come apart for tire removal and installation.

Follow the tire changing procedure as described under *Tire Changing, 1984 ATC110 and ATC125M* in Chapter Eight in the main body of this book. Use the bead breaker to break the tire loose from the rim as described in this procedure, then remove the tire from the rim with tire irons and rim protectors.

10

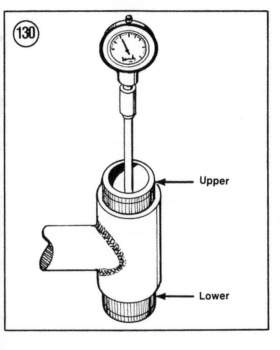

Upper

Lower

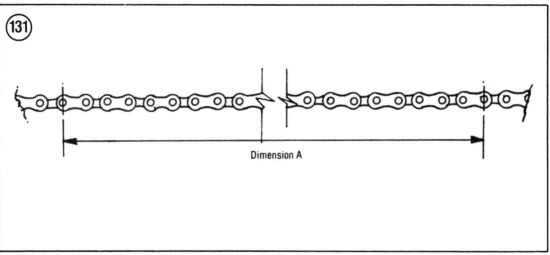

Dimension A

Table 17 FRONT SUSPENSION TORQUE SPECIFICAIONS

4-WHEEL MODELS		
Item	N·m	ft.-lb.
Front lug nuts		
70 cc	24-30	17-22
125 cc	50-60	36-43
Front hub nut		
70 cc	55-65	40-47
125 cc	60-80	36-43
Handlebar		
Upper holder bolts	24-30	17-22
Lower holder nuts	40-48	29-35
Steering shaft		
Holder nuts 70 cc	24-30	17-22
Shaft nut 70 cc	50-60	36-51
Shaft bearing locknut	40-60	29-43
in frame 125 cc		
Tie rod		
End nuts	35-43	25-31
Locknuts		
70 cc	35-43	25-31
125 cc	25-31	18-22
Kingpin		
Nut 70 cc	30-40	22-29
Bolt and nut 125 cc	50-60	36-43

Table 18 FRONT SUSPENSION SPECIFICATIONS (4-WHEEL MODELS)

Item	Service limit
Steering shaft	
Bushing ID 70 cc	22.8 mm (0.90 in.)
Bushing ID 125 cc	25.7 mm (1.01 in.)
Bushing OD 125 cc	35.0 mm (1.38 in.)
Steering shaft bushing area on shaft	
70 cc	22.0 mm (0.87 in.)
125 cc	25.3 mm (1.00 in.)
Steering knuckle pivot points 70 cc	
Upper	15.40 mm (0.606 in.)
Lower	16.90 mm (0.665 in.)
Kingpin bushings in frame 70 cc	
Upper	15.69 mm (0.618 in.)
Lower	17.19 mm (0.677 in.)
Kingpin OD 125 cc	17.90 mm (0.70 in.)
Kingpin bushings in front axle ID	18.17 mm (0.715 in.)

CHAPTER NINE

BRAKES

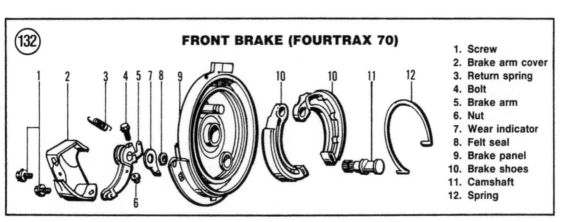

FRONT BRAKE (FOURTRAX 70)

1. Screw
2. Brake arm cover
3. Return spring
4. Bolt
5. Brake arm
6. Nut
7. Wear indicator
8. Felt seal
9. Brake panel
10. Brake shoes
11. Camshaft
12. Spring

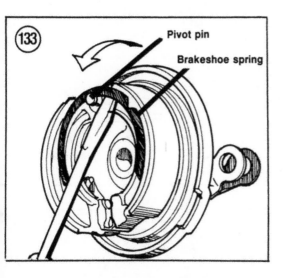

Pivot pin

Brakeshoe spring

FRONT DRUM BRAKE

Disassembly (Fourtrax 70)

Refer to **Figure 132** for this procedure.

1. Remove the front wheels as described in this supplement.
2. Remove the cotter pin and axle nut. Discard the cotter pin.

> *WARNING*
> *Do not inhale brake dust. It may contain asbestos, which can cause lung injury and cancer.*

3. Pull the brake drum straight off the brake shoes and brake panel.

4. If reinstalling the existing brake shoes, mark them "F" (front) or "R" (rear) prior to removal so they will be installed in their original position.
5. Use a wide-blade screwdriver and remove the brake shoe return spring (**Figure 133**) up and off the anchor pin.

> *NOTE*
> *Place a clean shop rag on the linings to protect them from oil and grease during removal.*

6. Remove the return spring from the holes in the shoes and remove the shoes from the pivot pin.
7. Remove the screws securing the brake arm cover and remove the cover.
8. Move the brake arm back to the applied position and disconnect the brake cable from the brake arm.
9. Slide the brake panel straight off the steering knuckle assembly.
10. Unhook the return spring from the brake arm.
11. Loosen the bolt securing the brake lever to the camshaft.
12. Remove the lever, wear indicator and felt seal.
13. Remove the camshaft.
14. Inspect the brake components as described in this supplement.

Assembly

1. Grease the cam and anchor pin with a light coat of molybdenum disulfide grease; avoid getting any grease on the brake plate where the linings come in contact with it.

10

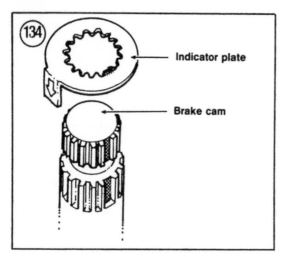

Indicator plate

Brake cam

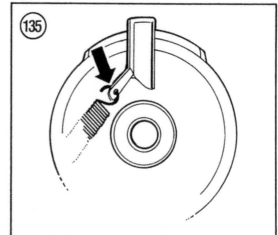

2. Install the camshaft into the brake panel.
3. Soak the felt seal in clean engine oil and install the felt seal.
4. Align the tab on the wear indicator with the groove in the camshaft (**Figure 134**).
5. Align the punch marks on the brake lever and camshaft and install the brake lever. Push the lever all the way down and tighten the bolt and nut to 4-7 N•m (3-5 ft.-lb.).
6. Install the return spring onto the brake lever and onto the tab on the brake panel as shown in **Figure 135**.
7. Install the brake panel straight onto the steering knuckle assembly. Align the recess in the backside of the brake panel with the tab on the steering knuckle. This is necessary for proper brake operation.
8. Move the brake arm back to the applied position and connect the brake cable onto the brake arm.
9. Install the brake arm cover and align the cover tab with the brake panel groove. Install the screws and tighten securely.
10. If reinstalling the existing brake shoes, refer to marks made during disassembly and install the shoes in their original position.

NOTE
*If new linings are being installed, file off the leading edge of each shoe a little (**Figure 136**) so the brake will not grab when applied.*

11. Install the brake shoes onto the pivot pin and push against the camshaft. Install the brake shoe spring into the hole in each brake shoe.
12. Place a broad tipped screwdriver under the brake shoe spring and place the tip of the screwdriver on the pivot pin.

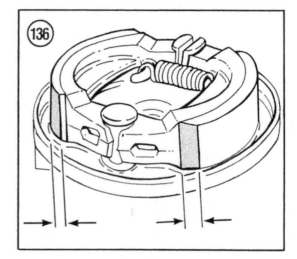

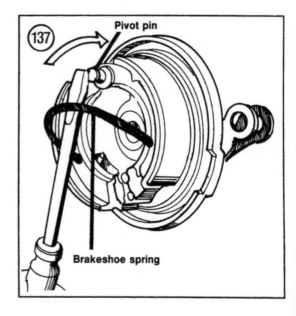

Pivot pin

Brakeshoe spring

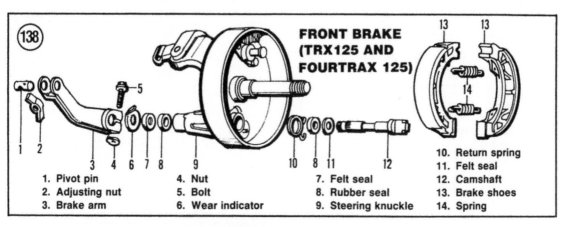

FRONT BRAKE (TRX125 AND FOURTRAX 125)

1. Pivot pin
2. Adjusting nut
3. Brake arm
4. Nut
5. Bolt
6. Wear indicator
7. Felt seal
8. Rubber seal
9. Steering knuckle
10. Return spring
11. Felt seal
12. Camshaft
13. Brake shoes
14. Spring

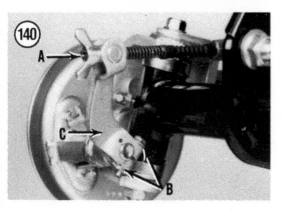

13. Pivot the screwdriver up until the spring slides off the screwdriver blade and onto the backside of the pivot pin (**Figure 137**). Remove the screwdriver.

14. Slide the brake drum straight onto the brake shoes and brake panel.

15. Install the axle nut and tighten to the torque specification listed in **Table 17**. Install a new cotter pin and bend the ends over completely.

16. Install the front wheels as described in this supplement.

17. Adjust the front brake as described in this supplement.

Disassembly (TRX125 and Fourtrax 125)

Refer to **Figure 138** for this procedure.

1. Remove the front wheel as described in this supplement.

2. Remove the cotter pin and axle nut (**Figure 139**).

WARNING
Do not inhale brake dust. It may contain asbestos, which can cause lung injury and cancer.

3. Pull the brake drum straight off the brake shoes and brake panel.

4. If reinstalling the existing brake shoes, mark them "F" (front) or "R" (rear) prior to removal so they will be installed in their original position.

5. Remove the brake shoes from the backing plate by firmly pulling up on the center of each shoe.

NOTE
Place a clean shop rag on the linings to protect them from oil and grease during removal.

6. Remove the return springs and separate the shoes.

7. Completely unscrew the adjusting nut (A, **Figure 140**) from the brake cable and brake arm.

8. Remove the bolt and nut (B, **Figure 140**) securing the brake lever to the cam.

9. From the backside of the brake panel, remove the brake lever (C, **Figure 140**) and wear indicator. Remove the felt seal and rubber seal from the recess in the brake panel.

10. From the front side of the brake panel, remove the camshaft, washer and return spring (A, **Figure 141**). Remove the felt seal from the recess in the brake panel.

11. Inspect the brake components as described in this supplement.

10

Assembly
(TRX125 and Fourtrax 125)

1. Onto the front side of the brake panel, perform the following:

   a. Soak the felt seal in clean engine oil and install the felt seal into the recess in the brake panel.

   b. Install the camshaft, washer and return spring (**Figure 141**).

   c. Locate the end of the return spring (**Figure 142**) onto the raised tab on the brake panel.

2. Onto the back side of the brake panel, perform the following:

   a. Soak the felt seal in clean engine oil.

   b. Install the rubber seal, then the felt seal into the recess in the brake panel.

   c. Align the tab on the wear indicator with the groove in the camshaft (**Figure 134**) and install the wear indicator.

3. Align the punch marks on the brake lever and camshaft (**Figure 143**) and install the brake lever. Push the lever all the way down and tighten the bolt and nut securely.

4. Grease the camshaft and pivot post (A, **Figure 144**) with a light coat of molybdenum disulfide grease; avoid getting any grease on the brake plate where the linings come in contact with it.

> *NOTE*
> *If new linings are being installed, file off the leading edge of each shoe a little (**Figure 136**) so that the brake will not grab when applied.*

5. If reinstalling the existing brake shoes, refer to marks made during disassembly and install the shoes in their original position.

6. Hold the brake shoes in a "V"-formation with the return springs attached and snap them in place on the brake backing plate. Make sure they are firmly seated on the backing plate (B, **Figure 144**).

7. Slide the brake drum straight onto the brake shoes and brake panel.

8. Install the axle nut and tighten to the torque specification listed in **Table 17**. Install a new cotter pin and bend the ends over completely.

9. Install the front wheels as described in this supplement.

10. Adjust the front brake as described in this supplement.

Drum Brake Inspection

1. Thoroughly clean and dry all parts except the linings.

2. Check the contact surface of the drum (**Figure 145**) for scoring. If there are grooves deep enough

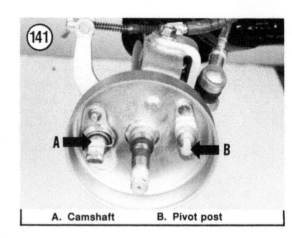

A. Camshaft   B. Pivot post

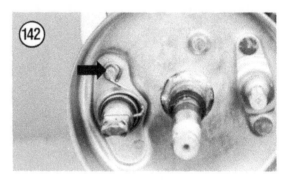

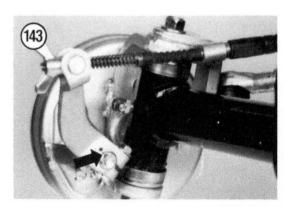

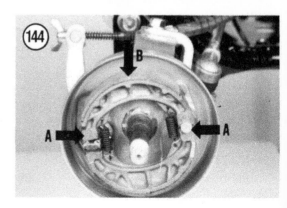

to snag a fingernail, the drum should be reground and new shoes fitted. This type of wear can be avoided to a great extent if the brakes are disassembled and thoroughly cleaned after riding the vehicle in water, mud or deep sand.

NOTE
If oil or grease is on the drum surface, clean it off with a clean rag soaked in lacquer thinner—do not use any solvent that may leave an oil residue.

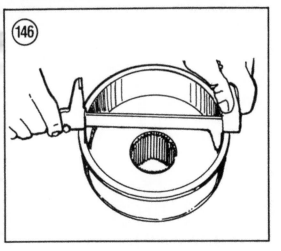

3. Use a vernier caliper (**Figure 146**) and check the inside diameter of the drum for out-of-round or excessive wear. Turn the drum if it will still be within the service limit dimension. Replace the drum if it is worn to the service limit listed in **Table 19** or greater.

4. If the drum is turned, the linings will have to be replaced and the new linings arced to the new drum contour.

5. Inspect the linings for imbedded foreign material. Dirt can be removed with a stiff wire brush. Check for traces of oil or grease. If they are contaminated, they must be replaced.

6. Measure the brake linings with a vernier caliper (**Figure 147**). They should be replaced if worn to the service limit (distance from the metal backing plate) listed in **Table 19**.

7. Inspect the camshaft lobe and the pivot pin area of the shaft for wear and corrosion. Minor roughness can be removed with fine emery cloth.

8. Inspect the brake shoe return springs for wear. If they are stretched, they will not fully retract the brake shoes from the drum, resulting in a power-robbing drag on the drums and premature wear of the linings. Replace as necessary and always replace as a pair.

9. Inspect the bearings in the brake drum as described under *Front Hub/Brake Drum* in this supplement.

REAR BRAKE
(FOURTRAX 70)

The rear brake is basically the same as that used on the 1978-on ATC70. Follow the procedure for the 1978-on ATC70 in Chapter Nine in the main body of this book and refer to **Figure 148**.

FRONT DRUM
BRAKE CABLES

Brake cable adjustment should be checked periodically, as the cable stretches with use and increases brake lever free play. Free play is the distance that the brake lever travels between the

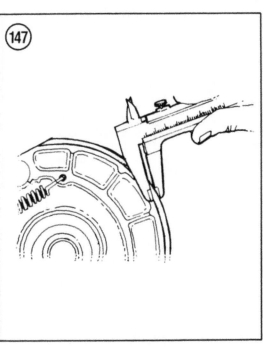

10

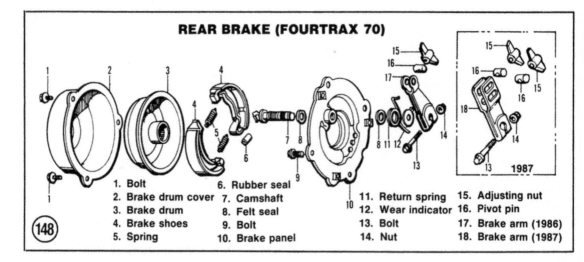

REAR BRAKE (FOURTRAX 70)

1. Bolt
2. Brake drum cover
3. Brake drum
4. Brake shoes
5. Spring
6. Rubber seal
7. Camshaft
8. Felt seal
9. Bolt
10. Brake panel
11. Return spring
12. Wear indicator
13. Bolt
14. Nut
15. Adjusting nut
16. Pivot pin
17. Brake arm (1986)
18. Brake arm (1987)

1987

released position and the point when the brake shoes come in contact with the drum.

If the brake adjustment, as described in the Chapter Three section of this supplement, can no longer be achieved the cable(s) must be replaced.

**Front Brake Cable Replacement
(Fourtrax 70)**

Refer to **Figure 149** for this procedure.

1. Place the ATV on level ground and set the parking brake. Block the wheels so the vehicle will not roll in either direction.

2. Remove the front fender as described in this supplement.

3. Remove both front wheels as described in this supplement.

4. To remove the primary brake cable, perform the following:

  a. Remove the screw securing the front brake lever to the boss on the right-hand side of the handlebar.

  b. Disconnect the brake cable from the brake lever.

  c. Completely unscrew the adjusting nut from the lower end of the brake cable at the equalizer arm.

  d. Remove the pivot pin from the equalizer arm and withdraw the brake cable from the equalizer arm. Don't lose the spring on the end of the cable.

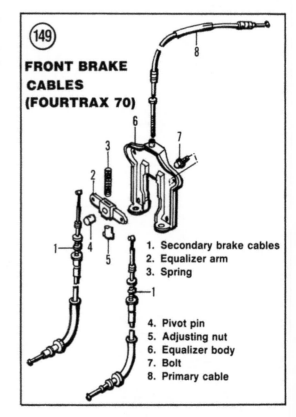

FRONT BRAKE CABLES (FOURTRAX 70)

1. Secondary brake cables
2. Equalizer arm
3. Spring
4. Pivot pin
5. Adjusting nut
6. Equalizer body
7. Bolt
8. Primary cable

NOTE
Prior to removing the cable, make a drawing (or take a Polaroid picture) of the cable routing through the frame. It is very easy to forget once it has been removed. Replace it exactly as it was, avoiding any sharp turns.

  e. Remove the primary brake cable from the top of the equalizer body and the frame.

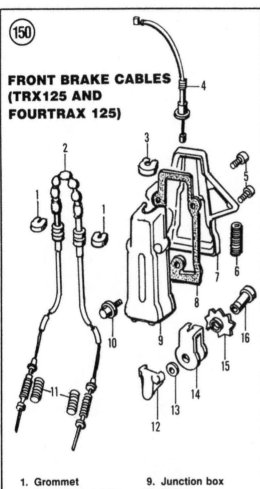

**FRONT BRAKE CABLES
(TRX125 AND
FOURTRAX 125)**

1. Grommet
2. Secondary cable
3. Grommet
4. Primary cable
5. Phillips screw
6. Return spring
7. Junction box plate
8. Gasket (1986)
9. Junction box
10. Bolt
11. Spring
12. Guide pin
13. E-clip
14. Junction plate
15. Sprocket
16. Pin

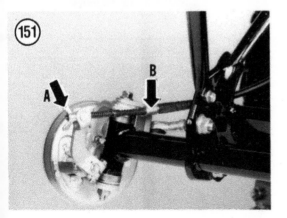

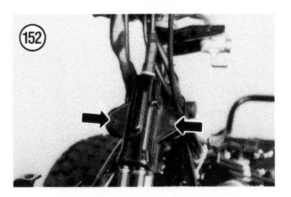

NOTE
*There are two secondary brake cables
and they may be replaced individually
or as a pair. If the ATV has been ridden
hard or has a lot miles on it, replace
both cables as a pair.*

5. To remove the secondary brake cable(s),
perform the following:
  a. At the brake panel on the wheel, move the
brake arm back to the applied position and
disconnect the brake cable from the brake
arm. If necessary, repeat for the other brake
assembly.
  b. Loosen the locknuts and adjusting nut and
disconnect the secondary brake cable(s) from
the equalizer arm.
  c. Remove the brake cable(s).
6. Install by reversing these removal steps, noting
the following.
7. Lubricate the new cable as described under
Control Cables in Chapter Three in the main body
of this book.
8. Adjust the brakes as described in this
supplement.

**Front Brake Cable Replacement
(TRX125 and Fourtrax 125)**

  Refer to **Figure 150** for this procedure.
1. Place the ATV on level ground and set the
parking brake. Block the wheels so the vehicle will
not roll in either direction.
2. Remove the front fender as described in this
supplement.
3. Remove both front wheels as described in this
supplement.
4. Completely unscrew the adjusting nut (A,
Figure 151) from the brake cable and brake arm.
5. Withdraw the brake cable from the brake arm.
6. Remove the brake cable from the bracket (B,
Figure 151) on the steering knuckle.
7. Remove the bolts (**Figure 152**) securing the
junction box to the frame.

10

8. Turn the junction box around to gain access to the backside of the box.

9. Remove the Phillips screws (**Figure 153**) securing the junction box plate. Remove the plate and on 1986 models the gasket.

10. Carefully pull the brake cable assembly out of the junction box (**Figure 154**). Do not damage or lose the rubber grommets on the brake cables where they enter the junction box.

11. Remove the guide pin from the junction plate.

12. Remove the E-clip from the pin.

13. Push the pin out of the sprocket. Remove the sprocket and secondary brake cable assembly from the junction plate.

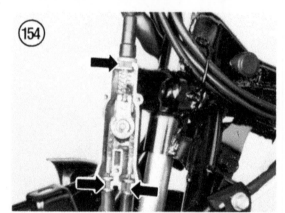

14. Remove the secondary brake cable assembly from the frame.

15. If necessary, compress the spring at the end of the primary brake cable and remove the cable from the junction plate. Don't lose the return spring.

NOTE
Prior to removing the cable, make a drawing (or take a Polaroid picture) of the cable routing through the frame. It is very easy to forget once it has been removed. Replace it exactly as it was, avoiding any sharp turns.

16. Remove the primary brake cable from the brake lever on the right-hand side of the handlebar. Remove the brake cable from the frame.

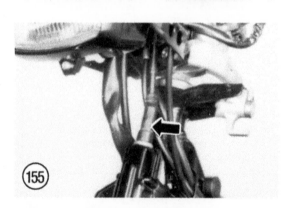

17. Install by reversing these removal steps, noting the following.

18. After new brake cables are installed, a preliminary adjustment must be performed prior to attaching the junction box plate and reinstalling the junction box onto the frame. At this time perform *New Brake Cable Preliminary Adjustment, TRX125 and Fourtrax 125* in this supplement.

19. Apply a coat of multipurpose grease to the sprocket, guide pin and the interior groove in the junction box cover prior to installation.

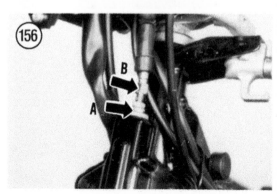

20. Lubricate the new cable as described under *Control Cables* in Chapter Three in the main body of this book.

21. Perform the final brake adjustment (mainly a free-play adjustment) as described in the Chapter Three section of this supplement.

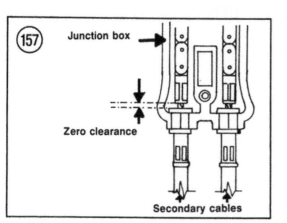

157

Junction box

Zero clearance

Secondary cables

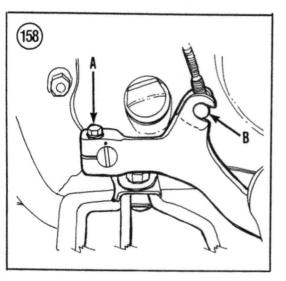

158

A

B

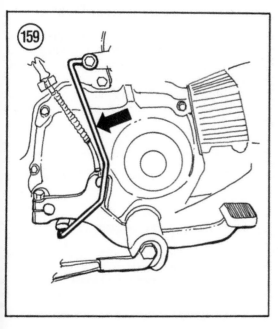

159

New Brake Cable Preliminary Adjustment (TRX125 and Fourtrax 125)

1. Slide the dust cover (**Figure 155**) up on the primary brake cable.
2. Loosen the locknut (A, **Figure 156**) on the primary brake cable adjuster.
3. Turn the cable adjuster (B, **Figure 156**) *clockwise* all the way down to the junction box.
4. Turn both brake adjusting nuts (A, **Figure 151**) on the brake arms until there is zero clearance between both secondary brake cable ends and the junction box (**Figure 157**).
5. Again turn both brake adjusting nuts (A, **Figure 151**) on the brake arms until both front wheels are locked by the brakes.
6. Turn the cable adjuster (B, **Figure 156**) *counterclockwise* until there is zero free play at the brake lever on the handlebar.
7. From this point, turn the cable adjuster *counterclockwise* an additional 2 1/2 turns and tighten the locknut (A, **Figure 156**).
8. On 1986 models, install a new gasket on the cover plate.
9. Loosen both brake adjusting nuts (A, **Figure 151**) an equal number of turns until the brake arms have 3 mm (1/8 in.) of free play.
10. Check the brake lever free play as described in the Chapter Three section of this supplement.

REAR BRAKE PEDAL (1987 FOURTRAX 70)

Removal/Installation

1. Place the vehicle on level ground and block the front wheels so the vehicle will not roll in either direction.
2. Remove the bolts securing the rear brake cable guard (**Figure 159**).
3. Loosen the *lower* adjustment nut on the brake cable. This is to allow slack in the cable.
4. Remove the bolt (A, **Figure 158**) securing the brake pedal to the pivot shaft.
5. Remove the brake pedal from the pivot shaft.
6. Disconnect the cable (B, **Figure 158**) from the brake pedal and remove the pedal.
7. Install by reversing these removal steps, noting the following.
8. Align the punch mark on the pivot shaft with the brake pedal and install the pedal. Install and tighten the bolt to 24-30 N•m (17-2 ft.-lb.).
9. Adjust the rear brake as described in this supplement.

10

Table 19 FRONT WHEEL BRAKE SPECIFICATION (4-WHEEL MODELS)*

Item	Specification	Wear limit
Brake drum ID		
70 cc	85.0 mm (3.35 in.)	86.0 mm (3.38 in.)
125 cc	110 mm (4.3 in.)	111 mm (4.4 in.)
Front brake lining thickness		
70 cc	3.0 mm (0.12 in.)	1.5 mm (0.06 in.)
125 cc	4.0 mm (0.2 in.)	2.0 mm (0.1 in.)

* Rear brake specifications are the same as previous models of the same engine displacement.

CHAPTER ELEVEN

BODY (4-WHEEL MODELS)

This chapter was not included for previous models and is added to cover the more complicated fender assemblies on the 4-wheel models.

Front Fender and Front Carry Handle (Fourtrax 70)

Removal/Installation

Refer to **Figure 160** for this procedure.

NOTE
Special bolts are used to attach the front fender to the frame. These bolts have a shoulder that stops the bolt against the metal frame without putting excess pressure on the plastic fender. Do not substitute another type of bolt or the bolt holes in the plastic fender may be fractured if the bolt is overtightened.

1. Place the ATV on level ground and set the parking brake.
2. Remove the bolts and nuts securing the rear fender to the foot peg guard on each side.

3. From under the seat, remove the bolts securing the seat/rear fender assembly to the frame.
4. Pull the seat/rear fender assembly up and toward the rear.
5. Remove the handlebar assembly as described in this supplement.
6. From within the wheel well housing, remove the bolts and nuts securing the front fender to the front carry handle and to the fender supports on each side.
7. Remove the fuel filler cap and cover the opening with duct tape.
8. Remove the bolts securing the rear portion of the front fender to the frame next to the fuel tank.
9. Carefully pull the front fender assembly up and off the frame.
10. To remove the front carry handle, remove the bolts securing the front carry handle to the frame and remove the front carry handle.

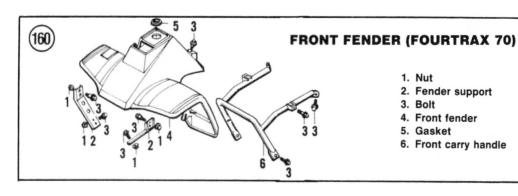

FRONT FENDER (FOURTRAX 70)

1. Nut
2. Fender support
3. Bolt
4. Front fender
5. Gasket
6. Front carry handle

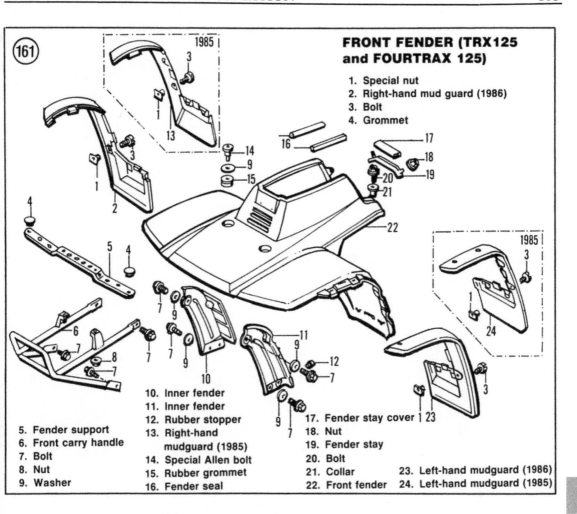

(161)

FRONT FENDER (TRX125 and FOURTRAX 125)

1. Special nut
2. Right-hand mud guard (1986)
3. Bolt
4. Grommet

5. Fender support
6. Front carry handle
7. Bolt
8. Nut
9. Washer

10. Inner fender
11. Inner fender
12. Rubber stopper
13. Right-hand
    mudguard (1985)
14. Special Allen bolt
15. Rubber grommet
16. Fender seal

17. Fender stay cover
18. Nut
19. Fender stay
20. Bolt
21. Collar
22. Front fender

23. Left-hand mudguard (1986)
24. Left-hand mudguard (1985)

10

(162)

11. Install by reversing these removal steps, noting the following.
12. Tighten all bolts securely.

Front Fender and Front Carry Handle (TRX125 and Fourtrax 125) Removal/Installation

Refer to **Figure 161** for this procedure.

NOTE
Special bolts are used to attach the front fender to the frame at some loctions. These bolts have a shoulder that stops the bolt against the metal frame without putting excess pressure on the plastic. Do not substitute another type of bolt or the bolt holes in the plastic fender may be fractured if the bolt is overtightened.

1. Place the ATV on level ground and set the parking brake.
2. Remove both front wheels (A, **Figure 162**) as described in this supplement.
3. Remove the special bolts, washers and nuts (B, **Figure 162**) securing the front fender to the front carry handle and the frame.
4. Remove the fuel tank as described in this supplement.

NOTE
***Figure 163** is shown with the front fender removed for clarity.*

5. Remove the bolts (**Figure 163**) and washers securing the inner fenders on each side and remove both inner fenders.

6. Carefully pull the front fender assembly up and off the frame.

7. Remove the fender support from the frame.

8. To remove the front carry handle, remove the bolts (**Figure 164**) securing the carry handle to the frame and remove the carry handle.

9. Install by reversing these removal steps, noting the following.

10. Make sure the locating pins on the front fender are indexed properly into the holes in the inner fenders.

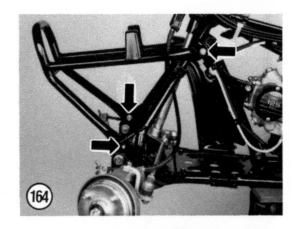

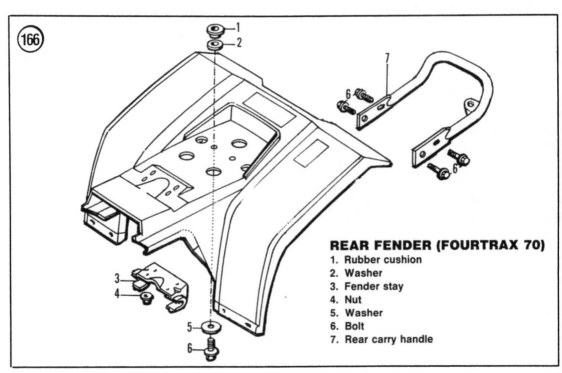

REAR FENDER (FOURTRAX 70)
1. Rubber cushion
2. Washer
3. Fender stay
4. Nut
5. Washer
6. Bolt
7. Rear carry handle

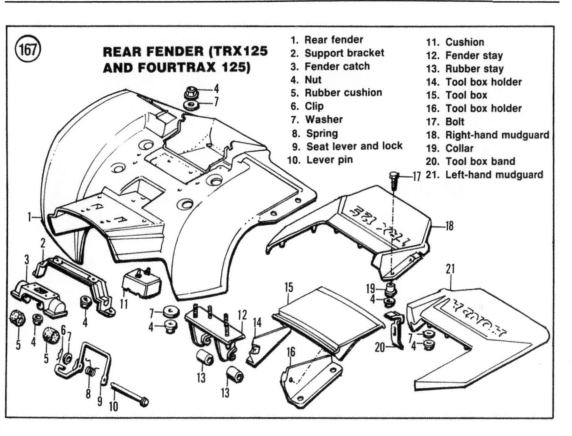

REAR FENDER (TRX125 AND FOURTRAX 125)

1. Rear fender
2. Support bracket
3. Fender catch
4. Nut
5. Rubber cushion
6. Clip
7. Washer
8. Spring
9. Seat lever and lock
10. Lever pin
11. Cushion
12. Fender stay
13. Rubber stay
14. Tool box holder
15. Tool box
16. Tool box holder
17. Bolt
18. Right-hand mudguard
19. Collar
20. Tool box band
21. Left-hand mudguard

11. Don't forget to install the fender support (**Figure 165**) between the fender and the frame.

12. Tighten all bolts securely.

Seat/Rear Fender Assembly and Rear Carry Handle (Fourtrax 70)

Refer to **Figure 166** for this procedure.

1. Place the ATV on level ground and set the parking brake.

2. Remove the bolts and nuts securing the rear fender to the foot peg guard on each side.

3. From under the seat, remove the bolts and collars securing the seat/rear fender assembly to the frame.

4. Pull the rear of the seat/rear fender assembly up and toward the rear. Remove the seat/rear fender assembly.

5. To remove the seat from the rear fender, perform the following:

  a. From the underside of the rear fender, remove the nuts securing the mounting bracket and seat to the rear fender.

  b. Remove the seat from the rear fender. Don't lose the washers and cushions located between the rear fender and the seat at the location of the bolts removed in Step 3. They must be

reinstalled in the same location upon assembly.

6. To remove the rear carry handle, perform the following:

  a. Loosen, but do not remove the bolts securing the muffler to the frame.

  b. Remove the bolts securing the rear carry handle to the frame on the right-hand side. One of the bolts also holds the muffler in place.

  c. Remove the bolts and collars securing the rear carry handle and tool box to the frame on the left-hand side. Don't lose the collars as they must be reinstalled in the same locations.

  d. Remove the rear carry handle.

7. Install by reversing these removal steps, noting the following.

8. Tighten the bolts securing the seat/rear fender assembly to the frame at the rear to 10-14 N•m (7-10 ft.-lb.). Tighten all other bolts and nuts securely.

Rear Fender and Rear Carry Handle (TRX125 and Fourtrax 125)

Refer to **Figure 167** for this procedure.

1. Place the ATV on level ground and set the parking brake.

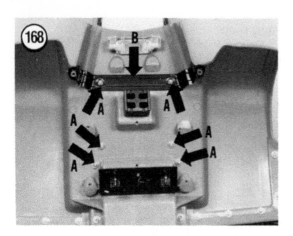

2. Pull on the seat release lever on the right-hand side of the seat.

3. Carefully pull the front portion of the seat up slightly and then forward to disengage the seat and rear fender assembly from the rubber cushions on the frame.

4. Remove the seat and rear fender assembly from the frame.

5. To remove the seat from the rear fender, remove the nuts and washers (A, **Figure 168**) securing the seat to the rear assembly and remove

remove the seat and the front support bracket (B, **Figure 168**).

6. To remove the rear carry handle, remove the through bolt (A, **Figure 169**), washer and nut and the bolt (B, **Figure 169**) on each side. Remove the carry handle (C, **Figure 169**) and tool box (D, **Figure 169**) assembly from the frame.

7. Install by reversing these removal steps, noting the following.

8. Tighten all bolts securely.

INDEX

11

1973-1974 & 1978-1982 ATC70

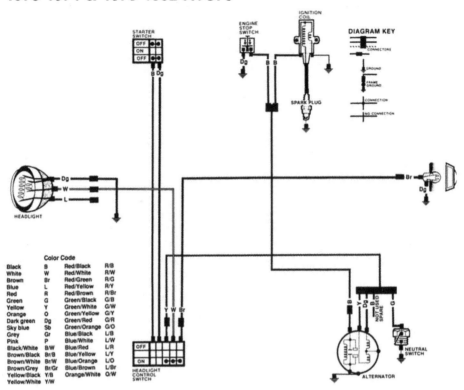

1983-1985 ATC70

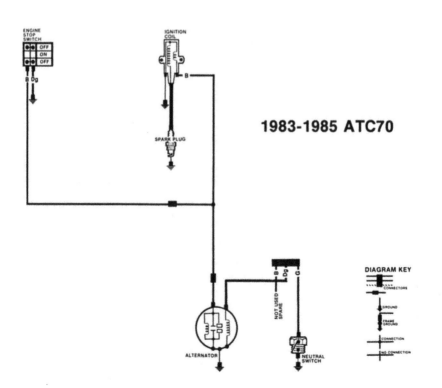

1970-1978 ATC90

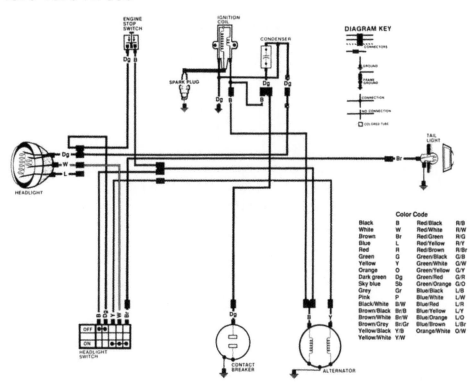

1979-1980 ATC110

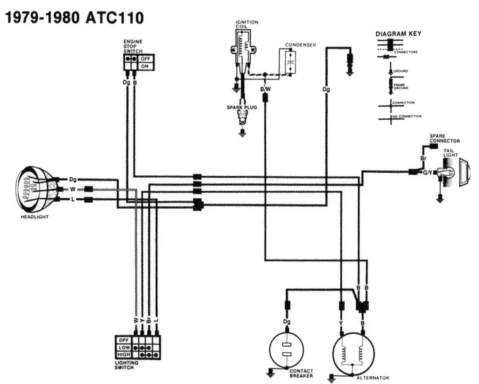

12

1981 ATC110

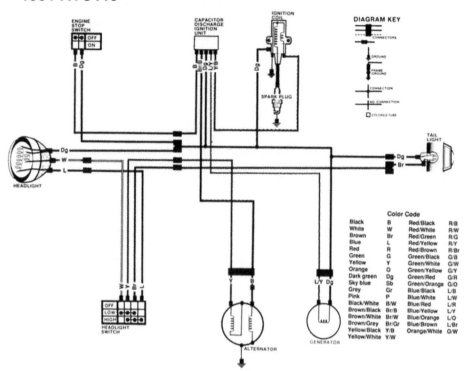

1982-1984 ATC110

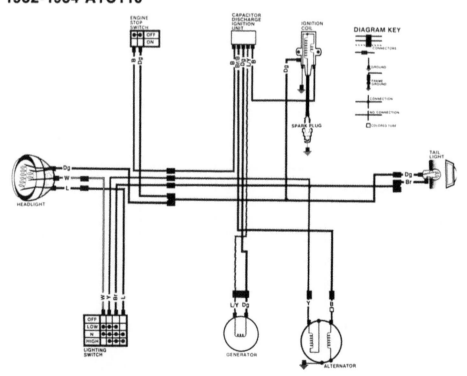

1984 ATC125M

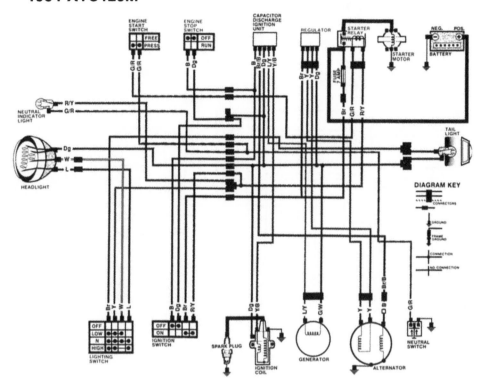

1985 ATC110

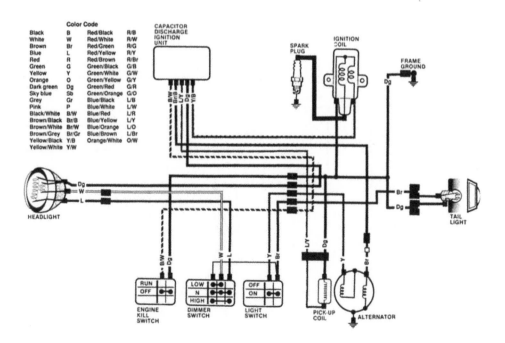

12

1985 ATC125M

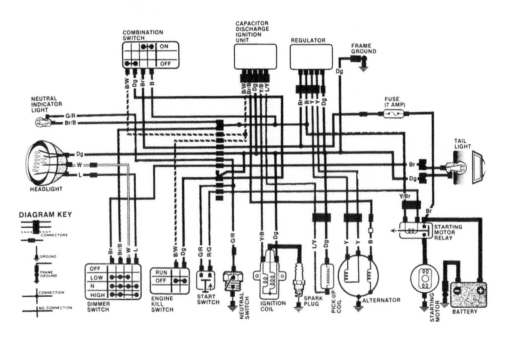

1986 Fourtrax 70

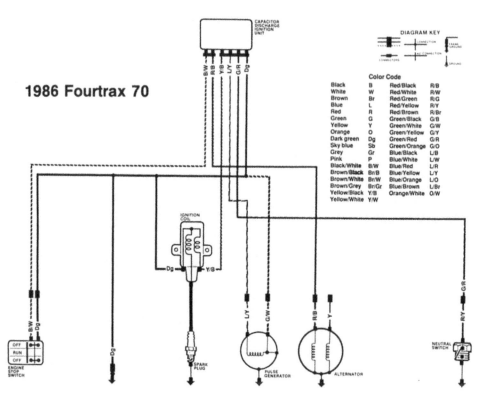

Color Code

Black	B	Red/Black	R/B
White	W	Red/White	R/W
Brown	Br	Red/Green	R/G
Blue	L	Red/Yellow	R/Y
Red	R	Red/Brown	R/Br
Green	G	Green/Black	G/B
Yellow	Y	Green/White	G/W
Orange	O	Green/Yellow	G/Y
Dark green	Dg	Green/Red	G/R
Sky blue	Sb	Green/Orange	G/O
Grey	Gr	Blue/Black	L/B
Pink	P	Blue/White	L/W
Black/White	B/W	Blue/Red	L/R
Brown/Black	Br/B	Blue/Yellow	L/Y
Brown/White	Br/W	Blue/Orange	L/O
Brown/Grey	Br/Gr	Blue/Brown	L/Br
Yellow/Black	Y/B	Orange/White	O/W
Yellow/White	Y/W		

1985 TRX 125

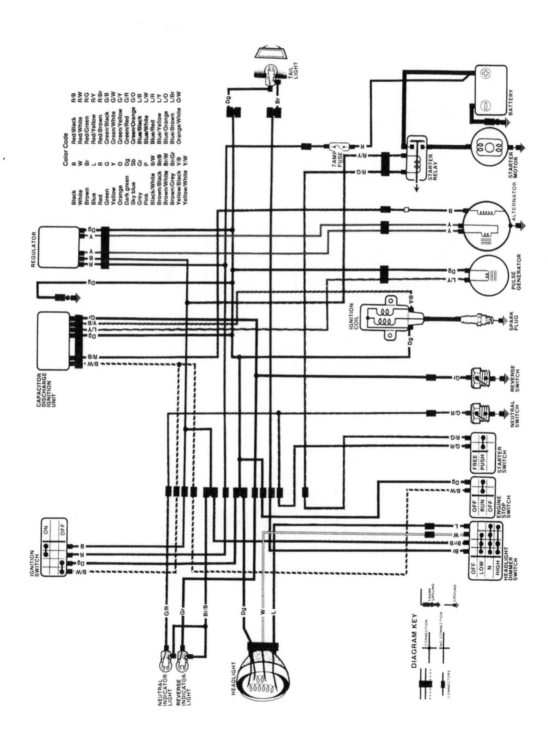

1986 Fourtrax 125

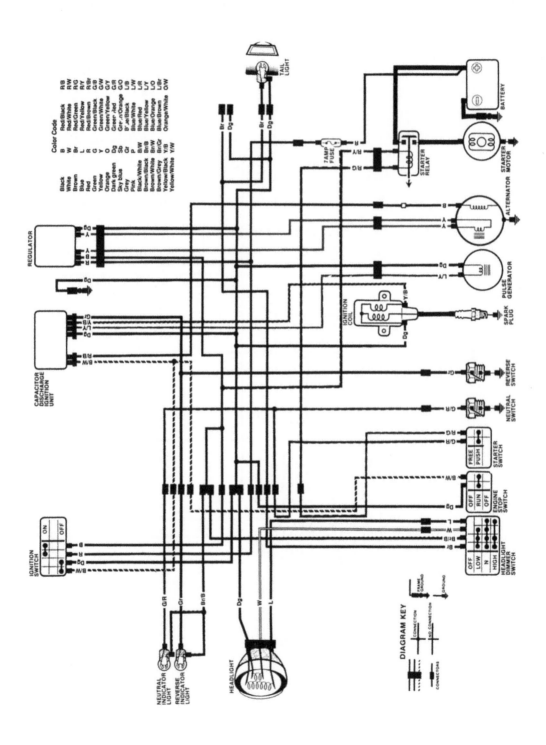

1987 Fourtrax 70

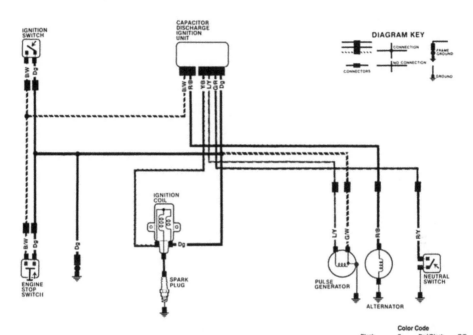

Color Code

Black	B	Red/Black	R/B
White	W	Red/White	R/W
Brown	Br	Red/Green	R/G
Blue	L	Red/Yellow	R/Y
Red	R	Red/Brown	R/Br
Green	G	Green/Black	G/B
Yellow	Y	Green/White	G/W
Orange	O	Green/Yellow	G/Y
Dark green	Dg	Green/Red	G/R
Sky blue	Sb	Green/Orange	G/O
Grey	Gr	Blue/Black	L/B
Pink	P	Blue/White	L/W
Black/White	B/W	Blue/Red	L/R
Brown/Black	Br/B	Blue/Yellow	L/Y
Brown/White	Br/W	Blue/Orange	L/O
Brown/Grey	Br/Gr	Blue/Brown	L/Br
Yellow/Black	Y/B	Orange/White	O/W
Yellow/White	Y/W		

1987 Fourtrax 125

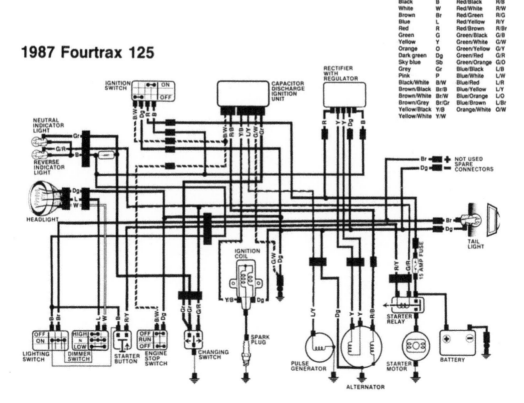

12

NOTES

MAINTENANCE LOG

Date	Hours	Type of Service

Check out *clymer.com* for our full line of powersport repair manuals.

BMW

M308	500 & 600cc Twins, 55-69
M502-3	BMW R50/5-R100GS PD, 70-96
M500-3	BMW K-Series, 85-97
M501-3	K1200RS, GT & LT, 98-10
M503-3	R850, R1100, R1150 & R1200C, 93-05
M309	F650, 1994-2000

HARLEY-DAVIDSON

M419	Sportsters, 59-85
M429-5	XL/XLH Sportster, 86-03
M427-3	XL Sportster, 04-11
M418	Panheads, 48-65
M420	Shovelheads, 66-84
M421-3	FLS/FXS Evolution, 84-99
M423-2	FLS/FXS Twin Cam, 00-05
M250	FLS/FXS/FXC Softail, 06-09
M422-3	FLH/FLT/FXR Evolution, 84-98
M430-4	FLH/FLT Twin Cam, 99-05
M252	FLH/FLT, 06-09
M426	VRSC Series, 02-07
M424-2	FXD Evolution, 91-98
M425-3	FXD Twin Cam, 99-05

HONDA

ATVs

M316	Odyssey FL250, 77-84
M311	ATC, TRX & Fourtrax 70-125, 70-87
M433	Fourtrax 90, 93-00
M326	ATC185 & 200, 80-86
M347	ATC200X & Fourtrax 200SX, 86-88
M455	ATC250 & Fourtrax 200/250, 84-87
M342	ATC250R, 81-84
M348	TRX250R/Fourtrax 250R & ATC250R, 85-89
M456-4	TRX250X 87-92; TRX300EX 93-06
M446-3	TRX250 Recon & Recon ES, 97-07
M215	TRX250EX, 01-05
M346-3	TRX300/Fourtrax 300 & TRX300FW/Fourtrax 4x4, 88-00
M200-2	TRX350 Rancher, 00-06
M459-3	TRX400 Foreman 95-03
M454-4	TRX400EX 99-07
M201	TRX450R & TRX450ER, 04-09
M205	TRX450 Foreman, 98-04
M210	TRX500 Rubicon, 01-04
M206	TRX500 Foreman, 05-11

Singles

M310-13	50-110cc OHC Singles, 65-99
M315	100-350cc OHC, 69-82
M317	125-250cc Elsinore, 73-80
M442	CR60-125R Pro-Link, 81-88
M431-2	CR80R, 89-95, CR125R, 89-91
M435	CR80R &CR80RB, 96-02
M457-2	CR125R, 92-97; CR250R, 92-96
M464	CR125R, 1998-2002
M443	CR250R-500R Pro-Link, 81-87
M432-3	CR250R, 88-91 & CR500R, 88-01
M437	CR250R, 97-01
M352	CRF250R, CRF250X, CRF450R & CRF450X, 02-05
M319-3	XR50R, CRF50F, XR70R & CRF70F, 97-09
M312-14	XL/XR75-100, 75-91
M222	XR80R, CRF80F, XR100R, & CRF100F, 92-09
M318-4	XL/XR/TLR 125-200, 79-03
M328-4	XL/XR250, 78-00; XL/XR350R 83-85; XR200R, 84-85; XR250L, 91-96
M320-2	XR400R, 96-04
M221	XR600R, 91-07; XR650L, 93-07
M339-8	XL/XR 500-600, 79-90
M225	XR650R, 00-07

Twins

M321	125-200cc Twins, 65-78
M322	250-350cc Twins, 64-74
M323	250-360cc Twins, 74-77
M324-5	Twinstar, Rebel 250 & Nighthawk 250, 78-03
M334	400-450cc Twins, 78-87
M333	450 & 500cc Twins, 65-76
M335	CX & GL500/650, 78-83
M344	VT500, 83-88
M313	VT700 & 750, 83-87
M314-3	VT750 Shadow Chain Drive, 98-06
M440	VT1100C Shadow, 85-96
M460-4	VT1100 Series, 95-07
M230	VTX1800 Series, 02-08
M231	VTX1300 Series, 03-09

Fours

M332	CB350-550, SOHC, 71-78
M345	CB550 & 650, 83-85
M336	CB650, 79-82
M341	CB750 SOHC, 69-78
M337	CB750 DOHC, 79-82
M436	CB750 Nighthawk, 91-93 & 95-99
M325	CB900, 1000 & 1100, 80-83
M439	600 Hurricane, 87-90
M441-2	CBR600F2 & F3, 91-98
M445-2	CBR600F4, 99-06
M220	CBR600RR, 03-06
M434-2	CBR900RR Fireblade, 93-99
M329	500cc V-Fours, 84-86
M349	700-1000cc Interceptor, 83-85
M458-2	VFR700F-750F, 86-97
M438	VFR800FI Interceptor, 98-00
M327	700-1100cc V-Fours, 82-88
M508	ST1100/Pan European, 90-02
M340	GL1000 & 1100, 75-83
M504	GL1200, 84-87

Sixes

M505	GL1500 Gold Wing, 88-92
M506-2	GL1500 Gold Wing, 93-00
M507-3	GL1800 Gold Wing, 01-10
M462-2	GL1500C Valkyrie, 97-03

KAWASAKI

ATVs

M465-3	Bayou KLF220 & KLF250, 88-10
M466-4	Bayou KLF300, 86-04
M467	Bayou KLF400, 93-99
M470	Lakota KEF300, 95-99
M385-2	Mojave KSF250, 87-04

Singles

M350-9	80-350cc Rotary Valve, 66-01
M444-2	KX60, 83-02; KX80 83-90
M448-2	KX80, 91-00; KX85, 01-10 & KX100, 89-09
M351	KDX200, 83-88
M447-3	KX125 & KX250, 82-91; KX500, 83-04
M472-2	KX125, 92-00
M473-2	KX250, 92-00
M474-3	KLR650, 87-07
M240-2	KLR650, 08-12

Twins

M355	KZ400, KZ/Z440, EN450 & EN500, 74-95
M360-3	EX500, GPZ500S, & Ninja 500R, 87-02
M356-5	Vulcan 700 & 750, 85-06
M354-3	Vulcan 800 & Vulcan 800 Classic, 95-05
M357-2	Vulcan 1500, 87-99
M471-3	Vulcan 1500 Series, 96-08
M245	Vulcan 1600 Series, 03-08

Fours

M449	KZ500/550 & ZX550, 79-85
M450	KZ, Z & ZX750, 80-85
M358	KZ650, 77-83
M359-3	Z & KZ 900-1000cc, 73-81
M451-3	KZ, ZX & ZN 1000 &1100cc, 81-02
M452-3	ZX500 & Ninja ZX600, 85-97
M468-2	Ninja ZX-6, 90-04
M469	Ninja ZX-7, ZX7R & ZX7RR, 91-98
M453-3	Ninja ZX900, ZX1000 & ZX1100, 84-01
M409	Concours, 86-04

POLARIS

ATVs

M496	3-, 4- and 6-Wheel Models w/250-425cc Engines, 85-95
M362-2	Magnum & Big Boss, 96-99
M363	Scrambler 500 4X4, 97-00
M365-4	Sportsman/Xplorer, 96-10
M366	Sportsman 600/700/800 Twins, 02-10
M367	Predator 500, 03-07

SUZUKI

ATVs

M381	ALT/LT 125 & 185, 83-87
M475	LT230 & LT250, 85-90
M380-2	LT250R Quad Racer, 85-92
M483-2	LT-4WD, LT-F4WDX & LT-F250, 87-98
M270-2	LT-Z400, 03-08
M343-2	LT-F500F Quadrunner, 98-02

Singles

M369	125-400cc, 64-81
M371	RM50-400 Twin Shock, 75-81
M379	RM125-500 Single Shock, 81-88
M386	RM80-250, 89-95
M400	RM125, 96-00
M401	RM250, 96-02
M476	DR250-350, 90-94
M477-3	DR-Z400E, S & SM, 00-09
M384-4	LS650 Savage/S40, 86-07

Twins

M372	GS400-450 Chain Drive, 77-87
M484-3	GS500E Twins, 89-02
M361	SV650, 1999-2002
M481-5	VS700-800 Intruder/S50, 85-07
M261-2	1500 Intruder/C90, 98-09
M260-2	Volusia/Boulevard C50, 01-08
M482-3	VS1400 Intruder/S83, 87-07

Triple

M368	GT380, 550 & 750, 72-77

Fours

M373	GS550, 77-86
M364	GS650, 81-83
M370	GS750, 77-82
M376	GS850-1100 Shaft Drive, 79-84
M378	GS1100 Chain Drive, 80-81
M383-3	Katana 600, 88-96 GSX-R750-1100, 86-87
M331	GSX-R600, 97-00
M264	GSX-R600, 01-05
M478-2	GSX-R750, 88-92; GSX750F Katana, 89-96
M485	GSX-R750, 96-99
M377	GSX-R1000, 01-04
M266	GSX-R1000, 05-06
M265	GSX1300R Hayabusa, 99-07
M338	Bandit 600, 95-00
M353	GSF1200 Bandit, 96-03

YAMAHA

ATVs

M499-2	YFM80 Moto-4, Badger & Raptor, 85-08
M394	YTM200, 225 & YFM200, 83-86
M488-5	Blaster, 88-05
M489-2	Timberwolf, 89-00
M487-5	Warrior, 87-04
M486-6	Banshee, 87-06
M490-3	Moto-4 & Big Bear, 87-04
M493	Kodiak, 93-98
M287	YFZ450, 04-09
M285-2	Grizzly 660, 02-08
M280-2	Raptor 660R, 01-05
M290	Raptor 700R, 06-09

Singles

M492-2	PW50 & 80 Y-Zinger & BW80 Big Wheel 80, 81-02
M410	80-175 Piston Port, 68-76
M415	250-400 Piston Port, 68-76
M412	DT & MX Series, 77-83
M414	IT125-490, 76-86
M393	YZ50-80 Monoshock, 78-90
M413	YZ100-490 Monoshock, 76-84
M390	YZ125-250, 85-87 YZ490, 85-90
M391	YZ125-250, 88-93 & WR250Z, 91-93
M497-2	YZ125, 94-01
M498	YZ250, 94-98; WR250Z, 94-97
M406	YZ250F & WR250F, 01-03
M491-2	YZ400F, 98-99 & 426F, 00-02; WR400F, 98-00 & 426F, 00-01
M417	XT125-250, 80-84
M480-3	XT350, 85-00; TT350, 86-87
M405	XT/TT 500, 76-81
M416	XT/TT 600, 83-89

Twins

M403	650cc Twins, 70-82
M395-10	XV535-1100 Virago, 81-03
M495-6	V-Star 650, 98-09
M281-4	V-Star 1100, 99-09
M283	V-Star 1300, 07-10
M282-2	Road Star, 99-07

Triple

M404	XS750 & XS850, 77-81

Fours

M387	XJ550, XJ600 & FJ600, 81-92
M494	XJ600 Seca II/Diversion, 92-98
M388	YX600 Radian & FZ600, 86-90
M396	FZR600, 89-93
M392	FZ700-750 & Fazer, 85-87
M411	XS1100, 78-81
M461	YZF-R6, 99-04
M398	YZF-R1, 98-03
M399	FZ1, 01-05
M397	FJ1100 & 1200, 84-93
M375	V-Max, 85-03
M374-2	Royal Star, 96-10

VINTAGE MOTORCYCLES

Clymer® Collection Series

M330	Vintage British Street Bikes, BSA 500–650cc Unit Twins; Norton 750 & 850cc Commandos; Triumph 500-750cc Twins
M300	Vintage Dirt Bikes, V. 1 Bultaco, 125-370cc Singles; Montesa, 123-360cc Singles; Ossa, 125-250cc Singles
M305	Vintage Japanese Street Bikes Honda, 250 & 305cc Twins; Kawasaki, 250-750cc Triples; Kawasaki, 900 & 1000cc Fours